The History of Work

Richard Donkin

palgrave
macmillan

First published 2001 as *Blood, Sweat and Tears* by Texerey

This edition published 2010 by
PALGRAVE MACMILLAN

Palgrave Macmillan in the UK is an imprint of Macmillan Publishers Limited,
registered in England, company number 785998, of Houndmills, Basingstoke,
Hampshire RG21 6XS.

Palgrave Macmillan in the US is a division of St Martin's Press LLC,
175 Fifth Avenue, New York, NY 10010.

Palgrave Macmillan is the global academic imprint of the above companies
and has companies and representatives throughout the world.

Palgrave® and Macmillan® are registered trademarks in the United States,
the United Kingdom, Europe and other countries.

ISBN 978–0–230–23893–0

This book is printed on paper suitable for recycling and made from fully
managed and sustained forest sources. Logging, pulping and manufacturing
processes are expected to conform to the environmental regulations of the
country of origin.

A catalogue record for this book is available from the British Library.

A catalog record for this book is available from the Library of Congress.

10 9 8 7 6 5 4 3 2 1
19 18 17 16 15 14 13 12 11 10

Printed and bound in Great Britain by
CPI Antony Rowe, Chippenham and Eastbourne

To the memory of my sister, Janet

CONTENTS

This book is huge. In every good sense of the word. It certainly belongs on the bookshelf of every leader and every scholar in the area of management and organizational life; but even more than that, it demands to be read closely. The stories it contains are enlightening, the questions it asks are profound, and the conclusions that it offers are sure to explode many of our most sacred assumptions.

An outstanding journalist and observer of human institutions, Richard Donkin has rare qualifications for leading readers on a journey of an immense historical scope. I want to emphasize for a moment the significance of this, because I am convinced that one of the secret scandals of contemporary organizations is the *ahistoricity* of its managers. The nature of work has always been changing; once it did so gradually and steadily, and now it does so at a breakneck pace. When Heraclitus observed 2,500 years ago that "there is nothing permanent but change," he had no way of conceiving exactly how right he could be. Yet a manager's ability to shape change, to make change work for us and not against us, is negligible unless one has a grasp of how change has already left its imprints on human industry. History is indeed one of the most significant laboratories for management theory, and Donkin unlocks the door to that laboratory and leads us on a remarkable guided tour.

Donkin shows how we have become "slaves to work" at precisely the time that most of us living in the industrialized world have been delivered from the oppressive yoke of manual labor. Our liberation has ironically led to a new and perhaps more troubling form of bondage. "Our lives are choked with work," he writes. "How did it get like this?" He then proceeds to address the matter skillfully over the course of several hundred pages.

Our concept of work, as he observes, lags several decades behind the current reality; our outdated concept is founded on an agricultural and industrial past, and has been reinforced by a centuries-old theological and cultural sanctification of a manner of work that is no longer even performed by most of us.

He offers an encyclopedic examination of the scientific, societal, and mythic progressions of work. Everything is explored here: the first forms of work, performed by our ancestors eons ago; the development of the modern "job"; the simultaneous blessing and curse of industrial innovation; serfdom, slavery, and child exploitation; and of course the new and dizzying computer era characterized by what I call Information Overload Anxiety.

Over the course of this historical journey, Donkin never loses sight of the central issues that he wants to leave each reader alone to wrestle with. Seeing where we have come from and sensing where we might be headed, he exhorts us to find new ways to think about the very nature of work and how we measure and reward it. Can we do so, he asks, in a manner that allows humans to express their full range of gifts in the classical Greek ideal? Can we keep women and men from being victimized by social and technological change, and can we help people who are so depleted by their treadmill work pace that they have forgotten the greater purposes of their work?

Even beyond these soul-sized matters, I have found myself in recent years telling leaders and academics that there are a number of specific questions about work that will need to be answered soon. Among them: Will the best organizations of the future be smallish, ramshackle clusters of individuals or large federations? Are there limits to the value of the so-called "high-involvement" and "self-managed" approach that is finally winning acceptance in so many organizations? What are we as a society to do with disparities in talent? What about the once-cherished Social Contract between employers and employees? Do we have or even need one single theory of organizational change? And finally, how do we find balance in our lives? I believe that Richard Donkin's book is of considerable use in helping us to address all these sorts of questions.

Most significantly, it is by walking us through the ages that he helps us to perceive the enormous significance of our own day. In his *Report to Greco*, Nikos Kazantzakis points out an ancient Chinese imprecation: "I curse you; may you live in an important age." And indeed we are all damned, encumbered, and burdened, as well as charmed, exhilarated, and fascinated by this curse. What a time! No small measure of credit goes to Richard Donkin for allowing us to understand this anew.

WARREN BENNIS
Distinguished Professor of Business Administration
University of Southern California

Acknowledgments

I owe thanks to many people for their help in the production of this book. The *Financial Times* library staff provided constant support and advice. I would particularly like to thank Pedro Das Gupta, Peter Cheek, Neil McDonald, Bhavna Patel, David Snaddon, and Philip Powell. In the *F T* Tokyo Bureau, Mitsuko Matsutani, Nobuko Juji, and Paul Abrahams ensured that my Japanese research program ran like clockwork. My warmest thanks also to Jackie Hare in the *F T* London office for her patience, hard work, and understanding as a friend and colleague. Many other *FT* colleagues deserve my thanks. I would single out: Martin Neilson, Bernie Flynn, Helen Timpson, and Celia Clack; Richard Lambert for letting me go; and John Ridding for bringing me back. Pradeep Jethi gave me some much-needed insights into the publishing market.

David de Haan, the Deputy Director of Ironbridge Gorge Museum Trust, took time out to explain the Darby dynasty, and Lorna Davidson, of New Lanark Conservation Trust, shared her extensive knowledge of Robert Owen. Peter Starbuck, probably the UK's most knowledgeable individual on the life and work of Peter Drucker, prompted many new avenues of inquiry. Robert Taylor, employment editor of the *Financial Times*, has proved a reliable source of expertise. Martin Wood at Board-level Interim Executive explained to me the history and significance of interim management. Charles Handy, Peter Drucker, and Joseph Juran all spared time to share with me their personal philosophies. Stephen Blinkhorn and Robert McHenry provided much needed clarity on the usefulness and limitations of psychometric testing. Chris Dyson, Lex Melzer, and Russell Hobby of Hay Management Consultants allowed me to tap their considerable experience of the competency movement and executive pay. Eric Duffelen and Duncan Brown, of Towers Perrin, were equally helpful in extending their pay expertise. Geoff Armstrong and his staff at the Chartered Institute of Personnel and Development remained consistently helpful throughout. The British Library staff deserve enormous praise for the way they deliver one of the world's greatest research services. I must also thank here the librarians at the Elton Collection, Ironbridge; the Henry Ford Museum, Greenfield Village; the Chicago History Society; the New Harmony Library; the Wiener Library, London; the Germantown History Society; Bethlehem Library; and Woking Library.

Will and Kenneth Hopper took time out of their own project on the contribution of Japanese management to make some telling points on the development of scientific management in the USA and Japan. Liz Ann Borden, Hugh Torrens, and Crispin Tickell gave their time, explaining the story of Mary Anning. The archivists at Lucent Technologies shared with me some valuable documents on the work of US engineers helping to restore management discipline in post-Second World War Japan. Masaharu Matsushita found time to outline his memories of the Civil Communications Section seminars, while Professor Hajime Karatsu of Tokai University loaned me his copy of the groundbreaking NBC documentary *If Japan Can Why Can't We*. Yoshihiro Kitadeya lent valuable assistance at Matsushita Electrical. My thanks too to David Erdal for sharing his perspectives on cooperative working in Italy and Dr David Hill at the University of Manchester, who explained the background to the Julian Work Calendar. Dr Barry Alpha, Timothy Bottoms, Jerry Mission, and Vol Norris made my trip to Kawanyama so worthwhile and enjoyable. John Lord, an expert flint knapper, provided a living link to the skills of the Neolithic Age, and Mark Roberts was happy to relive for me the excitement of the Boxgrove discoveries.

I want to extend a special thank you to Chay Blyth, David Tomkinson, the management of 3Com, the company, and my fellow crew members on board *3Com*, the yacht, for delivering a never-to-be-forgotten experience which inspired a number of the ideas in this book. Valuable inspiration and support was also extended by Clare Neal, who helped me to clarify the issues surrounding my career break.

Warm thanks also to Dennis Kilcommons, a great writer and one of my oldest friends, who enlightened this story with his extensive knowledge of the Luddite movement. Philippe Falle, another great friend and a fine photographer, endured an exhausting and sometimes harrowing trip to the east of Poland in winter, which would have been an impossible undertaking without his help. Above all I must thank Warren Bennis, whose friendship and advice have been immeasurable in helping me to handle the Byzantine dealings of the international publishing market. Finally I want to thank my wife, Gillian, for her encouragement, understanding, and sensitive support in reading the manuscript as it developed, and my children, John, Robert, and George, simply for being there.

RICHARD DONKIN

My grandmother was a strong woman, unfaltering in her judgment on the merits of work. "Make way for the workers," she would say as my father came home from the steel works wearing his blue overalls and cloth cap, a knapsack hanging from his shoulder. Dad received a hero's welcome in marked contrast to the disdain that grandma displayed for my own efforts at school. "There's too much education," she insisted. "There will always have to be the workers." I knew what she meant by this. There was something solid and reassuring about the blue-collared masses filing from the factory gate. There was a sense of order and continuity punctuated by the factory hooter and the unchallenged certainty of the clocking-on machine.

From 1945 to 1975 my father worked as an electric welder for the same employer, a steel fabrication company. Returning from the army to claim back his job at the end of the Second World War, he found a young woman, dressed in overalls, doing the work he used to do. So he married her, and she returned willingly to the chore-filled domestic existence of the housewife.

The steel works was a dirty, cold, noisy place. Dad worked there for most of his adult life, unquestioning, carrying out his job. Sometimes he worked during the day and sometimes he worked nights. It didn't matter much. Little natural light was able to filter through the shed's grime-covered skylights.

Just after the war his main job involved making angle brackets for the holds of Grimsby fishing boats, allowing the crews to separate their catches. For this he was paid a "piece rate" – a fixed price for each bracket based on the time it could be reasonably expected to take an individual to complete the work. My father worked quickly. "We made good money on that job," he said. Later his welding work switched to constructing girders in a way that maintained their strength while reducing their steel content. Some days the work was so hot his welding shield collected his sweat like a bucket.

Mum and dad's first child was a daughter they called Janet. On a rare outing, they took her to the seaside as a four-year-old. There, playing in the waves, she contracted polio. The disease withered one of her legs and left her with an acute curvature of the spine and one functioning lung. My parents had no car, so the care and upbringing of a disabled daughter and two energetic boys must have been a struggle. But it never seemed so. There was never any talk of layoffs or redundancy. Our family life was relatively free of such anxieties.

This was that golden age of almost full employment after the war. Not until dad had retired in the mid-1970s did the axe begin to fall among the smokestack industries in the North of England. The steel works closed, the Grimsby trawlers were broken up and scrapped or sold. Those great industries – textiles, steel, shipbuilding, and coal mining, stalwarts of Britain's Industrial Revolution – all began to crumble. Many of those queuing for benefits had never known unemployment.

Grandma was dead by then. She had gone to her grave unflinching in the certainty of her beliefs. How meaningless and hollow her mantra had become. "There will always have to be the workers." We knew who the workers were. They were the factory masses, usually unionized, blue-collared labor. The *Financial Times* was the first UK newspaper to recognize their strength with its daily labor pages, packed with stories of disputes, pay deals, and trade union news. Six journalists, dedicated to labor reporting, were supplying this demand when I joined the newspaper in 1987. Today there is no individual brief for employment. Instead there is a business and employment editor. The labor pages have gone because labor, as we knew it only 30 years ago, no longer exists. The lines of men and women streaming from the factory gates have dwindled to a trickle, the massed ranks of years gone by have faded like ghosts into the computerized, robot-dominated machine shops of automated manufacturing.

Something has happened to the way we work, something far more fundamental than changes arising from deregulation and the easing of industrial relations' legislation. Grandma was right in one sense. There are still people working and there is still work to be done, but not so much that would fit with her notion of work.

Once there was work, and what we understood as work was what we were paid to be doing. Today there is what we do, and sometimes the benefits to our employer of what we do are unclear. Sometimes it is difficult to think of what we do as work, and sometimes there seems to be so much work to shift that we feel overwhelmed. Once we may have left our work behind. Today we take it with us in our cellphones, our BlackBerries, our memory sticks, and our computers. Our working life is woven, warp across weft, into the texture of our domestic existence.

For 15 years now, the subject of work has been my work, writing on all the things that people do to find workers (recruitment, headhunting, testing), all the things that are done to encourage work (pay raises, promotion, incentives, perks, recognition), and all the ways that people are moved out of structured budgeted work (downsizing, redundancy, firing, and outplacement). The more I write, the more I ask myself this recurring question: Why on earth do we do it? Why, at least, do we do so much of it? Whenever I have confronted the question *why?*, my response has been, wherever possible, to get back to first principles. This is not so easy with work. It has been around far longer than the human race itself, emerging in its organized form in the practices of our early ancestors.

Today we seem to take the need to work for granted. Some would argue that it is a psychological necessity. Many would argue that the only reason they work is to earn a living. What is a living? One definition might be an income sufficient to house, clothe, and feed a family unsupported by welfare supplements. But average incomes in Western industrialized society among the ever-broadening middle class can provide a standard of living far beyond that definition. So maybe we work to progress in some way, to better our children and ourselves.

This may help to explain why – in addition to our paid work – we work in the garden, wash the car, decorate the house, and make the beds, even why we carry out voluntary work in the community. Some of this work may be necessary to maintain domestic order, but some might more properly be called lifestyle enhancement. In some cases we may be filling some inner need for recognition and respect that we cannot obtain in our paid work. It is clear that we work for many different reasons. But work we do, heads down, fulfilling daily routines and rituals in the belief – often without any great conviction – that somehow our contributions are helping to make a better world.

We grew up during the last half-century in the certainty that all the great technological advances – robots, computers, the Internet, the silicon chip – would save labor and thus create more leisure time. Today we are no longer so sure. Just as motorways created more traffic, technology has created more industries and yet more work. There seems to be an exponential relationship between what can be described loosely as "progress" and work.

In the first part of the twentieth century this might have seemed a good thing, because the regulated structure and factory-based nature of manufacturing employment dictated that more work equated to more jobs. These jobs were needed for growing populations, boosted by health improvements and as yet unchecked by reliable and widely available contraception. But the last decade of the twentieth century witnessed a dismantling of this structure and an erosion of the concept of the job, that neat package of work which had defined much of the employment of the previous two to three hundred years. The first decade of the twenty-first century has only reinforced the trend with the globalization of work through the offshoring of labor, increased labor migration, and the commoditization of many jobs.

Such changes have led to a belief that in the new century the influence of computers and the Internet is creating a watershed in the way we work as fundamental as that of the Industrial Revolution and the earlier Agrarian Revolution ten thousand years ago, when people developed the ability to raise crops.

While academics argue over the evidence for changes in work systems – the debates have been running for several years over whether job turnover is increasing or whether the rise in flexible working really is as marked as some have suggested – society across the Western world appears to be dividing increasingly into the haves and have-nots. This is not, however, simply a picture of rich and poor or employed and unemployed. The United States is witnessing the phenomenon of the working poor, people whose work provides them with insufficient income on which to live. At the same time there are chief executives of big publicly quoted companies who have seen their salaries and bonuses rise so much that they are earning 500 times more than their lowest paid employees. The redistribution of wealth has begun to look like "trickle up" rather than "trickle down."

The craziness is that some of these highly paid individuals are working such long hours they rarely have the opportunity to step outside their jobs and enjoy a moment's leisure. There used to be parts of our lives we could devote solely to play and leisure, but these precious days, once sacrosanct, have been invaded by the new communications of the work place. So often today, play is no longer divorced from work. I have sat alongside an FTSE 100 company chief, fishing by the riverbank – a form of work in itself, converted into relaxation – listening to him giving instructions on his cellphone. Standing next to him was a Scottish ghillie – the river keeper employed by the landowner to look after the water and assist the anglers. "Ghillie" is a Gaelic word, meaning "servant." On the river, however, the ghillie is the master of the company boss.

Out of his business environment the executive is happy to assume the role of apprentice. This change of role is subtle but significant. We must recognize that we have different roles in different situations. In Finland, schoolchildren are teaching their teachers in computing skills. In the new workplace authority is invested in knowledge, and knowledge is dissipated throughout society. It is not the exclusive preserve of the rich or the privileged.

Work has come to dominate the lives of the salaried masses, so much so that they are losing the ability to play. It is as if the world has become split into two societies – one with the means to enjoy leisure but not the time, and one that has the time but not the means.

Of course people still have their sports and pastimes. But when the salaried classes play today, they often condense their leisure into "leisure snacks." A party that would once have lasted all evening is shortened into a two-hour cocktail session. Meanwhile, "work snacks" are taken during leisure hours, as deals are negotiated on cellphones during breaks in the football game. Either way, the chunks of available time in today's "sound-bite" society are shortened to match our shrinking attention span.

In his book, *The Time Machine*, H. G. Wells imagined a future society which at some stage in its development had taken divergent paths, one in which the hedonist aristocracy and leisure seekers had devolved into a people of childlike innocence and naivety – he called them the Eloi – and one in which the laborers and mechanics, a manual underclass, had degenerated into troglodyte cannibalistic Morlocks trapped in a nether world of darkness and noise. He need not have worried. The laborer now seems as endangered a species as the blue whale.

Neither has the aristocracy prospered. The middle class has inherited the earth. It is a class that has successfully blended the industry of the Morlocks with the domestication of the Eloi, as dependent on its work as a cow is dependent on its field. The big difference is that cattle are herded into the field, whereas people go willingly and shut the gate behind them. We have become willing prisoners in what Max Weber, the German economist, called the "iron cage" of consumer and production driven materialism.[1]

At the dawn of a new century, as we travel on the commuter train, wearing our suits, reading our newspapers, and carrying our briefcases, are these troglodyte traits beginning to erode the roots of happiness in an insatiable pursuit of wealth and position? It was W. H. Davies, the itinerant poet, who wrote: "A poor life this if, full of care, We have no time to stand and stare."

Some years ago Juliet Schor, a Harvard economist, discovered in the research for her book, *The Overworked American*, that in the twenty years to 1992 the working hours of the average employee in the USA had increased by the equivalent of one month per year. Americans were choosing money over time.[2] Something appears to have gone terribly wrong with the way we work. The UK's Royal Society for the Encouragement of Arts, Manufactures and Commerce went so far as to publish a report, *Redefining Work*, which called for radical reforms to the infrastructure of society underpinning traditional forms of working.[3]

We have reached the stage where the way we work needs not only new definitions but also new explanations and understandings. It is important not just for us as individuals but for those who employ our skills. People today are often described as assets. Is that what we are – living, breathing assets, trapped and cocooned in the corporate and public sector webs that generate our incomes?

Charles Handy, the management writer, had predicted a portfolio society where people would live a kind of freelance existence, bundling together bits of work rather than holding down a traditional job. This seemed a logical alternative to the job, driven by demands for an individual's expertise, but as any actor or freelance writer can attest, the portfolio does not help when seeking a mortgage on the strength of it.

Only those portfolio workers who can demonstrate consistent employment over several years are going to be regarded by lending institutions on equal terms with those who have so-called permanent jobs. The infrastructure supporting the way we work has not caught up with this technological revolution, placing extraordinary pressures on the working lives of those in temporary or short-term positions.

Technology now allows a growing proportion of the population to work where it chooses, but attitudes to work remain rooted in the "nine to five" office model. Even the language of work draws upon outmoded definitions. The phrase "working from home" seems contradictory to many who associate home with leisure and domestic concerns. It is as if there is a great demarcation in time and space that many believe they must cross in their daily commute. Even those who have made the psychological break into home-working are struggling, faced with the need to stay in touch with others.

For millions of working people the emancipation promised by information technology has failed to materialize. Instead they find themselves ensnared by the demands of modern communication and the Internet. Voice mail, emails, the BlackBerry, and instant messaging have disrupted the environment for concentrated work.

In the information society work can be invisible. How do you reward the employee who is "thinking" over a work-related problem? Is this "thinking" not work? And what of the office gossip who might perform a more effective communications function than any management memo? Is that work?

There is a desperate need for a new psychology of work, a thorough dismantling of the old demarcations between work and leisure. Just as sports professionals are paid for what they enjoy doing, there must be some recognition by all employers that work can be fun and that there is a corporate necessity to make it so. At John Lewis, the UK retailer, the happiness of employees is considered a management priority.

There's the nub of it. Work can be stressful and taxing and boring and painful, but it can also be fun. So should we feel guilty for having fun in our work? Perhaps not, but we do, because most of Western society has become immersed in the Protestant work ethic – an ethos that has defined work for many people for hundreds of years, creating the belief among most of us that work is toil, that it is actually something we would rather not be doing but that we know we must do, nevertheless, because therein lies salvation; there is virtue in its accomplishment. This is the ethic that leaves no confusion about work, because work is categorized, pigeonholed, and defined. This is the ethic that defines work for work's sake, the ethic of job creation.

Challenging the Protestant work ethic, particularly in American society, has become a heresy. Suggesting that we might enjoy more leisure time, or asking the question "Why do we work?," is looked upon with scorn and suspicion, as the language of the shirker. In the world described by the Protestant work ethic there are those who work and those who are idle, and some of those who are idle, we all know, are idle because they choose to be, and idleness from choice is a sin.

But what of those whose work has been in vain or misdirected or downright destructive – scientists who struggle all their working lives on some false premise, architects who create ugly tower blocks, loggers who destroy the rain forest, soldiers whose work and expertise involve taking life in some pointless war?

What, also, of those whose work has been wasted – designers whose ideas are dismissed, writers whose books are not published, painters who destroy their work in despair? Some of this can be explained as training or necessary preparation for some later great work. It was the American artist J. A. McNeill Whistler who reminded a critic that his fees were based on "the knowledge of a lifetime." But much effort, indeed, is lost or misdirected in the makework society.

It sometimes seems as if there is no longer any working class. We are all middle class now. Yet, asked in a recent UK survey to describe their status, most people opted for the definition "working class."[4] Why should we be surprised at such results when work has come to dominate our existence? Dual-income couples toil in offices to finance private schooling, to pay for nannies to rear their children, gardeners to tend their lawns, and domestic cleaners to keep their houses. Work has run out of kilter. It is messing up our lives.

People are yearning for the opportunity to regain some balance in their lives but governments and companies appear blinkered to this daily struggle. Social security systems are structured for a society of employed and unemployed. Yet impoverishment is everywhere, not the grinding poverty of hunger and hopelessness, but the poverty of riches. Our lives are choked with work. How did it get like this?

The aim of this book is to examine, using a historical perspective, the evolution of work from the earliest times and the impact of great watersheds of development. It will look at early societies, slavery, the guilds, the creation of trade secrets, and the influence of religion on work, examining the humanist ideals of the great Quaker industrialists and the ideas of theorists like F. W. Taylor, Max Weber, Elton Mayo, Mary Parker Follett, Peter Drucker, and W. Edwards Deming. It will look at where we have been and where we are going. Finally it will suggest some ideas for adjusting our outlook on work and its role in our lives.

CHAPTER 1

Hands to the Grindstone

> Two roads diverged in a wood, and I –
> I took the road less traveled by,
> And that has made all the difference.
> (Robert Frost, 1874–1963)

Some years ago on a hike in the English Lake District with my two eldest sons, we struck out off the path to climb a scree slope on the southern side of Pike O'Stickle, a conical peak near the head of the Langdale Valley. The steep slope is covered in shards of hard blue rock. Some of the pieces have distinctive chips down a narrow edge, signs that they were once worked by a human hand. These are the discards from a Stone Age axe quarry sited where the hard rock outcrops near the peak.

Just how the rock was mined and worked is unknown. The outcrop is nearly two thousand feet above the valley floor. A small shelter has been hewn into the rock nearby. It is not known whether the shelter was associated with the workings, but what is quite clear is that the mine was used regularly for extraction and the preparation of axes.[1]

Was this an early form of production line in which experts created tools and passed them on or traded them with other communities nearby?[2] However the work was achieved, whether it involved individuals, specialist teams, or family groups, it was industry in every sense of the word.

But by the Neolithic period we should expect such organization. This, after all, was the period when people were constructing Stonehenge. To find the origins of work itself we must look back much further, since our ancestors had been perfecting recognizable skills far earlier than the Stone Age, possibly to the very dawn of humanity when hominids were beginning to spread out of Africa. Was life at that time really so "solitary, poor, nasty, brutish, and short," as Thomas Hobbes would have it?

The notion of humanity's miserable existence in an early struggle for survival has long proved attractive to those who are unable to conceive of evolution as anything less than progressive. The evidence for continual improvement seems overwhelming, particularly in technology, where only the very earliest inventions such as the ability to create fire, make rope, and tie knots continue to evade our detection. The evidence accumulated from the discovery of flint and stone artifacts, however, means that we now know from discoveries in Tanzania's Olduvai Gorge that our ancestors had learned to use rudimentary tools as early as 2,500,000 years ago.[3]

We have come a long way since then. But what kind of route did we take? Was it forever onwards and upwards? Is the way we live now immeasurably improved from that which existed when the differentiation between man and beast may have been little more than the combination of inventiveness, chance, and motivation? Sufficient evidence is emerging from remains of human activity going back 500,000 years to suggest that early hominids may have struggled less than fashionable thinking would once have had us believe. So much so that we may have to alter the way we think about progression and regression. Even the ability to walk on two feet has been seen to have its drawbacks, although Graham Richards, the anthropologist, perhaps went too far when he wrote some years ago that bipedalism did not so much free the hands as enslave the feet.[4]

But the comment did remind us that progression in one direction can and often does lead to regression in others. One person's technological revolution is another person's de-skilling. Is this always for the best? Richards's point was probably meant to be mischievous. The ability to walk gave our ancestors the opportunity to spread themselves over a far greater range. It gave them the flexibility to come down from the trees at will. Walking would have been gradually transformed by evolution from an acquired to an innate ability and, for some, to a joy. Most of us can experience the joy of walking, even today. Why, then, do people continue to be obsessed by the idea of taking short cuts?

This is one of the underlying questions of this book, one that the members of some households and the directors of some businesses might ask themselves occasionally. Why take a short cut when you enjoy walking? The answer of course is that we must forget the enjoyment when the short cut allows us to get there faster, beating the other guy, the one who for some unfathomable reason chose the path less traveled by. But what happens when we get there? Is the "being there" as good as the getting there? When Neil Armstrong put his foot on the moon he spoke of "one small step" and "one giant leap." It was the step, the leap, the getting there that occupied his mind.

The artifacts of prehistory cannot possibly tell us everything about the lifestyles, the character, and the priorities of our ancestors, but, as we shall see, they do provide clues which can be matched with what we know about the lifestyles of those who have not obviously changed their patterns of living beyond those offered by hunter-gathering.

The Yir Yoront tribe of Aborigines who live at the mouth of the Coleman River on the Cape York Peninsula in Northern Australia had not developed technologies beyond stone axes before their first contact with European missionaries in 1903.[5] They were genuine hunter-gatherers, relying on game and fish that they caught and vegetables they found growing wild in the bush. Their axes were made from stone quarried four hundred miles to the south, but they were able to trade for them through a succession of middlemen.[6] Their currency was spears tipped with the barbs of stingrays. Who is to say that some similar trade did not occur in Neolithic Europe?

Was this hunter-gathering lifestyle necessarily so arduous? Richard Lee, an anthropologist who spent fifteen months with a tribe of Kalahari bushmen, noted that the adults spent no more than two or three days each week finding food.[7] Men who were out of luck in the hunt would give up and spend time talking with their neighbors or dancing. The Hadza people in Africa managed to limit their hunting to two hours a day, on average, preferring to spend more time in diversionary pursuits such as gambling. "Hadza men seem more concerned with games of chance than chances of game," wrote Marshall Sahlins, the anthropologist, who went so far as to describe hunter-gatherers as "the original affluent society." What would Thomas Hobbes have made of such remarks?

The Yir-Yoront do not make any great distinction between work and play. They do have a word – "woq" – that is used to refer to various tasks and chores.[8] But the chores – this woq – did not include hunting. Hunting, the most fundamental activity in a hunter-gathering society, was not viewed as work.[9] Work in this society seemed to be viewed as something they would rather not be doing. Isn't this concept – something I would rather not be doing – one of the most recognizable definitions of work for most of us? And what if it is? Surely in our sophisticated world, we may argue, there is nothing we can learn from people, whether ancient or modern, whose lives were so basic. How can we compare the needs and desires of hominids with our own? Mankind has marched so confidently through the millennia that its earliest experiences can be nothing but an imprint in our genes. Or are we closer to our origins than we think? Perhaps we can learn something from the meager evidence left behind by our ancestors of their existence.

It is not so long ago that we described these early people as subhuman. There were those detractors who seized upon the romantic notion of man the hunter – John Dryden's "noble savage" – only to have their judgment questioned by theories suggesting that early hominids were scavengers who competed with hyenas and other carnivores foraging for the remains of some fresh kill.[10] The debate over humanity's progression along the pecking order continues, but evidence is accumulating to suggest that, if scavenging was practiced, the hominid had also become a hunter by the time he moved out of Africa.

The 1997 discovery in Schöningen, Germany, of three 400,000-year-old wooden spears, the oldest complete hunting weapons found to date, is surely enough to restore man the hunter to his pedestal. The spruce spears, one of which measured seven feet in length, were surrounded by the remains of at least fourteen horses. These remains showed signs that the horses had been butchered, suggesting that the archeologists had found some kind of preparation station, where spears were sharpened for the hunt and meat from successful kills was cut up and possibly cooked for consumption.[11]

It now appears that the first hominids to colonize northern Europe were not, as some had thought, opportunistic scavengers reacting to circumstances in a haphazard fashion. They were hunters with an element of sophistication and organization in the way they went about their work. We have not only discovered man the hunter, but man the worker. Is it too fanciful to believe that these hominids could have formed pioneering bands of colonization? They may have included the most skilled and adventurous spirits of their time.

The wooden spears mentioned were constructed with care. The tips were carved from the base of the tree where the wood was hardest and most dense, weighting them perfectly for throwing. Similarly, albeit at a much later date toward the end of the Stone Age, the Lake District site had been chosen specially because of the quality of the stone. The outcrop can only be reached after some tough climbing.

Some of the most convincing evidence of highly skilled work, dating back some half a million years, has been discovered in quarry sites at the West Sussex village of Boxgrove in the UK, where archeologists have unearthed eight hundred flint handaxes. Some were expertly created and some, as Nick Ashton, a flint tool specialist at the British Museum points out, were less well made, "as if experts and novices were working side by side."[12]

The dexterity needed in hand-axe construction should not be underrated. The process used to work a flint nodule by striking away shavings – usually using a bone hammer – until the required shape and sharpness have been achieved is called flint knapping. Francis Wenban-Smith, an archeologist who has mastered these knapping skills, describes hand-axe construction as an art. He likens the skill to playing chess, because the axe-maker needs to think some five or six moves ahead when making blows to shape the tool.[13]

Most of the Boxgrove hand-axes, though ovate with one pointed edge, have a tapered shape, like that of a discus, sharpened around their entire perimeter. When the Boxgrove archeologists asked a professional butcher to use one for cutting meat, he handled it with ease. The shape allowed him to cut with comfortable sweeping motions. He found he did not need to hold it firmly, which might have led to him suffering cuts to his hand. It is possible that the flints may have had some other use, but all the evidence at Boxgrove points toward butchery.

Mark Roberts, the site director, has described the butchery area as a meat-processing site.[14] The evidence is compelling. Unlike many other paleontological sites, this one involved examining an almost perfectly preserved level of land. The land, buried by debris from a collapsed cliff and successive layers of glacial deposits, had been virtually undisturbed for 500,000 years. The flints were found where they had been discarded. From the arrangement of shards of flint on the ground it was possible to detect in which position the knapper had been sitting as he worked on the tool.

Knapping is an acquired art. John Lord, an expert knapper who often gives lessons to students, says that even after a week's practice novices are rarely competent enough to fashion a hand-axe with the level of skill used on the Boxgrove axes. "The one thing these early people had which we lack today," says Lord, "is time. They could take the time to make their tools properly." While the sex of the toolmakers is not known, Lord believes that some may have been women. "Women seem to pick up the skill more quickly than men," he says.[15]

In their book, *Fairweather Eden*, Michael Pitts and Mark Roberts describe the way that the archeological team at Boxgrove was able to map out a specific area. From the positioning of flints around the bones of a horse they were able to reconstruct what must be one of the earliest examples of people engaged in organized work. Grooves made from the butchery were clearly visible in the horse bones. "The horse rose from the drawings, heavy on the ground," they write, "surrounded by squatting figures, knapping their flint knives." With justifiable pride they note that "nowhere, never, had anyone before seen anything like this. Not for half a million years, anyway."[16]

The site was based on a plain at the foot of chalk cliffs on an area of land that in even earlier times had been covered by the sea. Whether those who worked there lived in the immediate area or on a higher and more protected site nearby is unknown, but the excavation found no remains of burial or habitation. Two teeth and a tibia were found, confirming beyond doubt the hominid presence. Were these early commuters who walked home to a safer shelter after a day of hunting and foraging on the plain? Clearly the dexterity of these hominids cannot be dismissed as the brutish efforts of beasts at the lower end of the evolutionary scale. People and their ancestors have been capable of applying their brains to carry out work for hundreds of thousands of years. The ingenuity of the people who created houses from mammoth bones at a number of sites in eastern Europe twenty thousand years ago demonstrates that the art of building has a long and creative history.[17] Would specialization have been attached to the work of some individuals, designated as builders, perhaps?

This seems to have been the case among those responsible for cave art. The seventeen-thousand-year-old cave paintings at Lascaux, in southern France, were created by individuals who could demonstrate real artistic talent. They displayed a mastery of techniques such as stenciling and the use of shading to create a three-dimensional representation. Working by the light of tallow lamps, the Lascaux artists showed so much technical ability that Professor André Leroi-Gourhan, a specialist in French prehistoric art, has described them as "professionals."[18] Craftsmen, he believes, would have been released from other duties to create these paintings.

By the time they began their work they could already draw on thousands of years of experience. Paintings found in the Chauvet Cave in the Ardeche, dated some thirty-two thousand years ago, reveal that even at this stage people had developed an ability to create a faithful representation of shape and form. They also understood the rules of perspective. The finest illuminators of medieval manuscripts could not reproduce anything like this realism. The Aurignacian people responsible for this work were also carving ivory figurines of animals and fantasy figures, such as man-beasts. Such figurines, dated to the same period as the Chauvet cave paintings, have been found in the Volgelherd and Hohlenstein-Stadel sites in the Danube river valley. A bone flute has been found in a further cave at Geissenklosterle.[19] By the time that art appeared at Lascaux, people were already weaving textiles.[20]

We know from the Renaissance that when a particular talent, such as painting, is prized by a society, it can stimulate a cultural flowering in which skills and abilities are transferred across whole populations, but these skills may not always be retained where societies are exposed to the ebb and flow of competing influences. According to Alice Kelly, an aboriginal woman interviewed in *National Geographic* magazine, "all Aborigines are born artists." She told her interviewer: "You would be too, but your culture has driven it out of you."[21] It seems that at various stages in human history people have developed remarkable skills then lost them. Either that or the skills have simply been discarded as no longer important. We must reassess our attitudes to early societies. As our knowledge of unrecorded history accumulates we begin to understand the sophistication of Stone Age people. They had become accomplished hunters, farmers, and artists. They had medical skills and had developed rituals and spiritual beliefs. They understood the seasons and weather patterns. They towered over the land, conquerors of their environment.

Stone Age society was witnessing the emergence of industrial people. The ability to quarry and mine, for example, had become both specialized and organized by the time that Neolithic people began constructing the flint mines at Grimes Graves in Norfolk (where axes from Langdale, some 300 miles away, have been discovered, reinforcing the notion of a healthy Neolithic trading society) somewhere between 2,800 and 1,800 BC.

By these dates humanity had created or embarked on some of the greatest undertakings in history. They had built the city of Ur and its great ziggurat, the pyramids at Giza, and the stone circle of Stonehenge. How did the earliest industries emerge? Were people born to work? Was work a means to an end? Or had work, even then, become a necessary constituent of self-fulfillment? The experience of the Yir Yoront suggests that the development of the tool pre-dates any real understanding of work as a concept. There was what needed to be done. It was a way of life. As Richard Lee and Irven De Vore wrote after a 1966 conference in Chicago had renewed interest in early lifestyles: "Cultural Man has been on Earth for some two million years; for over 99 percent of this period he has lived as a hunter-gatherer." They called the hunting way of life "the most successful and persistent adaptation man has ever achieved."[22]

So how did he ever come to be carrying a briefcase, following a dress code, and pushing buttons on a keyboard? And was it for the best? In the 1950s Carleton Coon drew a Neanderthal man wearing a trilby hat to emphasize how close he was in looks to modern people, suggesting we wouldn't look askance if we saw him on the subway. The only thing about the cartoon that looks out of place today is the trilby.

But there may be something else out of place. Would the Neanderthal have the same way of thinking as those of us who were reared in households where the nearest thing to hunter-gatherers are those whom we describe as the breadwinners? If we look back to these earliest times we can see that work itself has a history, changing in nature and understanding, just as language, customs, and fashions have changed throughout the ages. What can this history tell us about the way we approach our work today?

One important lesson is that the way we organize work should not be taken for granted. Does work need a boss, a leader, some director of operations? Or can it simply happen, driven by need or desire or a spirit of cooperation? What can we learn from what has been discovered about the patterns of early societies?

Many contemporary paleo-archeologists and anthropologists are coming around to the idea that the history of civilization is not characterized by a steady upward curve of progress and that progress itself must be defined with some care if we understand its meaning as an ascent from barbarism. There is growing evidence that some of the earliest societies had learned to coexist in a harmonious relationship.

The late Marija Gimbutas aroused controversy among archeologists when she made a case for the existence of a pan-European civilization oriented toward women. This civilization, she believed, flourished for three thousand years between 6,500 and 3,500 BC. Discoveries of female effigies at many Stone Age sites, and the arrangement of some burial sites which seem to represent the female form, have led to a hypothesis that many European Stone Age communities were centered on the woman as the giver of life. Ms Gimbutas – supported, it should be said, by sections of the feminist movement – used these discoveries to argue against a model of civilization based on a warrior-led hierarchical political and religious organization overseeing a complex division of labor.

Societies had shown they could thrive, she argued, based on balanced and cooperative arrangements between men and women. Certainly the archeological discoveries at Çatal Hüyük in Turkey, a Stone Age town founded more than eight thousand years ago, suggest that Stone Age people were capable of organizing themselves with a degree of complexity sufficient to support a community estimated at about seven thousand people. Çatal Hüyük's buildings were mudbrick constructions around timber frames. The town was built close to a volcano, an important source of obsidian, used for making cutting tools and mirrors. The people were capable of making pottery and fabrics. One wall painting was created in the image of a geometric textile pattern.

As Richard Rudgley points out in his book, *Lost Civilizations of the Stone Age*, "This shows that woven rugs, what we now know as kilims, were innovations of the Stone Age."[23] Other artifacts and iconography suggest that the people of this site, too, engaged in the worship of some mother goddess. Exactly what led to Çatal Hüyük's abandonment, after a period of settled development spanning more than a thousand years, is not clear, but it seems that this civilization, like the much later Roman Empire, was overtaken by people who, to put it simply, chose to live differently.[24]

These changes are so often characterized as barbaric invasions that we have become accustomed to view history as a story of conquest. Even the combined genius of Stanley Kubrick and Arthur C. Clarke, in the opening to the film *2001*, portrayed the first hominid discovery of the tool as a type of weapon to be used as a source of dominance of one group over another. As the sun rises to the tune of *Thus Spake Zarathustra* by Richard Strauss an animal bone is transformed in the mind of an ape into a weapon with which it can subdue its enemies. The interpretation is understandable enough. Innovation, throughout the history of the last five thousand years, has so often been spurred by conflict and the urge of one society to prevail against another. Be it the longbow or the tank, there seems to be a common purpose of domination.

Weaponry and warfare pre-dated the society of Çatal Hüyük for sure. The earliest evidence of human conflict has been found at Waddi Kubbaniya in the Nile Valley, Egypt, where archeologists have found the twenty-thousand-year-old skeleton of a man killed by spears.[25] At that time, most of Europe was in the grip of the last Ice Age, which would have forced people together in areas such as the Nile flood plains, where they could still find food. Conflict most probably arose out of competition for resources. When the ice retreated, providing increased living space, it could well have created the conditions for a settled society.

Kubrick was engaged by the idea of humanity's inability to control a propensity to violence. His suggestion that our ancestor first picked up a stick in order to beat another ape over the head, however, is not supported by observation of the use of tools in the animal kingdom. Laying aside Kubrick and Clarke's entertaining notion that human invention was triggered by aliens, their interpretation of this transformational discovery overlooks the overwhelming evidence from the earliest hominid-related archeology that the tool, not the weapon, is the defining symbol of humanity. Surely the plowshare came before the sword.

The tool, after all, is simply a device to achieve an aim more effectively. Given that basic human needs are food, warmth, and shelter it seems reasonable to suggest that the first tools were used in the pursuit of such needs and that their use as weaponry, beyond that of hunting, was a later development. The tool, we now know, is not the sole preserve of humans. Neither is the division of labor. Chimpanzees have been observed using stones to crack nuts and sticks to search out termites.[26] Meerkats have a cooperative arrangement in which they interchange roles, sometimes burrowing for food, sometimes acting as lookouts. Do meerkats or chimpanzees regard their tasks as work? Did pit ponies who rarely saw the light of day as they pulled their heavy loads, and do carrier pigeons and guide dogs for the blind, have any idea that what they are doing would be, in human terms, classed as work?

The major distinction is that the chimpanzees are either helping themselves or working for the benefit of their social group, whereas the animals pressed into the service of people are constrained to do the bidding of others. Only people appear to have recognized at some stage in their history that things they were doing initially to sustain and enhance the quality of their lives could be regarded as work. In that sense humanity is unique. But when did work begin to take on its biblical definition as a burden, something that man, in his punishment, would be compelled to suffer "in the sweat of thy face?"[27]

The grindstone so clearly associated with monotonous labor can be dated back almost fifty thousand years.[28] By the time the Natufian culture of the Levant, that flourished between 10,500 and 8,000 BC, had demonstrated the capabilities to process grain with mortar and pestle and store harvests in settled sites, the daily grind was already a well-established constituent of domestic living.

At the dawn of the dynastic period of ancient Egypt, the age in which some historians would have us believe that civilization began,[29] manual work, at least, had already come to be recognized as something to be avoided by those privileged enough to escape its clutches. Moreover, people had discovered that the slingshot could be aimed as readily at an opponent's head as it could at a threatening wolf.

They had tasted conquest. They had begun to enslave each other. If ever there had been an Eden where people did what they had to do, free from any compulsion beyond that of satisfying their most basic needs, by the time the first Pharaohs assumed control over upper and lower Egypt, any semblance of such an age of innocence had passed.

Accumulating knowledge of prehistoric society is reshaping our understanding of the past. It may also begin to influence our thinking about organizations and the way we work. Is there a "natural state" for the organization? Is a hierarchical, status driven society a natural progression of mankind or a successful deviation that has held sway over the most creative yet, at the same time, destructive period of our existence? Is it time for us to consider some different path, one that, though less traveled, might lead us to a better accommodation between the way we work and the way we live and enjoy our lives?

The creatures that came down from the trees and began to roam upright over the land appear to have developed something beyond the need simply to survive. Uniquely they had the ability to oppose the forefinger precisely to the thumb. They were handy people and they seem to have moved with a sense of purpose. If anything drives our organizations today it must be in a similar sense that what they are doing has a common purpose to improve the lives of all those involved with the endeavor. If they fail to fulfill this objective, then they, like some species of hominid, will in time reach their own evolutionary dead end. What evidence of their industry will the great commercial undertakings of the twentieth century leave behind them?

CHAPTER 2

Fettered Lives

Slavery they can have anywhere. It is a weed that grows in
every soil.

(Edmund Burke, 1729–97)

Whenever we try to create categories for anything we lose something. We lose the subtle shading, the variety that exists in almost
every aspect of life. How often do we become angered or frus-
trated when faced with a check-box questionnaire offering us
no choice that really fits the description we want to apply to the
subject? Well, this box, we decide, is the closest, so we compromise or settle for checking the standard questionnaire miscellany
box marked "other."

I found myself encountering similar frustration as I began
to open this chapter with the observation that at some stage in
his evolution the hunter-gatherer abandoned a nomadic lifestyle for the more secure arrangement offered by subsistence
farming. I am sure this is true for some, but not for all. Hunter-
gathering was not necessarily an exclusive activity. Some people
who farmed would continue to hunt. Some people who roamed
nomadically would plant crops. Some would roam continuously; some would put down roots for a while then roam some
more; some would put down roots and settle in one spot for the
rest of their lives. These stages in human evolutionary behavior were witnessed by the earliest European colonists of New
England, who noticed that the native people both planted crops
and hunted.[1]

When historians talk, therefore, about the Agrarian Revolution
or the Industrial Revolution, they are talking about a large-scale
change in lifestyles but not an exclusive change. The Industrial
Revolution did not put an end to farming, just as the Agrarian
Revolution did not put an end to hunter-gathering or nomadic
lifestyles.

The urge to categorize and define – very much a feature of masculine left-brained thinking – continues to create problems and unnecessary arguments. Did, for example, civilization begin with the ability to write and govern – two of the traditional pointers – or did it begin with some relaxed acknowledgment of certain "human" rights or behaviors grouped around some common purpose such as collective security or mutualism?

If we accept the traditional view of civilization, that it emerged with the recognizable features of the ordered state, we must accept that one underlying feature of those states – the systematic use of slave labor – did not recognize the most basic of human rights, those of freedom of movement and freedom of expression. We do not know when it was that man came up with the idea of enslaving his fellow man. But it is a stage in human history as fundamental to our development as any technological discovery.[2]

We might surmise that slavery only occurred after certain patterns of living had been established and certain technologies were refined enough to determine the physical character of enslavement. A true nomad, for example, can have few material possessions if his livelihood depends on following migrating herds. Slavery in a mobile hunter-gathering tribal society would have been less desirable, partly because the most important work of the tribe involved hunting. Giving your slave a weapon for the hunt would not have been the brightest of ideas. There were few chores that did not involve tools easily adaptable as weapons.

North American Indians who hunted the buffalo on the Great Plains had no tradition of slavery. If they fought with neighboring tribes their captives would be slaughtered or set free. But then, as we have seen with the Yir Yoront, the hunter-gatherer may have had an ill-defined concept of work. It may well be that an initial notion of work, that which defines it as something to be avoided, emerged between the sexes. Women were not as physically suited to hunting because of their comparative lack of strength. They would also have the maternal duty of feeding their young. Both issues remain to undermine workplace equality to this day. But these deficiencies and responsibilities would not have precluded the gathering of wild vegetables and berries. It seems likely that women, therefore, would have been the first to explore ways of preparing, preserving, and cultivating food. They, after all, suffered the greatest inconvenience in following the hunt.

Men did the hunting and most probably butchered the meat. These are the areas of food preparation in which men tend to maintain the strongest interest. Even the most domestically challenged male who views the kitchen strictly as a female domain will transform himself into chief cook and provider if a modern family decides to have a barbecue. Give him a pan and a gas stove and he doesn't want to know. Give him some charcoal, firelighters, and tongs and he is happiness personified. Was there some evolutionary event that equipped the human male with a barbecue gene?

In his book, *The Selfish Gene*, Richard Dawkins speculates on the way ideas can be transferred almost like viruses across populations. He calls these ideas "memes." Building on this idea, Susan Blackmore has suggested in her book, *The Meme Machine*, that such cultural ideas can evolve and reproduce within the mind. Douglas Adams toyed with the theory in his *Hitch Hiker's Guide to the Galaxy*, in which Mr Prosser – council employee and direct male-line descendant of Genghis Khan – is unable to explain his attraction to fur hats or his regressionary images of axe-wielding horsemen. So was the early division of labor a matter of natural selection, sexual preference, or possibly both? We can only speculate.

We do not know, of course, whether women were the first to experiment with grindstones, but we do know that the ability to create surplus food and to live in one place created new tasks, new chores, new work. A place needed to be kept clean, there was a need for building skills, woodworking skills, and all the skills and accumulating of knowledge associated with agriculture.

When people began to settle they were, however unwittingly, creating the conditions for slavery to exist. The idea of sparing a foe's life in return for his labor might have begun to appeal where a need for extra labor had been identified and where a surplus existed for its support. The late Moses Finley, a Cambridge-based historian, identified three conditions he considered necessary for the development of slavery: the private ownership of land requiring a permanent workforce, the development of commodity production and markets, and the scarcity of any alternative internal labor supply.[3]

Certain technological developments would also have been necessary. Wood and rope would have been sufficient to secure an individual's imprisonment, although the ability to create metal chains would have added a new dimension of security. The domestication of animals was not achieved overnight. Neither was the domestication and enslavement of humanity.

By the time the slave had become an accepted part of society in the Greek and Roman eras, the ways and means of maintaining large numbers of people in slavery were well established. A further important feature of mass slavery was the desire and ability of one society to conquer and subjugate another. Could it be that humanity's capacity for war was derived from some innate urge to remain mobile and hunt?

Whether or not Marija Gimbutas was correct in her belief that European Stone Age society had perfected an egalitarian idyll, it was a way of life that was unable to defend itself from the horse-borne and warlike Kurgan tribes who swept into Europe from the steppe lands to the east. Whatever customs had prevailed throughout the Stone Age were swept away by a hierarchical and status-driven society that would become the dominant model for human relations. The physically strongest of the humans – the men – established themselves at the head of this society. Male thinking, male concerns, male attitudes would shape what men, without a trace of irony, would come to recognize as civilization.

The economies of the greatest of classical civilizations – those of Greece and Rome – were founded on the most uncivilized of human conditions: slavery. For hundreds of years in Greece and Rome slavery was the most common form of manual labor. These were slave societies – the two most ancient of five slave societies identified by Finley. (The other three were the United States, the Caribbean, and Brazil.) In classical Greece and Roman Italy, even skilled labor was often carried out by slaves. Some were employed in a professional capacity as doctors and teachers. By far the greatest use of slave labor, however, was in agriculture, a common feature of slavery wherever it has been used throughout history.

That Roman slaves were chained, whipped, and subject to gross physical abuse is well documented. This did not make for

happy slaves and led to several serious revolts, the most famous
of which, led by Spartacus in 73 BC, was brutally suppressed, the
bodies of the executed captives lining the routes into Rome so
that all could witness the futility of insurrection.

The unease of the slave owner – best summarized, perhaps,
by a Roman proverb which held that the number of your enemies
equaled the number of your slaves – created a thirst for some
better rationale for the management of slaves. In *De re rustica*,
which must surely be one of the earliest examples of the management textbook – it was written in the mid-first century AD –
the agricultural writer, Columella, outlined guidelines for the
treatment and management of slaves.[4] Its philosophy was very
much that of the stick and the carrot.

Columella's approach was driven by expediency. People will
respond most positively, he reasoned, if you treat them well and
give them some promise of reward. Sick slaves need careful attention, he wrote. Those working inside a villa need ample kitchen
space to accommodate their households. Their cells, although
fitted with chains for the hours of darkness, should have some
opening for natural light; slaves need also to be provided with
sturdy clothes to allow them to work in all weathers. Even some
consultation with a slave is desirable, he argued, since it gives the
impression that the slave master is interested in the slave's work,
thereby generating greater enthusiasm on the part of the slave.

The motive behind these methods is clearly stated: "Such justice and consideration on the part of the owner," says Columella,
"contributes greatly to the increase of his estate."[5] Is this what
many hundreds of years later would be described as enlightened self-interest? Such thinking would not be out of place in
the "family friendly" employment policies of today's companies.
Should we, therefore, identify Columella as the father of human
resources management as we know it?

Maybe not. Keith Bradley says in his book, *Slaves and
Masters in the Roman Empire: A Study in Social Control*, that
Columella's advice was not unique in Roman society. Others such
as Varro, Cato, and Seneca recognized the benefits to be gained
from the humane treatment of slaves. But the management theory
was designed as a means to an end. As Bradley points out: "It
is quite clear that Columella's recommendations on the treatment

of slaves were designed to promote servile efficiency as the key to economic productivity in a situation where the owner's profit from the agricultural production was a dominating principal."[6]

None of Columella's guidelines could ensure productivity. "Slaves could not simply be forced to work by virtue of their subject status," writes Bradley, but "their social contentment had to be secured as a prelude to work efficiency and general loyalty." In fact productivity was not a significant factor in Columella's advice. A slave's output seemed to be less of a concern than his behavior. *Fides et obsequium*, loyalty and obedience, were the most sought-after underlying qualities.[7] Columella went further than other theorists when he recommended that the slave owner could hold out the prospect of freedom as the strongest incentive for good and faithful service.

Bradley is at pains to emphasize that none of these ideas influenced the general view of slaves among the ruling classes as idle and feckless. Again this has parallels in some of the entrenched attitudes among those twentieth-century employers who allowed their labor relations to be conducted in an atmosphere of mutual distrust. That Columella's ideas did not enjoy universal or lasting support was demonstrated centuries later by Frederick Douglass, a former slave whose moving stories of slave mistreatment proved to be a powerful influence on the US abolitionist movement.

A skilled orator, Douglass noted in 1855 that different levels of treatment could produce a hierarchy of aspirations: "Beat and cuff your slave, keep him hungry and spiritless, and he will follow the chain of his master like a dog; but feed and clothe him well – work him moderately – surround him with physical comfort – and dreams of freedom intrude. Give him a bad master, and he aspires to a good master; give him a good master and he wishes to become his own master."[8] This seems to echo the popular nineteenth-century tenet that if you "spare the rod you spoil the child," an attitude born in the same Protestant stable.

There is no doubt that the practice of slavery underpinned the great classical empires of Greece and Rome. But these slave societies were not sustainable. The very success of slavery, where slaves became part of almost every area of employment outside the military and the senate, may have been one of the principal ingredients of Rome's demise. The citizens of Rome had lost any work ethic they once possessed. Their lifestyle was so corrupted, so hedonistic, that they were no longer capable of defending their overstretched empire. We can see the development of something resembling Wells's Eloi and Morlocks. The relatively sophisticated and, in terms of administration and infrastructure, advanced society within Rome's walls had become supine, physically a civilization but spiritually and morally retarded.

While its citizens on the streets were sedated by the Colosseum's increasingly degrading spectacles, beneath the city, hidden in the catacombs, human morality and decency were preserved among a gradually strengthening troglodyte population – the persecuted Christians. But, unlike the Wellsian vision, Rome's underground Christians were the vulnerable ones, hiding from the ruling elite who could enjoy the daylight.

Rome's fickle, leisure-loving populace, a degenerating society enfeebled by its very success and wealth, began to weaken at the center, so that when the northern hordes under Alaric crossed the Rhine and marched on the world's greatest city in AD 410, they discovered a population that had grown flabby and debased, a society that, in spite of – or even because of – its grandeur, was evaporating within a moral vacuum of its own making. Roman society dissolved because the will to preserve it had disappeared.

This is not to say that Roman society was replaced by an industrious Germanic code. Tacitus saw it differently. The Visigoth was action personified in war, but after the fight was over he liked to take life easy. Tacitus wrote: "When the state has no war to manage the German mind is sunk in sloth. The chase does not provide sufficient employment. The time is passed in sleep and gluttony. The intrepid warrior, who in the field braved every danger, becomes in time of peace a listless sluggard. The management of his house and lands he leaves to the women, to the old men, and the infirm. He himself lounges in stupid repose, by a wonderful diversity of nature exhibiting in the same man the most inert aversion to labor, and the fiercest principle of action."[9]

This passage from *Germanica* is more than simply an interesting early example of the pot calling the kettle black. It suggests that even in Roman times there was a recognition of the merits of industry and a dissatisfaction with the unadulterated pursuit of leisure. Is this a precursor of the Protestant work ethic? The Greek poet,

Hesiod, certainly appeared to be thinking on these lines in his *Works and Days*, some 828 lines of friendly advice for the working man in the eighth century BC, when he wrote: "Work is no disgrace: it is idleness which is a disgrace."

Slavery did not disappear with the fall of Rome. The very word "slave," from the eastern European *Slav*, is passed down from the continuing trade in European slaves, often with North Africa, that persisted into medieval times. The Latin word for slave, *servus*, became the basis of "serf." Most historians seek to distinguish the status of "serf" from that of "slave," arguing that the serf was the master of certain possessions – farm buildings and agricultural tools – even if they did not belong to him. But the same could be argued for some slaves. The most helpful distinction might be to think of the slave as a chattel, a possession, a tradable commodity, whereas the serf was more a unit of production who had some measure of protection from the lord and greater autonomy over his working hours, so long as he delivered the goods.

The distinction is muddied and possibly irrelevant outside academic circles, where the classicist may feel that slavery comes into his territory, leaving serfdom for the medievalist. Over time it may have been economic rather than any emancipatory concerns or pressures that allowed the practice to wither. Adam Smith noted in the *Wealth of Nations*: "It appears from the experience of all ages and nations, that work done by free men comes cheaper in the end than that performed by slaves."[10]

More important than the concept of slavery, perhaps, is the concept of freedom. Only when you understand what it is to be free can you determine whether your condition is that of the slave. Ancient Greeks who consulted the Delphic Oracle could see definitions of the four elements of freedom inscribed on the walls of the shrine. The free man, said the Oracle, could represent himself in legal matters, would not be subject to seizure and arrest, could do what he wished, and could go where he wished. All of these factors, of course, needed to be interpreted within the bounds of the law. William Lim Westerman, another classicist, argued that the reversal of these factors could define the condition of slavery in ancient Greece. The Greek slave, therefore, must be represented by a master, be subject to seizure and arrest, must do as his master orders, and cannot go where he pleases.[11]

The difficulty for those seeking to arrive at a modern interpretation of classical slavery is that it was possible in Greece for people to fill some of these definitions in part. Thus there were different degrees of slavery, and there was no sharp dividing line between slavery and freedom. Some slaves in industrial towns, for example, lived together, away from their masters. Some could attain a degree of elevation in their social rank. According to Finley, "the efficient, skilled, reliable slave could look forward to managerial status."[12]

The difference between slavery and freedom has taxed philosophers throughout the ages. In *De cive*, published in 1642, Thomas Hobbes decided that the free man was subservient only to the state.[13] The slave, he concluded, was an individual who was subservient to his fellow man as well as to the state. This is not so very different from Aristotle's observation that "the condition of a free man is that he does not live under the restraint of another."[14]

Free men in ancient Greek society tended to work on their own. Where people were employed in groups they tended to be slaves. A classical Athenian dragged into the twenty-first century might struggle to determine the status of a corporate employee working under managerial control – under the restraint of another. Are these free men and women, he might ask, or are they slaves to their jobs or to their employers?

He would be even more flummoxed to discover that these people are paid for their work, that they are free to leave their employment, can live where they wish, and can possess a passport so that they can go where they please. They even have rights when faced with arrest. Yet he might, nevertheless, decide that they are something less than truly free. Perhaps he would return to his contemporaries, confiding to them that "slaves have come a long way these past 2,500 years."

They had come so far that even freedom had taken on new definitions. Franklin D. Roosevelt had a stab at it in a speech in January, 1941. He dreamed of a world founded on four freedoms: "The first is freedom of speech and expression – everywhere in the world. The second is freedom of every person to worship God in his own way – everywhere in the world. The third is freedom from want – everywhere in the world. The fourth is freedom from fear – anywhere in the world."[15] It was a noble dream and, as yet, unfulfilled.

Fear and want – are these not two of the biggest factors driving the modern employee? If these were removed, the employer would need to revise his recruitment and management systems. We shall see in future chapters that these conditions are indeed disappearing, posing new challenges for those who need to secure the employment of people.

In a society dominated by work, where the need for work is greater than it has ever been, our liberty begins to be defined by our willingness or otherwise to do that work. St. Paul said: "If any would not work, neither should he eat."[16] This would suggest that the option of working or not working is not at issue. We must work. We expect it of ourselves. The modern debate is not so much about the need for work but about the quantity and quality of work expected of the individual.

In ancient Greece and Rome there were no great expectations of the common laborer. And yet the quality of some work continues to amaze us. The potter's art, the sculptor's skill, the mastery of masons and the Roman road maker still hold us in their thrall. The achievements of these societies were so great; it is with reluctance that we must recognize their denial of basic freedoms to so many under their control. Branding to the faces of those slaves ordered to work in the mines or fight in the arena was only outlawed by Constantine in AD 315. Branding, he decreed, should only be carried out on the legs or hands. Some slave owners reacted by fitting their slaves with bronze collars inscribed with the names and addresses of their owners.

It was not unknown for slaves to escape. Thucydides estimated that more than twenty thousand Athenian slaves fled during the Peloponnesian War of 431–404 BC. But slave revolts were rare, even in Roman society.[17] The degree to which Greek and Roman slaves accepted their status is difficult to discern but there is little evidence from contemporary accounts in these societies to characterize the plight of slaves as some kind of class struggle, as Karl Marx insisted in his *Communist Manifesto.* "The history of all hitherto existing society is the history of class struggles," wrote Marx. "Free man and slave, patrician and plebeian, lord and serf, guild-master and journeyman, in a word, oppressor and oppressed, stood in constant opposition to one another."[18]

Marx was as wrong about these status relationships as Hobbes was about the life of prehistoric hunter-gatherers. Marx should not have characterized either ancient slavery or those later working relationships as a class struggle. There was nothing of the oppressor about the habit of Greek estate owners sitting down at the table with their slaves after the harvest to share a celebratory meal. Tokenism it might have been; patronizing, maybe. But is it any more so than the invitation by modern corporate directors to an employee to share their lunch table? Having received and partaken of such invitations, I have found them mildly patronizing but harmless, hardly the stuff of oppression.

It is a pity that Marx did not look further into the past than Greek and Roman societies. He might have found some cause for optimism in Neolithic society, possibly even in Egyptian society. Although the Egyptians practiced slavery we do not know the exact status of the army of workers engaged to work on the pyramids. Pyramid building may have been a form of national service, an obligation similar to military conscription. The pharaohs could certainly expect ample labor to be released from the land every year at the time of the Nile flood. Construction of the pyramids may have used some slaves, but the masonry skills needed to create the Great Pyramid at Giza were those of the experienced artisan. Levers, not brute strength, were the most likely method used in jacking up the individual blocks of stone, weighing about two and a half tons each.[19] Each hewn block needed to be dressed to the correct proportions. This was the work of experts.

Experts were also engaged on the building of the henge monuments across Europe in predynastic times. Gimbutas argued that henges, such as Stonehenge in England, were the products of communal efforts. Such large-scale work, she maintains, had to be based on a society's social and religious systems. Indeed, she identified the ability to organize communal work on a grand scale as one of the chief characteristics of the culture of the megalith builders.[20] There is no evidence that this work had anything to do with oppressors or the oppressed. Quite the opposite: the evidence points to a settled society. It is difficult to envisage the completion of so ambitious an undertaking in any other circumstances.

If the Greek slaves described by Marx felt oppressed, awareness of their plight does not appear to have communicated itself
to the loftiest of classical thinkers. Slavery was such a fact of life
it was deemed hardly worth mentioning by some of the greatest
philosophers of their age. Socrates, Plato, and Aristotle, the "big
three" of Greek philosophy, saw it as their role in life to question,
challenge, dissect, and criticize almost every aspect of the human
condition. But they rarely mentioned slavery. Indeed, the Greeks
had no defining word for work. The word *ponos*, meaning something painful, was used to describe unpleasant work.[21] Another
word, *ergon*, described a task and tended to be applied to agricultural activities. The word for leisure, *scholia*, had its opposite in
ascholia, literally "not leisure."

Scholia is the root of our word "school." It seems fitting that
leisure and learning should be linked in this way. Edith Hamilton,
a writer on Greek society, explained the Grecian philosophy that
"given leisure, a man will employ it in thinking and finding out
about things. Leisure and the pursuit of knowledge, the connection was inevitable – to a Greek."[22] But the Greeks did not dig-
nify work with a verb of its own. Profitable enterprise, the work
of merchants and traders, was distrusted and their numbers were
restricted. Priority in Greek society was extended to the warrior
class and the political decision-makers. All other members of
society were part of what Plato called "the multitude."

Wedded as he was to the notion of hierarchy, Aristotle believed
that the highest form of existence was the rational being – someone
like Aristotle himself in fact. No surprises there. Here was a man
so sure of his intellect that he declared with certainty that women
had fewer teeth than men, without ever bothering to count them.
The function of lower beings, he argued, was to serve this rational
man. Slaves, consisting mainly of barbarians, were, by their nature,
best suited for the service of thinking man as "living tools." This
is the paradox of Greek society, that freedom and free thinking,
as Moses Finley observed, walked "hand in hand" with slavery.
"The cities in which freedom reached its highest expression –
most obviously Athens – were cities in which chattel slavery
flourished," he wrote.[23]

Perhaps there is something in the attraction of opposites.
Perhaps it has something to do with relativity – that it is possible

to perceive freedom most clearly where it does not exist. The closer you come to one condition, the more readily you appreciate and understand its opposite. This applies to every walk of life. Every chef should know that the most vital ingredient of gastronomy is the appetite. Without hunger, the grandest of meals is no more than a distraction. But when the appetite kicks in, the meanest slice of buttered toast can send the taste buds into rapture.

Certainly freedom must be viewed as a relative concept. Modern-day sports teams are made up of individuals whose loyalty and commitment are secured by a contract covering a period of time. They earn vast sums and yet they are traded for money just as slaves were traded, and they are expected to perform on the field like gladiators for the edification of crowds. They also live under the restraint of another – their coach – and they are fined or reprimanded if they commit any indiscretions in their private life that might put their club in a bad light. If their performance falters, then they go, often on free contracts but usually guided by agents working to a single axiom, immortalized in the film *Gerry McGuire*, as "show me the money."

In spite of such comparisons I do not intend to suggest here that there is anything akin to slavery in the contemporary employment contract. Slavery is a product of subjugation, whereas the long hours in today's office culture are the product of voluntarism born of habit.

We are locked into a system, a mentality, that regards hard work and long hours as vital for maintaining or enhancing our standard of living. We have become slaves to work. The galley chains are psychological. We manacled ourselves and threw away the key in the conviction that we should never desire to free ourselves. Did not Franz Kafka write in *The Trial* that "it's often safer to be in chains than to be free"? But the work has proved unrelenting, and doubts are beginning to undermine our old certainties. Now, at last, as we look hopefully into the future, we are starting to analyze the mentality that binds us to our jobs. Freedom and slavery, we may conclude, are relative forces, the yin and yang of work.

The most enlightened employers now understand the need for freedom in the workplace and are releasing their workforces from the tyranny of set hours, the strictures of managerial control, and the limitations of the fixed workplace. Many traditional businesses are struggling under such conventions. The static business that persists with traditional management–employee relationships and contracts will not flourish. Neither will the static employee. The best of these businesses will linger, of course. They may even merge and linger, continuing the pattern of corporate development among the giants of the late twentieth century; merge and linger like persistent weeds, like slavery itself. But they will have to take their place as unloved giants in a new corporate order, as their nimble offspring take wing and fly. The alternative is to devolve their operations so that they resemble a federation of interests bound together by common values and a common purpose. A new generation of multiskilled mobile employees will accept nothing less.

CHAPTER 3

Job Creation

The life so short, the craft so long to learn.

(Hippocrates, 460–377 BC)

On a visit to Boston during the late 1990s I was viewing an exhibition of mummy portraits from the Fayum area of Egypt, spanning the first three centuries AD. Three of the pictures were mounted together. They were each painted about a hundred years apart and appeared to show a steady progression of the skill of the artists, each one an improvement on the last. It was not until I examined the dates more closely, matching them to the pictures, that I realized the most accomplished portrait was the oldest and the most naive was the most recent. Rather than progression it appeared as if there had been some kind of regression in skills.[1]

The Fayum district had been settled partly by Greek soldiers, who had fought for successive Ptolemaic kings, and partly by Egyptian laborers. By the time Egypt fell under Roman control the Fayum population consisted of a mixture of Greeks and Egyptians at various stages of integration. The people of Fayum combined a belief in the after-life – celebrated in elaborate Egyptian funerary practices – with a Greek heritage and Roman administrative practices. Fayum mummies were complemented by Greek-style portraiture, and the portraits are truly remarkable. As Euphrosyne Doxiadis pointed out in a recent critique: "It is not until some fifteen centuries later, in the faces painted by Titian or Rembrandt's depiction of his own features as he saw them reflected in a mirror, that the same artistry that characterizes many of the anonymous painters of the Fayum was witnessed again."[2]

It is as if, after the Fayum paintings, the artistry and knowledge of the Western world had been swallowed in some giant barbarous chasm. At least this is the way it is often portrayed. But the gap of some hundred to two hundred years between the fall of Rome and the first surviving monastic writings in Europe, popularly known as the Dark Ages because of the scarcity of documented knowledge, should not be viewed as some black hole. If writing was barely preserved in the monastic orders on the western fringes of the old Roman Empire, there was a continuation of certain other skills. One need only look at the Alfred Jewel, fashioned for King Alfred, or the *cloisonné* work and the armorial workmanship uncovered in the seventh-century Sutton Hoo Anglo-Saxon ship burial in the East of England to understand that some of the finest of craft skills were maintained throughout this period.[3]

Ability never deserted mankind, but some things were lost. The understanding of form, mastered in part by the prehistoric cave painters, then rediscovered and perfected by the Greeks, had already diminished in translation to Roman civilization. It was never transferred to the Celtic illuminators, whose artistic skills in abstract forms and knot patterns are unquestioned. Techniques were also lost in other areas such as building and medicine. Embalming, for example, would never again reach the peaks of sophistication attained about 1,000 BC. Modern-day funeral directors can only look back in awe to the professional skills of the ancient Egyptian embalmers, who were part of a professional elite that included builders, stonemasons, and architects such as Imhotep, the first named architect.

Why have great skills been lost periodically throughout history? There seems to be a conspiracy of obsolescence, usually involving a combination of common influences – fashion, innovation, and price. Mummification and all the funerary trappings that went with it was a costly process, but this does not seem to have undermined the practice. Quite the opposite. Skills diminish when a practice spreads out to a wider audience, where new practitioners enter the market and begin to compete on price. In these circumstances quality and artistry take a nosedive.

This process was at work in ancient Rome, just as it is in television program making today. Quality only survives at the innovative fringe. The demands of the mass market reduce once-proud industries to the lowest common denominator. The real losers are those who take pride in their work, who are forced to speed up, cut corners, and use inferior materials. Their craft debased, they feel the emptiness of lost satisfaction and some move on to other media in search of the intrinsic reward of a job well done.

When workmen controlled their craft in guilds they could resist those market forces that tended to erode good workmanship with incessant demands for cheaper, simpler, ready-made products. The workmen held the key to something precious – their skill – and it was jealously guarded. The guilds emerged at a time when most manual work was organized within the feudal system, when most agricultural workers had to content themselves with the status of peasants. But their work was beginning to be dignified within the Church in the thirteenth century. Thomas Aquinas drew up a hierarchy of professions and trades, depending on their value to society. At the top was agriculture, then the handicrafts. He placed commerce at the bottom of the list.[4]

The guilds were merely consolidating and developing this new-found status, protecting their members and establishing a rate for the job. Part trade union, part trade organization, the guild derived its name from the Saxon verb *gildan*: to pay. Although the guild achieved its most elaborate definition in medieval London, the banding together of workers by specialism was common across many Western European towns and cities during the same period. Guilds in one form or another continued to play an important role in regulating work and trade in many other parts of the world. In Turkey, for example, they were known as *Esnafs*. Even today tradesmen and women in China and India would be familiar with the guild structure.

Guilds were an important grouping in the evolution of work because they regulated not only the work itself but also the particular enterprise, helping to keep wages steady and maintaining standards where otherwise commerce and trade would have been bedeviled by shoddy workmanship and cheating. Consignments of thirteen, the so-called "baker's dozen," emanated from these concerns for fairness.[5]

Craft skills need to be transferred from expert to apprentice. Only so much of any manual technique can be communicated in textbooks and diagrams. Shape, form, sound, texture, the characteristics of light, appeal to our emotions in a way that is difficult to emulate in the written or spoken language. Wine tasters drain the dictionary of every adjective in an attempt to communicate the difference between one vintage and another. Their descriptions are a poor substitute for the human olfactory sense.

Only a master of the craft can effectively communicate the mystery of his or her talent. That word, "mystery," is introduced deliberately because it derives from the Latin word *misterium*, meaning professional skill. It was used as an alternative word when referring to the guild.[6]

In London's liveried guilds, a seven-year apprenticeship would enable an individual to consider himself a journeyman, leading to the most sought after status of freeman. A freeman could work in comparative safety, protected by right from impressment into the armed forces. But he might still be in trouble if he were to return to the town or village of his birth. Simon of Paris, a free citizen of London, so respected within the city confines that he had served as a chamberlain and alderman, even Sheriff in 1302–03, found that his reputation did not extend to Norfolk and his home village of Necton. When he returned there in 1308 he was arrested and jailed by the bailiff, acting on behalf of the local landowner, who claimed that Paris was a runaway serf. It took Paris four years to secure his release and extract damages from his accusers.[7]

The case was not isolated. For the best part of four hundred years after the Norman Conquest in 1066, the English persisted with a feudal system that restricted the rights and privileges of ordinary working people. In Russia such a system continued up to the Bolshevik Revolution of 1917.

The feudal system that gradually replaced slavery in Western Europe between the fall of Rome and the re-emergence of state administration was simply another way of controlling and maintaining a pool of manual labor. People did not get up in the morning with a burning desire to till the fields. They did it because they had no choice but to do it. The Julius Work Calendar, a monastic manuscript created in Canterbury some time around 1020, outlines in pictures, month by month, the agricultural chores of the average village laborer shortly before the Norman Conquest in England.[8] The chores did not change with the conquest, but the lowly status of the peasant was confirmed and institutionalized.

There were differences of status in pre-Conquest England. The *Domesday Book*, the methodical village-by-village record of the spoils of the Norman victory, sometimes refers to slaves and at other times mentions serfs and villeins. Serfs were not traded as slaves, and the true slave was becoming a rarity in England at the time of the Conquest.[9] The villein and the serf were effectively one and the same. Both serfs and villeins were tied to their estate or manor in the service of a lord, and to obtain the status of freeman they had to pay for it. But for hundreds of years the strictest control over most people's lives continued and, however efficient a peasant farmer became, as long as his status remained that of the villein, he had to pay through the nose. He paid money to the landlord when he wanted to marry off his daughter and he paid for the right to plow his land. His family paid with their best animal when he died. The second best beast went to the parson.[10]

The villein was the lowest of the low. That the word for a criminal – villain – should be derived from the name applied to the medieval tied worker demonstrates that the sort of work that might dirty the hands was throughout this period associated with people of the basest nature. (The distinction was so important in China that the ruling and merchant classes grew their fingernails – often protected by elaborate casings – in order to distinguish themselves from those who needed to carry out manual labor.) A document outlining the laws of Henry I of England, written around 1120, describes the villein as a "*viles et inopes persone*," a despised and subordinate class, regarded by French courtly writers, at least, as the antithesis of the code of chivalry.[11]

The evolution in the status of work was slow, at times almost imperceptible, in the medieval English landscape. Serfdom and villeinage did not end overnight. They faded away. As serfdom gradually disappeared in the fifteenth and sixteenth centuries there were frequent attempts by landowners to make money from this change of status, but their power of control was waning.[12] While there remains some debate over the demise of serfdom and its causes, the rise of the towns, whose inhabitants were protected by charter from outside interference from other landowners, played a significant role. The landowner needed to weigh the risk of too draconian a form of control against forcing a worker to up sticks and move to a town. The influence of self-interest, one of the most enduring human traits across the ages, should never be underestimated.

The gradual abandonment of the system and the substitution of fees, fines, and levies for rents paid by tenant farmers was the better outcome for all.[13] Land was farmed more efficiently and the landlord could free himself from managerial responsibilities. There was never much evidence, anyway, with one big exception, that most medieval landowners had either the interest or skills in estate management.

The big exception, the huge exception, was the Church. Church estates were not only extensive, their administration was effective and knowledgeable. Administration in the Roman Catholic Church survived in far better shape after the collapse of the Roman Empire than Roman administration elsewhere across Europe, where it persisted for a time in pockets but never recovered any cohesion.

The Church not only maintained the linguistic links with ancient civilization, including many of the most important works of Roman and Greek literature, it preserved and developed skills, such as viticulture and building, that might otherwise have been lost. Church building continued in land occupied by the Visigoths and the Franks, who had both converted to Christianity. The Cathedral of Lyon, for example, founded around 470, was said to have been supported on a forest of columns with gilded paneled ceilings. The surviving church of San Juan Bautista at Banos de Cerrato was built in 661 during the Visigoth occupation of Spain. In these buildings, the common Roman structural form of the basilica was preserved, indicating that many of the most complex architectural skills were maintained.

The monasteries became oases of learning. At the same time they were structured centers of organized labor, whose leaders maintained the administrative skills and disciplines of the Roman official. The Church had sensibly retained these valuable aspects of Roman society (as a memorable scene in the film, *The Life of Brian*, acknowledges by posing the question: What have the Romans ever done for us? Not everything Roman had been rotten). The monasteries represented not only an intellectual elite, but also an employing elite. They were the McKinsey, the J. P. Morgan, and the Goldman Sachs of their day. Unlike these latter-day institutions, the monasteries did not offer individual wealth but spiritual wealth to those who were willing to combine learning and worship within a strictly disciplined pattern of living.

Life for the monks living under St. Benedict's Rule was and still is highly structured. The first Benedictine monastery, established at Monte Cassino in Italy in 529, was run to strict written guidelines governing times and types of work and prayer that are still in use today. A typical monastic day would start at 2 a.m. in winter (1 a.m. in summer), beginning a stringent timetable of periods for reading, worship, and work.[14] The reading would be biblical and the worship, under the Latin heading, *Opus Dei*, could be draining.[15]

Much of the work at that time is likely to have involved writing, translation, or artwork, so the opportunity to do some physical work must have come as a welcome relief. Even the abbot could take pleasure in such work. This is made clear in an assessment of Bede, written by Eastorwine, a young abbot in the monastery at Jarrow in Northumbria, where Bede was ordained as a priest in 703:

> He remained so humble and like the other brethren, that he took pleasure in threshing and winnowing, milking the ewes and cows, and employed himself in the bakehouse, the garden, the kitchen, and in all the other labors of the monastery . . . Often, when he went out on the business of the monastery, if he found the brethren working, he would join them and work with them, by taking the plough-handle, or handling the smith's hammer.[16]

Bede's fraternal approach to his fellow monks, his love of physical labor and his willingness to eat with everyone on one level without any consciousness of station, were as rare then as they are now. For all the moves toward single status working these issues remain valid today. Bede would have recognized the cell-like work style of Andy Grove, the chief executive officer of Intel, the computer chip company, who insists on working in a cubicle among his fellow employees, even if there may have been a gulf in the gentleness of their respective approaches.

Indeed, there are many similarities between the work styles of those early monasteries and those of the businesses in Silicon

Valley, California. They share a passion for the storage, generation, and dissemination of information, and neither was too worried about ostentation in the workplace. If Bede can teach us anything today it is that real authority comes from within, not from badges or titles or the size of your desk, your office, or your company car.

The early Church leaders were tough and resourceful. They had to be, or the Church would not have survived. In a divided and crumbling Roman Empire the Church moved like an acquisitive conglomerate in a corporate bear park, as it sought to establish some unity among its disparate branches. When Augustine came to England in 597 he re-established contact with the monastic tradition that had survived in Wales, Cornwall, and Ireland, had moved into Scotland, and would soon be established in Northumbria. These Irish and Roman traditions were not formally unified until the Synod of Whitby in 664, when the most pressing items on the agenda were the dating of Easter and the monastic hairstyle. Augustine monks had the familiar banded tonsure, while the Celtic monks preferred to shave the front part of their heads from ear to ear, leaving the rest to grow long.

Church advances suffered from periodic invasions and consequent reversions to paganism, but no single group of Norse or Germanic people succeeded in dominating Europe persistently enough to snuff out Christianity. The Huns came closest when their leader, Attila, reached as far west as Orleans, in present-day France, in 451. Attila was the archetypal mobile leader, never staying in one place for long. In today's management terminology he was a typical virtual worker, hot-desking – or rather hot-tenting – his way across Europe, dismissing the trappings of power in a way that would be applauded by most of today's technology entrepreneurs. Although the Not-so-Dark Ages are characterized by images of invading hordes from the North, pagan beliefs, supported as they were by an oral tradition, proved unsustainable against the power, learning, literature, and culture of Christendom.

Just how potent this power could be is illustrated by the Viking infiltration of France. Between 885, when Norse longships first sailed up the river Seine to Paris, and 1066, when William of Normandy arrived in England, the Normans had been completely

Francified. Fierce and warlike they may have been, but they were French-speaking converts to Christianity. Anglo-Saxon culture was equally sophisticated. The Bayeux Tapestry, one of the most extraordinary pictorial records of any era, was almost certainly created by English seamstresses.

By the time that Charlemagne became king of the Franks in the eighth century, the Church had grown as powerful as any Roman emperor. Its power was not absolute but its influence was undeniable in binding the peoples of Europe together in a common religion. When Charlemagne knelt in St Peter's, Rome, on Christmas Day 800 to take mass, he was approached, apparently quite unexpectedly, by Pope Leo III and proclaimed Emperor of the Holy Roman Empire. How could Charlemagne refuse? The gesture was charged with meaning, signifying that the title was in the gift of the pontiff. Leo had unilaterally established the patronage of territorial rule in the papacy. It had been implied, of course, from the time of Constantine, but here it was demonstrated in full public view.

The Roman Catholic religion had assured its ascendancy as the official religion of Western Europe. But it did not yet have all the trappings of ideology. It was very much a tool of control. When William of Normandy landed on the English coast at Pevensey in the autumn of 1066, his army assembled behind the papal banner. He secured control of the English throne by force but it was underpinned by papal support.

The Church commanded respect in England but often attracted resentment among those who came under its control. This resentment simmered for centuries, and sometimes boiled over into open dissent, even rebellion. When Wat Tyler headed the Peasants' Revolt in 1381, many of his grievances were aimed at the Church and Church estate management, which maintained the feudal system of villeinage as strongly as any English peer.

Tyler's demands for the confiscation of Church lands, indeed all his demands, were accepted in a face-to-face meeting with Richard II within the walled City of London. But the whole negotiation was a sham. The meeting had lured Tyler away from his fellow workers and he was provoked into a fight by the king's supporters. Armed with nothing more than a dagger, he was fatally wounded by the Lord Mayor's sword thrust and, although he was taken to hospital by his friends, the mayor had him dragged outside and beheaded shortly afterwards.[17] The privileges attained by London's merchant artisans were not about to be usurped by a common laborer, even if many in the rising, like Tyler, as his name implies, were tradesmen themselves.

The revolt may have had most of the hallmarks of armed insurrection but it was not a revolt in the proper sense of the word. It was not an attempt to oust the king. It was a determined effort to force reforms. Up to that point, the peasant had been regarded as an inconsequent individual whose opinion counted for nothing. His earnings had risen after the Black Death in 1348 when the English population was severely reduced – possibly by as much as a half – but labor laws were quickly introduced to curb wages.[18] The final straw was a tax levied on every individual over the age of fifteen to raise money for the king's military campaigns.[19] The disproportionate effect of the tax on those who earned very little was contrasted with its insignificance for the wealthier classes.

Just as there were poor farmers, there were poor priests, and one of them, John Ball, became the spokesman of the revolution, articulating popular resentment in the slogan:

> When Adam delved and Eve span,
> Who was then the gentleman?[20]

Ball, the agitator, emphasized to people that their tied status was little better than slavery, particularly when their standard of living was compared to that of the rich.[21] The insurrection failed to alter the system but it did make the ruling class aware that working people were not happy to maintain the status quo.

The demographic impact of the Black Death cannot be ignored either, because it increased demand for people to work the empty fields. It also meant that the serf who ran from the village to the city was not going to be questioned by those city-based employers who were desperate for his services. In the long run the competition for workers from the growing towns and the organization of trades perhaps did more than anything to erode the feudal status of the English peasant.

The shift in the balance of economic power to the towns was not smooth. The towns suffered a setback with one of the earliest forms of medieval mechanized industry – the fulling mill. Fulling, the process of pummeling cloth by hand or foot in water as part of the finishing process, was mechanized in the twelfth century, using a wooden roller with protruding blocks that proved more effective than muscle power in kneading the cloth. The use of waterpower to turn the rollers led to the adoption of the term "mill" for mechanized industry. The term had been associated previously with grinding flour between stones. It also meant that the mills were set up in rural areas at the headwaters of rivers. These were not popular developments among working people. The people whose livelihoods depended on hand fulling pleaded for some kind of restraint against the new technology. But their pleas were ignored.[22]

So crucial was the process that many weavers were attracted out of the swelling towns and began to cluster around the mills. It was the beginning of the textile mill communities and it weakened the town-based weaving guilds. It did not break the power of the Church, since the monasteries remained prominent landowners. Indeed, some of the fulling mills were on monastery land. The monasteries were big employers, calling on armies of peasants to service their way of life. The traditional landowners, including the Church, enjoyed the spoils of the growing textile industry, and many monks forgot their monastic ideals and lived in "lazy comfort."[23] However, the concentration of skills, shared both by free people and serfs, fostered a growing independence of character among the weaving communities.

It is not surprising, therefore, to find these centers receptive to religious Nonconformism when it began to emerge as a doctrinal force after Martin Luther delivered his first reformist challenge to the Roman Catholic hierarchy in the form of ninety-five theses launched in Wittenberg in 1517. Whether or not, as legend has it, they were pinned to the church door, the accusations of financial, doctrinal, and religious abuses found ready support in like-minded clerics and intellectuals across the continent.

Luther's later appearance at the Diet of Worms to stand face to face with the Emperor Charles V, and refute charges of heresy with a lengthy, impassioned, and eloquently argued speech, must have been one of the most dramatic scenes of the Middle Ages. Luther was the face of the working man, a son of toil, commanded like Adam to work in the sweat of his brow. The emperor was the potentate accustomed to subservience in every layer of society. To witness the intellect of this ultimate personification of the turbulent priest must have chastened those whose faith in the divine right of kings had been unshakable.

There was, however, an ugly side to Protestantism that did not have Luther's blessing. His dissent unleashed outbreaks of thuggery and violence directed at the churches and cathedrals. Stained glass windows and woodcarvings were wrecked as bands of Protestants vented their anger on Roman Catholic imagery. The toiling peasant could relate to a God who, the Bible said, had demanded work in atonement for the original sin. How else could Paradise be regained? Surely not by honoring the riches and gilded purple robes of the Roman Catholic Church.

A broader understanding of the Bible was promoted by Luther's translation of the New Testament into German, John Calvin's translation into French, and William Tyndale's translation into English. At the same time there was the opportunity of exploiting the ability to disseminate the printed word in volumes that had been impossible before Johannes Gutenberg's development of interchangeable metal type in 1450.

The ground had been prepared for a new type of religion, one that revered the teachings of the Bible, that combined religious devotion with a code of ethics, revoking excess and extolling the virtues of hard work in devotion to God. "Luther placed a crown on the sweaty forehead of labor," wrote Adriano Tilgher.[24] If Luther opened the door to this new Christian ethic, then John Calvin made it palatable to the wealth creators. Shorn of the condemnation of usury and distrust of capitalism, Calvin's Protestantism, according to the historian R. H. Tawney, was "perhaps the first systematic body of religious teaching which can be said to recognize and applaud the economic virtues."[25] Here is the difference as Tawney sees it: "The Roman Church, it was held, through the example of its rulers, had encouraged luxury and ostentation: the members of the Reformed church must be economical and modest. It had sanctioned the spurious charity of indiscriminate almsgiving: the true Christian must repress mendacity and insist on the virtues of industry and thrift."[26]

This was the key to its social acceptance across the entrepreneurial classes of northern European society. Within Calvin's doctrine it was possible to both pray and prosper, as long as you were prepared to forgo the frivolities and corruption permitted in Catholic circles, and as long as you were prepared to reinvest your wealth for the benefit of society. Only a select few – The Elect – would make it to paradise, hence the holier than thou approach of competing sects, each vying to be purer than the others.[27] Today we can see this same competition in the workplace, where the secular goal is a seat on the board or a year-end bonus. The Islamic world seems to have reached a similar dogmatic stage of the cycle, as moderate and orthodox strains struggle for ascendancy.

In sixteenth-century England there was cant on both sides of the religious divide, not least that displayed by Henry VIII. Henry had always regarded himself as a good Catholic, and in 1521 he was awarded the title "Defender of the Faith" by the Pope for putting his name to a book defending the seven sacraments of the Catholic Church against Luther's doctrinal attack. Rarely has a title been so ill deserved. In order to divorce his wife, Catherine of Aragon, he was prepared to break with Rome and sanction the formation of a Church of England.

Some, like Thomas More, himself a critic of the papacy, were not prepared to renounce their Roman Catholic faith and died for their beliefs.[28] Protestantism may have defined a work ethic but it was never confined to Protestants alone. Few could match More's fervor and commitment to his church and his work. Yet More sought to define a society where the daily routine of labor did not dominate people's lives. In his *Utopia* there were no social classes and no idle people. All men took turns at different kinds of work, finishing the necessary tasks of the day in six hours and spending the rest of their time pursuing their personal interests.

Roman Catholics were quite clearly capable of strenuous work and commitment, but their worldview differed fundamentally from that of the Protestant. "The true Catholic can never feel a mission to change by his work the face of the Earth and of society," wrote Adriano Tilgher, "for is he not already in this life a member of a society which cannot be changed because it is already perfect and divine?"[29]

There was no divine assumption in Protestantism. This religion defined a way of life and it was not about to relinquish its hold on English society. However, the Church of England was seen by some as no more than a watered-down version of the Church of Rome. Bishops still wore miters and gaudy, gold-threaded robes. The true Nonconformist demanded a much simpler communion between humanity and God. Of all the Nonconformist sects to emerge in England, including those of Congregationalism and Presbyterianism, Tawney identifies Puritanism – an ideal that was not confined to any particular sect – as the most influential movement of the seventeenth century.[30]

"Puritanism, not the Tudor secession from Rome, was the true English Reformation, and it is from its struggle against the old order that an England which is unmistakably modern emerges," he writes. Tawney's prose borders on the lyrical when he goes on to say:

> Immense as were its accomplishments on the high stage of public affairs, its achievements in that inner world, of which politics are but the squalid scaffolding, were mightier still. Like an iceberg which can awe the traveler by its towering majesty only because sustained by a vaster mass which escapes his eye, the revolution which Puritanism wrought in Church and State was less than that which it worked in men's souls, and the watchwords which it thundered, amid the hum of Parliaments and the roar of battles, had been learned in the lonely nights when Jacob wrestled with the angel of the Lord to wring a blessing before he fled.[31]

This is passionate stuff. It begins to explain the psychological grip that the Protestant work ethic would sustain for the next four hundred years, a grip that has become so powerful in the psyche of the Western industrialized world that it is beginning to take on the character of a stranglehold, no longer simply coloring our views but choking our judgment. It remains the surviving omnipresent altar in a secular world to which we make our daily sacrifice of unremitting toil. Luther would be shocked at such secularism but he might draw some comfort from its Biblical antecedents.

Today we work as if our souls are responding to some inner program. The software for this program was conceived in earlier generations, back in the Reformation, and it came in a large black book – Bible black. Its message was profound and apparently in conflict with the mysticism and majesty of the Roman church – but its influence on northern European society cannot be overstated. The Bible was learning, it was instruction, it was political and potentially seditious; and it was much, much more. It was a "must have" possession for the chattering classes. It was trendy and hip. It was cool.

CHAPTER 4

The New Religion of Work

All true work is religion.

(Thomas Carlyle, 1795–1881)

Throughout the sixteenth century the Bible became the intellectual bread and butter of northern Europe. Translations into the vernacular, spread by the new medium of printing, created a Bible culture that dominated everyday lives. In England Henry VIII complained to Parliament that it was "disputed, rhymed, sung, and jangled in every ale house."[1]

The vernacular Bible was like the Microsoft Windows of its generation. Within a hundred years of the English Reformation you could have found a Bible in every home. People opening its pages might well have asked themselves, "Where do I want to go today?" But its intellectual impact was far more significant because, unlike computer software, unlike the Internet with its amorphous and disparate content, the new medium of the printed page was delivering an extensive body of instruction, a moral ideology, previously modified for most people who had been forced to settle for the clergy's selective interpretations. In its Latin form, the Bible was the instrument of authority. In its vernacular form, throughout Europe, it became an instrument of debate, dissent, and, ultimately, conflict.

There was another side to its appeal. The first versions were banned. It was forbidden fruit. But once tasted, its message was so seductive that some would go to the stake rather than recant their opposition to the Catholic hierarchy.

Secret gatherings in opposition to the Church of Rome had existed in England since the late fourteenth century, when John Wycliffe, the first man to translate the Bible into English, began to outline a theological approach that would inspire the declarations of Martin Luther. Those who followed Wycliffe's line, the Lollards, were active in the professional, merchant, and artisan classes. The Lollards, who took their name from a pejorative Dutch term for mumbling, were as much a political movement as they were religious. They shared the same distrust of the Church that had been apparent in the Peasants' Revolt and earlier in the writings of Geoffrey Chaucer and the fable of Piers Plowman, but their movement was secretive in the face of suppression throughout the fifteenth century. As Christopher Hill, the historian, points out: "In the fifteenth century the mere fact of owning and reading the Bible in English was presumptive evidence of heresy."[2] When William Tyndall's English translation of The New Testament appeared in the next century – a printed publication, not scripted like Wycliffe's – it added to the fermenting opposition to Catholic doctrine.

Lutheran and Calvinistic teaching brought Lollardy out into the open, and the dissolution of the monasteries left the way clear for its dissemination within various forms of Nonconformism, including Puritanism. The dissolution of the monasteries, begun in 1536, legitimized Protestant dissent. It also created an opportunity for the existing landowning gentry and the moneyed merchant class to buy up tracts of land confiscated from the monasteries.

While the social order was shifting at the highest strata of society, the birth of English Protestantism was a hesitant affair. No sooner had churchwardens rid their churches of all their imagery and ostentation in the reign of Edward VI – Henry's only son and successor – than they were commissioning new icons and decorations under the succeeding reign of Edward's Catholic sister, Mary. When she died after eight years on the throne the churchwardens began the process of removing the imagery all over again under the Protestant rule of Elizabeth I.

Reform was moving too slowly for the Puritans, who continued to reject surviving Anglican practices. Taking the sacrament at an altar, baptizing babies with the sign of the cross on their foreheads, the wearing of vestments, lighting of candles, and veneration of crucifixes were all considered to be founded on superstition and idolatry.

Almost every facet of life was subjected to rigorous biblical interpretation. This would culminate in the formal challenge by Parliament to the hitherto self-perpetuating "divine right" of kings.

In the meantime Puritan thought began to establish itself among the general population, if not always at court. As Hill puts it: "It was a cultural revolution of unprecedented proportions, whose consequences are difficult to overestimate."[3]

The Bible was not protected by copyright. In this sense Bible study, translation, and interpretation were free for all, a magnet for intellectuals, the Internet of its time – without advertising. Its distribution, however, was subject to commercial factors. The popular Geneva Bible of 1560, an English translation based on Calvin's interpretation and including a preface by him, had a widespread and pervasive influence partly because it was much cheaper than other versions. Initially smuggled into England, it was sometimes referred to as the Breeches Bible because it told readers that Adam and Eve made "breeches" to cover their nakedness. It was not so much the textual passages that worried the established Church but the political dissent contained in the marginal analysis. The word "tyrant," for example, was used frequently in the Geneva Bible but could be found nowhere in the Great Bible that had been ordered by Henry VIII and approved by the bishops.

The Bible created popular debate about the nature of worship but this was not welcomed by the Establishment. Henry VIII had a statute passed that abolished "diversity of opinions." Ordinary men and women were forbidden to read the new Bible. The only impact of such laws was to drive the debate underground and increase its potency. Religious discussion had never been so fashionable.

While Calvinism took root in Scotland under the guidance of John Knox, the English Puritans were regarded with some suspicion throughout the Elizabethan era. With little prospect of overturning Anglican society in England the opportunity to create a Protestant Utopia, free from oppression, in the New World began to attract some of the most orthodox followers of Puritanism.

The earliest attempts at colonization met with mixed fortunes. The first English colony – on Roanoke Island, America, from 1584 to 1587 – was abandoned; the second to arrive there was lost without trace. The 150 colonists, abandoned for three years because of the English Privy Council's refusal to spare ships needed to fight the Spanish Armada, had disappeared by the time relief arrived. These early colonists were a different breed to the Puritan families who arrived later. They were adventurers and speculators lured by the prospect of finding gold. They knew little of farming.

Later groups, like the Jamestown colonists sent out in 1607 by the Virginia Company, were established with the intention of creating tobacco plantations. Many died. Some have pointed to the absence of farming skills or of any desire to work hard among the Jamestown colonists, but the conditions they were facing would probably have overwhelmed the most determined of settlers. There is evidence from tree ring studies that Virginia experienced severe droughts in those early years of colonization.[4] In spite of these hardships there was some tobacco planting, and the first shipment was sent back to England in 1616. Three years later colonists were buying black Africans from Dutch slave traders.

So, at a time when serfdom would still have been in the memories of some older English farm workers, the familiar experience of tied labor was renewed. It was not yet slavery, in theory. It never would emerge as slavery for white settlers, many of whom began their life in the colonies as indentured servants, working off their passage. Some of the first black settlers had the same status initially and should have been released from their obligation after a five-year period. In practice many had taken on new financial burdens and could not afford to become free landowning farmers. Some who secured land suffered reversals in their fortunes as racial attitudes began to harden. Whatever the original intentions of the white farmers the early employment practice of indentured labor soon slipped into slavery, with black workers bought and sold as chattels.

But another kind of colonist would soon arrive to the north at New Plymouth where a group of plainly dressed families stepped down off the *Mayflower* on December 11, 1620. These were Puritans, zealous Calvinists, some of whom had been living in exile in the Netherlands. They were not welcome in England, not by the Church establishment anyway. Their intention was to create their own Christian Utopia in New England. They had come to work because the Bible had told them how God had worked to create Heaven and Earth. They had come, in the words of John White, a Dorset clergyman who helped organize a subsequent expedition, to "propagate" religion.[5] John Winthrop, one of the most prominent of these early Puritan settlers, compared his voyage with the flight from Egypt to the Promised Land. Idleness would not be tolerated. Indeed it was made a punishable crime by legislation passed in Massachusetts in 1648.[6]

This was a new age of colonization and most of the colonists were possessed of the Protestant ethic that would shape a continent. A similar story was unfolding at the same time in Ulster, where thousands of Presbyterian Scots accepted an English invitation to colonize the north of Ireland. There seems to be a marked difference between the industry of these Nonconformist colonizing streams and those that began elsewhere as penal settlements.

Although the colonists might not have seen it this way (such was their antipathy to the Roman Church), they carried with them the same spirit that drove the monastic pioneers of the Dark Ages. The big difference is that their convictions were underlined with a latent power. They had the technology, organization, and strength of arms to be the top dogs in this vast new territory. Before them were uncounted miles of forest and plain occupied by people who were ill equipped to resist. But taming this land would not be easy, and the first settlers faced a similar struggle for survival to that of the early Church in a war-ravaged and fading Roman Empire. The supplanting of a moral, ethical, and religious code born out of resistance and dissent would give this new American society the backbone it needed to prevail.

If Tawney believed that Puritanism's struggle with the old order provided the nucleus of modern England, what would he have made of the impact on the United States of the Pilgrim Fathers in New England? My own belief is that Puritan influence in the modern American psyche is immense. Historically it created a distinct, powerful stream of intolerant Protestantism that was not mirrored by the experience of northern Europe. This radical Nonconformism continues to define the North American work ethic today.

Most of Europe developed some religious tolerance after a period of conflict, inquisition, and bloodletting. This spirit tempered zealous behavior on both sides of the religious divide. The Counter-Reformation in England, in which the Roman Catholic

Church sought to reform itself, helped to mend fences, but there was little hope of reconverting Protestant England. Not even force of arms could dislodge the Protestant establishment that finally consolidated itself in the 1689 Bill of Rights. Among other measures, the bill debarred Roman Catholic claimants to the throne. The English Cultural Revolution was complete. In England there was the Counter-Reformation, but there was no reversion to the Church of Rome.

It is as if a culture, to be all pervasive, needs either the full commitment of its adherents or some colloquial recognition. This popular appeal, that might lend a comfort factor to those living under the cultural influence, has extraordinary powers of conversion. The speed of conversion can be alarming and potentially devastating, as the German people discovered in 1933. In most circumstances, however, the change is positive and decisive. It worked with the Vikings in northern France in less than 200 years. It worked again in medieval England when the English language eclipsed the use of French, although there was some marrying of the two. The English peasant continued to farm his cows, pigs, and sheep, while the French-speaking master ate beef, pork, and mutton.[7] The power of familiarity worked also on the English in Ireland during the Elizabethan era, when laws were passed to deter English settlement beyond a boundary – the "Pale." The Irish way of life had been found to be so appealing that many English families had "turned native."

This did not happen in Ulster among the colonizing Presbyterian Scots, because their faith demanded full commitment. Religion in itself, of course, often had both of these constituents – commitment and colloquial appeal. When backed by these powerful motive forces it might be said that the only force strong enough to stop the spread of Christianity was that of another great monotheistic religion such as Islam.

Where the moral argument, a sense of commitment and colloquial appeal coincide strongly, as they did in Protestantism, founded on moral and ethical opposition to practices which the new Bible readers believed had gone beyond the original teachings of Christianity, there is a duality of popular belief and pragmatism. It is religion with its sleeves rolled up.

We can begin, then, to see two of the defining elements in the Protestant work ethic. There is the ideology, the Biblical guidance, and there is the practice, the example, the determination to pursue a moral code, to find salvation through work. Some of this feeling was apparent in the lifestyle of the Venerable Bede, mentioned earlier. In Bede's case the practice came from within. He did what he did without thinking, because he knew it to be right. He enjoyed the freedom of manual work, and those who worked with him enjoyed his presence. It was demonstrating what Robert Greenleaf, the management writer, would call "the Power of Servant Leadership" in his book of the same name.[8]

The Puritan ethic, however, had lost Bede's gentleness. It was a severe, formal, and pious code pursued with the utmost conviction and certainty. By the end of the English Civil War and the beheading of King Charles I in 1649 it was manifest in the extreme. The celebration of Christmas was proscribed, churches were vandalized, and the stern face of Puritanism became as set as stone in the Gorgon's glare.

No wonder the English breathed a collective sigh of relief at the restoration of the monarchy. The Nonconformists lost their grip on government, and the reformed Anglican church grew in confidence under Charles II. The new spirit of tolerance in the Reformation should not be overstated. The more extreme of the Nonconformist radicals found little freedom to practice their religious beliefs. But that did not deter all of them. If anything it provoked greater certainty and defiance among many of those who were driven by their convictions. This is because there are other defining elements in the Protestant ethic: it strengthens in adversity and it celebrates the triumph of the human spirit. Nowhere is this more apparent than in John Bunyan's *Pilgrim's Progress*, an allegory that relies wholly on the colloquial and unashamedly identifies with the little man.

Protestantism was a cultural and intellectual revolution of a power and intensity every bit as great as that recognized in industry and innovation during the eighteenth century. The latter could not have occurred without the former. The change was on a scale unknown, even in classical Greece and Rome, because it was a revolution of the masses, a triumph on behalf of, and exploited by, the masses. The vernacular Bible stimulated greater literacy. It was as if a whole nation had been captivated by the Holy Spirit of the Bible, and its influence was all pervasive. The first Sunday schools relied heavily on biblical passages for basic instruction. The rote learning of the alphabet, for example, used biblical references:

> A is an angel who praises the Lord,
> B is for Bible, God's holy word,
> C is for Church where the righteous reside
>
> . . . .
> G is for Goshem, a rich and good land,
> H is for Horeb where Moses did stand.[9]

Biblical instruction was even included in mathematical problems:

> There were seven days between the birth of Jesus and his circumcision, and five days from the event to the Epiphany, the time when the star led the Gentiles to worship the Holy Child. How long was it from the Nativity to the Epiphany?[10]

The thirst for literacy – so that you, too, could read the Bible – took a great leap forward in the mid-sixteenth century, when the first cheaper versions of the Bible became available. Even those who could not read immersed themselves in Bible discussion, as Henry VIII noted in exasperation. Among the most despised of the newer sects in the seventeenth century was the Society of Friends, nicknamed Quakers by a magistrate when he was advised by George Fox, the movement's founder and guiding spirit, that he should tremble at the name of the Lord.

The powder had hardly dried on the flintlocks of Cromwell's victorious New Model Army at the end of the English Civil War before Fox began his mission among the hardy farming communities of northern England. He was an extraordinary individual, described by those who admired him as a genuinely good man; but he was a good man with attitude. His preaching was confrontational and disruptive. Often he would stand up in his pew to contradict some point in another preacher's sermon. It was the riskiest form of protest. Disturbing the status quo, particularly

during a church service, was rarely welcomed among congregations who valued order and custom above aggravation. Fox was
beaten up by one mob after another. He stood up and invited the
blows with almost foolhardy courage.

His example won converts but it also invited new waves of
persecution. "They go like lambs without any resistance," wrote
Samuel Pepys in his diary. Not until the Toleration Act of 1689
were the Quakers left to worship unhindered. Even then they were
barred from many areas of employment. They were prevented by
statute from entering the universities and professions and from
engaging in traditional trades or crafts in the older corporate towns
that had independent charters allowing them to regulate trades.

Their stance against fashionable clothing meant that fashion
trades, tailoring, and lace making could not be considered potential careers for a Quaker in the movement's formative years. The
clergy was also out, because Quakers refused to pay tithes – the
church tax that demanded a tenth of a parishioner's income in
money or kind. They refused to take the oath in court, so that
ruled out the legal profession. For the same reason they could
not enter the military or politics. Other judicial arrangements
were denied them: they could not sue for their debts, defend
themselves, or give evidence in a court of law.

All in all the Quakers had made themselves well-nigh unem-
ployable. Yet so many of them prospered in proportion to their
numbers, even when their growth in England was beginning to
recede. The extent to which Nonconformists prospered in relation
to the rest of the population has been measured retrospectively
by academics. Everett Hagen compiled a table from the names of
inventors listed in Professor T. S. Ashton's book, *The Industrial
Revolution 1760–1830*.[11] After researching the religious background of the inventors, Hagen found that while Nonconformists
comprised 6 percent of the combined population of England,
Scotland, and Wales, they were responsible for more than a third
of the inventions listed in the book. As David McClelland, the
psychologist, pointed out later, one in ten of the inventors on
Hagen's list were Quakers, suggesting a mini-sphere of industrial
excellence and invention.[12]

The Quaker ability to prosper in business was even more
apparent in Philadelphia. Quakers made up a seventh of

Philadelphia's population in 1769 but accounted for half of those who paid more than £100 in taxes that year. Of the seventeen wealthiest individuals, eight were Quakers of good standing, four had been raised as Quakers, and another owed his business fortune to a Quaker grandfather. So more than three-quarters of this wealthy elite had Quaker backgrounds.[13]

How was it that the members of this minority extremist sect did so well in industry and business? They were hardworking, but that was true of most Protestants; it was part of the Protestant ethic. Hard work by itself would not make their fortunes. They ran a tight organization and were well structured. They were great bookkeepers, making records of all the judgments that went against them and perceived wrongs done toward them. In a way it was their alienation, as a society within a society, that created the conditions for commercial success.

They had a unified belief system, they watched each other's moral progress, and they founded schools for their children. They supported their fellows generously in trouble and spent time in each other's company, forming business partnerships, often cemented by marriage. In modern management parlance they were great networkers, but it was not networking born out of the desire to exploit another's usefulness. There was a strong vein of mutuality and self-help that made virtues of trust and fairness in their dealings. These carried over to their business activities outside Quakerism.

This last point cannot be stressed too strongly. This was a period when trust among tradespeople generally was not high. The guilds, formed to regulate their respective trades, had begun to attract criticism from rank and file tradesmen, who argued that they had become focused on the interests of their wealthiest controlling members, many of whom had given up practicing their particular trade in order to concentrate on various speculative ventures.

In one case, silk-weavers were forbidden by London's Guildhall to sell their products in City inns and forced instead to make deals with shopkeepers, who, together with the merchants, were determined to maintain their grip on city trade. Such restraint of trade and the poorer economic conditions at the end of the Civil War forced hundreds of craftsmen into lower skilled work such as laboring, portering, or chimney sweeping. The rank and file guild members attempted to overturn the constitutions of their liveries to make the organizations more democratic but they met with no success. In the latter half of the seventeenth century they began to form their own separate organizations that were the forerunners of the trade unions.[14]

The very success of the merchants heading the London liveried guilds had created class divisions. Now these ruling executives were perceived by many of their membership not as champions of their trades but as a merchant oligarchy controlling the companies, fixing wages, prices, and conditions, often to the advantage of their individual businesses. Ordinary tradesmen who had fought on the side of Parliament in the Civil War were attracted to the Leveller manifestos of pamphleteers like John Lilburne, who began to define their demand for voting rights for all men, with calls for "sovereignty of the people," as a class struggle.

The selfishness and distrust that began to characterize the established trade organizations proved a big advantage for the fledgling Quaker businesses. Even if people did not agree with their religious views they knew they could respect these people and the moral code that permeated their business dealings. If the list of exclusions for potential advancement looked comprehensive, the Quakers found plenty of possibilities in the new industries that had taken root in the one hundred years before the Civil War. Paper milling, gunpowder production, cannon founding, brass making, sugar refining, alum and copper smelting, and the mining of zinc ore and copper had all become organized industries during this period.[15] This, remember, was an era that began some two hundred years before the 1760s, the date most academics seem to agree marked the beginning of the Industrial Revolution.

The 1760s, in fact, saw more of a technological revolution, which accelerated the growth of industry; though it had been growing steadily since the Elizabethan era. It is no surprise, then, to find Quakers establishing themselves in the metalworking and smithing industries. One family, the Lloyds of Birmingham, became so entrenched in ironworking that they could afford to run lines of credit for their customers through their own bank. The provincial origins of Lloyds Bank provided a competitive alternative to City finance. So did the bank set up by David Barclay, another Quaker. The English Quakers built successful industries in iron founding, finance, chemicals, and confectionery. Not all industries were open to Quaker exploitation – arms manufacturing was out because of their growing pacifist beliefs. But the fashion for chocolate from the Americas was too new to create any line of dissent, and since the eating of chocolate was just about the only vice that did not meet with Quaker opposition it was virgin territory for their commercial development. Thus Fry & Sons, Cadbury, Rowntree, and Huntley & Palmer all owed their origins to Quaker development.

Quaker sons and daughters moved into industry with remarkable success. Here was the birth of industrial man and woman in mind and spirit. It was not the birth of achievement. Humanity had accomplished so much already without this Protestant ethic. The Pyramids, for example, stand testament to human willpower, discipline, and method. But the work of building pyramids, castles, and cathedrals was different in this respect: it was not guided by any belief in the work per se but by the product of the work. This new ethic celebrated work in its own right.

Nowhere was this more evident than in North America, and it contributed significantly to molding the embryo of a nation. The opportunity for this influential involvement in the beginnings of modern American society arose under William Penn, successor to George Fox in the Quaker movement. Penn had the advantage of a university education. The son of one of Oliver Cromwell's admirals, Penn was asked to leave Christ Church College, Oxford, because of his religious leanings. Unlike his fellow Quakers, however, he was accepted at the court of Charles II, who granted him American land seized from the Dutch.[16] Whether this was in appreciation of his father's achievements or whether it was a politically motivated gesture to rid England of Quakers is not known, but it is known that thousands of them and other Nonconformists flocked to the new lands.

Philadelphia, the capital of the state that the king announced would be called Pennsylvania, quickly became the largest city in North America, an entrepôt of displaced people from all over Europe. The Quakers were joined by Huguenots from France, Baptists from Wales, Dutch and German Protestants, even persecuted Roman Catholics from Maryland, all attracted by the state's "liberty of conscience," a declaration that allowed freedom of worship.[17] No wonder Samuel Adams described his country as the "last asylum."[18]

The Quakers were only a single grouping in the mostly Protestant ethnic mix whose rights were enshrined in the Declaration of Independence, signed on July 4, 1776 and proclaimed in public four days later in Philadelphia's State House Yard, as the Liberty Bell was rung defiantly for the first time. But their influence in shaping the American work ethic is immense. The Quakers and their Nonconformist cousins ensured that hard work would be venerated, embodied within the American dream in a self-generating virtuous cycle of industry and toil. Not even invention could deny the contribution of honest-to-goodness hard work in the American mind. As Thomas Edison would insist a hundred years later: "Genius is ninety-nine percent perspiration and one percent inspiration."[19]

After independence the Americans would need to look to their own inventiveness and industry. There would be a gap because the spark would be ignited in England. Just how it happened, how this revolutionary work ethic created an industrial spirit that would traverse the world, can be studied in microcosm among the Quaker community.

Max Weber, in his work *The Protestant Ethic and the Spirit of Capitalism*, concentrated on stressing the causal links between Protestantism and capitalism. His claim that capitalism was based on Protestantism is sound enough, but it may be more accurate to say that modern capitalism was based indirectly on religious intolerance. The adversity created by intolerance drove many of the early achievements of the Protestant ethic. Among Quaker businesses capitalism was employed as an efficient tool of the work ethic, lubricating industry, making the virtuous cycle spin more rapidly. Capitalism was a logical extension of industrial efficiency. It was a means to an end but wealth creation was not the end in the formative Protestant enterprise. Wealth was a welcome by-product, useful only in as much as it could be invested in extending the enterprise. Its meaning would change, but in the hands of these Protestant business pioneers it was as yet subordinate to the religiously inspired values that shaped the body corporate.

The way these values would manifest themselves in a small Shropshire community and in factory systems of employment would soon become apparent. Religion created opportunities for men and women to earn their daily bread, not only by the sweat of their brows, but in a way that would be organized and system-ized to the advantage mostly of those they served. It had taken the parcels of work called jobs and structured them in shifts, controlled by employers, promising regular wages and the pros-pect of continuous employment. The job we recognize, the job our parents knew, was taking shape.

CHAPTER 5

The Most Important Pile of Bricks in the World

A trade is not learned through words, but by experience.
(Richard Sibbes, 1577–1635)

Most religions have their altars, the focus of worship and contemplation, and there is no more fitting altar for the religion of work than Abraham Darby's forge at Ironbridge in Coalbrookdale, an unassuming village set in undulating farmland not far from England's border with Wales. Protected today by a canopy and bathed in floodlights, this crumbling brick structure is the womb that gave birth to industry on a scale that would transform the way people lived and worked.

Industry was advancing across Europe by the turn of the eighteenth century when Darby used the rebuilt forge to make iron using coking coal for the first time. Throughout the century, British businessmen and inventors would create or develop knowhow or innovations drawn from the European well of ideas and knowledge. Why was it happening in Britain more than anywhere else? A twentieth-century comparison might be made with the advances in Japanese manufacturing since the end of the Second World War. The Japanese may not have led the way in inventions, but the way they exploited and built on innovation propelled their economy beyond most of those in the West. The Japanese people had a work ethic of their own, not one that relied on the individualism of Protestantism but one that could harness social cohesion in the Confucian tradition.

Like Confucianism, Protestantism expected its adherents to observe a code of behavior, not so much on the spiritual plane as in daily life. The rules were different in Catholicism. They were there to be broken – and they *were* broken, but there was always the safety net of the confessional and absolution. The wonder and otherworldliness of Catholicism tended to stifle innovation. The scientists, Copernicus and Galileo, for example, were censured for suggesting that the Earth was not the center of the universe.

In 1642, the year that Galileo died, another great scientist was born, this time into Protestant England – Isaac Newton. The contrast between the treatment meted out to Galileo and the way Isaac Newton and his followers were able to develop their science is striking and significant. Galileo had been imprisoned within his own home by the Inquisition. Newton, on the other hand, was allowed to pursue science and mathematics for its own sake. Protestants wanted applications. Newtonian theory was fine because it was useful. It allowed people to make things that could be sold for profit. It fostered progress.

The business driver in Protestantism left little time for wonder and theory. It required application, not just of individuals but of the tools, systems, and ideas that came into their hands. They may have admired the curiosity of Leonardo da Vinci, but the Protestants had a duty to improve the human condition.

The economic and cultural root system of Europe was becoming highly developed and divergent, tapping and nourishing different wells. Those two great trading centers, Florence and Venice, bolstered by a strong Flemish tradition that in painting pursued its own methods, for climatic reasons preferring tempera then oils to fresco, had stimulated a Renaissance in art and architecture that fired European culture and aesthetics for hundreds of years. Spain, Portugal, the Netherlands, and England (with France playing catch up) had used their maritime traditions to push out the frontiers of discovery, laying the foundations of empire that would impose European culture, not necessarily for the better, on the lands they claimed for their respective crowns.

The secrets of previous generations, protected by established organizations – the Church and guilds – could no longer be maintained in these communities of self-interest, as people left them, taking their knowledge with them, or as state legislation eroded their independence. People like Marco Polo, Sir Walter Raleigh, and Hernan Cortéz had extended Europe's reach. There was an internationalization of interest, and ideas and discoveries began to tumble over themselves. The accumulation of new knowledge and the rediscovery of old knowledge were so over-whelming that no country, no government, no institution could hope to keep a lid on it. This was not for the want of trying, especially outside Europe.

In the mid-seventeenth century Japan all but closed its doors on the outside world for three hundred years, maintaining a single trading outlet with the Dutch. Elsewhere in the world there were too many avenues, too many possibilities, too many connections for secrecy to prevail. The tree of knowledge is aptly named. Like the spreading roots of a flourishing plant, determined to seek out the richest source of nutrients, people were dividing and exploring different paths, and those paths that found some opportunity for learning or profit – or both – divided and spread most rapidly.

Religion, politics, claims and counterclaims, led to wars, stimulating developments in tactics, organization, and technology. "War is nothing more than the continuation of politics by other means," said Karl von Clausewitz, the military strategist. He was wrong. War is much more than politics by other means. It was, and still is, an instrument of innovation, whose fruits may be applicable in many fields.

Advances in metallurgy, shared across Europe in the 1556 publication of Agricola's *De re metallica*, an influential book that outlined many hitherto-secret processes, were exploited nowhere more effectively than in England, and by no one more influentially than Abraham Darby and the Darby dynasty of ironfounders.[1] Darby was a giant of eighteenth-century industry and, although there is little evidence that he devised revolutionary systems of employment, his contribution to the means of production and his Quaker ideals, shared by others who would influence the field of workplace human relations, should not be minimized.

Rarely can anyone claim innovation in isolation, and Darby was not a man alone, but his work embodied the spirit of what would become known as the Industrial Revolution. If anyone deserves the mantle of father of this Revolution it is he, even though there are persuasive arguments that the "Industrial Revolution" is something of a misnomer if interpreted as some great leap forward in the history of mankind. We have already noted the industrial strides made during the Elizabethan era. Should they be considered part of the Revolution? Some historians have pointed to the years between 1760 and 1830 in Britain, the years often quoted as spanning the Industrial Revolution, as a period of low economic growth.[2] This should not be so surprising. Change is never easy. It involves experiment and failures. There is an argument that the benefits of these changes might have been enjoyed more profitably by others who had no experience of the birth pains. But does this mean we should rid ourselves of the popular images of the Industrial Revolution, the images of mills and chimneys, belching smoke, punching pistons, flywheels, and the hiss of steam?

Historians have given us labels for certain periods – the Dark Ages, the Reformation, the Renaissance. It is not unreasonable for another generation to challenge such labeling, to suggest that progressive change should not be put in boxes. But history is punctuated by events. Luther may not have started the Reformation, but he pointed out to us that there was something in the air. We experience this same recognition when we look at the work of Raphael, Michelangelo, and Leonardo da Vinci. It was as if these men, in their own way, had experienced moments of understanding just as profound as the one that provoked Archimedes' excited leap from his bathtub, exclaiming "Eureka" when he realized that his body displaced water. We know, too, that there was something in the air when we look at the developments of James Watt and the inventions – and their application – of the textile innovators such as John Kay, Richard Arkwright, and James Hargreaves.

What was that something? It was change, so palpable you could sniff it, feel it, almost shape it in your hand. It was emotional, exciting, and frightening. It put people on the move, it worried governments, and it made men kill. The historian G. M. Trevelyan epitomizes the resistance to change in his *English Social History*, where he describes the England of the eighteenth century as "a land of elegance" where "as yet there was no great development of factories, producing goods wholesale, ruining craftsmanship and taste, and rigidly dividing employers from employed."[3]

Trevelyan does not appear to be a great fan of mass production. This is the scene he portrays of a land before factories:

Under these happy conditions, the skilled hands produced, for the ordinary, market goods of such beautiful design and execution that they are valued by connoisseurs and collectors today: china, glass, and other ware, silver plate, books beautifully printed and bound, Chippendale chairs and cabinets, all sorts of articles for ornament and use. Even the commonest type of grandfather clocks that told the time in farmhouse kitchens were simple and effective in design, the outcome of a tradition followed with individual variations by innumerable small firms. Architecture was safe in the plain English style now known as "Georgian." In those days all buildings erected in town or country, from town halls and rural mansions to farms, cottages, and garden tool-houses, were a pleasure to the eye, because the rules of proportion, in setting doors and windows in relation to the whole, were understood by common builders. Those simple folk, by observing the rules of proportion laid down for their guidance in Gibbs's handbooks kept hold of a secret, afterwards lost by the pretentious architects of the Victorian era who deserted the plain English Georgian style to follow a hundred exotic fancies, Greek, Medieval, or what not, and were book-wise in everything concerning their work, except the essential.[4]

Trevelyan, writing with hindsight, is suggesting that the English were about to "lose it," just as other societies had lost it before them. It is a different perspective from that of the rags-to-riches entrepreneurial elite who would view every new industrial development as "progress." Trevelyan's portrait may be colored somewhat by the nostalgia of the time – he is writing just before the Second World War – but clearly he is unimpressed by the march of industrialization. He writes of a great age of artisanship that had reached its zenith. He writes of art and architecture that collapsed into Victorian mannerism. Few of those undergoing these changes could have understood their collective magnitude throughout that century, but they undoubtedly knew that change was happening at a rate impossible to control or calculate. So when the historian Arnold Toynbee popularized the term "Industrial Revolution" in a series of lectures in 1884, he knew he was dealing with something that had indeed the sniff of revolution. No wonder the label stuck.

All revolutions have a genesis, some spark or event that triggers a series of other transformational events. History is littered with wars, treaties, coups, and countercoups, but some of the most lasting influences on civilization – the birth of Christianity, for example – have humble origins. So it was with the Industrial Revolution, whose origins can be traced to one man's desire to make a better cooking pot.

The brick-built forge in Ironbridge is a fittingly humble shrine at which we may pause and contemplate the events that would change the lives of so many people, that would channel that Protestant energy and define the industrialized world. We find the qualities of humility and honest endeavor, and more, in this forge, the culmination of Abraham Darby's determination to make a cheap and serviceable cooking pot. Darby was a pot maker, pure and simple, yet the discoveries and processes he began, further developed by his son and grandson, would help to change the world. Darby would become a master forger – *the* master forger of the eighteenth century – father of a new Iron Age. His first breakthrough in pot manufacturing was to take a more economical form of brass molding used by the Dutch and adapt it for molding iron.

The Dutch method used sand for the molds. These were reusable and therefore cheaper than the loam or clay molds in general use at the time. Cheapness was the key. The problem was that molten iron – far hotter than brass when poured into the sand molds – caused a buildup of gas that would burst them apart. Darby's assistant, John Thomas, suggested making air holes in the sand to allow for the greater heat of the iron.

The work was so secret that Darby blocked up the keyholes to the doors of the forge.[5] Rivals offered to double John Thomas's wages if he joined them, but he stayed loyal to Darby. While there is no doubting Darby's desire to make money, it is worth noting the wording of his 1707 patent for casting iron pots. It reveals a social consciousness in line with the Quaker ethic while at the same time stressing the potential importance of the process for the nation in foreign exports:

A new way of casting iron bellied pots and other iron bellied ware in sand only, without loam or clay, by which iron pots and other ware may be cast fine and with more ease and expedition and may be afforded cheaper than they can be by the way commonly used and in regard to their cheapness may be of great advantage to the poore of this our kingdom, who for the most part use such ware, and in all probability will prevent the merchants of England going to foreign markets for such ware, from whence great quantities are imported and likewise may in time supply foreign markets with that manufacture of our own dominions.[6]

Was this the greatest stride forward in civilization since Gutenberg's development of the printing press? There were similarities. Gutenberg's invention was a refinement of printing that allowed interchangeable metal type. It made printing cheaper and much more efficient, leading to an explosive spread of printed knowledge and stimulating an unheralded desire for literacy among the populations of Europe. Most great inventions, in fact, tend to be refinements. Watt's steam engine was a refinement on earlier machines, and he would refine it further to deliver rotary power. Darby's development created the raw material for a new age of invention. It was just the first of a series of momentous strides in ironworking made by members of his family. Within two years Darby had moved his operations to Coalbrookdale, taking advantage of a derelict forge in a traditional ironmaking area.

Hitherto, charcoal had been the fuel used in iron and brass forging. Traditional iron forges scattered around the English Midlands relied on large swathes of coppiced woodland. About 2,500 acres of woodland were needed to sustain a single forge. This prevented the concentration of iron production, because charcoal could not be transported in bulk without crumbling. The geology of Coalbrookdale, with outcrops of clay, iron ore, coal, and limestone, offered resources on the doorstep. The only restriction to expansion was the supply of charcoal, but Darby had ideas for improvements to the forging process that would overcome the problem. Coke is made from coal, covered and heated at high temperatures to change its structure. Its advantage over coal is that it also burns at high temperatures. The vital component was coke.

Darby began smelting iron ore in January, 1709. If this was the birth of the Industrial Revolution, and it may be as good a date as any, it was a revolution that started quietly. The first smelting was carried out using the conventional charcoal fuel, but the scarcity of wood for charcoal led Darby to experiment with other fuels. He tried coal, but it burned too quickly and not hot enough. It may well have been some earlier experience with malt mills that led him to experiment with coal and coke in forging, since brewers had perfected the way of making coke.[7] At some stage in that year – we don't know when – he had some coal coked into cinder. What was good for drying malt, he reasoned, might work with iron.[8]

He found that locally mined coal, low on sulfur content, worked best. The local iron was also good for casting because it was high in silica and low in phosphorus. Although Darby did not understand the chemistry, he realized he was making fine cast iron that could make pots with far thinner walls than any made previously.

Within a year these cheap "bellied" pots – the sort we associate with witches' cauldrons – were transforming the domestic market for cookware. People who might have previously scraped enough together to buy a single pot could now own more than one. The trade should not be trivialized. There was a time in England when the habit of boiling a pot in one place was a symbol of residence and freedom. It was part of English law.[9] The Quaker business ethic meant that Darby did not set a price for his pots but asked a buyer to name a fair price. This underlying fairness in the way the Quakers did business is one of the defining characteristics of their success, establishing a strong link between honesty and customer loyalty that remains as valuable today as it did in Darby's time.

Darby opened more forges nearby and built cottages for his workers. These were among the first row houses associated with industrial production. When Abraham Darby died in 1717, his partners carried on the work until Abraham Darby II took control. The son was as inventive as his father, gradually building his understanding of the process and developing a new ironworking method that would propel the revolution even further. This was wrought iron.

Cast iron was strong but brittle. Wrought iron, made by elongating and mangling the hot metal and beating out the carbon responsible for cast iron's fragility, was bendable and flexible. Coalbrookdale continued to make cooking pots, but soon it was also making iron rails and wheels for the new locomotives. It made steam boilers and the first iron frames used in factory buildings, allowing the owners to concentrate their production in far larger multistoried factories.

By the mid-eighteenth century there were other iron producers. Hundreds of people were exploring the potential of this new product that had allowed steam power to come of age. How had something like a simple cooking pot done so much to liberate the almost explosive inventiveness of the age? The answer is quite simple – because it was cheap. The first steam engines, like the first computers, were complex, expensive machines. Many of their working parts were made of brass, and brass was expensive. Iron was much cheaper, and the Darbys' quality improvements made it viable in steam engine construction. Refinement of innovation at lower cost was the key to the widespread adoption of steam power. This combination of factors has proved itself time and again in the marketplace. Innovation is moribund without it. Abraham Darby's iron smelter was as crucial to developments in the eighteenth century as the silicon chip was to computing nearly three hundred years later.

The forge itself is not much to look at. Its history is inscribed in lintels set in the brick structure at different dates. The first, dated 1638, was placed there by the Brook family who established the charcoal furnace. Later lintels were added by Abraham Darby III, when he enlarged the structure to manufacture the cast iron for the bridge that gives Ironbridge Gorge its modern name. Otherwise the structure looks little more than a pile of bricks. David de Haan, deputy director of the Ironbridge Gorge Museum Trust, puts it into perspective: "Essentially it's the most important pile of bricks in the world."[10]

Some may argue differently, inspired perhaps by excavated walls, such as those of biblical Jericho (now equally decrepit) or the Great Wall of China; great structures both, but they did not change people's lives in the same way as this new age of iron and steam. In this small Shropshire valley at the beginning of the eighteenth century, the smell of change was once more in the air. It was a sulfurous smell borne on choking fumes that constricted the lungs and stung the eyes. It was the smell of progress. We can see change happening in Abraham Darby's lifetime. His daughter-in-law, Abiah Darby, contrasts the economy of Coalbrookdale before and after the arrival of her family: "This place and its environs was very barren, little money stirring amongst the inhabitants. So that I have heard they were obliged to exchange their small produce one to another instead of money, until he came and got the works to bear, and made money circulate amongst the different parties who were employed by him."[11]

Something else was happening in this period. Darby and his industrial successors were creating the job, as we would recognize it for the next three centuries. The job was changing, almost imperceptibly, from a piece of work that needed doing, to something that began to be perceived as a constant source of employment and income packaged by the parameters of time. Looking at Darby's cashbook in the first year of the forge's operations, you can see it developing. Much of the early work is bought in. Individuals are contracted for specific tasks. Sometimes they bring their materials with them as trader-contractors. But very quickly you begin to discern a small core of regularly paid individuals, five at first, growing to a dozen or more by the end of the year.[12] There is no clue to their working conditions, although the amounts they are paid usually (but not always) correspond week by week. This is still a long way from uniformity, but it is beginning to look like regular employment.

Some regular employment at this time, mine work for example, was contracted out, typically using middlemen called charter masters. It would be wrong to describe these people as professional recruiters, because they were quite unprofessional. They often ran pubs and stores called truck shops, and on paydays their tardiness in distributing the wages was legendary. The idea was to keep the workers hanging around long enough to chalk up some credit in the pub or to buy some of the overpriced goods in the shop.[13] The mine owners were slow to realize that they should "have no truck" with these people.[14]

In spite of these abuses, employment was settling into a daily pattern. Instead of working from dawn until dusk for intensive periods defined by a specific project such as the harvest, people would rest at the end of their shift. The next day there would be another shift. The work was a constant in a mushrooming economy where demand fueled production and production fueled demand. It would be a mistake, nevertheless, to say that the Industrial Revolution created "the job." It changed the job, making it the most recognizable feature of employment and the handiest of words to describe an individual's employment. But the word "job," like most of the words describing employment, has a long and evolving history, sometimes obscure in origin.

The *Oxford English Dictionary* suggests that "job" may share its origin with the word "gob," meaning a small parcel of something in the mouth. Gradually it came to mean a heap of material, specifically so in the mining industry, where it was used to describe both a mining cavity and the pile of mined material. It does not take a great stretch of the imagination to see how the act of creating the pile and the cavity could become a "gob" or a "job." The words covering occupation (even "occupation" itself) began to take on their modern meaning during this period. The salary – from the Latin *salarius*, a word that had first been applied to the payment given to Roman soldiers for the purchase of salt (*sal*) – had come to be used as a term for a priest's stipend but was not yet in general usage. Words like "recruitment" and "wage" had military origins. "Work" had Teutonic origins and "trade" evolved from its original Old German meaning of following a path.

Workers did not yet "clock in," but the clock began to increase in importance, both in governing the length of the working day and in proportioning pay. The marine chronometers of John Harrison, a contemporary of the Darbys, had greatly advanced the accuracy of timekeeping in the first half of the eighteenth century, but telling the exact time was not necessarily the most important feature of early factory timekeeping.

Mills relying on water to drive their machinery would sometimes use a two-faced clock.[15] One face would tell the real time and the second face would tell the time for which an individual would be paid. This "factory time" was governed by the flow of the river that worked the machinery. If the flow slowed, so did production. The elongated hours measured by the clock geared to the water flow were used, therefore, to calculate the excess hours that employees would need to work to make up their pay.

It was a novel form of flexible working, allowing manufacturing employers and employees to plan more efficiently for peaks and troughs in production – not so very different from the "hours banks" introduced in the late-twentieth century, which allow workers to save up hours worked as overtime, so that they can be taken later, ideally during a slack period. Unlike hours banks, however, the system of employment governed by water clocks was wholly one-sided. This form of variable factory time meant that the worker would be in place whether the water, and thus production, flowed or not. In the early factory system, time was in the power of the factory master, often the only individual in possession of a watch. According to the historian E. P. Thompson, factory masters would sometimes cheat their workers by putting the clocks forward in the morning and back at night. One worker with a watch had it taken from him because he was telling his fellow workers the time of day.[16]

The introduction of clocking on by workers using a recording clock in the early 1800s prevented either workers or employers taking advantage of work-time expectations. According to Lewis Mumford, the American sociologist who died in 1990, this precise control of time in factory production was a natural progression from the regulated strictures of St. Benedict's rule. The monasteries, said Mumford, had helped to give enterprise the "regular collective beat and rhythm of the machine; for the clock is not merely a means of keeping track of the hours, but of synchronizing the actions of men" so "time-keeping passed into time-serving and time-accounting and time-rationing." Thus, he concluded, "the clock, not the steam engine, is the key machine of the industrial age."[17]

The factory, in the sense of a building in which manufacturing work was concentrated, had come of age. The word was originally applied to the place used by merchants or factors to carry out their foreign trade. Unlike the mill, which was associated with a mechanical function, the factory was associated, first and foremost, with the boss, the controller of production. Mill and factory would become synonymous. But it is significant that the factory was the place where the manufacturing entrepreneur would concentrate his production. Its main advantage over home-based production, at least until economies of scale became apparent, was probably that of concealment and protection of the new machinery from those who might imitate or destroy it.[18]

The theft of industrial secrets was becoming an international issue. When John Lombe took a job in 1717 at a silk factory in Livorno, Italy, his express intention was that of copying the silk spinning machine on which he was working.[19] He worked by day, and by night he copied every single detail of the machine, before hiding the plans inside a bale of silk bound for England. Within four years John and his brother, Sir Thomas Lombe, had established a factory on an island in the middle of the River Derwent in Derby. The Italians had been using these machines for at least three centuries before the secrets were brought to England, but the Italian enterprises were confined to relatively small mills. The Lombes built a five-story factory, employing some three hundred people, including skilled female Italian operators recruited from their hometown of Livorno. A warrant was issued in Italy for John Lombe's arrest, but he was well away from Italian jurisdiction. He may not, however, have been out of the Italians' reach. He died three years after his factory went into production, and there is a story that he was poisoned by an Italian assassin, possibly one of the women operators.[20] The espionage game, then as now, was a perilous business.

Silk spinning would remain a specialist industry in England. The potential for wool and cotton was far greater. No wonder then that the most ambitious of individuals applied themselves to improving the manufacture of these more serviceable textiles. One of the first important breakthroughs was made by John Kay, who invented the flying shuttle. The shuttle could work so quickly that thread manufacture could not keep up with it until Hargreaves responded by inventing his spinning jenny in 1767. Within the space of about fifteen years the technology of the textile industry was transformed in a series of logical leaps.

The jenny could only make thread strong enough for the weft – the short thread carried by the shuttle. The next breakthrough would be to make a machine capable of spinning the stronger warp, which stretched over the length of the loom. Kay, a clockmaker, would give his assistance to Richard Arkwright, a barber turned wigmaker and itinerant trader in human hair, who was intent upon making a perpetual motion machine. According to his landlord he was seeking to win the prize offered by the

British Parliament to anyone who could find a reliable way of calculating longitude.[21]

Perpetual motion eluded Arkwright, but with Kay's help he did design a useful spinning frame that could make the stronger warp thread. When he exhibited the frame at Preston Grammar School it was not well received by self-employed weavers worried about its potential to destroy their jobs. Others possibly saw an opportunity to steal the idea and pursue their own manufacturing operations. This was the textile entrepreneur's dilemma and remains the innovator's dilemma to this day. How do you display your invention to potential backers and yet conceal it from imitators? Who can you trust? The danger is that in business the gamekeeper can sometimes turn poacher.

Arkwright's first spinning frame used horsepower, but he soon switched to waterpower in a purpose-built cotton-spinning factory established in 1771 by the side of the River Derwent in Cromford, Derbyshire. The machine was renamed the water-frame. By the latter half of the eighteenth century the British textile industry was awash with inventions. Samuel Crompton's Mule (1774) was devised as a hybrid of the water-frame and the spinning jenny, and Edmund Cartwright's power loom (1785) took advantage of James Watt's improvement in steam power. By 1780 the UK had 120 textile factories, mostly in Lancashire and Yorkshire. But they far from dominated the trade. This was still a labor-intensive, household artisan industry. The power loom did not work well at first, and handloom weaving prevailed for a while. But the bargaining power of the handloom weavers had been destroyed by the yarn manufacturers and cloth merchants. The days of relative prosperity and independence for the artisan weaver were coming to an end.

Only when mechanization began to impact on wages, as it did after the turn of the century, did worker resentment of textile machinery boil over into violence and outbreaks of frame breaking. There was similar unrest in France when Joseph Jacquard invented an improved loom in 1804. He was mobbed and almost drowned by the weavers of Lille, who destroyed his new invention. The destruction, wherever it occurred, was short-lived, sporadic, and organized. The British government response to frame breaking was that of a nervous administration, reeling still from revolution in the

American colonies. Fearful of any repeat of the events that had led to revolution in France, suspicious of anything that smacked of insurrection on its own soil, the British government ensured that the North of England towns were garrisoned against a potential threat from within. Troops would fire in anger. Men would fight and die for the right to work. The ethic that defined a spirit of endeavor was pumping the heart and boiling the blood. Something would have to give.

CHAPTER 6

Secrets of the Dumb Steeple

Man is a worker. If he is not that he is nothing.
(Joseph Conrad, 1857–1924)

John Booth was dying. The loss of blood from his leg, shattered by a musket ball, had been too great. He was a young man, just nineteen, a harness maker from Halifax in the West Riding of Yorkshire. It hadn't even been his quarrel, but passions were running high, and when volunteers were sought to fight on behalf of the hand shearers John Booth was with them. His father had been a shearer before joining the priesthood and still did the odd shearing job. It was a good job and had been well paid before the machines arrived. Machines did not put food on the Booth family table. The issue was that simple.

But was it worth dying for? As Booth's life ebbed away, a clergyman called Hammond Roberson stooped over him, eager to hear him speak. Roberson was not ministering absolution. He wanted information. He wanted names. Who were Booth's accomplices? Who were these so-called Luddites who thought they could terrorize manufacturers into abandoning their wage-saving mechanization?

This was the North of England, April, 1812. Britain was at war with France and America. Its best troops were abroad, and unrest had broken out in the manufacturing centers of Nottingham, Lancashire, and Yorkshire. The Luddites at the heart of the trouble were named after a Nottingham apprentice, Ned Ludd, who set about his stocking frame with a hammer when threatened with a whipping for working too slowly. Their tactic was to send threatening letters in "General" Ludd's name to potential victims. If machinery was not dismantled by its owners, the Luddites did the job themselves. First it had been the stocking-frame breakers in Nottingham, then the weavers in Lancashire, then setting fire to mills in protest over the threat posed to work and pay by the new power looms at a time of sharply rising food prices.

Finally it was the Yorkshire shearers, a well-paid industrial elite whose job was to crop the newly made cloth with large and heavy steel shears. Their work was becoming scarce and poorly paid. Worker hostility was discriminatory, aimed not at all at the mill owners who installed machines, but at those who did so while lowering their rates of pay.

William Cartwright, the owner of Rawfold's Mill in the Yorkshire village of Liversedge, had done just that. He was a determined man – his character was the inspiration for Robert Moore, the hero of Charlotte Bronte's second novel, *Shirley*, based around the events of April 12, when perhaps between a hundred and two hundred men, including John Booth, met in darkness at a local landmark, the Dumb Steeple, about three miles from the mill. They were desperate men, fortified by their convictions. They were not poor. They were not starving. Not yet anyway. But they had plenty to lose.

The West Riding Luddites had already claimed a victory against Cartwright when they intercepted and destroyed a batch of shearing frames on their way to the mill from the manufacturer, Enoch and James Taylor. The company not only made the frames, it also made the hammers that were used to smash the frames. For one business, at least, the Luddite risings were a healthy source of profit all round.

The men who met at the Dumb Steeple were organized and probably well drilled. They marched with hammers, clubs, and a few small arms. But Cartwright was waiting with five soldiers, assigned to protect the mill, and four of his own men, all armed. The mill had been reinforced in case of attack and the raiders could not get in. The battle lasted twenty minutes. When the Luddites gave up and dispersed they left two of their group, John Booth and Samuel Hartley, lying, mortally wounded, in the mill yard.

The two men were taken to a nearby public house and questioned, but they belonged to a group where the imposition of secrecy was vital. All its members were under oath to keep silent. The local parson, Hammond Roberson, was on the side of the owners and hoped to win the dying men's confidence. When Booth beckoned him closer, he knelt to hear his confession.

"Can you keep a secret?" asked Booth, his voice beginning to falter.

"Yes," said Roberson.

The priest brightened until Booth replied with his dying breath: "So can I."[1]

Charlotte Bronte's mill owner hero was foreign-born, the son of a Flemish textile family that had fallen on hard times. But the real Cartwright was from the same stock as those who opposed him. In different circumstances you could imagine him leading the riot. Owners and employees possessed the same ethic but were capable of directing it differently, depending on their position.

Class distinctions had become acute by this time. Charlotte Bronte acknowledges as much when her heroine, Shirley Keeldar, turns on some local gossips:

"Fine, rich people that have nothing to do, may be partly excused for trifling their time away: you who have to earn your bread with the sweat of your brow are quite inexcusable."[2]

At which section of society is Bronte's rebuke directed – rich or poor? Perhaps it is at both. The track of her mind is further revealed by a question from one of the villagers:

"Should we never have a holiday because we work hard?"

"Never," says Shirley, "unless you knew how to make a better use of it than to get together over rum and tea, if you are women – or over beer and pipes, if you are men, and talk scandal at your neighbours' expense."

The Protestant morality comes shining through, governing the way that people are expected to work and the way they should spend their leisure time.

The clergyman in the novel and his fictional parish was drawn from that of St Peter's Church, Hartshead, where the Bronte sisters' father, Patrick, had been curate at the time of the Luddite attack. The Luddites would have marched close by the church, as they do in the novel.

The Rawfold attack was a turning point in the Luddite unrest. The killings demanded tit for tat revenge, and a mill owner was waylaid and murdered near Huddersfield soon afterward. Luddites were rounded up and tried. Executions and transportations were carried out across the industrial North. Luddism had failed but the name would continue in the language to refer to anyone unsupportive of new technology.

Resistance over, the mill owners consolidated their power, installing steam powered machinery in their factories. Within the next fifty years the independent artisan/traders all but disappeared from the industrial scene, although they continued to thrive in the growing service industry and in general trade.

Handloom weavers, who had numbered almost a quarter of a million in 1820, had dwindled to no more than twenty-three thousand in 1856. The great piece halls – large, square, refectory-sized buildings consisting of small offices where merchants and manufacturers met to trade pieces of cloth – were transient constructions whose productive life was finished within twenty or thirty years. As an experiment in small-owner capitalism it failed, swept away by mechanization and the concentration of production in mills.

This was the British experience at any rate. In Ireland the industry outlook was quite different, as a British government inspector discovered when he interviewed Irish cottage-based textile workers to make comparisons in a parliamentary inquiry into the demise of handloom weaving in England. The inspector estimated that the Irish weaver's year consisted of two hundred days. The 165 days off were made up of fifty-two sabbaths, fifty-two market days, twenty-six days for wakes and funerals (calculated on the basis of half a day per death and the assurance that "it's a poor neighborhood that there wasn't one death a week") and sundry days for holidays, birthdays, and saints' days.[3]

Although the Irish cottage workers lived in "filth and squalor," said the inspector, "they were contented." He added: "The Irish weavers as a body seem to love freedom and a potato rather than factories and better food."[4] The remark was published just two years before the Irish potato famine, when such observations would have been unthinkable. But it demonstrates the gulf in attitudes informed mainly by differences in religious dogma. It has little to do with the difference between Celt and Anglo-Saxon. The real divide is religious in its ancestry. Its power is inescapable, shaping the values of generations, however they may frame their individual beliefs. The Ulsterman, whether godly or atheist, carries his unshakable Protestantism, not as a burden but shouldered proudly and paraded in the confident assurance that his iron will has been hammered on the anvil of hard work.

In the same way the Methodist miners of South Wales love to celebrate their unity, strength, and comradeship in poetry and song.
Work for these communities is not a curse but a birthright.

By the turn of the seventeenth century mass employment had
become a privilege to be dispensed as such by the new industrialists who began to dominate the everyday existence of those who
worked in their mill communities. At Cromford Mill, Richard
Arkwright's workers were urged to sing in his praise:

> Come let us here join in one,
> And thank him for all favours done;
> Let's thank him for all favours still
> Which he hath done besides the mill.[5]

The mill owner now had the whip hand and many were prepared to use it. Much of the mechanized work could be carried
out by women and children, whose labor came more cheaply than
men's. Women, by tradition, had been spinners, using hearthside
wheels or the distaff, a stick full of wool from which the operator
could spin the yarn onto a hand-held spindle. Typically the distaff
stick would be secured with one end stuck into the woman's girdle.

The earliest spinning machines, operating twelve spindles,
were incorporated alongside the domestic textile trade, supplying
yarn to handloom weavers. This is the trade that was still pros-
pering as the Luddites moved to protect their improved status and
incomes in turn-of-the-century weaving. Later, larger, factory-
based machines allowed one woman or child to control spinning
on a hundred machine-mounted spindles at any one time. By then
the cottage industry was in decline.

Children were brought from poorhouses to work in the mills.
They were sent to the silk mills as young as five years old,
because their hands were perceived as potentially more dexterous
in handling the fine silk yarn. Why were children used arbitrar-
ily in these new factories? In *Centuries of Childhood*, Philippe
Aries suggests that childhood is a comparatively modern concept,
and that children used to be perceived as young adults.[6] But this
cannot alone explain the attitude to child employees. The British
Factory Commission reports on the new industries suggest that
there were serious concerns about child labor in some quarters in

the 1830s, when factory owners were building up their businesses. But in the places where it mattered, in the factories themselves, across the industrial belt of northern England, commercialism appears to have blinded those who controlled them to any great social concern.

The new employers, often former laborers themselves, had little to lean on in terms of custom and practice. Dealing with large numbers of people, usually women and children, working together in a systemized fashion and in a confined space was alien to both manager and employee. This is not offered as justification for ill treatment but it does help to explain how ill treatment could arise. The mill-owning families, such as the Arkwrights and the Strutts, were considered good employers among their peers. The Strutts, who started their textile empire in the Nottinghamshire hosiery business, moving later into cotton spinning, took children from the age of seven, which was considered more than reasonable in the second half of the eighteenth century.

A glance at the records kept by these mill owners, listing reasons for fines (the Strutts did not allow corporal punishment in their mills) imposed on employees, shows the extent to which the factory floor discipline and behavior could relate to that found in some of the earliest schools. Fines were imposed, for example, for such misdemeanors as "idleness and looking through window," "riding on each other's back," "terrifying S. Pearson with her ugly face," "sending for ale into the room," "neglecting his work to talk to people," and "rubbing their faces with blood and going about town to frighten people."[7] These were neither model employers nor model workers. The long lists of fines demonstrate the parameters of the work ethic. It was there in the industrialists, but in many of the workers it was barely skin-deep, often because the workers were children, who needed to play, not work.

Finding people to work these early Derbyshire mills was not easy. Some of the job advertisements emphasized the rural charm of the Derwent Valley in the hope that they would stir some nostalgia for the countryside among first generation townies. One newspaper advertisement placed by the Darley Cotton Mill said: "Wanted, families, particularly women and children to work the said mill. They may be provided with comfortable houses and every necessary convenience either at Darley or Allestry;

particularly a milking cow to each family. It is a very good neighbourhood for the men getting work who are not employed in the manufacturing." The lure of a milking cow to a former farm laborer had the same attraction as a company car would have to a traveling salesman today. Other popular incentives included allotments or potato plots. The concept of a piece of land for personal subsistence is an ancient one.

Finding separate work for men, often constructing or running properties on the mill owners' private estates, was another way in which these entrepreneurs filled their mills with the wives and children of tradesmen. The whole family then could be conceived as an economic unit. For this reason, Arkwright's mill houses were built on three stories, to allow a man to work a single loom in the top room. So many of the necessities of life – housing, groceries, coal – were provided by these mill employers that employees often received no more than a sixth of their wages in cash. It meant that families became as tied to their place of work as their ancestors had been in service to the Lord of the Manor.

Richard Arkwright lost his earliest attempt to protect his patent, and the spinning business became a free-for-all. As the technology spread, and steam power allowed the machinery to move into towns and cities, the reasonable living conditions for the earliest mill workers were not sustained. Parliament was forced to intervene in a bid to regulate the textile working regime.

Factory Commission reports from the period quote one spinner saying that, but for the Factory Acts, the competition among mill owners was severe enough to force round the clock working with no breaks other than for meals. Even Quakers, often lauded as humanitarians, were capable of pushing their workers too hard. In the first volume of *Capital*, Karl Marx quotes a report of a prosecution in June, 1836 against some Quaker mill owners in Batley, Yorkshire, who kept boys aged between twelve and fifteen at work from six in the morning on a Friday until six in the evening on the Saturday, with no respite except an hour for sleep and some breaks for meals. The Quakers were fined £20.[8] Objections to child labor needed to overcome widespread indifference in general society. This seems clear from an examination of one specific area of child employment – the climbing children used to clean out the chimneys of large houses.

The employment of climbing children had begun as a solution to a problem caused by an increasing use of coal in the seventeenth and eighteenth centuries. House chimneys began to appear in sixteenth-century England, when the idea of using enclosed chimney breasts to take smoke from a hearth set alongside a wall was introduced from Italy. Coal began to be seen as a viable alternative heating fuel as mining techniques improved and wood became scarce. But chimneys needed cleaning.[9] The work was originally done by servants, but dedicated chimney sweeps began to appear in the Elizabethan era. Large wood-burning fireplaces with their broad chimney breasts were not well suited to coal burning, which required a strong air flow and a good draw on the fire to work effectively. This meant that in later centuries openings for old chimneys were contracted in size, and new chimneys were built altogether narrower to prevent the discharge of smoke into people's living rooms.[10]

The chimney sweep's solution to the physical difficulty of tackling narrow flues was to use children, some apprenticed as young as four and five. One sweep, Thomas Allen, told a parliamentary inquiry that his career had begun when he was aged three and a half.[11] Boys and girls were used for the job. Two girls, the daughters of a sweep called Morgan, were employed to clean the chimneys of the Royal Family at Windsor Castle.[12] Some flues were quite spacious but some were so narrow – as tight as seven inches square – that only the tiniest of children, often stripped naked, could be used to squeeze through the gap. They had to move with their arms extended. One slip and they could find themselves jammed.

The sweeps used a variety of methods to persuade their young charges to do the job. Sometimes it was the promise of plum pudding when they reached the top, sometimes it was the threat of a beating. More extremely, some of the most brutal of the master sweeps were known to set straw on fire in the grating or to prick the feet of the children.[13] The competing options of stick and carrot in their many guises have been an enduring form of motivation throughout history. But when the job is as unremittingly punishing as that of the child sweep the discussion of motivation seems redundant.

There were stories of children stolen from their parents. Some were sold by their families. Others were taken from workhouses.

The word among master sweeps was that in Liverpool you could find any quantity of children you needed. The trade in people had re-emerged on Britain's streets, even if transactions were made quietly beyond public scrutiny. The evidence was strong enough to convince a magistrate in Leicester. "I am satisfied," he wrote, "that great numbers of these children are regularly bought and sold; and that practically they are as complete slaves as any negro children in South Carolina." This statement would have some resonance in court. The treatment of black slaves in the former colonies was a hotly debated issue in the UK abolitionist movement in the early nineteenth century, after Britain had taken the lead among the slave-trading nations by banning slave traffic in 1807. But the magistrate was right, if he believed that self-righteousness would be misplaced so long as British children continued to be exploited as chimney sweeps.

Chimney passages ran through the superstructure of large houses like a maze feeding into fireplaces throughout the house. This explains how young Thomas Allen came to lose his way and find himself in an unfamiliar bedroom. It also helps to explain why it took the best part of a century to pass legislation effective enough to ban the use of children. Time and again the owners of these large houses, many of whom sat in the House of Lords, would obstruct attempts to legislate.

Humanitarian pleadings were not strong enough to move the legislators, one reason why The Society for the Necessity of Superseding Climbing Boys took a different tack by offering a reward for anyone who could produce an effective cleaning machine. The society believed that the prospect of financial gain would prove the most effective driver of innovation in the chimney sweeping business.

Tests on one machine proved particularly effective.[14] One of its few drawbacks was that it struggled to remove the soot that accumulated in horizontal flues. This kind of flue was quite commonly used among the gentry to preserve the symmetry of their elegant rooms. Members of the House of Lords, faced with altering their houses or preserving the status quo, preferred the latter option and continued to resist reforming legislation.

They had the master chimney sweeps on their side. Fearful that mechanization would either put them out of work or introduce unwelcome competition, the sweeps were assiduous in collecting evidence to support their cause. Not all this evidence, however, was so helpful. One sweep stressed the importance of boys for extinguishing chimney fires. If the boys knew what they were doing and protected their heads with clothing, he said, there was no reason why they should be burnt.[15]

But boys were burnt. Deaths among the chimney sweep children from fire or suffocation were not uncommon, neither were debilitating illnesses such as "chimney sweep's cancer" and physical deformities of the knees and ankle joints. Sweeps rubbed brine into the bleeding knees and elbows of their new charges until the skin had hardened.[16] Many children were forced to sleep in the sweeps' cellars alongside bags of soot. Some children, and their masters for that matter, contracted scrotal cancer, caused by ingrained soot. Chimney sweep's cancer, identified by Percival Pott, was the first recorded occupational cancer.

Often young sweeps were not washed from one year to the next, but at least they saw the daylight. Those who toiled blindly in the mines often saw little or no daylight for weeks on end. Some were employed as "trappers," opening and closing the air passages into the mines. The trapper children often sat in the darkness in a hole hewn into the side of the passage by the trap doors which it was their job to operate for twelve hours at a stretch. Other children were used to fill skips with newly mined coal, and some either pulled or pushed the mine cars along the galleries. Those who pulled were often harnessed by the waist like huskies tied to dog sleds. A girdle was passed round the naked waist and a chain ran from the carriage, between the boys' or girls' legs, allowing them to drag the skip along.

One eight-year-old girl described how she would sometimes sing if one of the miners had been kind enough to hand her a scrap of candle for some light, for in the dark "I dare not sing then." [17]

This then was the legacy of Abraham Darby and James Watt. The revolution that had unfettered capital, sparked invention, and unleashed a tide of industry that transformed the Western world was not created without a price. The indifference to such suffering was not universal, but the displays of callousness among the established hierarchies were breathtaking.

It was not just callousness. There were some among the Lords who were convinced of their own righteousness in resisting reform. Lord Lauderdale, one of the most vociferous opponents of legislation to stop the use of child chimney sweeps, urged that reforms should be left "entirely to the moral feelings of perhaps the most moral people on the face of the earth."[18] Who were these people? He was referring, in fact, to the British and, by implication, the ruling gentry in British society.

Repeatedly, the cause of vested interest, be it the gentry or the artisans themselves, overruled the plight of society's weakest members. It wasn't even as if the coal industry was threatened by cheaper imports. Market forces did not help the child laborers and neither did innovation. It was the persistence of reformers like William Wilberforce, Lord Shaftesbury, and others, often those who had survived childhood miseries undertaking such work, that finally held sway.

The use of chimney sweep children was rare outside the UK. No other nation dallied as long as Britain in its efforts to outlaw the practice. Child labor was a cheap and effective response to a problem posed by one of the new technologies at a time when society was ill equipped to respond to the social implications of such change. But this was not the first time, nor the last, that society and legislators would respond either slowly or inadequately to the social upheavals resulting from technological change.

The piecemeal advance of labor regulation relative to national social and economic factors has assumed a fresh significance in the so-called "global marketplace" of today, where mass-selling fashion items might be made by sweatshop labor and child labor working in conditions that do not conform to Western regulations. The practice of child labor cannot always be judged against Western cultural expectations. Should we, for example, boycott the import of Persian rugs handmade by children, knowing that the creation of the rug is a family affair, in which the skills are passed down from generation to generation? Is the young weaver learning his craft at the loom in some way disadvantaged when compared to his Western counterpart, or is he simply taking his place in the world?

The judgment will probably rely on the strength of world opinion. If the market rejects Nike training shoes because of allegations that some of them have been made by child labor, then Nike must address its labor sourcing. And market forces are beginning to shape company policies. Manchester United supporters, for example, expressed some unease at the club's £302.9 million ($450 million) kit supply deal with Nike in 2002 precisely because of the past allegations against the company. Manchester United has a policy of not dealing with any country that allows breaches of child labor regulations.

The rule of cause and effect is beginning to replicate change that was once confined to a national stage. The stage where Britain's Industrial Revolution was played out was a microcosm of economic acceleration. The surge in economic activity had increased the need for industrial labor at the same time that mechanization in agriculture had reduced demand for farm work. Land enclosure was also depriving village laborers of their opportunity to farm their own animals on common land. As E. P. Thompson put it: "In village after village, enclosure destroyed the scratch-as-scratch-can subsistence economy of the poor."[19]

Enclosure did not happen overnight, but it became an escalating practice in the eighteenth century, as landowners sought to limit, even remove, the rights of tenant farmers and cottagers that had been established over the long history of the manorial feudal system. Common land had in many cases been farmed for centuries by the same families, often working at their own pace. The transformation of their social contract from one of servitude to subsistence farming, then wage labor, was probably the biggest influence on the enclosure movement. The landowners wanted to formalize their ownership of the land out of self-interest, and their domination of the parliamentary system, whether as Tories or Whigs, allowed them to pass hundreds of private enclosure acts throughout the eighteenth century before the system was simplified in the General Enclosure Act of 1881.

Enclosure of large tracts of land, alongside farm mechanization brought about by inventions such as the threshing machine and Jethro Tull's seed drill, which had been in use since 1701, allowed significant economies of scale. Rents rose and farm profits increased in this industrialization of the land, but small farmers often lost their independence. Those who were enclosing the land regarded this as a good thing, noting that independence had enabled some of these small farmers to work less. They had their small house and a piece of land, and they were comfortable. This comfort was destroyed by enclosure, as a 1794 report looking at Shropshire observed favorably. With enclosure of the common, wrote its author, "the labourers will work every day in the year, their children will be put out to labour early," and "that subordination of the lower ranks of society, which in the present times, is so much wanted, would be thereby considerably secured."[20] The subordination was "so much wanted" because the English landowning class had been horrified by the French Revolution of 1789.

The further impoverishment of people who were already struggling to supplement their meager earnings with what they could eke out of the land was bound to create discontent. The laborers who lived in the tiny Dorset village of Tolpuddle were hardly brimming with seditious intent when they met under a sycamore tree in March, 1834 to discuss their grievances against the local landlords. But that is not how the law saw it.

The wages for farm laborers in Tolpuddle had been reduced from nine shillings a week in 1830 to eight shillings, then seven. One of the villagers, George Loveless, called a meeting of fellow workers. Firstly they approached the vicar to act as an intermediary with their employers to seek some assurances over their wage rates. When that failed they turned to the recently formed Grand National Consolidated Trades Union, a body set up by Robert Owen, the textile entrepreneur turned social reformer. Two of its members came to Tolpuddle and shortly afterwards the Dorset men established their own organization, the Friendly Society of Agricultural Labourers.[21]

The landowners took fright and sought help from Lord Melbourne, the then home secretary. Trade unions had been legalized ten years earlier, so the employers pursued a different course. The new membership had bound themselves to the union with oaths, a common practice at the time, when organizations sought to preserve some secrecy over their discussions. The Mutiny Act of 1797, which forbade the taking of "unlawful oaths," was invoked to arrest and charge Loveless and five others. They were tried the next month and each received the maximum sentence possible – seven years' transportation to Australia. The case was a cause *célèbre*.

In response, Owen mustered a "Grand Meeting of the Working Classes," which drew ten thousand people. This was just fourteen years after cavalry had charged an open gathering demanding franchise reforms in St Peter's Field, Manchester, killing fifteen people. The government-sanctioned action was forever afterwards known as Peterloo. There would be no overreaction a second time. Another meeting in London swelled to thirty-thousand, and a delegation petitioned the government. Melbourne refused to accept the petition but he would receive further notice that his strategy had seriously misjudged the mood of the nation when the protest began to grow.

William Cobbett, the social commentator, and several members of Parliament took up the campaign for a pardon. Melbourne's successor, Lord John Russell, proposed a conditional pardon that would require the men to remain in the colony for various periods. Finally, he bowed to pressure and granted a full pardon in March, 1836, two years after the men's arrest. Some did not get back home until the fourth anniversary of their trial. The men were hailed as martyrs and still are by the trade union movement. Tolpuddle remains as a piece of historical grit, never buried and never forgotten by those who continue to press the cause of freedom of association.

The trade union movement was formed in response to widespread abuses in working conditions and pay across the oldest and newest sectors of employment. Karl Marx and Friedrich Engels believed it would be only a matter of time before the working classes repeated the pattern of the French Revolution in Britain. Engels had witnessed conditions in the Manchester cotton factories at first hand. But the poverty of Britain's nineteenth-century city-dwelling working class was highlighted nowhere more graphically than in the *Morning Chronicle* articles on the London poor written by Henry Mayhew. Among a wide range of working people interviewed and surveyed by Mayhew, few were as destitute as women needleworkers, who routinely resorted to prostitution in an effort to survive. One woman told him how her baby son's legs had frozen to her side as she sat with him throughout the night on a doorstep. Even the workhouse had rejected her without an order for admission.[22] Work for many people among the London poor offered no hope of salvation, no future. Wages in far too many cases were insufficient to allow any reasonable standard of living. The levels of exploitation in the frantic search for profit had sunk beyond any recognition of human decency.

The mill-owning class, which in many cases had risen from the very people it now sought to suppress, is often portrayed as heartless and uncaring, and justifiably so, but there were exceptions whose concern for their workforces would influence a vein of humanity in factory management. In its earliest manifestations it often took on the form of philanthropy, the generous owner basking in the glow from his munificence. But in some, like Robert Owen, entrepreneur, social reformer, and utopian dreamer, there was a genuine philosophy, a genuine desire to build a better world from the success of their enterprises. Owen, like Benjamin Franklin, was an internationalist. From a promising start in a small Scottish community he pushed out his ideas across the Atlantic, where the spirit of hard work, individualism, and tolerance had been bound together with the twin pillars of democracy and meritocracy in an eloquent constitution.

The United States was not yet one nation and could not be while people were subjugated in the South; but when the internal reckoning was over, destructive as it was, the pace of change would pick up so dramatically that the quarreling states of Europe would be staggered by America's economic transformation from an agricultural and slave-plantation base to an industrial powerhouse. The hardworking Protestant immigrants who played such a pivotal role in America's transformation were gradually making an impact as they pushed westwards in search of Utopia. Some would find their Utopia, planting the seeds of communism in the swelling belly of the capitalist state.

This communist experiment would enjoy a brief yet extraordinary success in a quiet rural backwater by the Wabash River in southwest Indiana. The small town erected here would become inextricably linked with the ambitions and ideals of Robert Owen. A thousand miles of land and three thousand miles of ocean separated the rugged Scottish valley at New Lanark, where Owen made his fortune, and the pioneering community of German Lutherans, creating their tiny version of Eden on the fringe of the Great Plains. Their town was called Harmony, and it captured Owen's imagination. So much so, that he bought it.

CHAPTER 7

The Silent Monitor

> The object of human existence, as of all that has life, is to be happy.
>
> (Robert Owen, 1771–1858)

Walking along the carpeted corridors of the smart new hotel conversion in the center of New Lanark, a small community nestled on one side of the upper Clyde Valley in the Scottish Lowlands, it is difficult to believe that it once housed banks of textile machines. Only the smell of oil-soaked cloth that permeates the very fabric of the building reminds you of the industry that thrived within its walls, where women and children once stood barefoot, minding their spinning mules.

But this was no ordinary mill community. New Lanark was different, so much so that poets and potentates flocked to its gates. The Wordsworths came here. So did the poet Robert Southey, and so did the Grand Duke Nicholas, soon to be Tzar of Russia. There were other mills with state-of-the-art machinery, and the workers' dour sandstone tenement houses were hardly out of the ordinary. They had no sanitation and no running water. Water was drawn from wells, and chamber pots were slopped out in communal middens. The conditions, nevertheless, were far better than those in the slum-ridden cities. But the visitors had come for something else. News had spread of what would be hailed as a pioneering experiment in social engineering. The real exhibits were the workers themselves.

The villagers worked long days but in the evenings they had the opportunity to study in the mill-based school. Child labor had been phased out for all under the age of ten, and children were schooled from the moment they were able to walk. New Lanark was the embryo of a social model that would influence educationists and organizational thinkers the world over, the blueprint for a succession of communities inspired by its example.

Some four thousand miles away in Harmony, Indiana, the social ideas would be developed further but never on the scale envisaged by their originator, the Welsh-born entrepreneur and social idealist, Robert Owen.

Long since claimed by the international labor movement as one of its founding fathers, Owen has been neglected by business theorists, dismissed as a runt in the capitalist litter. In the roll call of great industrialists – Arkwright, Brunel, Carnegie, Du Pont, Ford, Sloan – there seems little room for Robert Owen, and yet his rise to prominence was as impressive as that of any of these illustrious entrepreneurs. The difference that marks him apart is that he broke all the rules. For years he had pursued the accumulation of wealth while revolutionizing management practices and proving that it was possible to run a textile business without wringing out every ounce of sweat from the workforce. Then he sold up and turned his back on the UK to concentrate his efforts on the small community of Harmony he had purchased in the southwest corner of Indiana, renamed New Harmony.

This second, more fundamental experiment in the United States exposed the limitations of intellectuals – today we would probably call them knowledge workers – left to work alone, as if in a vacuum. It highlighted the imbalance that occurs when knowledge is not harnessed to purposeful, practical production. There are two views of Owen's New Harmony experiment. One points to the community's many firsts – it had the first kindergarten in the USA, the first elementary school, the first free public library, and the first civic dramatic society. The second view, assessing its success as a utopian society, must conclude that it flopped – a grandiose idea on paper that simply did not work, because the brainpower of its intellectuals could not transcend the achievement of the honest graft and piety that had established this hitherto thriving rural community.

The architect's plans for a Harvard-style campus with a large quadrangle of Gothic proportions were never realized.[1] Frankly there was no one capable of building it. The irony is that before it was renamed and remodeled, Harmony had harbored a successful, hardworking community. When Owen bought the town for about £75,000 ($119,000)[2] he acquired a twenty-thousand-acre estate, later extended to thirty thousand acres, that had been a thriving settlement of dissenting Lutherans – industrious souls, driven from their native Germany by religious persecution.

Harmony was the second town established by the followers of George Rapp, a self-styled prophet who had pursued a separatist strain of Lutheranism in his native Württemberg. Rapp was preparing his followers for the Second Coming of Christ and wanted, therefore, to model their behavior on early Christian practices. The idea, shared by other religious separatist groups such as the Shakers and the Moravians, was to live in the purified state outlined in the Acts of the Apostles: "And all that believed were together, and had all things common" (Acts 2:44). He was particularly influenced by Johann Valentin Andreae's *Christianopolis*, a seventeenth-century novel that envisaged a Christian republic based on communal living.[3] Put simply, the Rappists were Christian communists.

The freedom of worship promised by the United States' Declaration of Independence offered an escape from the civil censure of Württemburg. Rapp's first community in Pennsylvania, established in 1804, was a stopgap. He wanted something better, something that could deliver the ideal conditions for farming and viticulture. Not until he discovered the land abutting the Wabash River on the fringe of the as-yet-unexplored Great Plains, ten years later, did he believe he had found the perfect place to create a balanced and self-sufficient economy. By that time the community was fully incorporated, its members pooling their finances and property in accordance with its Articles of Association. In return for their labor, cooperation, and an adherence to the rules, the Harmonists would benefit from educational provision, food, clothing, and other goods they would need to maintain a simple lifestyle.

Harmony could draw on a useful mixture of practical skills and trades. The town had smiths, masons, carpenters, coopers, brewers, and farmers, supplemented by specialists in textiles, dyeing, printing, and engineering. In fact there were people skilled in maintaining every facet of healthy village life. They worked cooperatively, building each other log cabins at the new site and later replacing these timber houses with brick-built dwellings made to a defined standard and size and situated within a gridiron-style town plan. Harmony was a planned community, and as an economic unit it was a resounding success. The Harmonists had orchards under glass to grow exotic fruits and they had a steam engine that operated a cotton mill and threshing machine.

The workers were roused by the blowing of French horns. They would go outside to fetch their milk from a cart touring the street. Pinned on the cart were work assignments for the day. Some work was routine. Where work demands varied, some would be assigned to help others in a particular task. People would sing as they worked, and the town band would sometimes play to accompany their labors. Freshly cut flowers would be arranged in vases placed on workbenches to brighten up workshops. This was communism flourishing in the heartland of nineteenth-century America. Within a few short years the Harmonists had established a standard of living that was superior to that of almost any community in the country. It was known as "that wonder of the West."[4] When the Indiana State Legislature ran into financial difficulty it was bailed out by a loan from Harmony. The Harmonists exported many of their goods, finding markets overseas.

But there were internal strains within George Rapp's community. In 1807 its members had committed themselves to lives of celibacy. When children reached the age of fourteen, their parents were encouraged to allow them to live separately in communal dormitories. Some of the people rejected this idea, and Rapp continued to perform marriages, acknowledging that celibacy might be considered a step too far, but there were social pressures to conform. Behind this conformity, bonding the society, underlying its unity, was a religious communion anchored by a deep-seated faith that Christ would be coming any day.

Christ did not come, and Rapp, partly, perhaps, responding to some growing communal disillusionment and partly in recognition of the better prospects for trade to the north, decided to move his community once again, this time to the village of Economy, just north of Pittsburgh. The town of New Harmony was advertised in the European press, and Robert Owen bought it. Most of the Rappists had packed their bags and left by the time Owen arrived in 1824 with a retinue of intellectuals and educators on the keel boat *Philanthropist*, popularly described as "the boatload of knowledge." Most of them were teachers, influenced by Johann Pestalozzi, the Swiss educator and advocate of "learning by doing." Pestalozzi's book, *Leonard and Gertrude*, pursued the idea that education should be shaped for each individual child. It rejected the widespread practice of rote learning to reinforce the memorization of facts. Life in the keelboat offered Owen's band of academics plenty of scope for learning by doing. At one stage the boat had been icebound in the Ohio River, just seven miles from the new community of Economy. The practical Rappists came over to pull it free.

Few would have disputed that Owen had brought with him some of the sharpest intellects of the age, but in practical terms they were useless. So were many of the other newcomers, who often came either as speculative settlers or as freeloaders, dazzled by the idea of joining the Owenite experiment. Few of them knew how to brew beer or how to weave or turn a plough. This so-called Preliminary Society consumed more than it produced. Few crops were harvested and housing was in short supply and badly maintained. Owen had sold half the town to his partner in the venture, the Scottish-born geologist, William McClure, but the two men soon disagreed about the way the community should be organized.

After investing most of his fortune on the New Harmony experiment, Owen began to sell parcels of land to other groups who formed splinter communities. Beset by financial squabbling and starved of practical labor, the community might have died on its feet, yet its social and intellectual life actually flourished. Three schools, headed by Pestalozzian teachers, were educating some four hundred children. Lectures, balls, and concerts continued unabated, but within three years Owen had left, disaffected with his partners, proclaiming the experiment a failure.

New Harmony continued, however; not, perhaps, in the way that Owen had envisioned but in a way that suited its inhabitants. Today the town has a modest tourist industry based on the two consecutive utopian experiments. Owen himself returned to the UK, chastened but undeflected in his beliefs. If New Harmony was thousands of miles from New Lanark, the intellectual ideals of its inhabitants were light years away from those of the Scottish mill workers.

The Scots were not idealists but economic migrants. Some had arrived in New Lanark destitute, turned out of their smallholdings in the Highland clearances. In many ways their plight was not so different from that of the immigrant Rappists. Their story at New Lanark began not with Owen but with his father-in-law, David Dale, who established the New Lanark Mills in 1785 as a joint venture with Richard Arkwright, whose Cromford Mill had already demonstrated the potential for concentrating production in purpose-built factories. Dale was keen to exploit the new technology in Scotland and believed the fast-flowing water beneath the Falls of Clyde would provide the perfect power source.

The partnership did not last long beyond the end of a patent dispute that led to Arkwright losing the sole rights to his invention. Some of the New Lanark workers were trained on the Arkwright machines in Cromford before they were joined by the new workforce, which included hundreds of young children procured from the Glasgow poorhouses. The transaction securing their employment consisted of a promise of work, housing, clothing, and education for the children in return for their labor. Such promises were widely abused by mill employers but not by Dale, who was concerned for the welfare of his employees. So the New Lanark that Robert Owen took over on January 1, 1800 could already boast employment conditions somewhat better than those in the emerging northern English textile belts of Lancashire and Yorkshire.

Some impression of just how bad conditions were for most factory children at the time can be obtained from a visit to Kirkburton parish churchyard near Huddersfield in West Yorkshire. A spartan column contains the names of twelve children between the ages of five and sixteen who perished together in a nearby mill fire. The mill owner had locked them in – a common practice used to ensure the workers would stay at their looms. The fire started when a candle was knocked over. The newspaper report of the tragedy mentioned the damage to the mill owner's business before it mentioned the deaths. Factory and plant was expensive. Life was cheap.[5]

Robert Owen was well acquainted with such callous and single-minded pursuit of wealth in the new industries. He himself had been apprenticed as a ten-year-old to a Lincolnshire-based dressmaker. Within ten years he had risen from shop assistant to mill manager, after working for a time manufacturing textile machinery. The machine was the spinning mule invented by Samuel Crompton. The mule combined the best features of Arkwright's water-frame and Hargreaves's spinning jenny. The machinery-making business lasted no more than a few months, but it gave Owen some vital exposure to the most advanced industrial technology of the age. This, more than any other experience, would have increased Owen's stock in the eyes of older industrialists. Here was a young man, not yet twenty, who had a complete familiarity with the new technology that was transforming textile production. The choice was stark for industrialists – they either mastered the technology or they went under.

In spite of his demands for a salary of £100 a year when he applied for the manager's job at Drinkwater's Bank Top Mill in Manchester, Owen soon demonstrated his worth. Not only did he prove himself capable of handling five hundred workers, he sought out the best quality cotton for spinning. He also began to exchange ideas with some of the most formidable brains in the North of England as a member of the Manchester Literary and Philosophical Society. Hopes of a partnership in Drinkwaters did not materialize, so he left to form another business, the Chorlton Twist Company, with a group of established businessmen.

On a business trip to Glasgow, Owen met Caroline Dale, David Dale's daughter, who took him to see the cotton mills at New Lanark. "It is a truth universally acknowledged, that a single man in possession of a good fortune must be in want of a wife," wrote Jane Austen in the opening passage of *Pride and Prejudice*. Another universal truth, she might have noted, is that one of the fastest ways to a fortune for any single man is to marry the boss's daughter. In Owen's case the marriage was accompanied by a £3,000 dowry.

Owen married Caroline in September, 1799. Within four months he and his partners had bought New Lanark mills from David Dale, and he was moving into the village.[6] Owen had already pursued concerns for the welfare and health of workers at Bank Top – he was a committee member of the Manchester Board of Health. Now he would begin to put his ideas into practice on a much larger scale. First, however, he moved to improve efficiency, sacking the existing management and installing a new manager brought in from Bank Top. The new regime imposed strict controls on costs and quality, clamped down on bad timekeeping, and dismissed workers who had reputations for drunkenness, persistent absenteeism, or dishonesty.

Frederick Taylor, the man whose ideas would structure the workplace in a way inconceivable to Britain's early textile barons, would have smiled sublimely at Owen's recordkeeping, which measured input, in terms of hours worked and wages paid, against output. Owen also introduced a little gizmo, his "Silent Monitor." This consisted of a four-sided rectangular block of wood suspended near every worker. Each side was painted a different color – white, yellow, blue, and black. Whichever color was turned to the front represented an assessment of the conduct of the individual on the previous day. White denoted "super excellence" in conduct, yellow equated to "moderate goodness," blue represented "a neutral state of morals," and black stood for "excessive naughtiness." The previous day's conduct, highlighted on the monitor, was also noted in a "book of character." The most marked difference between this signposting and the much later time-and-motion practices of scientific management is that the Silent Monitor was never intended to measure performance or output. It appeared instead to be a record of temperament or behavior, an early psychological bellwether. If you kept your nose clean, the least you could expect was a blue. You also had a right of appeal against a supervisor's assessment.

The Silent Monitor's concern for behavior recalls the overriding Roman concern for loyalty and obedience. Behavior, or what schools would call "conduct," has been emphasized persistently in any workplace where control has been a prominent feature of management. Modern parallels with the Silent Monitor can also be drawn with the way some call-center operatives are monitored in telephone conversations with customers. The more sophisticated forms of call-center monitoring involve "listening in" by supervisors who will make behavioral observations, checking for tone, delivery, friendliness, and helpfulness as much as they are measuring the time of the call and efficiency.

The Silent Monitor was a powerful psychological tool. Few people would enjoy seeing their behavior recorded in something that might be interpreted by the religiously inclined as a book of atonement. Owen himself professed no religious beliefs. In fact he was a strong critic of the many competing sects, denouncing religions as "the great repulsive powers of society ... ever-burning firebrands wherever they exist."[7] Such views would ultimately alienate him from the governing Establishment in Westminster.

At various stages during his management of the mills Owen cut the working day from twelve to ten hours, and from the very beginning of his term at New Lanark he started to phase out the "pauper apprentices." A school had already been established by David Dale before Owen arrived. Dale's intention was to ensure that the children received an adequate education while at the same time laboring in the factory. Owen's ideas were far broader. In his plan education would replace any commitment to undertake physical labor. His theory was that education was the key that could release society from poverty and crime. To this end in 1809 he unveiled plans for a school on what had earlier been envisaged as a vacant mill plot. Another plot he sought to use was for the construction of his "Institute for the Formation of Character." The social experiment was about to begin in earnest – but not without opposition.

Owen's partners were horrified that he was proposing to build schools on plots that could otherwise enable production capacity to be enlarged by 50 percent. There were four mills on the site and enough plots for six. But the limited building space within the confines of the steep-sided valley would not allow room for both schools *and* extra mills. New Lanark was a profitable enterprise, but the partners argued there was scope to make it far more profitable. They removed Owen from the mill management and decided they would seek to buy him out. None had accounted for his single-mindedness. Owen was that rare individual, a cunning businessman with social ideals. Armed with a pamphlet setting out his ideas of building a business that would pursue concerns for the social, moral, and educational welfare of its workforce, he succeeded in attracting new backers, most of them Quakers, who agreed to take no more than a 5 percent return on their investment. Profits hitherto had been in the region of 15 percent – the sort of shareholder value that would be demanded by managements of large public companies in the latter days of the twentieth century.

Owen and his Quaker partners outbid his former backers when the mills were placed on the open market, and he returned to New Lanark in 1814. His speech on the opening of the institute two years later reveals the extent to which his thinking was taking shape. Like many people at the time he was intrigued by Millenarian concepts – the idea of achieving a lengthy period of good government ensuring happiness and prosperity for all. "What ideas individuals may attach to the term 'Millennium' I know not," he wrote, "but I know that society may be formed so as to exist without poverty, with health greatly improved, with little, if any, misery, and with intelligence and happiness increased a hundred fold: and no obstacle whatsoever intervenes at this moment except ignorance to prevent such a state of society from becoming universal."[8]

These were heady words backed up by employment policies and an attitude to education that were as revolutionary as the factories themselves. Owen's declaration that children would attend school rather than work was not initially welcomed by his workforce, who viewed the family as an economic unit. Children in school could not be wage earners. But those were the terms. The school became a shop window for Owen's ideas. Children, dressed in white gowns, laundered communally every three days, would drill in the work yard and dance and sing in the institute, often in front of invited audiences. Such was its fame that any young gentleman embarking on a grand tour of Europe would make sure New Lanark was somewhere on his itinerary.

Owen's progressive education eschewed the use of books. He wanted learning to be enjoyable, one reason why he advocated dancing at the beginning of classes. Cynics might conclude that without book learning, New Lanark's mill children would be deprived of the breadth of education that might give rise to subversion. Owenite society preserved the status quo to a great extent.

The management writer, Lyndall Urwick, described Owen as "the pioneer of personnel management."[9] Urwick's observation was based partly on Owen's conviction that paying attention to employees was as vital as making sure that the plant and equipment were in perfect working order. "Many of you have long experienced in your manufacturing operations the advantages of substantial, well-contrived, and well-executed machinery," wrote

Owen in an essay directed at factory managers. "If then, due care as to the state of your inanimate machines can produce such beneficial results, what may not be expected if you devote equal attention to your vital machines, which are far more wonderfully constructed?"[10] Columella, the Roman expert on agricultural work practices, would have applauded his logic. This business argument for the humane treatment of employees would seem as pertinent in the third millennium as it was in Owen's time and in the era of Imperial Rome nearly two thousand years earlier.

Had Owen continued his involvement with New Lanark as a committed industrialist, driven by the pursuit of wealth, it is arguable that his ideas might have gained far greater currency with other factory owners – but the pursuit of wealth came to be of secondary importance to the pursuit of a better way of living for the whole of society.

Robert Owen and George Rapp were like the captains of distinctive ships sailing in different directions. As their paths crossed in New Harmony each scrutinized the other with a keen attention to detail, then each collapsed his telescope and continued on an unaltered course. Neither of their societies was perfect, yet each has lessons for the workplaces of today. The Harmonists showed that communal working among skilled people, concentrating efforts efficiently where they were most needed, could reap strong economic benefits. This small-scale communism, however, could only succeed when the organizational ground rules were clear and fair, and where there existed a powerful, uniting belief system.

Rapp's own belief system had a limited time span, finitely governed by the practice of celibacy. When the Harmonists died their society died with them. Their hard-earned wealth – millions of dollars – was squandered by a speculator who engineered the liquidation of their funds.[11] Owen never achieved his own idea of Utopia. He was never prepared to accommodate the ideas of others. But his experiment showed that a concentration of intellects could spark social innovation and transfer learning across a constituency. Its unity, however, could not be retained without a strong and bonding value system common to all those involved.

Owen was not the first to experiment with utopian societies, and he would not be the last, but he was the first among the new breed of entrepreneurial industrialists to create a rationale for socially concerned capitalism. He was the first social entrepreneur. He was also an autocrat. It was not all sweetness and light in his rural mill village. But the residents of New Lanark were willing guinea pigs. In the early days of the mills, labor had been in short supply. When a shipload of migrants bound for North America from the Isle of Skye were forced into Greenock by storms, David Dale had offered them alternative employment in his mill. Dale was dismayed that this rich source of labor for the emerging industries was being lost to the New World.

But the Highlanders found it difficult to settle in the cramped living conditions of New Lanark. Many continued to speak Gaelic and some left, unable to conform to the rigid regimes of factory work, overburdened perhaps by "excessive naughtiness." Owen was concerned for the happiness of his workers, but some social historians have interpreted this as a concern for docility,[12] just another version of *fides in obsequium*.

New Lanark and New Harmony were followed by other attempts at Owenite Utopias, none of which flourished. But Owen's seed of industrial and social integration was robust enough to influence other industrialists. Titus Salt, the worsted manufacturer, was well established as a wool magnate by the time he conceived the construction of the model industrial village of Saltaire, near Bradford in the North of England, in 1850.

House construction close to the factory had become essential to ensure a reliable pool of labor. Efficient factory operations required new work disciplines and a more rigid adherence to timekeeping. The demands of the new industries also created peculiar jobs. The "knocker upper," whose job it was to rap the bedroom windows of shift workers with a long pole in order to get people out of bed, was unknown in the agrarian economy.

Like his fellow paternalist, John Grubb Richardson, who built the village of Bessbrook in Northern Ireland to support his flax mill, Salt's religiously governed brand of paternalism – he was a member of the nonconformist Congregational church – became evident in the village layout. Neither Salt nor Richardson made any room for a public house or pawnshop.

These planned model villages were a marked contrast to the crowding of mills and housing in the growing cities, where mill workers lived in unsanitary conditions exacerbated by disease and factory pollution. If the housing was poor in the cities, the mills were often architectural masterpieces, reflecting the pretensions of their owners, who viewed themselves as the nineteenth-century inheritors of the traditions of the great class of merchants in Renaissance Italy.

Florentine and Venetian architectural features were copied throughout the textile belt. In Leeds, a few miles to the east of Bradford, mill owners commissioned chimneys replicating Italianate towers. A scaled-down replica of Giotto's campanile at the Duomo in Florence was built as a dust extraction unit at Colonel Thomas Harding's Tower Works, which used to make steel pins for wool-combing engines. A second chimney alongside is modeled on another tower in northern Italy. One of Salt's chimneys was based on the campanile of the church of Santa Maria Gloriosa in Venice.

The grandeur did not stop at Italy. A hundred yards from Harding's Tower Works is Marshall's Temple Mills, a masterpiece in classical revivalist architecture, which would look more in place on the banks of the Nile at Luxor than in the back streets of an English industrial city. Huge blocks of millstone grit were used to construct this factory, covering two acres, in the style of ancient Egypt. While Ignatius Bonomi, the architect, took great pains to model it on the Temple of Horus at Edfu, he had to insulate the roof to ensure the correct humidity inside for flax spinning. A layer of plaster was covered in pitch. Earth was shoveled on top to prevent the pitch cracking, and grass was seeded to bind the earth together. The final eccentric but practical ingredient employed to keep the rooftop grass in check was a small flock of sheep.[13]

If wealth is a measure of greatness, the industrialists of the northern English textile towns were worthy inheritors of the Florentine mercantile tradition. For many, however, their excessive wealth was only matched by their callousness. Benjamin Gott, a Leeds mill owner who built his mill upwind of the city in 1824, driving out the wealthier residents with the smoke from his chimneys, amassed works by Titian, Rubens, Caravaggio, Poussin, Canaletto, and Brueghel at his manor house. The gaudy juxtaposition of the squalid mill and artistic beauty is typical of the blinkered priorities of Gott and his fellow textile entrepreneurs. Gott's Bean Ing Mills heralded a grimy industrial epoch for the textile belt of northern England, where generations of millworkers' children would grow up in the belief that all stone was black.[14]

By the mid-nineteenth century the UK was indisputably the world's richest nation by head of population. At the time of the Great Exhibition of 1851 in London, only a handful of the exhibitors were US companies. But the industrial tilt had already begun. By 1870 the UK had been overtaken by the United States in its overall gross domestic product. America was growing rich on cotton. Eli Whitney's cotton gin, invented in 1793, had, in the words of Professor W. Wilson, "enabled even the unskillful slave to cleanse a thousand pounds of cotton of its seeds in a single day, instead of five or six pounds formerly." In one bound the American South had become the cotton field of the world.

The extent to which cotton production had enabled the United States to leap forward economically can be gauged in these statistics. In 1792, the year before Whitney's invention, US cotton exports totaled 138,328 pounds. By 1804 they had risen to 38 million pounds, and by the time of the Missouri Compromise of 1820, when the state was allowed to preserve its pro-slavery majority by prohibiting black settlers, they had risen to close on 128 million pounds. By that time the North and South were evenly divided over the Mason–Dixon Line, the boundary between freedom and slavery.

The United States lost no time in exploiting the European textile technology. In an attempt to subvert Arkwright's spinning machine patents, brass models were made of his machinery. The plan was to have them shipped out through France, but the models were seized in England and the agent involved was placed under bonds to remain in England for three years. Not to be deterred, the Pennsylvania Society for the Encouragement of Arts and Domestic Manufactures offered a reward for the introduction of the new machinery in the US. The advertisement in an English journal prompted Samuel Slater, a former worker at Arkwright's Cromford Mill, familiar with the water-frame, to leave the UK and set up a cotton mill in Pawtucket, Rhode Island, in 1793.

The secret was out. Cotton production and the mechanization of cloth manufacturing, coupled with improved transport, were putting cotton goods within reach of a wider market than ever before. The Deep South, which had hitherto persisted with slavery as much out of habit as anything, now had a powerful economic incentive to preserve its pool of slave labor. It was Roman civilization repeating itself.

As the New World was embracing servitude, the Old World was leaving it behind. The French had formally abolished serfdom and its feudal system in 1789. That aside, the US was poised to absorb the progressive ideas on economics outlined in Adam Smith's *Wealth of Nations.* Here was a fledgling nation, eager to investigate the most innovative thinking of the age. For a people bred on the purity and sanctity of honest toil, the soundly argued justification of profit in the *Wealth of Nations* was nothing less than manna from heaven, a blueprint for industry and commerce and a guiding text for the fulfillment of the American dream. It was no less important to those engaged in business than the Declaration of Independence had been to American republicanism. People of the stature of Benjamin Franklin were casting off the puritan mantle to enjoy the material benefits of wealth. "Is not the hope of one day being able to purchase and enjoy luxuries a spur to labor and industry?" he wrote. All the constituents for unprecedented economic growth were slotting into place; all except one. Not until the United States was truly united, with slavery consigned to history, could it assume the moral ascendancy that would help to make it the most powerful and influential nation on the globe.

Slavery was a growing issue on both sides of the Atlantic. The trade, which had grown up as private enterprise between seafaring traders and plantation owners, was coming under threat from a new intellectual class, often bolstered by private incomes from inherited wealth. Influential works such as Thomas Paine's *Rights of Man* (1791–92), Voltaire's *Candide* (1759), and Jean-Jacques Rousseau's *Social Contract* (1762) were outlining a liberal philosophy that would transform the social order.

The Puritan work ethic that had underpinned the institution of slavery was under threat from this liberal elite who, backed by new scientific and natural discoveries, would ultimately go so far as to question the most fundamental of biblical tenets surrounding the origins of humanity – Creation itself. The body of learning that would overturn this most precious of human beliefs developed in Victorian society, as one nation reached the pinnacle of its influence and another, like a precocious starlet brimming with talent and promise but as yet unsure of her audience, took its first tentative steps into the international spotlight.

CHAPTER 8

The Last Puritan in a Nation of Amateurs

Work is the grand cure of all the maladies and miseries that ever beset mankind.

(Thomas Carlyle, 1795–1881)

London's Natural History Museum is one of the city's finest examples of Victorian architecture, its neo-Gothic facade and interior elaborately decorated with colored stone inlays of flora and fauna. Conceived and commissioned by Sir Richard Owen – the man whose *Dinosauria*, published in 1842, introduced the world to a genus of bird-hipped reptiles that walked upon the earth before the Ark – the museum is a temple to the Age of Enlightenment. Through its halls walked the greatest minds of their day, men of stature, revered and honored for their knowledge alone.

Hung prominently on the walls are two of the museum's most treasured possessions, from Owen's personal collection. The fossilized ichthyosaur in one framed case and the plesiosaur in another must have caused a sensation when they first went on exhibition. Up to the mid-1990s a visitor could read of Owen's munificence on an inscription near the foot of each case. Most would probably have assumed that the great man had found them himself because there was no mention of any other finder or of the circumstances in which they were uncovered. This is because the finder was a woman with no extensive formal education who earned her living by trading in fossils. Her name was Mary Anning, described by the American biologist Stephen Jay Gould in his book, *Finders Keepers*, as "probably the most unsung (or inadequately sung) collecting force in the history of paleontology."[1] Outside paleontological circles Anning is not well known, and yet as children we have probably all recited her exploits in the popular tongue twister, "She sells sea shells on the sea shore," without knowing the origin of the words.[2]

Today her name is included in the exhibition reference, and her portrait hangs on the wall. Why did it take the best part of 150 years for the museum authorities to recognize Anning's work? We need look no further than this one example to demonstrate the persistence and range of prejudices in a society that has been content to stifle so much latent talent. How much human potential has lain unexploited and ignored by a privileged elite whose flagrant self-interest has been served by the preservation of long-standing rights and traditions? Even today in Britain's House of Lords we can find living proof of the power of birthright over individual merit. Not until 1999 was the hereditary privilege of Britain's peerage to influence the legislature finally abolished, and then not fully, since a rump of the most popular of the hereditary peers among their fellow sitting members was allowed to remain for a transitionary period.

Mary Anning would never have sought out such pomp. She was a true misfit, a square peg unfitted for the self-serving round holes of academia, created for the purpose of promoting and protecting academic interests among academics. Anning was a self-taught professional living and working in rural Dorset yet moving confidently among the grandest of amateurs in the so-called Age of Enlightenment. She was a modern woman so far out of her time that it is impossible to align her with other prominent women of the age. Although she lived in Lyme Regis at the same time as Jane Austen, there is no record of their being acquainted. For all the power of her writing, Austen was made for her time, a subtle commentator on the lives and vanities of her contemporaries in genteel society.

Anning was a country woman, lacking elegance or refinement, working either alone, chipping away with her hammer at rocks on the beach, or supervising workmen in the extraction of some of her most spectacular finds. She made, said Gould, "an astounding series of discoveries, including squidlike creatures with associated inkbags, a plesiosaur in 1824, and a pterosaur (flying reptile) in 1828. She directly found or pointed the way to nearly every specimen of importance."[3]

Owen was not the only naturalist to beat a path to her door. Almost every aspiring expert in this fledgling field of academia appeared to have cause at some stage to wander down to Lyme Regis to view the "curiosities" in Anning's shop: William Buckland, the Oxford geologist who had the distinction of providing the first dinosaur name – megalosaurus; Gideon Mantell, the GP whose find of iguanodon teeth (his wife was given them by workmen) led to the second dinosaur name; Sir Roderick Murchison, a military man and self-styled "Silurian King"; Henry De la Beche; and William Conybeare – all were recognized paleontologists among academic circles. In fact they *formed* these very same circles, each adding to the others' repute. But rarely did they give a nod of recognition in the direction of Mary Anning. One who did, De la Beche, delivered a eulogy after her death in his presidential address to the Geological Society in 1848, to "one who had to earn her daily bread by her labor, yet contributed by her talents and untiring researches in no small degree to our knowledge of the great Enalio-Saurians and other forms of organic life entombed in the vicinity of Lyme Regis."[4]

Beyond her sex, beyond her rustic antecedents, the most significant difference between Anning and her peers was her professional or academic status, or lack of it. She was a trader. Unlike the rest of them, she had to work for a living – "she sells sea shells," went the rhyme. The academic and professional classes did not relate their work so directly to payment. They did not tend to do the type of work that required them, at the end of it, to extend their hands for payment. This was far too grubby a notion. One Victorian commentator, T. H. S. Escott, thought that receiving money directly from clients was a sufficient distinction to place the professions of the solicitor and the doctor on a lower plane than those of barristers and the clergy, who faced no requirement to undertake such "vulgar" commercial transactions.[5]

An important by-product of industrial and commercial prosperity was the increasing comfort enjoyed not only by the wealth earners but also by those who aligned their own careers or lifestyles to the spending power of those who could afford their services. These were prosperous days for clergymen whose congregations were swelled by prominent landowners and businessmen, doctors whose curative powers were limitless in the service of the well heeled, or lawyers who provided the necessary legal adornments, advice, and safeguards to those who needed to protect their patents and transact business in a cut-throat environment.

The professional classes were coming of age. Their alliance with the industrialists was a marriage of convenience. Each possessed something the other craved. The professional had status and, almost inevitably, the benefit of a classical education. The industrialist had wads of money. Devoid of any common social circles, they created new ones, such as the Royal Society for the Encouragement of Arts, Manufactures and Commerce (RSA), founded in 1754, and Birmingham's Lunar Society, founded in 1764.

On one level these societies were attempting to fill a gulf in understanding of the sciences and social changes arising out of industrialization. The universities were so wedded to the classics and the merits of a classical education that the dons of Oxford and Cambridge might as well have been living in the clouds on Mount Olympus. As a way of illustrating the extent of this intellectual insularity, Thomas Henry Huxley, the champion of Darwinism, told a British parliamentary select committee of a question he posed at a dinner party of Oxford academics. "Would it be fair," he asked his fellow diners, "to say that anyone might have taken the highest honors at university and yet might never have heard that the Earth went round the Sun?" As one they replied, "Yes!"[6]

On another level, the societies were meeting places where like-minded individuals could keep abreast of each other's work. This was certainly true of the short-lived Lunar Society, where practical men like Matthew Boulton and James Watt could consider business applications for some of the most important new discoveries. The RSA, on the other hand, had a more eclectic approach, seeking solutions to problems as diverse as the synthetic production of alkali and the standardization of weights and measures. Both of these societies, however, were more practical in their approach than the Royal Society, which always had patronage at its base. No matter how ignorant the member of the aristocracy, his title and patronage alone would be sufficient to earn society membership.

Connections carried far greater weight than vocational qualifications among those seeking preferment, recognition, and prestige among the Establishment of eighteenth-century England.

As Kenneth Clark wrote in *Civilization*: "Eighteenth-century England was the paradise of the amateur; by which I mean, of men rich enough and grand enough to do whatever they liked, who nevertheless did things that require a good deal of expertise."[7] Among these gifted amateurs were Sir Christopher Wren, the architect, Sir Joseph Banks, the botanist, and Sir William Herschel, the astronomer, all prominent members of the Royal Society.

Fluttering butterfly-like between each of these organizations – the lofty Royal Society and the more down to earth RSA and Lunar Society – (at least in his correspondence) was the Boston-born Benjamin Franklin, one of the first great internationalists, as comfortable in his London home as he was in his adopted city of Philadelphia. It is to Franklin we owe what might be considered the first of that peculiarly American genre of management books that promise to reveal some secret path to prosperity, when the real secret is in writing and selling the book. *The Way to Wealth* featured a series of extracts from his *Poor Richard's Almanac*, an annual calendar-diary with tidbits of advice, jokes, and colloquial wisdom, appealing to the potential of the self-made man. "Remember that time is money," was one of its aphorisms. Its twin-pronged approach, stressing frugality and industry, was tailor-made for a people who had been weaned on the Protestant work ethic. It sold a quarter of a million copies in Franklin's lifetime, the second most popular book in the New England colonies after the Bible, and it made him rich enough to devote most of his time to the acquisition and transference of knowledge from the Old World to the New.

His familiarization with contemporary science in Britain and Continental Europe, culminating in his own celebrated experiments with electricity, took him into the most exalted scientific circles. He was awarded degrees from Harvard, Yale, William and Mary, Oxford, and St Andrews; he was made a Fellow of the Royal Society; and he was a member of some twenty-eight other learned societies. He established a bookshop importing scientific and academic pamphlets from England. "Let me have everything, good or bad, that makes a noise and has a run," he told his London contacts.[8] This conduit for the transference of ideas cemented relations and contacts at an intellectual, scientific, and industrial level that would defeat the best attempts of the British government to prevent the leakage of manufacturing know-how.

The Boston Tea Party in 1773, when colonists dressed as Indians hurled tea chests from British ships into Boston harbor in a dispute over the importation of tea, may have caused outrage in England at a political level. It may even have caused outrage in the streets. But the subsequent American War of Independence did not put an end to British and American collaboration. The dissenting tradition in Britain was alive and well in the eighteenth century, and the promise of a new life away from the restrictive laws, proscriptive Church, and claustrophobic confines of the British Isles would not allow an as-yet muted patriotism to prove too great an obstacle to emigration. What patriotic British fervor there might have been was traditionally reserved for the French, and it was a long time since the English archers had defiantly raised their two bow-string fingers to the massed ranks of French knights at Agincourt.[9]

The alternative to emigration for those who had elevated themselves above the bread line was entry into one of the professions, increasingly developing themselves into a class apart from those who would work by hand and muscle. Britain's Royal College of Surgeons was established in 1800. In the next fifty years, barristers, solicitors, civil engineers, architects, pharmacists, and actuaries would all form professional bodies in England as their ranks swelled.[10]

The professional class conveniently bridged the gap between the older landowning aristocracy and the self-made capitalists. These social divisions were far less prominent in the New World, to the great relief of those who settled there in search of a better life. The New England elite were doing their best to establish such divisions, but they would never emulate the increasingly stifling class system of the old country. They would never, for example, turn their backs on innovation and industry. Not so in England. By the nineteenth century some English commentators were beginning to voice reservations about their newly industrialized society. Anthony Trollope and Charles Dickens both harbored doubts about the way in which industry and commerce was heading. "Buying and selling is good and necessary," wrote Trollope in *Doctor Thorne*, published in 1858. "It is very necessary, and may, possibly, be very good; but it cannot be the noblest work of man; and let us hope that it may not in our time be esteemed the noblest work of an Englishman."[11]

John Stuart Mill crystallized these doubts when he pointed the finger at Thomas Carlyle's gospel of work that had been outlined in a collection of essays published under the title *Past and Present* in 1843. Carlyle had eulogized work as something venerable. "All true work is sacred; in all true work, were it but true hard-labor, there is something of the divineness," he wrote. Mill thought Carlyle was writing nonsense and said so: "Work, I imagine, is not a good in itself. There is nothing laudable in work for work's sake. To work voluntarily for a worthy object is laudable; but what constitutes a worthy object?" "Carlyle," wrote Mill, "revolves in an eternal circle round the idea of work, as if turning up the earth, or driving a shuttle or a quill, were ends in themselves, and the ends of human existence."[12]

Mill had identified correctly the focus of the Protestant universe. It was not God or the Bible or wealth or power, it was the ill-defined and by this time significantly secular ethic of work itself. Work was at the very core of human existence, something from which all men and women could derive some meaning. In the space of 150 years its influence would so dominate the everyday lives of most people on the planet that to defy its expectations and demands would be to invite the severest censure and opprobrium.

It would be too simple to suggest that Carlyle was a defender of the downtrodden, although early in his career some may have thought so. Reading his later pamphlets, it is difficult to conclude that he was ever their champion at all. But Carlyle's sanctification of manual labor had appealed to the thinkers among the disenfranchised mass of working men and women who felt alienated from the ruling class. He was as condemnatory of the idle rich as he was of the idle poor. Carlyle's concerns cut through the class lines. His was a world of polarities – good and evil, strong and weak, silence and chatter, honest endeavor and idleness. His views were so bound up with the work ethic and how it came to be perceived by the Victorians that they demand attention even today.

Born in Ecclefechan, Scotland, of staunchly Calvinist parents – his mother urged him to read a chapter of the Bible every day – Carlyle was probably the last of the Puritans and the first among

Victorians. There were no intermediaries between Carlyle and his God. His faith was absolute and did not require translation or interpretation. His uncompromising views, delivered in a cutting, discomforting, often brutal writing style, were laced with language of sparkling originality. Morose in his persona, provocatively insensitive in his invective, Carlyle could offend just about everyone, a Victorian Lenny Bruce who ultimately went too far with his audience.

Ralph Waldo Emerson, who had introduced Carlyle's work to an enthusiastic American readership, felt betrayed when Carlyle in one of his later pamphlets referred to America as a country that had "begotten, with a rapidity beyond recorded example, eighteen millions of the greatest bores ever seen in the world before."[13] This was just Carlyle being Carlyle. As Mark Twain observed: "At bottom he was probably fond of them, but he was always able to conceal it."[14] (Carlyle was consistent in his criticism. He dismissed the British population of twenty-seven million as "mostly fools.") He had not meant his disdain toward Americans to be taken too seriously, but it was. No wonder Emerson decided it was high time his fellow Americans should learn to go their own way and "extract the tape-worm of Europe from America's body."[15]

Earlier in his career it had seemed as if Carlyle was on the side of the masses, ridiculing, as he did, the "thousand crown, coroneted, shovel hatted quack-heads"[16] who had supported King Charles I against Parliament and Oliver Cromwell, one of Carlyle's greatest heroes. Carlyle had condemned the massacre of Peterloo and had railed against the workhouses and the growing inequality between rich and poor. Whereas Mill poured scorn on the notion of work for work's sake, Carlyle complained of industry for industry's sake. He saw nothing salutary about the headlong rush into production. "The world has been rushing on with such fiery ambition to get work and ever more work done, it has had no time to think of dividing the wages; and has merely left them to be scrambled for by the law of the stronger, law of supply and demand, law of laissez-faire, and other idle laws and un-laws – saying in its own haste to get work done, that is well enough."[17]

To the "Captains of Industry" (a term, like so many now in common usage, coined by Carlyle) he put an awkward question made for the new science of economics: "What is the case of your spun shirts? They hang there by the million, unsalable; and here, by the million are diligent bare backs that can not get hold of them."[18] It was Carlyle who first pointed to the "cash nexus" that had come to define transactional relationships in society. "We have profoundly forgotten everywhere that cash-payment is not the sole relation of human beings; we think nothing doubting, that it absolves and liquidates all engagements of man," he wrote.[19] But money, as Carlyle understood, had its limitations: "Love of men cannot be bought by cash-payment."

How could any of these defective transactional arrangements, he wondered, compare with the "blessed glow of labor"?[20] Work, with its "perennial nobleness; and even sacredness," argued Carlyle, could provide humanity's salvation. "Were he never so benighted, forgetful of his high calling, there is always hope in a man that actually and earnestly works: in Idleness alone is there perpetual despair."[21] There was more: "Labor is life. From the innermost heart of the worker rises his God-given force, the sacred celestial life essence breathed into him by Almighty God."[22] It was as if his Calvinism had been hammered into a single oaken pillar – the work ethic – which formed the support for the Carlylean universe. It set the moral tone of Victorian society and industry and underpinned the Victorian concern for self-help, the idea that men and women were bodily equipped with the key to their salvation – their labor.

Not everything that Carlyle said angered Mill. In fact the two men were friends for twenty years. Their relationship survived the most testing of incidents between literary figures. Carlyle had embarked on writing an account of the French Revolution, and Mill had loaned him both books and moral support. Five months' hard graft brought Carlyle to the end of the first volume. With a sense of unmitigated relief and elation at its completion he asked his friend to look over the manuscript.

Mill read the manuscript by his fireside. After reading a while, he put it down close to the fireplace and, for want of anything better, his housemaid had picked it up and used it to light the fire. All that remained were the scraps of four or five pages. Mill was mortified. So was Carlyle. "I remember and still can remember less of it than anything I ever wrote with such toil: it is gone, the whole world and myself backed by it could not bring that back: nay the old spirit too is fled. I find that it took five months of steadfast occasionally excessive and always sickly and painful toil. It is gone; and will not return."[23]

Had anyone been insensitive or mischievous enough at that moment to console Carlyle with the prospect of five more months of spiritual bliss, basking in the blessed glow of labor, he would probably have earned a punch on the nose. The great thoughts of the philosopher could soon dissolve in the cold face of reality, when suddenly work could be conceived as "sickly and painful." It was tough for Carlyle, embarrassing for Mill, but the newspapers loved the story. Mill sent Carlyle a cartload more books. Carlyle set to and wrote the book again. He even asked Mill if he wanted to read the new draft but Mill declined, waited until it was published, and gave the work a good review. It was the least he could do. He also sent Carlyle £200 in compensation, but Carlyle would only take half and later regretted keeping it after the two of them had fallen out.

That their views should diverge so markedly – Mill was a committed liberal, Carlyle was not – seems surprising in that both men had been appalled at the suffering of the working classes in the new industrialism.

In criticizing Carlyle's gospel of work, Mill was equating work with industry and the impact of free enterprise. Carlyle, on the other hand, was putting work on a pedestal, elevated above the machinations of industry, which he held in just as much contempt as his erstwhile friend. Mill was more the pragmatist and arguably the more humanitarian. In his own way Mill, too, was challenging the ideas of economic growth that Adam Smith had so successfully planted in industrial society. The end of economic growth, thought Mill, would be an improvement on a society scarred by Victorian working conditions.

He believed that "the ideal of life held out by those who think that the normal state of human beings is that of struggling to get on" was nothing more than "the disagreeable symptoms of one of the phases of industrial progress."[24] He looked forward beyond this stage of Protestant-driven industrialism to a New Age where concerns for quality, not quantity, would be paramount, "when minds cease to be engrossed by the art of getting on."[25] Had Mill arrived at the turn of the twentieth century he might well have wondered whether this New Age was almost upon us, but he may have been saddened, even angered, at the continuing overbearing presence of the Protestant work ethic, still planted at the center of the human universe, not dimmed but glowing ever brighter like an overheating star.

Mill envisaged a world where pleasure alone, not the intrinsic joy in work, would motivate human endeavor. From one angle the prospects looked promising during Voltaire's Age of Reason, which had witnessed a transformation in the arts, architecture, and innovation. But the world looked very different to the infant chimney sweep, weaver, and mineworker, and to those who still suffered the ugliest form of human exploitation in the slave trade, which had never prospered so much as it did in the eighteenth century, feeding the growing wealth and prominence of ports like Liverpool, Bristol, Lisbon, Nantes, Cadiz, Havana, and Rio de Janeiro.

Liverpool was the largest slave port in Europe, sending four thousand slaving voyages to Africa between 1700 and 1807. Anyone visiting a Liverpool chandler's shop in the eighteenth century would have seen handcuffs, leg shackles, iron collars, and restraining chains displayed in the window.[26] Britain had prospered from the international trade in people and America had been one of its most eager customers. Not all the slaves in America were black. Many of the European immigrants were redemptioners, poor settlers who forfeited their freedom to pay for their passage. On reaching the colonies they were sold into a form of slavery where they were indentured to work for a number of years until the cost of their passage had been redeemed.[27]

But distinctions arose very quickly between the status of black and white workers. A tiny minority of the first black settlers was freed. Two of them – Anthony Johnson and his wife, Mary – worked their way out of the indentured term and acquired their own farm. In *Africans in America*, Charles Johnson and Patricia Smith write that "the first Virginian colonists thought of themselves as Christians or Englishmen, not white people. The word white was not yet used to refer to a type of person . . . Black and white servants were oppressed equally."[28] As Johnson and Smith put it: "Sometime in the mid-seventeenth century, that changed.

Darker became wrong."[29] It seems that white settlers initially used the lack of Christian belief among black Africans to deny a right to freedom. When blacks converted to Christianity, their lower status became defined by the color of their skin. In 1639, the Maryland colony spelled out that a slave's freedom could not be achieved through Christian baptism.[30] Black slavery in America had now been institutionalized.

This return to chattel slavery, the ownership and trade in people, meant that African slaves, if they survived the terrible rigors of the ocean journey, tended to be kept in better conditions than the redemptioners, since they had a higher tradable value. A redemptioner working for a set term would be pushed hard by his owner, who wanted to extract the maximum labor before the term expired.[31] The living conditions of African slaves, however, have been a contentious issue. In his book, *Slavery*, Stanley Elkins challenged a long-standing argument that antebellum slaves were "better fed, better clothed, and better lodged" than northern laborers, highlighting the degradation suffered by many African women importuned by plantation owners and their sons.[32]

But it was the oratory of escaped slaves like Frederick Douglass, speaking to Northern audiences, that most powerfully exposed the cruelty of the slave system. One former slave, Josiah Henson, recalled seeing his father soaked in blood. His father's right ear had been cut off, and his back was severely lacerated from a hundred lashes. The whipping and mutilation had been his punishment for beating an overseer who had assaulted Henson's mother. This was reality for the African slave in America.

The trade in black African slaves had settled into a steady and profitable barter trade since the first slave ship, *Treasurer*, a Dutch ship, had sailed into Jamestown in August, 1619 with twenty slaves on board. A typical trade recorded by the master of a ship called the *Fortune* in 1630 enabled the exchange of its cargo of African slaves for eighty-five barrels of rum and five barrels of tobacco. Slavery, then, was promoting the production and trade in goods that people did not need and that arguably caused people more harm than good. It was a squalid equation in a squalid trade.

By 1863, just before the American Civil War, there were 4,442,000 African slaves in America,[33] But the slave trade was almost at an end. Britain's increasingly liberal middle class, united in sentiment with the egalitarian ideals of the Northern American states, whose labor market was based on the cash nexus and therefore immune to the economic pain of abolition, had swayed the rest of Europe into passing laws banning the trade in slaves. Even after abolition in Britain, however, some English slavers still tried to continue their trade. One slave ship, the *Brillente*, made ten illegal ocean crossings, carrying five thousand slaves to Cuba. Once, when surrounded by warships, the captain ordered on deck the six hundred slaves in his cargo. They were chained to each other by the neck. An anchor was attached to the chain and cast overboard, pulling every slave with it.[34]

In the knowledge that the trade was characterized by such inhuman behavior, how could anyone justify the continuation of a system in which one human being remained the chattel of another? Carlyle could and did so in a pamphlet on the "Nigger Question." (The first version had referred to the "Negro Question," but Carlyle thought it not quite offensive enough.) In this work he laments the breakdown of order in the West Indies after the British abolished slavery throughout its empire in 1834. Using a rationale that is driven by his fixation on the work ethic, Carlyle writes of former slaves sitting around on the plantations eating pumpkins while the sugar crops are left uncut because labor cannot be hired. "So cheap are the pumpkins," he writes, that "a Blackman, by working about half an hour a day (such is the calculation), can supply himself, by aid of sun and soil, with as much pumpkin as will suffice ... Supply and demand which, science says, should be brought to bear on him, have an uphill task of it with such a man. Strong sun supplies itself gratis, rich soil in those unpeopled, or half-peopled regions almost gratis; these are his 'supply'; and half an hour a day directed upon these, will produce pumpkins which is his 'demand'."[35]

If only Carlyle had applied a little cultural understanding he may have concluded that the former slaves had rediscovered Marshall Sahlin's original affluent society. The idea, however, of man finding contentment in fulfilling a simple need was anathema to an ideal that treated idleness as a sin. A man, said Carlyle, should be "emancipated" from indolence and whipped, if necessary, into doing the work he is fit for.[36] This was the line that forced Mill's trenchant rebuttal. If this had been an isolated exchange between two men of ideas it might have been ignored, but Carlyle was drawing from a deep well of conservatism. As Asa Briggs remarked in *A Social History of England*: "Carlyle's prophecies had been most welcomed when they were in harmony with existing prejudices."[37]

Carlyle was not only perpetuating what Syed Farid Alatas would call "the myth of the lazy native," he was defining laziness as a disinterest in supporting the demands of capitalism, even though he himself, some years earlier, had pointed to the folly of misdirected production. Some of Carlyle's ideals would re-emerge in Germany, but even as he wrote there was another man in another part of London framing a different proposal that would change the world: "From each according to his abilities, to each according to his needs."

The ideas of Karl Marx had little influence initially in the country he had made his home. The impact of his thinking was stronger in Germany and among the German migrants who flocked to the United States in search of work. Some of the earliest struggles between socialist idealism and the interests of capital would be fought out among the emerging industrial regions of the Midwest. The flash points were the railroads.

CHAPTER 9

The Yellow Dog Unleashed

The worker who strikes for higher wages does not do so simply because he is greedy and wants all the material comforts he can get; instead he seeks economic justice in which his labor is compensated fairly in relation to others – in other words that it be recognized for its true worth.

(Francis Fukuyama, b. 1952)

Pittsburgh, Saturday, July 21, 1877, the night that the American Dream lay shattered among the broken glass and rubble of the city's burning goods yards, the night that the spirit of entrepreneurialism and unrestrained capitalism clashed headlong with the demands of railroad workers for a fair day's pay. People were dying, caught up in the ugliest labor disturbances that America had experienced. The disturbances were put down by federal troops ordered to turn on their countrymen for the first time, just twelve years after the country had emerged from civil war. From the start of the dispute five days earlier to its end nine days later, more than a hundred people, some of them bystanders, would be killed in street fighting centered on Baltimore, Cumberland, Pittsburgh, and Reading.

The strike had started spontaneously among crews of the Baltimore and Ohio Railroad and quickly spread to other railroad companies, who demanded military protection. Unrest had been simmering for weeks, after rail companies had begun to reduce wage rates in response to a falloff in trade. Workers in other companies had accepted pay cuts, but when the Baltimore and Ohio Railroad followed the trend its workers rebelled, prompting those from other companies to join them. The protests escalated into rioting when strikers were confronted by the often heavy-handed deployment of troops.

In 1830, when Peter Cooper's locomotive, Tom Thumb, traveled thirteen miles on the Baltimore and Ohio Railroad, it

opened a new era of American industry. Wooden rails gave way
to rails made of iron, and iron rails gave way to steel as the rail
network grew outwards like a widening web. By 1850 there were
nine thousand miles of track, by 1860, thirty-one thousand miles.
At the time of the 1877 strike the Baltimore and Ohio Company
ran freight trains on a hundred miles of track between Baltimore
and Martinsburg. Its schedule for covering this distance on a
one-way trip was six hours. So the train crews were paid for six
hours' work and no more, even though the journey invariably
took longer, because of delays along the route, and could at times
take forty hours to complete.

The company had been running crews of five men – a fireman,
engineer, conductor, and two brakemen. This was regarded by most
operators as the bare minimum. The Northern Central Railroad
added a flagman to make a crew of six. The poorest-paid crewmen
earned between $1.17 and $1.58 a day, although the extra hours
forced on crews meant that some workers were receiving less than
a dollar a day and very often were averaging no more than fourteen
days' pay a month. The company made other savings by denying
sleeping quarters to the crews on the return journeys. It also dispensed with hostlers, men who would prepare the engine for departure and clean it up after it had reached its destination. These tasks
were passed on to the fireman, adding another two hours' work
for every journey, but again with no extra pay. A group of firemen
went to the company management to protest. All were summarily
dismissed. In another cost-cutting move the company removed one
of the brakemen, paring down its crews to four.[1]

When the management decided, therefore, to cut pay rates by
ten percent, in line with other operators, the crews had reached
breaking point. As the first train arrived at Camden station in
Baltimore on July 16 its firemen stepped off and refused to continue their duties.[2] The firemen of later trains followed suit, and
groups of men began to picket their co-workers, urging them
to join the strike. The men were not unionized, not effectively
anyway. A rail union did exist but its members met in secret, fearful of losing their jobs and being blacklisted if their employers
found out. The strike at Camden junction began with a minority
of dissenters whose action was quickly supported by others and
spread like brush fire through rail companies in eleven states.[3]

The whole rail network was paralyzed within four days. The Baltimore and Ohio management demanded military intervention when a mob began to gather in Cumberland on the Friday after the strike began, and the Maryland governor, John Lee Carroll, ordered the mobilization of state troops. Alarm bells, rung only in times of extreme emergency, were sounded in Baltimore to alert and muster the troops. But the bells alerted everyone else, and crowds poured into the streets. As soldiers pushed through people to reach their assembly point and armory at the corner of Fayette Street and Fort Street the mob turned angry and began to stone the building. The troops broke out and headed for a train that would take them to Cumberland. Nine people were killed and sixteen were injured as the soldiers tried to fight their way through the crowd. Many of the troops abandoned their weapons and fled, as the rioters began to set fire to coaches on the train. Order had broken down so completely in Baltimore that the government decided that troops were more urgently needed there than at Cumberland.

President Rutherford Hayes, a former Union general, sanctioned the use of federal troops sent out from Washington to bring order to Baltimore. The day after the Baltimore clashes, confrontations between troops and strikers in Pittsburgh boiled over into open fighting when rioters armed themselves with rifles and cannon. At the height of the disturbances some 30,000 people among Pittsburgh's 120,000 population spilled out onto the streets. Some were strikers, some were onlookers, and some were sympathizers with the strike who relished an opportunity to challenge military authority. The American constitution's endorsement of the right of its citizens to bear arms would rebound, not for the last time, against the efforts of state control. Private gun stores were looted, and some two thousand rifles and pistols were distributed among the protesters. About four thousand strikers and sympathizers, arranged in military order, were marched in separate columns along Pennsylvania Avenue and Liberty Street as far as Twenty-eighth Street, where troops were protecting a railroad crossing.[4]

Bayonets were fixed and shots fired into the stone-throwing crowd before a body of the troops retreated into a railroad roundhouse nearby. The armed rioters laid siege to the roundhouse with two captured field guns that they used to create a breach in the walls. Coal wagons, their contents soaked in oil, were pushed against the walls and set alight in an attempt to burn out the troops inside. Across the road under the illuminated letters of the YMCA building, the sign said "Prepare to Meet your God."[5] In an act of restraint that probably saved the lives of most of them, the troops did not fire out at the rioting mass outside the roundhouse. The scene must have made the Luddite attack on Rawfold's mill in England look like a minor altercation in comparison, but everything about this big country demanded action on a grand scale. The troops took advantage of the mob's brief distraction elsewhere to make a break from the building, leaving fifteen men dead behind them in the burning roundhouse. More were killed when rioters pursued the soldiers down streets and alleyways to the Allegheny River. More than forty civilians and troops were killed in the lawlessness, which ended the next day when the rioters were persuaded to give up their arms.

Some 120 locomotives worth $3 million were burned, and railroad property valued at about $4 million destroyed along fifty miles of track.[6] Overzealous reaction by troops in Reading led to more deaths, sometimes of people who were not involved in the dispute. A stray bullet killed one woman as she sat at her sewing machine.[7] In the ten-day duration of the strike, before troops restored order across the rail towns, the disturbances claimed the lives of more than a hundred people, with five hundred injured. It was the most violent industrial action in American labor history. It was more like insurrection than industrial action.

Life was cheap among the laboring masses, particularly among the gangs of Chinese engaged to lay track for the Central Pacific Railroad in the final push to create a transcontinental railroad. The Chinese were unpopular among track-laying gangs made up of European immigrants, because they worked for a dollar a day, fifty cents less than a European. They would also work in the harshest of conditions. Thousands of them died. The Chinese, like black Africans, were debarred from being members of the first trade unions, which were really self-interest groups, in the main representing white Anglo-Saxon artisans.

Growing union muscle would be at the heart of the next great railway strike, seventeen years on from the Pittsburgh and

Baltimore riots. This strike would set the trend for employer–union relations for years to come. Again the action was sparked by pay cuts, this time at the Pullman Palace Car Company.

Pullman is a name that has become synonymous with traveling luxury. Travel was a serious problem for Americans eager to share in the wave of expansion after the Civil War. It took three and a half days to travel from New York to Chicago by rail, a tortuous roundabout journey of thirteen hundred miles. The first sleeping cars lacked privacy and hygiene. Pullman's idea was to improve the sleeper and introduce greater levels of luxury to make the journey more comfortable for the increasingly wealthy business people moving between the cities.

Chicago in the mid-nineteenth century was a boom town. Its population had grown from 350 at the date of its incorporation in 1833 to 334,000 by 1871, the year of the Great Fire that killed nearly three hundred people and left a trail of devastation a mile wide and nearly five miles in length, engulfing seventeen thousand buildings. Days after the fire, the gritty spirit of Chicago's people was shining through. Wooden shacks sprang up to continue business. One real-estate trader put up a sign saying "All Gone but Wife, Children and Energy."[8] In the space of three hundred working days some three thousand brick and stone buildings had been erected, and in a further year Chicago had almost completely re-emerged from the ashes. By 1890 it was the United States' second largest city, with one million people.

George Pullman had been there in those early heady days of expansion. His father had a business that moved buildings physically – the whole building – from one place to another. George Pullman carried on the work. He also secured big contracts to lift buildings in Chicago when the city council decided it needed to lay sewers and drainage pipes and pave over the roads. The job would mean raising the roads, and the adjoining houses and stores would have to be lifted too. In one of Pullman's biggest jobs, he raised Matteson House, a city-center hotel, using 800 screwjacks in a coordinated lift.[9] As the jacks raised the building the resulting cavity was packed with timber supports.

When the lifting work came to an end, Pullman looked elsewhere and made money for a time running a hardware and food store for prospectors in the gold rush of 1859. But the most successful business was palace cars.[10] He built them and he ran them, profiting from the surcharge he made on top of the ordinary fare that went to the railroad.

Pullman created more than a business. He created a town of twelve thousand people just south of Chicago, dedicated entirely to the construction of his cars. He ruled his town, named after him, like a feudal landlord, the omnipotent industrialist who laid down the regulations governing the way his society would be run. According to one employee, "We are born in a Pullman house, fed from the Pullman shops, taught in the Pullman school, catechized in the Pullman church, and when we die we shall go to Pullman Hell."[11]

It followed similar lines to – although according to Pullman it was not inspired by – the British mill communities of New Lanark and Saltaire. Like the leaders of those communities, Pullman was a committed Nonconformist. His father had been a Baptist, his mother a Presbyterian. Both parents had turned their backs on the hellfire preaching that emphasized the wrath of God and placed their faith in a Universalist belief in a loving God. They were strict and conscientious Bible readers who taught their children a moral code gleaned straight from its pages. It stressed the importance of honesty, thrift, frugality, industry, and universal salvation. It also taught charity. But St. Paul's letter to the Corinthians did not appear to leave a deep impression on young George Pullman. If charity indeed was the greatest of all virtues it began where Sir Thomas Browne, the seventeenth-century Puritan writer, said it should begin: at home.

George Pullman's morality belonged with the New England radicals whose values were aligned with those expounded by John Dod and Henry Cleaver. Dod and Cleaver's explanatory books on the Bible espoused the duty of vocation against the sin of idleness.[12] The poor, they argued, should ask themselves whether their poverty was their own fault. This was Pullman's attitude when later he was asked to be charitable toward his workers. Dod and Cleaver had argued that servants should obey their masters as if they, the masters, were the greatest princes in the world. Pullman, as one of his biographies suggested, was "The Palace Car Prince."[13] He lacked the sense of philanthropy that underlay the communities of New Lanark and Saltaire. He made money out of his townspeople at every turn. He bought the 4,300 acres of land on which building work started in 1880 for $800,000. By 1892 the land was valued at $5 million. He even profited from vegetables fertilized by the sewage from his workers' homes.[14]

In two short years he had created what William Carwardine, the Methodist minister in Pullman, would later describe as a "civilized relic of European serfdom." Pullman arranged with the nearby community of Hyde Park to take water from its reservoir. Hyde Park charged 4¢ for a thousand gallons; but Pullman charged his tenants 10¢ for a thousand gallons – or $3,000 a month for water that cost him $1,200.[15] His annual profit on water alone was $21,000. For gas he paid 33¢ per thousand cubic feet, but charged his tenants $2.25.[16] His house rents brought in $500,000 a year, an 8 percent return on his investment.[17] Cheaper rents could be obtained in other towns, but anyone who moved out was more likely to lose his job. Preferment was given to Pullman residents. The same practice applied to promotion opportunities. The Reverend Carwardine knew one worker who, after deductions for rents and other overheads, received a paycheck of just 2¢.

Pullman never claimed any element of philanthropy in his decision to create his model community. He was guided by ideas designed to prevent the breakdown of relations between labor and capital. Specifically he was influenced by a Victorian novel, *Put Yourself in His Place*, by Charles Reade, which he read over and over again. Reade wrote of the industrial squalor in Hillsborough, England, a town, he wrote, which "is pock marked with public houses and bristles with high chimneys . . . stuck all over the place like cloves in an orange."[18]

Reade wrote of the callous treatment of labor by employers so typical of Victorian English mill communities. In his stories the employees respond by organizing secret trade unions and terrorizing factories and fellow workers in bomb outrages. Pullman read the book first in 1872 on a voyage over to England. Five years later the story must have returned to haunt him during the rail strike of 1877 when thirteen people died in Chicago over four days of rioting. One of Reade's characters is a benevolent and learned doctor who urges the entrepreneurial inventor hero to put himself in the place of the worker, hence the book's title.

According to Reade, applying scientific principles to production could have a three-pronged effect – delivering higher profits to owners, safer and more pleasant conditions for the worker, and an improved product for the company's customer. Pullman was convinced by the novel that the cooperation between capital and labor was to their mutual benefit. But how was he to set the working man on a path lit, as his had been, by the Protestant virtues of industry and thrift? Pullman's idea was to take his workforce out of an environment "pock marked with public houses" and place them in a clean, ordered community where everyone dressed respectably, everyone behaved respectably, and everyone knew and accepted their place in society.

He even applied discretion in his recruitment. Job applicants were set a written examination and had to disclose personal details – whether they were divorced or in debt, whether they drank alcohol or gambled – and explain why they had left their previous job. Pullman wanted a business staffed by model workers living model lives in his model community.

Investors would have no problem with the idea if it impacted encouragingly on the bottom line, but they were suspicious of any hint of philanthropy. Pullman believed, therefore, that returning a reasonable rate of profit from the running of the community was vital in retaining the support of shareholders in the Pullman Palace Car Company. He was pioneering an ideal in corporate labor relations, and like many new ideas it did not meet with universal approval. In the hard-nosed trading pits of the New York Stock Exchange it was not unusual for a trader selling Pullman stock to shout "How much for flower beds and fountains?"[19]

Pullman defended the park-like atmosphere: "With such surroundings and such human regard for the needs of the body as well as the soul, the disturbing conditions of strikes and other troubles that periodically convulse the world of labor would not be found here," he argued. Outlining his idea, he said: "A man who can bring his mind down to understand the simplest business proposition can fathom the Pullman scheme very easily. It is simplicity itself – we are landlord and employers. That is all there is of it."[20] This indeed was the nub of Pullman's scheme. But it would turn out that the role of landlord and employer created tensions that he had never envisaged. When he introduced a piece-rate system in 1886, the workers went on strike. It was short-lived, associated, like other strikes at the time, with a claim for an eight-hour day. But it served notice on the company that there were potential flaws in Pullman's social experiment.

According to Pullman's own counsel, Judge A. O. Lochrane, "People imagine that the town of Pullman is a white elephant to the company . . . that eats up the earnings."[21] The perception was mistaken when business was good and employees were earning enough to pay the higher than average rents. But when business faltered Pullman was left in a difficult position. His rival firms could shut up shop and lay off workers until times improved. Continuity of labor was an ideal to which the see-sawing fortunes of those engaged in capitalist enterprise could not yet aspire.

But Pullman needed continuity of labor to fund the community he had established. How else would rents be paid? How else would shopkeepers maintain their businesses? His worries had become those of the social entrepreneur responsible for a far larger family than his own, while at the same time being responsible to shareholders who cared only for the returns they could obtain on their capital. When the general economic depression of 1893 caught up with the company and business began to dry up, Pullman's solution was to continue competing for what few orders there were, even if he was taking orders at a loss. To minimize the impact to the company shareholders he cut the wages of his craftsmen and laborers.

This might have succeeded without industrial action, had he cut the wages of their supervisors and his own income accordingly. Another option was to tap the company's substantial reserves. But management salaries and those of the directors were maintained and, in the event, the reserves allowed the company to defeat its striking workers. A further problem was Pullman's aloofness from his workforce. He lunched with his fellow tycoons, people like Marshall Field, the department store owner, at the millionaires' table in the dining room of the Chicago Club. The work ethic and the profit motive were closely welded together in this society, and they were underpinned by the concerns of self-interest. They did not lend themselves to personal sacrifice or disinterested charity.

Andrew Carnegie, the Scottish-born railroad pioneer and steel magnate was made in the same mold. Carnegie's thinking reflected the work ethic coated with a veneer of capitalism. His career could have been plucked from the pages of a Horatio Alger novel. Alger wrote more than a hundred books for boys, all with the same theme of hardworking poor boy makes good. With titles like *Fame and Fortune*, *Bound to Rise*, and *Up the Ladder*, their message of riches within the grasp of anyone prepared to graft was absorbed by millions of teenage American boys.[22]

While Carlyle had preached the gospel of work, Carnegie delivered his personal *Gospel of Wealth*,[23] arguing that the wealthy had a moral obligation to serve as stewards for society. This was Carnegie's way of accommodating his great wealth with the idea of social responsibility. He didn't believe in inherited wealth, and before he died in 1919 he distributed more than $350 million, the biggest part of his fortune, to good works, such as funding education, libraries, and hospitals. Everything he did, from building his business empire to distributing the spoils of his entrepreneurship, was guided by a solid commitment to the work ethic. His idea was to help the industrious, "the best and most aspiring poor," not those who were "irreclaimably destitute, shiftless, and worthless."[24] Even in his philanthropy, Carnegie was a man who expected to get his own way.

Carnegie admired Pullman, but both men knew they would put one over each other if they could and delight in doing so. It was easy for them to believe that all people behaved in this way. If Pullman had mixed with his workforce, had spent time with the families who lived in his town, he may have begun to appreciate their problems. He might have put himself in their place and found that their ideals were not so far removed from his own. But he had allowed his wealth to elevate his concerns beyond those of employees. To the rank-and-file worker it seemed as if there was one law for the rich and another law for the poor. (Pullman, like many others of his rank, including Carnegie, had fought the Civil War by proxy, hiring a substitute to fight for the Northern Union in his place.)[25]

He claimed to understand his workers when he built the town. He told the *Cincinnati Enquirer* that "no question was more important to American society than (that of the) taste, health, cheapness of living, and comfort among the artisan class." However, his system of house rents denied them the opportunity to have a house of their own. He seemed to acknowledge this when he announced plans for an owner-occupied community nearby, but they never materialized.

Over five years, from 1888 to 1893, the wages paid to Pullman's workers were in many cases cut by 30 percent.[26] By the time the workers went on strike in the face of a wage cut in 1894, many had joined the recently formed American Railway Union. The union came under pressure to escalate the action, and about six weeks into the strike it called on its 150,000 members to boycott Pullman railcars. Since Pullman cars were present in almost every passenger train in the rail network, the action threatened to spread across the industry, particularly since the rail company owners rallied initially in support of Pullman. The boycott by other rail workers did not begin as a strike, but as each employee refused to handle a Pullman car he was discharged. Financially the industrial action was always a loser. In 1893 Pullman was capitalized at $30 million, with $18 million in cash reserves. It had returned dividends of 9.5 percent to its stockholders that year.[27]

A crowd turned out to see the first passenger train to leave Chicago after the boycott had been called. The train moved out without incident, as did the second and third trains. But any hopes that the action had been abandoned were premature. Within three hours, the network was frozen. By the fourth day of the boycott some twenty-nine railroads were tied up by the ban, losing some $250,000 a day.[28] The railway companies publicly supported Pullman but behind the scenes some were angered by his intransigence. One owner accused him of losing touch with his workers.[29]

American unions were only just beginning to find their feet at this time, emerging from alliances of craft interests, producer cooperatives, and a desire for mutual insurance. The first American trade union was called, somewhat romantically, the Knights of Labor. Formed in 1869, it later amalgamated with the American Federation of Labor led by Samuel Gompers. Neither of these unions could be described as radical. The Pullman boycott was led by the American Railway Union's president, Eugene Debs, who was anxious to stop the dispute breaking down into anything resembling the unrest and rioting of 1877. The anarchist bombing in Chicago's Haymarket Square in 1886 – sparked by unrest at the McCormick Harvester Company – had sent jitters through business and government and had not been forgotten. A bomb had been thrown at police as they tried to break up an evening meeting held to support demands for an eight-hour day. In the confusion that followed, eight policemen were mortally wounded, some of them apparently shot by their own men, who fired indiscriminately into the crowd.[30] An unknown number of protesters were also killed. Four of the rally's organizers were tried and executed for conspiring to overthrow the rule of law. Three others who were jailed were later pardoned when the governor decided their convictions had been unsafe.

It was in a climate of nervousness among Chicago's business elite, therefore, that the Pullman workers went on strike. Order was maintained at the start of the dispute, but riots did break out later. Three men were killed and seven injured when strikers damaged cars on the Baltimore and Ohio railroad. Another seven people were killed in Chicago.

The strike of 1877 had been put down by the military. The 1894 action was ended by the courts. Debs was served with a restraining injunction effectively preventing him from sending out telegrams to union activists and coordinators. When he and other officers continued to do so they were held to be in contempt and jailed. Without leadership, the action broke down.

If the Pullman workers thought that they would be forgiven they were wrong. George Pullman refused to reinstate the strikers, even though families in his so-called model community were beginning to starve. John Altgeld, the governor of Illinois, who visited the community and saw how the families were suffering, urged Pullman to cancel house rents for the period of the strike. He pointed out that it had cost the state $50,000 to protect Pullman's property during the dispute.[31] Pullman was immovable. "I do not doubt there are many cases of need caused by the refusal of the employees for two-and-a-half months to earn offered wages of more than $300,000," he wrote in reply.[32] In other words, the plight of the workers and their families was their own fault. Every word was wrapped in Puritan philosophy. Work was a divine gift and those who refused it were sinners. Pullman said in his negotiations with the workers that he thought of them as

his children. It was a patronizing remark, reflecting his own misguided self-aggrandizement.

George Pullman, a man who Andrew Carnegie described as
a "typical American,"[33] has been demonized in the eyes of the
American labor movement and in the eyes of many others, but
there were understandable reasons for the stance he took. He
headed a joint stock company. Any action that was not perceived
to be in the interests of shareholders could lead to a potentially
damaging sale of shares or stocks on the stock market. On the
other hand the company was probably more recession proof
than he maintained, in that much of its income came from the
surcharge he levied on the ticket prices of other rail operators.
In spite of his aloofness, in spite of the wage cuts, the strike might
still have been averted had there remained any trust between managers and workers. In talks between a committee of workers and
Pullman, the committee had been assured that none of its members would be victimized. But the next day three of the men were
laid off. The layoffs appear to have been ordered at shop-floor level
by a foreman who had no personal knowledge of the agreement.
It looked quite different to the workers and was sufficient to spark
a strike. Even then it was not like other strikes. There was no rampant mob. The workers played baseball on the green, although
some mounted pickets in case the company should try to draft in
strike-breaking labor. One newspaper journalist wrote: "Pullman
is called a model town. It now has on its hands a model strike."[34]

The strike did not stay that way, and Pullman's ideals were
buried in the acrimonious dispute that confirmed the investment
community's distrust of such social experiments. The workers had asked for their pay to be restored to the levels of three
years earlier or for their rents to be reduced. Pullman insisted
that they could not link their house tenancy agreements with
their employment contracts. But the workers were right to do so,
and he was wrong to see the issues separately. His original concept had linked living conditions with those of employment. How
could he then insist they were divorced in negotiation?

In fact they were more seriously intertwined than he cared to
acknowledge. Without earnings, without other disposable assets,
with savings depleted, and with credit denied to them by local
storekeepers, families quickly began to go hungry. Pullman

did not try to enforce rent arrears or evict his families until the strike had ended, but by that time many had deserted their homes, leaving the community in their hundreds to find work elsewhere.

The Pullman strike was a watershed in the relationship between capital and labor in the United States. With a few notable exceptions such as the Hershey Chocolate Company, established by a Mennonite family, social entrepreneurship would be viewed with suspicion and dismissed by most investors as a nonrunner. There would be few other experiments in company-run communities. The workers would be unionized to protect their interests and would conduct their negotiations with management in a spirit of mistrust. Employees and their labor would be regarded as cost items, as units of production that could be improved and operated in the same way as a machine. Pullman himself was so hated a figure at the time of his death in 1897 that his coffin was buried encased in a thick slab of concrete, lest anyone should try to desecrate his grave. The idea of a community of interest between capital and labor, of the social enterprise, of mutuality, had been abandoned in the burnt-out wreckage of Pullman's railcars.

Confrontations between unionized mobs and employer-recruited thugs or Pinkerton guards became commonplace.[35] Industrial anarchy had terrified employers since the so-called Molly Maguires, a secret society of Irish immigrant mine workers, had used terrorist tactics against mine owners in the Pennsylvania coalfields from the 1850s to the early 1870s. The widow Molly Maguire had earned a reputation in her native Ireland for armed resistance to landlords and bailiffs. She is said to have carried pistols strapped to her thighs beneath her petticoat.[36] Her followers, all Irish born Roman Catholics, were blamed for a series of assassinations of mine bosses in the American coalfields. The attacks ended when ten of the "Mollies" were tried and executed in 1875. The fear of organized armed resistance among workers meant that the criminal law of conspiracy was often used against striking laborers. Later, employers resorted to civil injunctions, arguing that strikes were a restraint of trade. Finally, as employers consolidated their power after the turn of the century, they began to insist that newly recruited workers sign so-called "yellow-dog" contracts that forbade union membership.[37]

A few employers made genuine efforts to understand the needs of manual workers. Whiting Williams, a vice president and director of personnel for the Hydraulic Pressed Steel Company of Cleveland, donned overalls and joined the ranks of working men for a while to experience their life at first hand. For seven months he worked in a variety of jobs – in steel mills, coal mines, a ship-yard, an oil refinery, and a railroad roundhouse. Williams noticed how a man's job impacted on his social standing. He did not find much evidence that pay made a big difference to the way people worked. "Beyond a certain point," he decided, "the increase of wages is quite likely to lessen as to increase effort."[38] Williams believed that money, like work, carried social value. The workers drew their strength from a feeling of togetherness, from the "wish to enjoy the feeling of our worth as persons among other persons," he wrote.[39]

But for every Whiting Williams who took the trouble to investigate shop-floor working conditions there were thousands who did not. When improvements were made they could often be costed in lives. Nowhere was this more apparent than in the cramped working conditions of the garment factories in turn-of-the-nineteenth-century New York. The ten-story Asch building on the corner of Greene Street and Washington Place in lower Manhattan was typical of those that made this area and the adjoining SoHo district the industrial center of the city. Dozens of clothing businesses were interspersed among the Greene Street blocks. Cramped into these layers of industry were hundreds of women working at long rows of sewing machines. Some five hundred women worked in the top three floors of the Asch building at the Triangle Shirtwaist Company, run by Isaac Harris and Max Blanck. The air in the machine rooms was dense with tiny particles of cotton. Offcuts were strewn across the floor. One spark was enough to send a flash fire through this highly combustible atmosphere. When it happened on March 25, 1911, the fire spread so swiftly through the eighth and ninth floors that many women were engulfed in flames where they stood. Some ran to the door on the ninth floor, but it had been locked to stop girls stealing cloth, just as the door had been locked nearly two hundred years earlier in the Huddersfield mill fire. The issues were the same – greed, neglect, ignorance. There were elevator cars, but they were too small to handle the crush and broke down. Young women, their dresses on fire, hurled themselves from windows in the panic. The horror of this fire, which killed 146 people, led to large-scale reforms in American labor and safety laws.

Reform rarely came from the top, but wealth was accumulated on such a scale amid this frenzy of nineteenth-century American expansion that some employers did find themselves wrestling with their consciences. Andrew Carnegie, the steel baron, defended the right of employees to organize in unions, drawing, perhaps, on memories of his father, a struggling Chartist weaver before the family emigrated from Scotland. But when it came to workers striking at his Homestead plant in 1892, his managers sent a barge full of armed Pinkerton guards to break through the picket lines. Seven civilians and three of the guards were killed. The tragedy was that the Pinkerton men belonged to the same working class as those they fought. Each man in his way was trying to earn a living. This was recognized by employers, but some betrayed no hint of conscience in their understanding of its implications. "I can hire one half of the working class to kill the other," said Jay Gould, president of Western Union, the telegraph and railroad company.[40]

Men were prepared to fight for the right to be rewarded for their skills. Their skills were precious, built up over many years, sometimes passed down from father to son. Employers might take away their jobs, but they couldn't take their skills. Surely not. The employers, however, had other ideas. Suppose they found a way to dispense with skills altogether? Suppose they could create a standardized worker? Maybe what was needed was the application of science.

CHAPTER 10

The Philadelphia Catechism

The only safeguard of order and discipline in the modern world is a standardized worker with interchangeable parts. That would solve the entire problem of management.

(Jean Giraudoux, 1882–1944)

Henry Dana, Jr. was a raw Harvard law graduate in 1834 when he walked up the gangplank of the *Pilgrim*, a brigantine sailing out of Boston on the hazardous voyage around Cape Horn that would bring him five months later to California. Dana had joined the ship as an ordinary seaman in an attempt to recover his health and eyesight. Reading the law had become impossible after an attack of measles, and the doctor's somewhat drastic advice had been to spend some time at sea as a curative.

Dana's experience, recounted in his book, *Two Years before the Mast*, is a classic account of on-the-job learning. Here was a young man, his education hitherto relying on the lecture theater and the textbook, suddenly finding himself in the harshest of environments with no opportunity to walk away. There was a new language to learn because a boat has its own terminology. There were the unusual working patterns of watches to maintain a twenty-four-hour work regime, and there was seasickness, a physical threshold that must be overcome if an individual is to be an effective sailor.

He soon discovered that the on-board work was unremitting. He quotes what he calls the "Philadelphia Catechism":

Six days shalt thou labor and do all thou art able;
And on the seventh, holystone the decks, and scrape the cable.[1]

Although Dana complains of the constant repetitiveness of the shipboard jobs, his sense of pride in his seamanship, as he finds his sea legs and gradually masters the on-board tasks and routines, is palpable, particularly when he compares the confident labors of his fellow seamen and himself, furling sails in heavy seas, with the anxiety of the passengers. "I will own," he wrote, "there was a pleasant feeling of superiority in being able to walk the deck, and eat, and go aloft, and compare one's self with two poor, miserable, pale creatures, staggering and shuffling about decks or holding on and looking up with giddy heads, to see us climbing the mastheads, or sitting quietly at work on the ends of the lofty yards."[2]

The curative worked for Dana. After two years he returned to Harvard and pursued his chosen career as a practicing lawyer. Forty years later another young man who was forced by failing eyesight to turn his back on a Harvard education might have sympathized with the ship passengers, as he found himself the butt of a skilled worker's scorn. The eighteen-year-old Frederick Winslow Taylor was a living embodiment of the Philadelphia Catechism – hardworking, eager to learn, and fascinated by detail. As an apprentice to a steam pump maker in Philadelphia he was asked by a foreman on joining the company if he knew "the rule." The rule was the foot rule used on the shop floor. It was a rule with no numbers, only lines engraved on its surface. The skilled workman could relate a measurement instantly to one of the lines, just as a good fisherman will tell you a hook size at a glance. Taylor did not know the rule. As Robert Kanigel points out in his biography of Taylor, *The One Best Way*, if he did not know the rule, "so far as any self-respecting mechanic was concerned, he knew nothing."[3]

Taylor was a man born for his time and for his country. The United States had quickly learned the secrets of textile manufacture and all the other technologies emerging in Europe's Industrial Revolution, but it was the processes developed midway through the nineteenth century that would power the country to a position of world industrial leadership that it would occupy for the whole of the next century.

No more than a handful of American companies were represented in Britain's Great Exhibition in 1851. But they made a strong impression on the British public, who in the reign of Queen Victoria were witnessing the extension of their empire across a third of the globe. That the upstart colonists across the

Atlantic could invent as well as copy the innovation of others was one of the sensations of the exhibition, drawing praise and admiration from the British press. What the press did not know was that Britain was about to hand over the baton of industrial innovation and production to its cousin on the other side of the ocean. The transfer was invisible and seamless. Britain would continue in the belief that its industrial might was unassailable, while the American dynamo fizzed into life, creating an industrial giant so concerned with its own affairs that it could afford to look benignly, almost naively, at the agitated nations of Europe, like Gulliver musing over the anxieties of the Lilliputians.

Among the Great Exhibition's American contributions there were Erastus B. Bigelow's power carpet loom, Alfred Hobbs's locks produced by Day and Newell, and the sewing machine invented by Elias Howe but produced by Isaac Singer, who had stolen Howe's patent. Howe had to fight in the courts for royalties, but it was Singer's name, not Howe's, that became synonymous with a machine that would transform domestic clothing production. There were Samuel Colt's repeating pistols and the Sharps rifle of Robbins and Lawrence, and there was Cyrus McCormick's grain reaper and Eli Whitney's cotton gin. Whitney was one of the most prominent industrial pioneers in the use of interchangeable parts, securing a contract from the American government as early as 1798 for the supply of muskets. But Whitney's earliest attempts at interchangeability were only partially successful. The process was refined and improved by Colt, whose gun factory at Hartford, Connecticut, was fitted with four hundred machines producing some twenty-four thousand pistols per year by the 1850s.[4]

The Great Exhibition was held in the Crystal Place, a huge edifice of steel and glass covering eighteen acres of London's Hyde Park. Among the exhibits was the finest wrought ironwork from the Ironbridge foundry. But the Darbys' ironwork, as wondrous as it may have been, would be obsolete as a construction product within four years, after an engineer called Henry Bessemer, working in the Yorkshire city of Sheffield, perfected a process for making hardened steel.[5]

The secrets of fine steelmaking had been known to the Japanese for hundreds of years, but the Japanese manufacturers concentrated their methods on sword production. It was a long and laborious process in which different qualities of steel were hammered together and treated in such a way that the sword maintained a hard cutting edge, combined with flexibility and durability. This artisan construction of a Samurai sword, immersed in tradition and spirituality, was far removed from the mass production of steel in a society that had launched itself headlong into industrial development.

The most important aspect of the Bessemer process is that it was cheap – like Abraham Darby's way of making cooking pots – and could handle steel in bulk. Bessemer had found that blasting air through molten pig iron could burn off most of the carbon. Controlling the air blow allowed a measurable quantity of carbon to remain in place, influencing the quality of the steel. Too much carbon and the metal was brittle, while burning off all the carbon – as Abraham Darby II had discovered – could, if the metal was reheated and beaten when hot, produce a malleable wrought iron.

Bessemer's development was just one of a series of improvements in steel manufacture within the space of a few years that made bulk steel production increasingly economical and much easier to control. The open hearth method of production devised by Friedrich and William Siemens in Britain and Pierre and Emile Martin in France, and the development of British-born Robert Mushet's manganese and tungsten steels, brought the steelmaking process under precision control.

These developments could not have been better timed for American expansion. As the Colt and the Winchester, deployed with murderous callousness, helped to obliterate the hunter-gathering way of life that had existed on the Great Plains for thousands of years, the railroads pushed westwards, their progress swiftened by the new hardwearing steel rails. Steel barons like Andrew Carnegie would accumulate personal wealth on a scale unsurpassed in the twentieth century.

Just as textiles became a transformational industry when Richard Arkwright and his contemporaries mastered the mechanics and organization of the factory system in yarn spinning, steel had become the industry to be in when Frederick Winslow Taylor moved his apprenticeship to the Midvale steel works on the industrial outskirts of Philadelphia in 1878. In doing so he was joining one of the technological pioneers of his time. The company had come into the ownership of William Sellers, whose machine tools had dominated Machinery Hall in the Philadelphia Centennial Exhibition of 1876. Sellers was the epitome of the Philadelphia Protestant, with an austere, functional approach to production. In Frederick Taylor he could not have found a better lieutenant. Taylor's father was a Quaker. His mother could trace her roots to a Puritan émigré who came over to Plymouth in 1629. Few Americans could be more imbued with the Protestant work ethic than Fred Taylor, described by one observer as a "whale of a New England conscience."[6] He neither smoked nor drank and he avoided coffee and tea, which he regarded as unnecessary stimulants.

Midvale workers were paid by piece rate. The more work they completed, the faster they earned, in theory. In practice, however, the piece rate system was abused on both sides. When the men began to earn too much, in the opinion of the employer, their rate would be cut. So, as often as not, the men worked within themselves knowing it would not profit them to work any harder. This practice was known as "soldiering," a term used by naval ratings in recognition of the exemptions from chores allowed their soldier passengers. The idea was to look as if you were busy while actually doing very little. Taylor noticed that workers were devoting time, expertise, even their intellectual abilities, toward achieving this aim.

He should not have been so surprised. Pacing yourself in the workplace has an ancestry even older than that of the Protestant work ethic and the capitalist ideal. Many industries accepted that people liked to work within themselves. Practices such as "Saint Monday" when workers did little work, if they bothered to show up at all, were commonplace. Men would work in bursts, then rest a little or have a break for drinking and conversation.[7] Work was still seen as a form of subsistence for those involved, rather than an acceleration of economic output in pursuit of ever-higher production levels and ever-higher profits for someone else. Soldiering might have been frowned upon, but it was accepted by many employers.

However, the soldiering culture was alien to Taylor's psychological make-up. He determined to end the practice when he was given some responsibility over fellow machinists in the Midvale tire-making shops, where steel tires for trains were made. These were metal casings fitted around the wheel so that when they wore out they could be replaced without any need to change the whole wheel. Taylor fired people who wouldn't work hard enough, but their replacements adopted the same easy pace. He threatened to cut pay rates, which only increased resentment, and when he speeded up machines some resorted to sabotage in order to slow them down again. Finally he imposed fines on those whose machines broke down.

Taylor's concern for an individual's output was already bordering on obsession, but this was only the start. The biggest obstacle to his attempts at management was his lack of technical knowledge, his inability to contradict an assurance by the "old hand" that an idea would not work. The only way to overcome this obstacle was to understand the metalworking process more intricately than those he was trying to manage. Taylor decided that the solution was to concentrate on the tool. Machinery doesn't answer back. Sellers agreed to Taylor's request to carry out a series of experiments on cutting tools. The experiments were undertaken with scientific rigor, adopting controls and avoiding the kind of assumptions and bias that can occur when searching for evidence to reinforce a particular theory.

He not only found the most efficient way of cutting metal but was able to support this with measurements and the essential calibrations that could be passed on to unskilled machinists. This broke the cabal. No longer could a skilled engineer pride himself on knowledge and ability that had been honed over a lifetime. Machining had been standardized. Unlike the machines that had wiped out the skills of the English shearers, Taylor's discoveries had no physical embodiment that could be smashed with a large hammer. His ideas were beginning to concentrate on method, on process – a way of working that could surpass all others.

If Taylor was aware of the psychological damage he was inflicting among the artisan workforce of Midvale it is not apparent in his lectures or papers. But his lifestyle did not include much capacity for reflection on such matters. He worked hard and studied hard six days a week, and on the seventh day he played hard. His daily regime was to rise at 5 a.m., work at Midvale from

7 a.m. to 5 p.m., walk home, have dinner, study until 11 p.m., then go for a run before sleeping for about five hours. This was a man in a hurry, not someone who could easily accommodate the idea of sedentary relaxation. His busy routine still allowed him sufficient time for playing tennis to a level that enabled him and his more talented doubles partner, Clarence Clark, to win the inaugural national championship of the newly formed United States Lawn Tennis Association in 1881.

During his earliest days as a foreman in 1880 he began making observations on the timing of jobs in his "Book Containing Notes of Importance."[8] This was an important feature for anyone in his position when fixing piece rates for jobs. The idea of recording worktimes in a far more detailed way grew during the next year, as he began to transfer the principles of measuring a machine's capabilities to measuring human capability. He used the same measurements – foot-pounds per minute, adopted by James Watt when measuring the horsepower of his steam engines. Taylor's first measurements on two workers asked to work at their full capacity on a variety of tasks for double pay produced inconsistent findings. Some jobs were performed far more efficiently than others.

The experiments were abandoned for a time, but in 1883 Taylor decided to take an even more detailed approach, timing specific elements of a task. This idea of breaking down work into its component parts is at the core of scientific management. Taylor understood that the component times could be added together to fix piece rates for many different jobs. But Henry Ford, the car maker, and his team of engineers realized that these "component jobs" could be jobs in themselves, and thus the turning of a screw on a moving assembly line could be an individual's sole job. It was this combination of a simplification of tasks, through work study, with moving assembly that created a manufacturing revolution while at the same time laying waste human potential on a massive scale.

Taylor was not the first to consider scientific method in the study of work. Baron Charles Dupin, the founder of several French mechanics' institutes – educational schools for workers that began to spring up in the United States, Britain, and France during the 1820s – had highlighted the need for work study in 1829. "We have been very much occupied in perfecting the machines and the tools which the worker uses in the economic arts. We have hardly attempted to improve the worker himself," he wrote.[9] In the machinery of production, said Dupin, the worker was in the first rank, "since he has the immeasurable advantage of being an instrument who observes and corrects himself, a self-stopping motor which functions with the motivation of its own intelligence and which perfects itself by thinking not less than by work itself."[10] Dupin was introducing two concepts, both of which had profound consequences for manufacturing businesses and the people who worked in them. The first of these concepts was the worker as an automaton, the worker as a human machine; the second was the application of scientific study to the functions of work.

It is not known whether Taylor was familiar with Dupin's observations, but the ideas could possibly have filtered through to him from Philadelphia's Franklin Institute, where William Sellers, the head of Midvale, had served as president, or he may have been drawn to the methods independently. There is a remarkable similarity in thinking between Taylor and Dupin. Improving the worker was central to Taylor's philosophy, and the idea that the worker could run almost like clockwork was apparent in Taylor's approach.

In fact clockwork was an essential component of Taylor's research. His principal technique of taking precision timings had only become technically possible in the nineteenth century. Although pocket watches have been dated back to the early sixteenth century, it was not until the eighteenth century that manufacturers began to experiment with making stopwatches.[11] The earliest stopwatches used a lever that stopped the second hand. They could not count elapsed time of any greater duration than a minute and did not have a reset device to bring the hand back to zero. It was not until 1842 that the Swiss watchmaker, Adolphe Nicole, patented a reset system. The more widely used three-press button system was patented in 1862.[12] So when Fred Taylor began to make stopwatch timings of work at Midvale in 1881, he was taking advantage of the latest technology.

When he passed on his ideas to others he had to explain the workings of the stopwatch and how to use it, such was its novelty. In advising one of his collaborators, Sanford Thompson, on the choice of a stopwatch in 1895, he describes the watch in detail, although he himself was still quite vague about its workings.[13]

The timing of work was so distrusted that Thompson devised a way of concealing watches in a book so that they would not be noticed by people engaged in their work. The book concealment is displayed in a diagram in *Shop Management*, the 1903 work in which Taylor first outlined his methods.[14]

Midvale workers complained that Taylor's ideas put their nerves on edge, making many of them irritable. Taylorism had increased stress in the workplace way before anyone came to use this term. Taylor told the workmen squarely that they were not being employed to use their brains. "I have you for your strength and mechanical ability, and we have other men paid for thinking," he told Charles Shartle, one of the engineers.[15] Shartle never accepted this argument and in time found personal success as an inventor and manufacturer.

Shartle would never fit the mold of Taylor's perfect workman. Only when Taylor's ideas were attracting the interest of other manufacturers did he find his ideal workman in Henry Noll. Noll was seen as the model laborer. He may have been the most important laborer who ever lived, thanks to the Spanish–American War that in the winter of 1899 led to rising prices for pig iron. Bethlehem Steel Works, Noll's employer, had a glut of the stuff. Some eighty thousand tons of it were stockpiled in a yard at the company's sprawling site in South Bethlehem, about fifty miles north of Philadelphia. The time was ripe to sell.

A ten-thousand-ton batch was quickly sold, and Frederick Taylor assumed the job of working out the best way of shifting it. Each "pig" or iron bar, just less than a yard in length, weighed ninety-two pounds. Loading the pigs onto railroad freight cars was backbreaking work. But Bethlehem had engaged Taylor as a consultant to achieve for the company the kind of efficiencies he had created at Midvale. Taylor assigned two managers, James Gillespie and Hartley Wolle, to help fix a piece rate for the job, based on an estimation of the time necessary to do the work. The seventy-five laborers in the pig-iron gang were working as well as handlers in any company. Each man was daily loading about twelve and a half tons of pig iron onto freight cars. Taylor believed they were capable of loading much more than that.

Stopwatch timings were carried out on a group of twelve workmen, handpicked from the pig-iron gang. Sometimes the men were asked to work steadily, and sometimes they were urged to work flat out for short periods. Flat out, one group loaded a car – sixteen and a half tons of iron – in fourteen minutes. This worked out to seventy-one tons per man per day, but it did not allow for rest periods.[16] There was little science in the arbitrary way that Gillespie and Wolle decided the men were capable of loading seventy-five tons a day, if pushed. The managers then installed a 40 percent allowance for resting, so that a daily level of forty-five tons per man was deemed achievable. It was guess-work, but Taylor made no objection.

This was the figure Taylor used to set the piece rate of 3.75¢ per ton. Anyone achieving the forty-five-ton target would earn $1.69, 50 percent more than most Bethlehem laborers received for a day's work. But there was a big drawback. Under the new system the average work rates achieved before the study would earn less than 50¢ a day. The men were onto a loser and they knew it. To achieve the target they would need to lift a ninety-two-pound iron bar and carry it up a plank into the car every thirty seconds – eleven hundred times a day.[17] It was a ridiculous expectation. When ten of them were picked to work under the new rate they refused, so Taylor fired them.

A number of concessions were made. Even so, the few loaders engaged to do the work rarely maintained the punishing rate for more than a day. Invariably they would fail to show up for work after more than a day or two. There was one exception – Henry Noll from the Pennsylvania Dutch community. For day after day he met the target, thus, in Taylor's eyes, vindicating the chosen rate. Noll was not feted, simply cited, in Taylor's speeches, and even then not by his real name, but as the fictional worker "Schmidt."

Schmidt was the archetypal laborer, a unit of production that could be measured, regulated, systemized, and incentivized. He was the only worker to see the loading job through and averaged between $1.35 and $1.70 a day, not quite the figure proposed by Taylor but not far off. Schmidt was never represented by Taylor as anything more than a laborer and then only as a "mentally slug-gish type." Henry Noll, on the other hand, was just a man, doing his best, sometimes excelling himself, while building his house in his spare time on a small plot close to the mill, and at other times falling into drink.[18] But it was Schmidt, not Noll, who excited the new Taylorist breed of management.

Scientific management had changed the manufacturing workplace for good. The trade-off for accepting such mechanized working conditions was the better pay rates that could be offered from the savings in production costs. Taylor suggested that a worker needed to be offered a rise of a least 30 percent to accept this controlled form of working, in which the individual suppressed his normal working rhythms, adopting instead the rigid practices laid down by a manager under the principles of scientific management.

But just how revolutionary was this scientific management? The military would not have found it so far removed from the types of drill that had been in existence since Roman times, when rigid discipline and close-order maneuvering so often gave armies a decisive advantage. The best-drilled crews in a man-of-war of the Napoleonic era were timed and worked until they carried out their actions like automatons. Equally the movements of loading and firing a musket were well understood and had been practiced to perfection by infantrymen since the sixteenth century.

Neither was the breakdown of work into specific tasks on a kind of assembly line particularly new. A division of labor in this way was noted by Dante and Marco Polo when they witnessed the construction and fitting out of warships in Venice in 1260. Each galley was towed down a canal between rows of windowed buildings. Workers stood at the windows handing out equipment and supplies as the vessel moved past.

Pero Tafur, who described the process in his book, *Travels and Adventures*, said: "I know not how to describe what I saw there, whether in the manner of its construction or in the management of the work people."[19] Not until the giant US program for the production of Liberty ships in the Second World War, when production lines ran a mile to the slipways, was there anything to match this process in sophistication. It is a pity that Tafur could not have created a handy label like "flow line" or "assembly line production." Had he done so, the penny might have dropped sooner among other manufacturers.

If the penny hadn't dropped, the pin had certainly done so for Adam Smith, who demonstrated that he was familiar with the division of labor in manufacturing when, in *The Wealth of Nations* in 1746, he described the way that pins were produced in Nottingham using about eighteen different operations. Smith understood the implications for mass production in the process. One workman, he wrote, would struggle to make one pin a day, but a group of ten workmen, dividing the task into separate and distinct jobs, could make among them more than forty-eight thousand pins in a day.

Pins were not the only products to involve a division of labor in their manufacture. Hatters would stand around an octagonal bench, each engaged on one of the different jobs – wetting, rolling, pressing, ruffing, and blacking – that went into working the steamed felt in hat making.[20] Button manufacture, which saw an upsurge in demand during the eighteenth century with the demise in fashion of the buckle, was another example. According to Lord Shelburne, describing the Birmingham toy trades in 1766: "There a button passes through fifty hands, and each hand passes perhaps a thousand in a day."[21]

The manufacture of buttons and pins seemed to lend itself to these arrangements. There was a mass demand for such objects, so any business that could churn them out in large quantities was going to have a competitive advantage. It was also important to make and sell such utilitarian products cheaply, so the economy of scale was vital to the success of the industry. Time and again with innovation, cheapness has been a vital constituent of the enterprise. Inventors sometimes wail at the way their ideas are exploited by others, while failing to understand that their idea is only a step in the process. It might not even be described as the first step, because the first step is the recognition of a need. The Victorians were masters at producing inventions that nobody wanted because, too often, they failed to understand this first step. John Harrison's superb nautical clocks would never have been made without the British Parliament stressing the importance of finding longitude and reinforcing this desire publicly with the offer of a lucrative reward.

Smith recognized the importance of a "need" to the success of any enterprise. A sixteenth-century proverb held that necessity was the mother of invention. But Smith went farther, suggesting that it was possible to create a need, to create demand where none had existed previously. This was a significant feature in the success of Henry Ford's approach to manufacturing. He made his cars efficiently, he made them cheaply, and he made a product that had become affordable to large numbers of people because the efficiencies he achieved allowed him to pay his production workers far better than any others.

The wage packet of Ford workers alone would not have been sufficient to support volume car production. But the knock-on effect of these higher pay rates throughout other industries raised the overall wealth of the growing mass of people working in the factory system. The so-called "working classes" had been supplied with the most important ingredient of consumerism – money to spare, or what economists prefer to call "disposable income," as if it was created to fritter away. (Some would argue that this is exactly what should happen to it in order to fuel the market economy.) The consumer society had been born. Singer was supplying it with sewing machines and Ford was supplying it with his ubiquitous Model T.

CHAPTER 11

Modern Times

> The working men have been exploited all the way up and down the line by employers, landlords, everybody.
>
> (Henry Ford, 1863–1947)

In 1909 a fully equipped Model T Ford tourer cost $950. In 1914 it cost $490, and in 1916 it cost $360. The earliest of these cars were produced by teams of assembly workers putting them together in one spot. In that first year the company made 13,840 cars. In 1914, when the car had begun to move along an assembly line, Ford made 230,788, and in 1916 it made 585,388. In seven years the motorcar had come of age. So had the conveyor-belt system of production that would be lampooned so effectively by Charlie Chaplin in the opening sequences of his 1936 film *Modern Times*.

The first Model Ts, made by stationary assembly, were put together at the company's Piquette Avenue Plant in Detroit. Output increased and costs began to fall when Ford expanded into a new plant at Highland Park, but production was still labor-intensive, until Ford's engineers began to experiment with a conveyor-belt system. The idea was to keep the workers in place and let the machinery do the moving. William Klann, one of Ford's engineers, had seen something similar in the Chicago meat-packing business, where whole carcasses hung from a moving line were progressively butchered as they were moved along. "If they can kill pigs and cows that way, we can build cars that way," said Klann.[1]

A moving assembly line was installed in the magneto department of Highland Park in the spring of 1913. A man would draw a component out of a bin, add it to the magneto, then slide the magneto along a waist-high shelf to a man at his side who added a different component. Where previously workmen had been familiar with the whole twenty-nine-component assembly, now each man's personal involvement was limited to one or two stages of the assembly. Workers could learn these simple tasks quickly and could rapidly become highly adept at carrying them out. The job had become less skilled and could be done in a shorter space of time.

Previously it had taken about fifteen minutes to put together a magneto. The new method reduced the assembly time by almost two minutes. Average production time fell farther when a motor-driven conveyor belt began to move the magnetos past the workers at a set pace. With refinements to the division of labor the average assembly time was brought down to five minutes, a third of the original time. The implications for staffing levels were obvious. Soon conveyor belts were moving throughout these sub-assembly departments. The natural next step was to introduce the system to the whole chassis.

The first moving chassis was winched slowly across the floor by rope, a team of six assemblers keeping pace with it and picking their parts from bins placed along its route. The chassis assembly time fell from twelve and a half man-hours before the installation of the winch to five hours and fifty minutes, and the time fell even more when workers were asked to stay in one position as the chassis approached them at waist height. Taylor's idea of breaking a task down and timing each element of the task was pursued to extremes by Ford engineers.[2] The fastening of a nut and bolt might be undertaken by three different workers – one to put in the bolt, one to put on the nut and one to tighten the nut on the bolt. In this way the average time needed to make a chassis fell to ninety-three minutes.

In 1911–1912 some 78,440 Model Ts were made by 6,867 workers. In 1912–13 a workforce that had doubled produced double the number of cars. But the ratio of new cars to workers would fall dramatically the following year, when the moving assembly line was introduced. Production doubled again, but the size of the workforce did not increase. In fact it fell from 14,336 employees to 12,880. This was the year that a new car could be bought for under $500 for the first time.

For the worker the change was incalculable. At work he was rooted to the spot, but outside work he and his family could move around at forty miles per hour in their new Model T. They could live outside town if they felt like it, free from the necessity to live in rows of worker housing close by the factory. But such freedom was illusory. The employee came to work at a set time, he worked to a set pace that could be increased at the employer's will, and if he thought at all while working, it was of other things, far beyond the workplace.

Some have sought to differentiate Fordism from Taylorism.[3] David Hounshell, a historian of mass production, says that Taylorism was trying to improve the efficiency of workers, whereas Fordism was trying to eliminate labor, where it could, by using machines. "Workers fed and tended the Ford machines. For Taylor the workers were the machines," he wrote.[4] Either way these systems, working in unison, amounted to a ghastly sublimation of the human spirit. That people could take pride in such an "achievement" only confirms the way moral priorities were distorted by competitive industrialism. No wonder that these systems created distaste among intellectuals.

Henry Ford did not see things this way. He was the emancipator, the visionary who had seen the car as a product for the masses, not just for the rich. Other carmakers were positioning their models upmarket. Ransom E. Olds, who had sold five thousand of his popular "Merry Oldsmobiles" in 1903, had been forced by his backers to steer away from the mass market and pitch his models at the same wealthy people who bought Henry Leland's Cadillacs. Ford, however, was convinced that the mass market could be breached if production costs could be reduced sufficiently to make an affordable car. His $600 Model N of 1906 had shown that it was possible to make a strong and powerful car delivering better value than other makes.

The car helped push Ford profits above $1 million in 1907, creating finance for the experimentation and development that would make the Model T not only a car that was inexpensive to buy, but one that was packed with innovative features. The four cylinder engine had the upright cylinder configuration pioneered in the Model A. But in the Model T, this robust little engine had been refined with a cylinder housing that could be split in two, creating a removable cylinder head, allowing easy access to the internal moving parts.

Ford was always the engineer, never happier than when he was in the workshop, tinkering alongside able assistants like the engineer, Harold Willis, who helped him develop the vertical cylinder engine. He left the sales and cash flow side of the business in those early days to James Couzens, a former coal yard clerk whose bookkeeper's discipline was essential in keeping the business on an even keel. It may well have been Ford's engineering obsession that blinded him to the dehumanizing aspect of assembly line work.

Ford saw himself as a worker-entrepreneur who had founded his business on his own abilities. There is some truth in this, but his first job, like that of Taylor, was secured through family connections, a biographical detail that Ford later tried to hide.[5] Neither Taylor nor Ford possessed sufficient personal humility for mutual recognition. Taylor had given a four-hour speech in Detroit to the management of the Packard company in 1909 heralding a fashion for work study in factories across the city, but Henry Ford was loath to give Taylor any credit for the moving assembly line. In fact he disclaimed "any dependence on scientific management," according to one of his engineers.[6] But Ford would say that. He was an egoist, like Taylor. Besides, there was always the risk that admitting to have borrowed an idea might land a business with a royalties suit. It would be absurd to believe that Ford engineers did not exploit the ideas of scientific management. The application of stopwatch timings to assembly work was in widespread use at the time.[7] One of the Ford engineers later confirmed that time-and-motion study was employed in establishing the assembly lines at Highland Park.[8] Everybody was doing it.

Taylor seemed equally unwilling to give much credit to Ford, referring on one occasion to his "cheaply and roughly made cars."[9] And yet, in spite of their apparent indifference toward each other, the two men were so alike. Ford did not share the Puritan/Quaker background of Taylor, and Taylor did not share Ford's notorious anti-Semitism; but Ford was from strong southern-Irish Protestant stock, and his family shared the same values and the moralistic education that molded Taylor. As a youngster, Ford, like most American children of his era, had been reared at school on "McGuffey Readers." The books of William Holmes McGuffey were a "reminder that this was a nation founded by Puritans," according to Robert Lacey in his book, *Ford: The Men and the Machine*, a history of the company. "Filled with dramatic illustrations and simple moral tales in which bad boys came to bad ends and good boys ended up president, they were used by schools in practically all thirty-seven states in the 1870s," he writes.[10]

Whether you were Henry Ford or a wrench-wielder at the end of the line, if you were a second- or third-generation American citizen in the 1900s, the chances were that you were familiar with McGuffeyland. How well these ideals corresponded to the work disciplines expected under the unsanctified marriage of Taylor and Ford is difficult to judge, but workmen came and went in their droves during that first year of assembly line production at Highland Park. Its labor turnover ran at 380 percent in 1913, exceeding 900 percent toward the year-end, forcing the company to recruit four thousand people a year for each thousand jobs. Many of them were the work-hungry immigrants from Europe flooding through New York's Ellis Island.

Ford quickly swallowed Taylor's dictum that "men will not do an extraordinary day's work for an ordinary day's pay,"[11] and on January 5, 1914 he made the unprecedented gesture of promising to return $10 million of profits to his workforce by raising wages to $5 for an eight-hour day, replacing two daily nine-hour shifts with a three-shift, twenty-four-hour, nonstop rotation. This was at a time when industrial workers were averaging $11 a week. It meant that thirty-six weeks' work would buy a car, not far from the purchasing power of a modern American automobile factory worker.

The publicity generated by the five-dollar day was phenomenal. The *New York Evening Post* called it a "magnificent act of generosity," the *Wall Street Journal* condemned it as "the most foolish thing ever attempted in the industrial world," and Henry Ford described it as "one of the finest cost-cutting moves we ever made."[12]

What Ford knew, and what the *Wall Street Journal* did not, was that the company had made enough profits that year as a result of cost reductions achieved by the moving assembly line to have paid each worker $20 a day. Instead some $11.2 million was paid to shareholders in dividends. News of the raise led to fifteen-thousand-strong crowds of jobless men standing outside the factory gates day after day that January, hoping for work. Resentment led to rioting that was only broken up when Highland Park police trained fire hoses on the job seekers.

Ford would surprise the world again when in November, 1929, a month after the Wall Street Crash, he again announced a pay increase for his workforce, in another attempt to engineer consumerism on a scale broad enough to allow the country to spend its way out of the threatening slump. But when this failed, he cut wages to less than those of his competitors. Ford was no paternalist.

Acceptance of Ford's terms that January in 1914 was the equivalent of a Faustian pact for the assembly line worker, sacrificing his individuality for the means to improve the material existence of his family and himself. This was a different image of the Promised Land than that created by the Pilgrim Fathers. It amounted to a stifling of what the philosopher, George Santayana, described as the "hereditary spirit" – that of the Pilgrim Fathers and other hardworking immigrants and pioneers – that differentiated the American people from those of the Old World.

If many working people turned their backs on the production line, those who acquiesced were fulfilling the Taylorist dream of a perfect manual worker fitted for the modern industrial workplace. The Taylorist message, in the form of scientific management, was spreading across the industrial world, creating new tiers of administrators who were needed to put it into practice. Taylor himself argued the need for a team of work-study experts to carry out his studies at Midvale, using the talents of people like Carl Barth, one of his collaborators, who invented a slide rule to help him make his calculations. Others, like Frank Gilbreth and his wife, Lillian, perfected the study of motion. Frank Gilbreth was so obsessed with efficiency he used it in his family life. He filmed his children washing dishes so that he could work out how they could perform the task more speedily. He fastened his vest buttons from the bottom up because that took three seconds instead of the seven seconds it took to go from top to bottom.[13] He applied shaving foam with two brushes to save time but abandoned an experiment with two razors when he lost time dealing with cuts to his chin.[14]

His children – the Gilbreths had six boys and six girls – were expected to submit sealed bids for odd jobs that might enable them to earn some spending money. The lowest bid received the contract. The extent to which this way of thinking became an obsession was apparent also in the last years of Frederick Taylor's life, when he spent much of his time watching the grass grow. He didn't simply watch the grass, he counted the individual blades per square inch in a series of more than eight hundred experiments designed to create the perfect lawn. Within a year or two, what Taylor did not know about grass was not worth knowing. Whether they were blades of grass or people, it made no difference to Taylor. His focus was almost entirely on process.

But process was crucial in creating new tiers of management, where inspiration and leadership became subordinate to method. In France Henri Fayol found that scientific management complemented perfectly his own administrative theories. In Germany they adopted the Taylor ideas with gusto, but then they would. Management was no longer a term used by Mrs Beeton to describe a way of looking after the household, nor was it simply a chain of command. Management had become a system of mass control in production by process, method, and textbook, something that had enduring appeal to the military mind. When British soldiers embarked at walking pace side by side across no-man's-land on the Somme in July 1916 they were conforming to method, suppressing their individuality for the greater good of the enterprise. Their sacrifice had become subordinate to the search for victory. War and sacrifice had always been as disciplined as the assembly line. Now there was consistency in factory and field. Lines of moving magnetos had been replaced by rows of graves marking lost lives and buried aspirations. The consumer society was consuming itself in the greatest conflagration the world had known.

By the end of the First World War, the Taylorist doctrine had spread across Europe, through France, Germany, and Russia. The Russians swung first one way and then the other as the Revolution of 1917 trampled the last vestiges of Czarist feudalism into the soil and seeded an ideology that venerated the efforts of working men and women. Vladimir Ilyich Lenin had been initially suspicious of Taylorism, describing it before the First World War as the "enslavement of humankind to the machine."[15] By 1918, after Lenin had led the Russian Revolution, he was urging its introduction into industry. He wrote in *Pravda*, "We should immediately introduce piece work and try it out in practice.

We should try out every scientific and progressive suggestion of the Taylor system."[16]

Unlike Taylor, who used a pseudonym for his ideal workman, Henry Noll, to stress the attributes of the system rather than those of the individual, Joseph Stalin, Lenin's successor, saw the potential in scientific management to glorify the worker in contrast to the ruling elite who had been overthrown in the revolution. It seems curious that the United States, a country that upheld the rights and freedoms of the individual, should be reticent to endorse the productive accomplishments of one of its working class. Under Stalin the most productive workers had become the icons of the Soviet system. The chosen few were elevated to hero status and handed many of the comforts, perks, and trappings of the ruling Politburo. The downside, for some, was the accompanying fear of the secret police that came with the special status package.

There could be no greater contrast to the Ford homestead, evoking romanticized memories of a pioneering spirit, than number 2 Serafimovich Street. This large block of luxury apartments on the embankment of the Moscow River, commanding unrivaled views of the Kremlin, was home to the Soviet elite under communist rule. Here it was that Stalin housed the most favored individuals in Soviet society. Here it was that a knock on the door in the early hours confirmed his fickleness, as the pendulum swung from patronage to purge.

To be allocated a Serafimovich apartment was to have arrived in communist Russia, but the price of success was a precarious existence, always living in fear, always looking over your shoulder. As people struggled to find enough to exist on in much of the country, the Serafimovich residents were pampered in comparison, with their private canteen, store, garage parking, nursery, and tennis court. They also attracted the close attention of the NKVD, Stalin's secret police, who had spy holes in every wall. Some of the biggest names in the Soviet administration came and went from this address in the 1930s. Those who went were rarely heard of again. Some six hundred officials were dragged away and shot in successive purges during the 1930s.[17]

The only ones who could live in relative safety were those whom even Stalin could not conceive as a threat, people like Alexei Stakhanov, the Ukranian coal miner and worker-hero, who at the age of twenty-nine was feted for his prodigious efforts in cutting 102 tons of coal in a single six-hour night shift in August, 1935. This was fifteen times more than a worker might cut away on an average shift.

It has been stressed subsequently that this was no ordinary shift but a deliberate, party-organized attempt to gain plaudits from the Soviet leadership. Stakhanov was also helped in removing the coal by two co-workers whose role was not fully revealed until the late 1980s. The admission delighted some modern writers who reveled in exposing the fraud.[18] The lie did not need to be exposed. Stakhanov's own account is comprehensive enough to leave the reader in no doubt of the phoniness of the claims. But these writers should be permitted their cynicism. Given a shovel, they could not shift a ton of coal in a month of Sundays.

The Soviet propaganda machine moved into overdrive to portray Stakhanov as an iconic figure for the Soviet worker. In a book, *The Stakhanov Movement Explained*, said to be "by its initiator, Alexei Stakhanov," the young miner, then aged thirty-three, describes his experience, first as a farmhand, then a shepherd, and finally a coal miner at the Central Irmino colliery in the Dombas region of the Ukraine. Using a pneumatic pick, his standard daily production rate in his earliest days amounted to about five tons of coal on an average shift, eight tons on a good day. After undergoing a course in using the pick, he raised his output to ten tons a shift. But there was still a big obstacle to better production levels. The coal hewers were packed too closely together, allowing insufficient elbow-room. Miners were getting in each other's way. Another problem was a lack of specialization. The hewers were using their picks for not much more than half a shift since they were also required to fix their own timber props to stop the roof from collapsing.[19]

Removing these handicaps, he wrote, allowed him to achieve the feat of 102 tons of coal in a shift. It seems self-evident from his earlier remarks that he had help in propping and coal removal. The most curious part of the account is that passing the hundred-ton mark was not enough. If we found that figure hard to believe, what should we make of his assertion that another worker the very next day achieved 115 tons, and another soon afterwards cut out 119 tons? But this is only the start, as another miner cuts

125 tons before his record is quickly overtaken by a different worker with 151 tons. Before we know it, Stakhanov himself has reached the two-hundred-ton mark. Does he call it a day at this stage? Well, no. Somebody else cuts 240 tons, then a worker called Artyukhin shifts 310 tons, eventually bettering this figure with 536 tons.[20] "No more than a few weeks elapse before miners hewing two hundred, three hundred or even more tons of coal with every shift could be counted by the dozen," writes Stakhanov.[21] By this time the newly created mythical status of the Dombas miner has reached farcical levels. Why did the Russians persist with such nonsense? Did they really believe that people in the West were going to believe it, or did they simply get carried away with the need to fabricate and exaggerate?

The great sadness of these ridiculous figures is that Stakhanov makes some points about the front-line production worker that would find favor some sixty years later among many of the most progressive managements in Western industry. Stakhanov explains his method: "It requires only a public spirited attitude towards one's work and a thorough study of one's machinery and technique. Stakhanovite work is a combination of manual and mental work. It enables the Stakhanovites to show their mettle, to display their faculties, to give free reign to their creative ideas; it signifies the victory of man over machine."[22] Compare this with Frederick Taylor's exhortations to the shop-floor workers at Midvale to speed up and work harder, echoed in thousands of management–worker confrontations the world over.

Meanwhile the term "Stakhanovite" has gone into the language, meaning someone intensely committed to sustained hard work. But that is not the way that Stakhanov saw it. His own interpretation was akin to what would come to be known in the trendy personnel management circles of the late twentieth century as "empowerment," outlined in great detail by the Harvard professor and management thinker, Rosabeth Moss Kanter.[23] It looks like the Russians got there first. Unfortunately they never practiced what Stakhanov was preaching. The idea of worker initiative was a sham. The idea of any kind of initiative in Soviet life was stifled by the reality of an oppressive regime where staying in favor could mean the difference between life and death. The working masses were the little people as far as Stalin was concerned. He referred to them as *vintiki*, meaning "little screws" and thought of them as nothing other than "cogs in the great state machine."[24] Stakhanov was the figurehead of the *vintiki*.

The hero treatment for Stakhanov rewarded him with an airy apartment in Serafimovich Street, so that everyone could see how communism celebrated the best efforts of brawn and muscle. Beyond his book he became the subject of a "Stakhanovite" conference, attended by Stalin and three thousand other "worker-heroes." Stakhanov could never cope with his celebrity status and lapsed into alcoholism. He died in 1977. But, unlike many of his neighbors in the Soviet era, he outlived Stalin. That alone must have been some kind of record.

The bogey of Marxism so overshadowed the management systems of Taylorism and Fordism that the leaders of democratic capitalist governments were oblivious to any similarities between the way these methods were applied in the West and the way they were adopted and merged into the Soviet system. The parallels were not overt. Marxism set out its stall as a political ideology concerned with the conduct of a society in its entirety. It was revolutionary in its aims, in its approach, and in its execution. Taylorism was never promoted as anything other than a process, a system for the management of work in the private enterprise. And yet its influence was felt across society, disturbing many intellectuals concerned at its potential for control and the way that it stifled ideas and ambition in the individual.

The systemization of the factory job across the industrialized world so appalled the writer Aldous Huxley that he envisaged in his futuristic novel, *Brave New World*, published in 1932, a future of standardized workers "hatched" into predestined social roles. The book described a future world of test tube babies and genetic engineering rigidly controlled and exploited by a dehumanizing industrialized oligarchy. The most basic workers in Huxley's World State are the Epsilons, whose labor is used to man the industrial production lines. These are the little people, the downtrodden, although in Huxley's story they know no better.

Huxley elevates Ford to the status of a deity. The book is set in the year 632 AF (After Ford). It was not difficult to portray Henry Ford in this way. His approach to business was like something out of the Creation as he developed an all-encompassing industrial empire with coal mines, iron mines, and forests in the United States and a rubber plantation in Brazil. In one Canute-like experiment he tried to create a bird reserve on his farm, installing hundreds of birdhouses and freeing six hundred pairs of imported English songbirds at one go. They all flew away.[25] Unlike Ford's workers, the birds had a choice.

The US government woke up to the pervasive influence of scientific management after a labor strike at Watertown Arsenal – sparked by attempts to time workers by stopwatch – and launched a congressional inquiry in 1912. Just two years earlier the system had been a relatively obscure idea known only among a few engineers, when a story known as the Eastern Rates case hit the headlines. Harrington Emerson, a Taylor disciple, had given evidence to the Interstate Commerce Commission investigating resistance by eastern seaboard shippers to an application by railroad companies to raise their freight rates. Emerson argued that if the railroads adopted scientific management they could save a million dollars a day on their operating costs.[26] The claim was headlined in the *New York Times*. Suddenly businessmen everywhere wanted to know if they could benefit from these ideas. Nor were the implications lost on the labor unions, who immediately perceived Taylorism as a threat to their members.

Taylor's idealistic stance before the congressional committee on Watertown was unconvincing. Even Taylor stalwarts must have been surprised at his insistence that "scientific management is not an efficiency device, nor is it any bunch or group of efficiency devices; it is not a new system of figuring costs; it is not holding a stopwatch on a man, and writing things down about him; it is not time study; it is not motion study."[27] "No," he said, scientific management was nothing less than "a complete mental revolution" of workers and managers. If this was really Taylor's belief, the world did not see much evidence of this revolution in attitudes.

Taylorism was a manual for management control. Sometimes this control became intimidating in the extreme. The workers who set themselves against Ford in the early 1930s knew only too well the power they were confronting. The heady days of 1913 had been replaced by a workplace as repressive as any in Soviet Russia, resembling a police state with spies, called "spotters," planted among the workforce to report on employee code infringements such as killing time in the washrooms or attempting to organize a trade union. Other snoopers went to the homes of workers, collecting data on their personal lives for Ford's "Sociology Department," which decided whether they were clean-living enough to deserve the bonus that made up part of the five-dollar day.

The Ford hunger march on March 7, 1932 was reminiscent of that occasion back in 1812 when the Luddites marched on Rawfold's Mill in the North of England. A hundred and twenty years later history was repeating itself, as three thousand protesters with labor grievances, waving red flags, marched on Ford's River Rouge Plant at Dearborn on the outskirts of Detroit. Unlike the Luddites, these hunger marchers were not armed. There was no destructive intent. They were met on the city boundary by armed Dearborn Police, and four of them were machine-gunned to death when fighting broke out. Harry Bennett, Henry Ford's right-hand man, had been remonstrating with Joseph York, a nineteen-year-old organizer of the Young Communist League, when Bennett was hit on the head by a rock thrown by another protester. Bennett pulled York to the ground, and when York stood up he was fatally wounded in a hail of gunfire. Some Ford workers who later joined the mourners at the men's funeral were dismissed when they came back to work.[28]

Taylorism and Fordism transformed factory working so completely that the systems together must be viewed as perhaps the most enduring societal change of the twentieth century, arguably more influential and wider ranging than the competing ideologies of fascism and communism, although the destructive impact of these political ideologies is seared far more deeply on the collective memory of the human race. Peter Drucker, the management writer, described scientific management as "one of the great liberating, pioneering insights," adding that "altogether it may well be the most powerful as well as the most lasting contribution America has made to western thought since the *Federalist Papers*. As long as industrial society endures we shall never lose again the insight that human work can be studied systematically, can be analyzed, can be improved by work on its elementary parts."[29] Drucker might have thought differently had he worked on a production line.

Unlike slavery, the Faustian deal with the production-line worker delivered cheaper products that became affordable to the working classes, who could indulge themselves in the novelty of disposable income. The choice was ours. We could save in the spirit of Victorian parsimony or we could squander our money on a growing variety of consumer goods. The luxury of an extra cooking pot in Abraham Darby's day had made way for hundreds of household gizmos and devices aimed at saving labor that previously had been unnecessary. Buying the car was only the start. Soon you could shampoo it, hose it, vacuum the interior, black its wheels, and stick a nodding dog on the rear parcel shelf. Happiness came in boxes with a flex attached. Like Walt Disney's dwarfs in the film, *Snow White*, we could sing our merry way to work and whistle when we got there.

Disney, like McGuffey, reflected the Protestant virtues inherent in hard wholesome work. The rhythmical ring of picks striking rocks was playing out an anthem to the values of industrious God-fearing America. The danger was not in work but in the temptation of reaching out for illusory delights that were not earned by work. So Snow White, like Adam, became one more victim of the tempting apple, oblivious to the poison stored inside. The Biblical curse on mankind was as potent as ever, and the only path toward redemption was to work, work, work. Work was good; work was uplifting. "There is joy in work," said Ford. "There is no happiness except in the realization that we have accomplished something."[30] In work you could find freedom, of a kind.

CHAPTER 12

Western Electric Discovers Motivation

> We can never wholly separate the human from the mechanical sides.
>
> (Mary Parker Follett, 1868–1933)

National Geographic magazine published a map of the world in October, 1998 drawn from night-time satellite images. Scattered like icing sugar over a freshly baked cake were thousands of white dots, what the map called "human settlement lights." Each white speck was itself made up of thousands of individual electric lamps. Light was so profuse in the industrial conurbations that the white dots were fused together, stretching like a Milky Way of electrical luminosity across the planet.

Had the same photographic composite been possible during the Christmas of 1879 there might have been a few yellowish dots from gas lighting in a sea of blackness. But if the cameras had been able to intensify their magnification over Menlo Park, New Jersey, they would have found that one of these man-made pools of light was the genesis of the galaxy of electric lights that pepper our world today. The forty light bulbs run off a dynamo were vastly outnumbered by the throngs of visitors. On New Year's Eve some three thousand people converged on the display, attracted by the promise of Thomas Alva Edison that the whole of Menlo Park would be bathed in light. He didn't quite make it, but there was enough to assure those who gathered there that humankind had made yet one more great stride in controlling his environment. No one who witnessed this marvel could have imagined that electric lighting would not only illuminate people's homes and streets but would stimulate a new avenue of thinking in workplace motivation, raising afresh the old debate over stick and carrot and the psychological value of workplace recognition.

That is precisely what happened. What became no more than a footnote in the story of lighting would open new paths of exploration in management and psychology. The way it happened was almost accidental and, in the birth of this new industry, an irrelevance.

Edison did not invent the electric light bulb, any more than Abraham Darby invented iron forging or the cooking pot. But, like Darby, he improved the existing technology, making something that was cheap and useful. It was no mere novelty. He told his visitors that soon they would be able to buy his light bulbs for 25¢ apiece and run them in their homes for a few pennies a day. The previous October, after hundreds of hours experimenting with different lighting filaments, he had watched the persistent glow from a piece of carbonized cotton bent into a horseshoe shape and sealed in an evacuated glass globe. Switched on in the early hours of October 22, it burned for thirteen and a half hours, into mid-afternoon. Later the same month he made an improved filament from carbonized paper.

Edison's light-bulb invention was a refinement of the incandescent lamp, but a crucial refinement at that. What he specifically created is a bit of a mouthful, but the authors John W. Howell and Henry Shroeder thought it worth defining precisely in their *History of the Incandescent Lamp*. He had invented, they wrote, "a lamp with a high resistance filament of carbon in a vacuum contained in a glass container closed at all points by fusion of the glass to the filament." As they pointed out, "this was the first incandescent lamp which was suitable for the system of general multiple distribution which solved the problem of the 'subdivision of the electric light.'"[1] The light-bulb refinement was just one of the world-record 1,093 patents filed either personally by Edison or jointly with others during his lifetime. His Menlo Park laboratory was a hive of industrious invention. Edison's collaborators were craftsmen and they called each other "muckers," reflecting the way they all "mucked in" or pitched in together.[2] They worked long hours, late into the night, punctuated by sessions on the organ at one end of the laboratory and weekend drinking bouts. It was an informal, freethinking atmosphere and Edison was one of the boys. "Hell, there ain't no rules in here! We're trying to accomplish something!" he said.[3]

The power of this informal atmosphere in creative teams was highlighted by Warren Bennis and Patricia Ward Biederman in their book, *Organizing Genius,* which observed how teams of specialists brought together for creative projects feed off each other. The animators who worked with Walt Disney and the nuclear physicists who worked with J. Robert Oppenheimer on the development of the atomic bomb were young and enthusiastic, "fueled by an invigorating, completely unrealistic view of what they [could] accomplish."[4] They did not need fine offices and had little time for hierarchies or dress codes. They thrived instead on a shared aim and the opportunity to work with a pioneer in their chosen field.

Edison was just such a figure. But his creative juices fed off a conviction that hard work sparked creativity. "He believes that unflinching, unremitting hard work will accomplish anything. It was this genius for hard work that fired me as a lad and made Mr. Edison my hero," said Henry Ford, who never forgot the inventor's early encouragement for his work on the internal combustion engine.[5] Ford had taken the opportunity to show Edison the plans for his engine in its early stages of development. Edison banged the table with his fist and said: "Young man, there's the thing. You have it." Ford recalled later: "That bang on the table was worth worlds to me. No man up to then had given me any encouragement."[6]

Edison was never credited with great administrative skills. Running companies was not his thing, and he quickly bowed out of the operations of General Electric, the company created to exploit the light-bulb breakthrough. But he was more than a gifted inventor. He had the vision to grasp the implications of his work beyond the finer points of the invention. Unlike many of his contemporaries – and the field of electric lighting development was almost awash with inventors obsessed with the idea of prolonging the glow they could create in their crude electrical filaments – Edison kept his eye on the big picture. A durable long-lasting light bulb was all well and good, but it would not work without a power supply. Connected lighting run from a central source had been pioneered by the gaslight developers. Companies like England's Boulton & Watt, which installed gaslights in the Phillips and Lee cotton mills in Manchester in

1806.[7] William Murdoch, an engineer, had found a way to distill coal gas, which he first used to light his home in 1792. Boulton & Watt had snapped up the man and his idea in the same way that an ambitious football club signs a promising young player for his potential.

Only when the company discovered that Phillipe LeBon had plans to light the whole of Paris with his gas Thermolamp did it give Murdoch the backing he needed to push his development forward. Phillips and Lee reduced their annual lighting bill, spent on candles, by more than two-thirds and found that the gaslights saved labor expended in the constant trimming of candlewicks. The gaslight was a big step, but equally important was the delivery of gas through pipes from a central station. When the London and Westminster Chartered Gas Light and Coke Company was established in 1812, it was the beginning of an industry that would expand and prosper for the next sixty-seven years, until the Menlo Park exhibition in fact.[8] The gas companies sent their spies to the Menlo event and one of them tried to short-circuit the display, but Edison had watchmen posted. The saboteur was caught and thrown out.

Edison arrived late to lighting experiments, but he came with his Menlo Park laboratory – the world's first industrial research and development center – and he had powerful financial support from people like J. P. Morgan, the banker.[9] But the backers insisted on evidence of commercial promise for any of Edison's inventions before their funds could be channeled into further development and production. They wanted to know whether this light bulb would sell. Potential patent litigation was less of an obstacle than industry domination, or, in this case, industry creation. Edison himself, already recognized as the inventor of the phonograph, was a big enough name to sell the new lighting, and his fledgling company, General Electric, promoted him heavily in its advertising as the "founding father" of the lighting industry.

But the industry needed something else, some great benefit of electricity over gas. The company was keen to hang its marketing on whatever evidence it could find to convince potential buyers that an electric lighting system was viable. General Electric would come to develop a marketing campaign based on the "science of seeing," a novel idea, suggesting that electric lighting

made work easier.[10] The science of seeing must have seemed at
that time as attractive as the notion of the paperless office would
be in the 1980s, and it was just as unrealistic. But if the concept
was going to sell electric lighting to companies, nobody in the
industry was going to quibble.

Nevertheless, there had been quibbling in the lighting industry.
More than quibbling. One apparently commercial decision amounted to outright censorship and helped to create confusion over a
seemingly innocuous set of experiments that continues to this day.
The focus of this industry displeasure was a series of studies centered on Western Electric's Hawthorne factory in Chicago.

Initially, at least, the supporters of scientific management
showed little interest in lighting. But two of Taylor's followers,
Alexander Church and Frank Gilbreth, theorized separately on
the possible benefits to production work of well-placed artificial
lighting. Church believed that poor lighting caused a "strain on
the faculties," suggesting that high-intensity lighting had an
"influence upon the spirits" of the workmen.[11] These are significant observations because they demonstrate a recognition that the
well-being, mood, and morale of employees could contribute to
their work. Columella, the Roman agricultural writer, had sensed
this hundreds of years earlier, but classical literature did not
feature highly on the reading list of those engaged in scientific
management. Its pioneers were practical people, not theorists.
Sometimes their work bore no more than a passing resemblance
to either science or management. There was much trial and error
and not a little speculation. Frank Gilbreth, for example, worried that glare and reflection of lighting caused tiredness among
workers. All workshop machinery, he said, should be painted
matt black. Later he changed his mind and said all workshop sur-
faces should be painted white.[12]

It should not be surprising that electric lighting found itself the
subject of scientific scrutiny. Frederick Taylor and his disciples
had created a mania for measurement across industry. The craze
had gathered momentum in November, 1910 after the Boston
lawyer Louis D. Brandies trumpeted his claim that the railroads
could save $1 million a day in the Eastern Rates case if they were
to adopt scientific management. Suddenly every business on the
block was buying stopwatches and notebooks.

When Taylor published his techniques in *The Principles of Scientific Management* the following year, he set the tone that would underpin process-driven manufacturing management for the rest of the century, so much so that "what can't be measured isn't worth doing" remains a popular maxim across company boardrooms today. Scientific measurement would give way to "benchmarking," "economic value added," "six sigma quality improvement," and a host of other jargon for controlling and refining the productive process. This was clipboard management delivering fascinating figures and measurable results, allowing all kinds of comparisons and calculations to convince whoever needed convincing of the merits associated with the scientifically proven one best way of doing things. It was boys playing with numerical toys.

Efficiency drives during the First World War, looking for ways of improving industrial output and quality, stimulated renewed interest in the relationship between high intensity electric lighting and production. William Durgin, one of Edison's lighting specialists, carried out some detailed tests in 1918 to highlight the link. The previous year a survey of ninety-three Chicago companies using electric lighting found that workshops were operating in lighting far poorer than that recommended by the industry. Durgin followed up the survey with tests in four factories, which suggested that better lighting could increase production by between 10 and 35 percent.[13] The results were encouraging enough to convince General Electric that it should increase its efforts to promote factory lighting and strengthen its already dominant position in the sector. Part of this dominance was achieved by populating various lighting research bodies with its own experts.

As General Electric's warehouses began stockpiling lamps during a postwar downturn in business, the impetus and funding for industrial lighting research were stronger than ever.[14] Experiments were carried out in more factories, including those instigated in 1924 at the Hawthorne works of Western Electric. Chicago had changed some since George Pullman had jacked its buildings out of the mud. This was the Chicago of the roaring twenties, a city of gangsters, speakeasies, and cars with running boards for gun-toting henchmen, as rival gangs vied with each other for control of prostitution, extortion, and bootleg liquor in defiance of Prohibition. The influence of some, such as Al Capone, even extended to the unions.[15] But away from the headlines, grabbed so often by fast-living, fast-talking, and sharply tailored gangsters, was another population, the silent majority intent on making a living to support their families.

Out on the two-hundred-acre site of the Hawthorne works run by Western Electric, some thirty thousand men and women were employed on assembly lines making telephone equipment. This small industrial metropolis, the equivalent of a good-sized town, was put together from sixty nationalities – a cross section of the new American labor force drawn from the millions of European immigrants. As the factory workers labored, the gangs were running their prohibition-busting schemes nearby, with Capone's operations headquartered half a block away and a couple of his gambling dens just across the street. Joseph Juran, the then Western Electric statistician who, with W. Edwards Deming, went on to become one of the heroes of the Japanese quality movement after the Second World War, would put his mathematical talents to use watching the actions of the roulette wheel operator in a gambling house called "The Shop." The operator's arm action was so repetitive that Juran won a hundred dollars working out the resulting improvement in the odds favoring certain numbers.[16] His method was overlooked: otherwise Japan's postwar miracle, together with one of its principal gurus, could have ended up swimming with the fishes in Lake Michigan.

The fluctuating fortunes of Al Capone were not the only distraction for the Hawthorne workers. Without realizing it, some two-thirds of the workforce would become the unwitting guinea pigs in perhaps the most extensive investigations into human motivation the world has known. The studies didn't start that way. Production rates and General Electric's insatiable desire to sell more lighting across manufacturing industry were at the heart of the first experiments. The psychology would come later, after the lighting industry tried to forget about the surprise results of the initial tests.

Tests were run in several places, including General Electric's Bridgeport Works and the Massachusetts Institute of Technology. The most rigorous experiments, however, appear to have been conducted at Western Electric's Hawthorne works, and it was these tests – three sets of experiments run at intervals between November, 1924 and April, 1927 – that caused the biggest fuss. The first experiments appeared promising: lighting was improved in some departments and productivity went up. The problem was that productivity also went up among teams where the lighting was *not* improved. One team managed to maintain output even when lighting was dimmed to the level of moonlight.

Western Electric's management was intrigued by the findings and wanted to know more. If it wasn't the lighting that made people improve their output, what was it? General Electric, on the other hand, saw no merit in continuing a program that was doing nothing to support its claim that better lighting delivered higher profits.[17] Quite the opposite. According to Clarence Stoll, the superintendent of the Hawthorne works who went on to become Western Electric's president, the final report, if it was ever completed, was buried. So the written results of the tests which gave rise to what the world would come to recognize as "The Hawthorne Effect" were never published.[18] George Pennock, the engineer in charge of the program, told Stoll: "The project is being allowed to die and it is hoped that it will be forgotten."[19] Pennock was unhappy about the decision. He and his fellow managers had other ideas.

Western Electric was not the kind of company to overlook something that might improve the well-being and, more importantly, the output of its workers. Like many other large companies during this era, it pursued the concept of cradle-to-grave employment, rewarding long service and loyalty. It ran an evening school for workers called the Hawthorne University. It ran an employee benefit and insurance plan and treated its workers to annual picnics. The picnic and the insurance plan were not supposed to be made for each other, but this was the way it turned out. In the summer of 1915, within two years of the plan's introduction, the company chartered six steamships for the annual picnic. One of the boats, the *Eastland*, capsized a few feet from its dock, killing 812 people – employees, their families, and friends.[20] Most of the victims were central European émigrés. The benefit plan was swamped, but the company paid an additional $100,000 for relief, and a collection among other Chicago businesses raised

$350,000 more. Western Electric stood by its workers in good times and bad.

The Hawthorne plant made telephone equipment for Western Electric's parent, AT&T. The corporate relationship had developed in a roundabout way from Alexander Graham Bell's invention of the telephone and Western Electric's agreement to manufacture it. The business arrangement did not mature quite so simply, but after a period of corporate jostling, early lawsuits over patent infringements, quarrels over manufacturing alliances, and the kind of posturing and skirmishing that tends to go with the turf when the players struggle for dominance in a nascent field of industry, Western Electric sold out to the American Bell Telephone Company, which became American Telephone & Telegraph, or AT&T.

As Chicago's biggest employer, Western Electric was an obvious choice for lighting experiments. It did not face the competitive pressures of its parent, since the Bell system bought everything it made. Its managers, therefore, were not prone to the sort of anxiety attacks and defensive responses that can be induced by falling sales. Like most companies of its size and stature it adhered to the principles of scientific management, so it would have been perfectly comfortable with the features of the initial lighting experiments. It shared none of General Electric's discomfort with the ambiguous findings. Nor did it display GE's disinterest in the idea that the experiments were causing some kind of psychological impact on employees.

A potential link between lighting and behavior had been suggested by Hugo Munsterberg in 1914. He had wondered whether psychological techniques could be used to evaluate lighting efficiency.[21] Western Electric had dabbled with psychology itself in 1915, when it invited Walter Dill Scott, a psychology professor at Northwestern University, to address its senior management in a series of lectures. Impressed by his arguments, the management asked Dill Scott to develop some tests that would look for creative potential among the company's engineers.[22] That same year, in what may well have been the world's first occupational psychometric tests, Western Electric's personnel director, Walter Dietz, used Dill Scott's methods to assess fifteen engineering graduates. Stanley Bracken and Heine Beal, far and above the highest scorers, went right to the top. Bracken became president of the company and Beal served as vice president.[23]

Most accounts of the earliest use of psychometric testing in recruitment and selection date its development to the US military after its entry into the First World War, but Dill Scott had introduced tests at Western Electric two years before selection testing was adopted on a broad scale in military recruiting in 1917. When the war ended, Western Electric began to broaden its use of testing in recruitment and selection. In 1923 it carried out tests on almost 8,500 employees.[24] An AT&T decision to concentrate group-wide research and development at Bell Telephone Laboratories, a purpose-built division set up in New York in 1925, reinforced Western Electric's own commitment to industrial research.

In 1927 Hawthorne had a mystery on its hands, and solving the mystery might provide another leap forward in the never-ending search for increased productivity. The company launched a new series of studies designed to explore the possible causes of the bizarre results of the lighting tests. Six women were drafted into the test area that had been created for the lighting experiments. This Relay Assembly Test Room was partitioned off from the main assembly floor. The researchers selected a sample of able and experienced employees to avoid the potential for attributing any rise in their performance to skill improvement as they learned the job. One of the women was designated a supervisor. Sitting on tall stools at a long workbench, each woman took about a minute to assemble the thirty-five parts in a telephone relay unit and drop the unit into a chute.

The new tests were quite distinct from the original lighting tests in their design. These tests were observing work patterns and behavior. Among the questions the investigators were seeking to answer were: Why does production traditionally fall off in the afternoon? Do employees get tired? Are rest periods or a shorter working day a good idea? What is the employees' attitude toward their work and the company? Will a change in working equipment affect their performance?

The women's work was monitored constantly. Their conversations were noted, they had frequent medical examinations, and the room temperature and humidity were also measured to check for any possible variables in their conditions. Although the women had been in a group scheme for piece work rates, they were put in a separate scheme and promised that they would be able to earn at least as much as they had done previously. They had other privileges denied to their fellow workers. Hawthorne had a tall tower that was off-limits to most people, but the relay test women were regular visitors as they popped in and out for research interviews.[25]

The second set of experiments in the relay room was already underway when George Pennock asked Elton Mayo, a Harvard Business School professor, if he wanted to cast his experienced eye over the various work team studies the company had established. Mayo was born in Adelaide, the son of an engineer. Abandoning medical school, he worked for some time as a journalist before taking up a partnership his father had bought for him in a printing firm. He combined the business venture with a return to studies in Adelaide, this time in psychology. His work led him into the treatment of shell-shock victims returning from the First World War battlefields. The experience in this relatively new area of psychotherapy influenced his thinking on the psychological adaptation of individuals to unfamiliar environments, be it the horrors of trench warfare or the more mundane but nevertheless wearing demands of the factory assembly line.

A successful lecture tour of North America led to funding from the Carnegie Foundation for three years studying in Philadelphia. Part of this involved looking at the impact of people's home lives and working conditions on employee turnover and productivity in various Philadelphia companies. Mayo had moved to Harvard in 1926, two years before receiving Pennock's invitation. He recognized at once that Western Electric was what many would regard as a "good employer," describing it as "a company definitely committed to justice and humanity in its dealings with workers, and with general morale high." The workers themselves might not have been so glowing in their praise but they knew the wages were competitive and the working conditions excellent. In addition to the insurance and school, they had the use of a cafeteria shared by employees and management, and an in-house hospital. Industrial unrest had not been an issue since the turn of the century, when a group of machinists had walked out, demanding union recognition and a nine-hour day. The management had stood firm on its rejection of unions but settled the dispute by reducing its daily shift by half an hour to the nine hours the workers had sought.

Mayo arrived, buoyed by a large grant from the Rockefeller Foundation and the sort of reception extended for a visiting company boss. He warmed to this red-carpet treatment, which included a room at one of Chicago's swankiest hotels and a chauffeured door-to-door limousine every morning. "The door is opened and Elton Mayo, formerly of South Australia, gets in and glides off to his alleged industrial researches," he wrote in a letter to his wife.[26]

The all-women relay assembly team was studied for five and a half years in total, up to the summer of 1932. Other teams were also studied. A similar group was segregated in the mica splitting room to look at the influence of individual rather than group piece-work incentives, and some time later a section of male operatives in a telephone wiring department had their routines monitored. Side by side with these experiments the researchers instigated an employee consultation program. Between 1928 and 1930 some twenty thousand employees were interviewed.[27] The later interviews allowed employees to range over topics of their own choosing, and this led the company to adopt employee counseling from the mid-1930s until it was replaced by union consultation in the 1950s.

By the time the workplace experiments ended the United States was in the midst of the Great Depression, and Western Electric was laying off thousands of workers. Mayo lamented the impact of layoffs on the workplace community with sentiments that would be echoed by social commentators some sixty years later. Given the climate of mass unemployment and harder-edged managements, it is hardly surprising that he stressed the need for companies to recapture the communal spirit that had characterized the increasingly productive work teams in the earlier Hawthorne experiments.

It would be wrong, however, to conclude that the experiments had discovered a recipe for workplace Nirvana. The very creation of teams sometimes led to resentment among other workers. This happened among colleagues of the relay assembly team, who complained that they were not getting the special attention meted out to the others. It also explains why one team had to be reabsorbed into the general workplace when other workers complained that it was getting preferential pay rates. (This short-lived relay assembly team was paid on the same individual basis as the mica splitting team. The incentives seemed to work, increasing productivity by 12.5 percent.)

The final study in the bank wiring room observed the working relationships among a group of male operatives. In this case the men were restricting their output with the knowledge and apparent approval of their supervisor. The experience seemed to echo Frederick Taylor's characteristically blunt assertion that "hardly a competent workman can be found who does not devote a considerable amount of time to studying just how slowly he can work and still convince his employer he is going at a good pace."[28] The men were soldiering. The company researchers interpreted the tardiness as a tactic arising from the suspicion of the workers that if they worked consistently faster their pay rate would be cut. Mayo argued differently, suggesting the go-slow was an unconscious group reaction to the lack of any incentive for them to work harder. Like the Three Musketeers the men found strength in pursuing a united strategy as a social unit.

These individual findings soon lost their definition under Mayo's repeatedly voiced conclusion that the puzzling responses to lighting changes had been stimulated by a conviction among the employees involved in the experiment that they were part of something special. They had been made to feel important, to feel wanted. They had a sense of togetherness and they were consulted. They did not feel like nameless automatons or cogs in the machine. They had become a social unit and they enjoyed the attention they received. When they were treated like human beings, anything was possible, even working in moonlight. This was the homily Mayo repeated in lecture after lecture. It was restoring the face of humanity to industrial manufacturing. Perhaps it was what people – managers and employees – whatever their commitment to scientific management, really wanted to hear. But did they believe it?

Mayo's arguments were greeted with a sigh of relief by those, like Aldous Huxley, who had feared the consequences of production-line working across society. The myopia of scientific management could focus only on production, sacrificing richness and beauty to the cavernous hunger of efficiency. Lillian Gilbreth, the wife of Frank, understood this. Lillian was as expert as her husband in the field of motion studies. She also studied psychology to complement their management work. Toward the end of her life she wrote:

> The people who started the scientific management movement did not have the advantage of an arts and letters background or training in philosophy, and they did not read or speak other languages fluently or travel a great deal. They were mechanical engineers, trained in the fashion of their time. They went into industry and devoted their lives to making the best use of their own and other people's time, energy and money. They did not realize that management was something that had come down through the ages and was being practiced in some form or another in every country in the world.[29]

Hawthorne was the backlash against Taylorism. But it did not stop work-study. It tempered it with a timely warning that people were not machines, but it did not deliver a neat formula or point in large neon letters to the one best way of people management. Across the industrial firmament, where scientific management had been delivered like commandments in tablets of stone, Mayo's arguments were received with caution bordering on suspicion. Scientific management had taken the work ethic and converted it into the shop-floor equivalent of a Gregorian chant. That was fine with company bosses. All they needed was a formula for productivity, not endless debates on the corporate family. Industrialists like Thomas Gradgrind in Charles Dickens' *Hard Times* were satisfied that "facts alone are wanted in life." The attitude prevails today in a continuing obsession with measurement and benchmarking.

The official account of the second series of Hawthorne experiments was written not by Mayo but by two of his collaborators, Fritz Roethlisberger, a Harvard academic, and William Dickson, a Western Electric engineer. Both, nevertheless, were under Mayo's influence. Mayo had strong concerns about the workplace long before his involvement at Hawthorne. He was convinced that long hours, poor working conditions, and bad posture created fatigue, stress, and potential industrial unrest, and nothing he saw at Western Electric persuaded him to change his mind. On the contrary he believed he had accumulated in the Hawthorne experiments the evidence for a counter-argument to Taylorism. Here was the stick with which he could beat the efficiency experts. Companies needed managers schooled in human relations, people with empathy, listeners, counselors. Companies needed the collaboration of their workers. The message was cooperation secured by recognition and job satisfaction. Hawthorne had supposedly demonstrated all of this. But had it really done so?

The management academics, Daniel A. Wren and Ronald G. Greenwood, suggest in their book, *Management Innovators*, that Mayo's strongly held views "shaded" Roethlisberger and Dickson's account.[30] They point out that Mayo changed his interpretation of the studies before his collaborators published their book. The social needs of the relay assembly workers were brought to the fore and their moneymaking desires were pushed into the background. Mark Putnam, the personnel manager involved with the team, had told *Business Week* that the chance to earn extra money was the prime reason for workers' increased output. In a memo to Mayo, Putnam had said: "Economic and financial factors are of considerable importance in the test room. The employees are anxious for high earnings."[31] Mayo chose to ignore this evidence, possibly for good reason. After all, the employees and their managers would say that, wouldn't they? This was Marx's cash nexus. More niggling still for Mayo, it supported Taylor's conviction that people had their price. However well founded these arguments may have been, Mayo's lack of objectivity, and the nagging suspicion held by some that he was manipulating the experiment to support his opinions, exposed the work to skeptical analysis.

Should we dismiss Harvard Business School's most celebrated case study as a dud, a piece of flawed research reported by a team of Johnny-come-lately academics who threw their objectivity out of the window and who were less than rigorous in their methods? I think we should. Mayo had his own agenda and he cooked the findings to make it fit, ignoring the sometimes contradictory conclusions of experienced company researchers. Eight years of research, that soaked up much of the $1.52m in grant funding awarded to Mayo's team, was wrapped up in a handy soundbite – "The Hawthorne Effect," the surprise result of dimming the lights on ladies who just wanted to be loved.[32]

It sounded so appealing, so simple, so human. It had to be true, and the most damning point of all is that it probably was. Before the first tests the women in the relay assembly team had been expressly ordered by their foreman not to talk to each other. This kind of autocracy disappeared as soon as they were engaged in the tests, which they greeted as a welcome release from the normal shop-floor regime. But it didn't disappear for good. Two of the team were later dismissed for talking too much.

Elton Mayo had his own theories about management–worker relations, and he used his interpretations of the Hawthorne experiments to reinforce and consolidate his preconceived views. But he did not establish the link between the new-found freedom of the test teams and higher productivity, not beyond the doubts of those who pointed to financial incentives. Hawthorne occupies a tainted pedestal in industrial research. For too long it was celebrated as a milestone in motivational studies – and perhaps it was – but in terms of convincing production managers it had barely left the starting block. As Bernard Bass and Gerald Barrett pointed out in *People, Work and Organizations*, changes to working patterns and changes in team membership at various stages of the investigation, compounded by the lack of any control group, meant that the Hawthorne studies had "very limited scientific worth."[33] The studies were influential, nevertheless, in the way that information about the experiments was distributed through the Marshall plan set up to finance post-Second World War industrial regeneration in Europe.[34]

Hawthorne had done enough to make a case for the human relations school of management, but would the evidence convince a sitting jury beyond reasonable doubt? Sadly, all these years after, the jury still appears to be out. The question for those obsessed with output (i.e. production managers) still comes down to what makes people work more productively – more money, the attention of others, or both? The failure to nail these points allowed the "us and them" syndrome of employee relations to prevail throughout the rest of the century. Human relations, nevertheless, had secured a foothold in the body corporate.

The debate had been joined, and it would rage never more fiercely than in the 1990s, when companies reached the global wall. Their markets were saturated. There was nowhere else to look but inward. Suddenly every company needed a shrink or the corporate equivalent – a management consultant. What were the implications of this introspection for work? The focus had turned full circle from the product to the producer. People once more were viewed as the potential heroes of the workplace. How did you find these heroes? Were they born or made? The debate has a lengthy history. It is the story of selection, nature versus nurture, and what makes people tick.

CHAPTER 13

Unnatural Selection

'Tis labor indeed that puts the difference of value on everything.

(John Locke, 1632–1704)

Frederick Taylor's work-study at Bethlehem Steel had demonstrated the value of careful selection in the recruitment of workers. One of the fundamental responsibilities of scientific management, he said, was to find the speediest and most competent workers fitted for the job. Selection of the fittest was doing a kindness to the others, he thought, since they would be miserable in a job they could not do so well. That they would have been even more miserable without work was hardly an issue for Taylor's industrial Darwinism. Before Taylor, job selection was arbitrary and crude. After Taylor it began to develop disciplines.

The investigations at Western Electric had shown that scientific methods in the nascent discipline of psychology could also be applied to the study of the behavior and abilities of workers. Factory owners had found there was room for improvement in physical output. Now they were finding there was room for behavioral improvement too. The workplace would soon be awash with a new army of silent monitors recording movements, watching, timing, interviewing. In the list of human rights upheld by the Constitution of the United States there may well have been the right to bear arms, but there was no right of privacy, not in the workplace at any rate. Workers were a rich source of interest. Scientists had learned to read their movements. Now they would try to read their minds.

According to Morris Viteles, one of the pioneers of twentieth-century occupational psychology, Walter Dill Scott, the Northwestern University psychologist who so impressed Western Electric's management with his lectures on the potential of psychological assessment testing, deserves star billing in the history of occupational psychology.[1] And yet his role in this field, perhaps because of his pioneering contributions to the advertising industry, is often overlooked, achieving not so much as a footnote in some accounts. It is a serious oversight. Dill Scott was the first individual to consider the use of psychology for increasing worker output, for improving the quality of work and for recruiting employees. In a groundbreaking volume, *Influencing Men in Business*, published in 1911, Dill Scott made some telling remarks about the importance of people in business. "The greatest business problems of our day have to do with the personnel of industry and the arts of guiding and influencing men in the achievement of business aims," he writes. [2] To do this he advocates the application of psychology. "It is the only science that can give us any sound information about human nature," he says.

These were bold statements at the time, made possible by developments in psychological testing in Germany, Britain, the United States, and France. The first of these developments was a series of psychological experiments run in London by Francis Galton, the half-cousin of Charles Darwin. Galton had been regarded by his parents as something of a child prodigy. Coming from a Quaker family who had converted back to the Anglican faith, Galton was the first of his line to be eligible for university, and his parents had high hopes of his future academic achievement. Although he was accepted to study mathematics at Trinity College, Cambridge, he was never among the elite, a devastating discovery considering the expectations of his family.

Later, when he visited a phrenologist to have his "bumps" read, the quack who carried out the examination suggested that Galton's intellectual capacities would be better exploited by doing some "rough" work. Galton took an opportunity for such work by heading a geographical expedition to Africa, at a time when expeditions were exciting the Victorian public. Between 1850 and 1852 he had led an expedition that mapped a large area of South West Africa. He could afford to make such journeys, since his inheritance ensured his financial security without the need to go out and earn a living. Galton was one of those financially secure new amateurs who could pursue their interests however they pleased, and he pondered at length whether to live the life of a country gentleman or apply his talents in some creative way. He chose the latter course.

After his return from Africa he began to show interest in human reaction times. Galton thought they might point to individual differences in thinking ability. The study of reaction times can be traced back to some astronomical observations made by Nevil Maskelyne, the Astronomer Royal at Greenwich in 1795. Maskelyne had dismissed his assistant for having the temerity to record the times of stellar transits – the time it took a star to cross a set distance in the field of a telescope – almost a second later than his boss. The error was simply a matter of their respective reaction times, but no one up to that point had given the matter much thought, and neither did Maskelyne beyond sacking his slower-reacting aide.

About twenty years later the German astronomer Friedrich Bessel, who happened to be interested in measurement errors, found an account of the Greenwich discrepancies and began his own study of the differences in human reaction times. His intention was to use his findings to eliminate errors in astronomical observations.[3] Bessel became the first man to work out accurately the distance from Earth of a fixed star – 10.9 light years for a star designated in Flamsteed's star catalog as 61 Cygni. But he didn't do any more work on response times.

Galton was interested in response times for quite different reasons. He hoped that studying the way that they differed could help prove his theory that people inherited the behavior and intellectual capabilities of their parents. During his travels in Africa – still considered the "Dark Continent" at the time – Galton had noticed the ethnic diversity of different tribal groups. On his return he was consulted occasionally by missionary groups for advice about the most suitable people for conversion to Christianity. There was a degree of nervousness among Victorian missionaries that tempered their enthusiasm for pushing out the borders of Christianity. The native stewpot, boiling the captured missionary over a campfire, was a popular image in penny magazines, not without some foundation. Cannibalism in Fiji inspired such fear among Europeans that when David Cargill, a Wesleyan missionary, was selected by his mission society to go there, the meeting was held in his absence. After he had settled in Fiji he went mad watching the locals playing football with human heads.[4] The circulation of stories like this in polite Victorian society did nothing to dispel the notion that Europe was occupied by civilized white supremacists surrounded by a world of savagery.

This was the common belief underlying Adam Smith's justification for capitalism. Smith, displaying little understanding of other cultures, had referred to "miserably poor" tribal societies without appreciating, as Carlyle did, the simplicity of their needs or the abundance of resources that often existed around them. Smith's northern European society was the best society and there was nothing the "civilized" world could learn from the "savage nations of hunters and fishers." It was the job of the educated to take civilization to the rest of the world.

Galton shared this view and believed that selective human breeding would help to achieve this happy state. In his science of eugenics he looked forward to a world where a society of intellectual aristocrats could be bred like pedigree poodles. In 1884, in an attempt to gather data supportive of his theory, he set up a series of tests in what he called his Anthropometric Laboratory at the International Health Exhibition held in London's South Kensington museums. Visitors paid threepence each to try out various exercises in Galton's Laboratory. Two records of their performance were taken by tellers, one for the person undergoing the tests and a duplicate for the scientist.

Galton was the first person to begin correlating figures – a practice that would become essential as psychologists strove to prove the validity of their tests. Validity – establishing that a test could measure what it claimed to measure – would be a long-running area of contention in psychological testing. Even today there are question marks over the value of some of the most widely sold personality tests. The significant question is not whether they can establish the personality traits of an individual undergoing a test, but whether they can predict future job performance from these findings.

Once Galton had collected his body of statistics it did not take a great leap to begin constructing the mechanics for their analysis. Galton was contacted by James Cattell, an American psychology student who had been studying under Wilhelm Wundt in Leipzig. Wundt had set up the world's first psychological laboratory in 1879, and many of the earliest psychology students clustered there before taking the teaching back to their respective countries. Dill Scott had taken his doctorate in psychology under Wundt before applying his ideas, first in advertising, then in selection.

Moving to England, Cattell set up his own Anthropometric Laboratory at Cambridge University and later devised his own mental tests, consisting of various response indicators. In one test, the subject had to name various colors in order while being timed with a stopwatch; in another, a random set of letters had to be repeated from memory; and in another a hard rubber tip was pushed against the subject's forehead until the tip began to cause pain. Sensitivity to pain was thought by Galton to be related to intelligence. But it wasn't. The tests were a failure. One of Cattell's students was able to show that there was no link between the tests and academic performance.

The pioneer psychologists were disappointed but not deterred by such results. The French-born psychologist, Alfred Binet, carried out some tests of his own, homing in on one of the Cattell tests, in which a set of dividers with rubber ends on the points was applied to the skin of the person undergoing the test, who was then asked if he could detect the separation without looking. As the points were moved closer together, the "twoness" of the points became more difficult to discern. Apart from observing the different distribution of nerves in the body, the experiments did little to advance medical science and nothing to advance psychology. But Binet became hooked on the subject. He began looking at the psychological theories of John Stuart Mill.

The young John Mill had ploughed his way through most of the Greek and Latin classics by the time he was twelve, when he wrote a book-length history of Roman government. He was a brilliant child, in the academic sense of brilliance, but he would have made a poor Artful Dodger, lacking social skills and basic practical know-how. He was hopeless at dressing himself and had still not learned how to brush his hair by the age of fourteen.

Mill had been taught at home, sharing a desk with his father, the philosopher James Mill, and he put his knowledge down to his father's teaching. From the lessons of his own experience he was attracted to the ideas of John Locke, the English philosopher, who held that the mind of a newborn child is a blank slate that receives impressions from its surrounding environment and develops ideas by association with external influences. The associationist ideas of Locke and David Hume had held sway for most of the nineteenth century. Their theories underlined Adam Smith's thinking, in that he believed the economic wand of capitalism could transform the less well developed societies, whose inhabitants he felt sure could be converted to the ways of civilization. "The difference of natural talents in different men is, in reality, much less than we are aware of," he wrote in the *Wealth of Nations*. "The difference between the most dissimilar characters . . . seems to arise not so much from nature as from habit, custom, and education."[5]

Behind these influences of habit, custom, and education were Locke's and Hume's ideas, expanded and developed by Mill. Contact with external stimuli made through the senses, thought Mill, could generate particular thoughts. A familiar smell, for instance, could trigger a memory or strengthen or magnify an idea. He saw the development of ideas as the formulation of a recipe, a mental chemistry pulling together various ingredients which could combine like a chemical reaction to form what he called a "complex idea." This was a contrasting avenue of thought to that of Galton.

These two different strands of thinking formed the beginning of what has ever since been referred to as the "nature versus nurture" debate, although people had been deliberating over the source and nature of the intellect for centuries. In 1637 René Descartes had famously declared *cogito ergo sum* – I think therefore I am – concluding that it was the power of reasoning that set man apart from the animals.[6] Cartesian dualism, the idea that body and mind were separate from each other, had been the stimulus for linking reactions to brainpower.

The study of reactions was leading nowhere. If some measure capable of distinguishing intellectual ability were to be devised, it would need some new avenue of exploration. This avenue was supplied by Alfred Binet, a French psychologist who, like Sigmund Freud, had studied under the neurologist Jean-Martin Charcot, director of the Salpêtrière Hospital in Paris. Charcot had established the first postgraduate center for psychiatric education at Salpêtrière. Both Binet and Freud were drawn to Charcot's investigations of hypnosis and hysteria. Freud trotted back to his home city of Vienna to develop the art of psychoanalysis, which would spread like an addiction, feeding the peculiar neuroses and hang-ups of a regressively Puritan American society. Binet, however, used the experience to broaden his associationist ideas, which had not hitherto allowed for the indirectness and variation of individual thinking. Binet made observations about the difference in people's ability to sustain their attention in some specific area. Experimenting with the reaction times of his two young daughters, he found that on average they reacted more slowly than adults, but not always. From this he concluded that the ability to sustain attention to a task was important and that children tended to have a shorter attention span than adults. He also noticed that children made different distinctions than adults between words. Confronted with the word "snail," an adult might say "mollusk," aware that the snail could be defined. But the young misses Binet said "squash it." Had they said "eat it," they might have taken their father's thinking into the area of cultural differences, but they did not – so thinking about cultural impacts on individuals, society, and finally on the workplace would have to wait a while.

Binet's observations of his daughters had further value. He noticed that each of them adopted a different approach to learning to walk. One of them, Madeleine, moved herself cautiously from one support to another, while the other, Alice, was more confident, "staggering like a drunken man" a few steps into the middle of the room. Madeleine's thoughtfulness, contrasting with Alice's impulsiveness, led Binet to conclude that people differed in the *way* that they thought.[7] People had different styles of thinking.

He continued to devise tests for his daughters as they grew up. Madeleine he described as *l'observateur* (the observer), while Alice was *l'imaginitif* (the imaginative one).[8] When asked as a teenager to describe a chestnut leaf, Madeleine recorded her observations about the color, size, and number of the follicles. She noted the "ramified nervures" of the leaf that enabled her to classify the tree as a docotyledon. Alice, on the other hand, wrote that the leaf had "fallen languidly in the autumn wind . . . Yesterday, hanging from the branch it awaited the fatal flow of wind that would carry it off, like a dying person who awaits his final agony."[9]

It is to Binet, then, that the modern personality test concentrating on thinking styles – the way that people approach their work – owes its development. It is to Binet also that we owe a thousand newspaper questionnaires on the lines of: "Are you an Alice or a Madeleine?" Defining the different types, or dimensions, of thinking style and devising a reasonably straightforward test for them was the next logical step, but the best efforts of Binet and his assistant, Victor Henri, working on a test for schoolchildren, failed to deliver anything that could be usefully related to children's educational performance.

With a different assistant, Theodore Simon, Binet began to look at ways of grading mentally subnormal children so that they could be educated in groups of similar ability. Binet and Simon developed a series of tasks of gradually increasing complexity. The idea was that all children could complete the simplest tasks, but as tasks became more difficult it was possible to arrive at a "normal" age for completing a particular task. This allowed the testers to determine that a child, for example, might be ten years old but, because of his or her performance in the test, might display the intellectual capabilities of a seven-year-old.

These were the first true intelligence tests and formed the basis for the intelligence quotient, or IQ, devised by the US psychologist, William Stern. Stern suggested that the mental age of a child could be divided by its chronological age to provide a "mental quotient." Lewis Terman, a Stanford psychologist, preferred to use the now familiar term, "intelligence quotient." An American version of the test, developed by Terman and called the Stanford-Binet test, would become the adopted measure of intelligence in the US school system for the next twenty years.[10]

The intelligence quotient was like a toy in the hands of psychologists. They couldn't leave it alone. One favorite pastime was to work out the possible IQs of long-dead academics like Mill, who was estimated to have had an IQ of 190, while Galton's childhood IQ was reckoned to have been 200.[11] Whether it was IQ or eccentricity that drove him – perhaps they are related – Galton at times seemed a caricature of the mad scientist. In an attempt to induce behavior changes in himself he stuck a magazine cartoon on a wall and convinced himself of its godlike capabilities, treating it with reverence. The experiment worked, and he became superstitious toward it, bestowing on it the power of reward and punishment. In an even riskier exercise he sought to investigate insanity by producing in himself a state of paranoia. He invested objects, whether living or inanimate, with the attributes of a spy. In a short space of time he was imagining that people and animals were watching him, intent on an act of espionage. Genius or oddball? This was a man who wanted to breed a race of superhumans, and he was not alone.

In the meantime, however, the power of IQ testing for selection, rather than selective breeding, was considered important enough to arouse the interest of government. The entry of the United States into the First World War led to a countrywide recruitment drive for the military. Robert Yerkes, president of the American Psychological Association, decided the Stanford-Binet test could be used not only for screening out educationally subnormal recruits but also for identifying the best performers for officer training. The Stanford-Binet test was not ideal for assessing large groups of people, some of whom would be illiterate, so two new tests were devised – the Alpha test for those who could read and the Beta test for those who could not. By the time of the Armistice in November 1918 some 1,750,000 men had taken either Alpha or Beta tests.[12] The wartime testing demonstrated the potential for testing on a commercial scale. If tests could find the best recruits for the military, why couldn't they find future managers and business leaders?

Walter Dill Scott had been making this very point at Western Electric in 1915, two years before the United States entered the war. He had already begun to run psychological tests at the company by April, 1917, when he was drafted onto the wartime committee that established the Alpha and Beta tests. After the war he devised the first officer selection test for the US Army. Meanwhile Western Electric began to use the army's Alpha test to assess men who were either applying for jobs or for transfers into clerical and production work.[13]

Dill Scott has received scant attention in the story of psychological testing and yet, with powerful reasoning, his business writing took the autocratic Victorian businessman by the scruff of the neck and dragged him into a new age of multifunctional management teams and specialist personnel. The growth of the joint-stock company meant that in the previous century even the likes of George Pullman had been forced to heed the concerns of stockholders who wanted to be assured that the managers of their businesses were pulling out all the stops to improve efficiency and competitiveness.

Frederick Taylor had pointed the way to more efficient methods of working, insisting that "a first-class man can, in most cases, do from two to four times as much as is done on the average."[14] Dill Scott recognized that such increases in output could not be engineered without first-class management. "Men who know how to get maximum results out of machines are common," he wrote, but "the power to get the maximum of work out of subordinates or out of yourself is a much rarer possession."[15]

As an example of human physical potential combined with the personal will to push himself to the limit, Scott quotes the achievement of Edward Payson Weston, who at the age of seventy walked from New York to San Francisco in 104 days without stopping. His best distance over twenty-four hours was eighty-seven miles. "We have a choice between wearing out and rusting out. Most of us unwittingly have chosen the rusting process," wrote Scott.[16] After reading of Weston's exploits we might be forgiven for deciding that rusting is better. But that would be inexcusable in a society driven by Protestant fervor. There are shades of the *Reader's Digest* in the wholesomeness of Scott's advice. You can feel the motherhood and smell the apple pie. You can visualize the figure of old Mr Weston marching ever onwards, like Forrest Gump, until he reaches the sea.

Scott's *Increasing Human Efficiency in Business* pulls a veil over the nineteenth-century sweatshop and unfolds the prospect of a more regulated, enlightened environment where care for human welfare is part of the productivity equation. He writes of loyalty to the company and of the "love of the game," the idea that work itself must appeal to the individual as something important and useful. Here was something novel. This was placing the emphasis not just on individuals to enjoy their work because it was their duty to do so; it was expecting employers to ensure that the work they supplied had some meaning.

Edison had achieved this at Menlo Park, but he did not run a production line where the urge was to make ever-increasing volumes, where speeding up the line could antagonize employees into disruptive action. The gulf between the ideal and reality in most workplaces remained as wide as ever. But people like Scott were beginning to increase their influence in the relatively new discipline of personnel management.

Hugo Munsterberg, like Cattell and Dill Scott a product of the Leipzig school, was another important early influence on workplace psychology. Munsterberg, who became the director of the psychological laboratory at Harvard University, described a program of industrial psychology when lecturing as an exchange professor at the University of Berlin around 1910 or 1911. Outlining the "big prize" that he believed was achievable in the study of occupational psychology, he envisioned a society where "mental dissatisfaction in the weak, mental depression and discouragement, may be replaced in our social community by overflowing joy and perfect inner harmony."[17] There is no sweeter song than that from the mouth of an idealist.

A humanist camp was developing strength, led by people like Elton Mayo and Mary Parker Follett. Follett was ahead of her time in her conviction that management and workers would need to cooperate more closely to move their companies forward. It didn't come easy to management then, and it still doesn't, but some companies have begun to pay more attention to Follett's ideas in recent years. In the interwar years she was sought out by businesses in an effort to improve their industrial relations. At that time, unions were becoming more organized and more politicized. The workshop had become a battleground between management and labor.

Manufacturing work on the Taylorized assembly line had lost the old pride and experience and magic of the artisan's skill. Work or the chance of work had been ravaged by depression. Consumerism and the cash nexus were maintaining order of sorts, where work was in supply. In Germany, work or the hope of work had propelled the sinister dogma of Nazism to power. Taylorist ideas in Japan had been swept aside by the militarist regime that set itself against anything that declared itself a science. Work in every industrialized country remained the vital component of production as man and machine combined, not in the pre-First World War artistic ideal of the Futurist movement but in a highly controlled and supervised atmosphere. Work and the promised deliverance of work were at the height of the political agenda the world over. Work could liberate. Work, said the Nazis, could make you free.

CHAPTER 14

Arbeit Macht Frei

> Consider whether this is a man,
> Who labors in the mud
> Who knows no peace
> Who fights for a crust of bread
> Who dies at a yes or a no.
> (Primo Levi, 1919–87)

Otto Ambros was one of Germany's most outstanding talents in the production of synthetic rubber. In the winter of 1940 he was asked by the head of his company to evaluate two possible factory sites for a new European plant. Ambros had been the protégé of Richard Willstaetter, the Nobel laureate for chemistry who had been driven out of his native country because of his Jewish faith. Now the laureate's former pupil was a board director of IG Farben, the chemical conglomerate and Germany's biggest company.[1] Its supervisory board leader, Carl Krauch, had approached him to check out the two potential sites. One site was in Norway. The other was in Polish Silesia.

The contract was vital for raising the production of Buna, the name given to synthetic rubber, to a level of 150,000 tons annually, an output considered essential if the German military was to be supplied with all its requirements for the planned attack on Russia. This would be the single largest project in the IG system, one to which the parent company would commit 900 million Reichsmarks, over $250 million at the time it was conceived.

Walking over the two sites, Ambros could see that the Norwegian proposal had several disadvantages compared to the alternative. The chances of sabotage in Norway were far greater, and any plant might be more easily hit by British bombers. The other site, conversely, looked ideal. It was flat and featureless scrub, pasture, and woodland. There was a coal mine not far away and the site was close to the convergence of three rivers, the railway, and an autobahn. The biggest advantage of all, however, was a ready supply of labor from a nearby concentration camp which the SS had plans to expand.[2]

Yes, thought Ambros, this factory site on the outskirts of a small town the Poles called Oświęcim would be the perfect location for corporate expansion. The Germans had another name for the town. They called it Auschwitz. The IG Auschwitz division was formed to handle the building and production, and Ambros was selected as director of rubber production alongside Heinrich Buetefisch, who would head up a synthetic oil plant on the same site.

Krauch, a former professor of chemistry at Heidelberg University, arranged with Hermann Goering, the Reichsmarschal, for the labor needed for the plant's construction. Goering approached Heinrich Himmler in February, 1941, requesting that the "largest possible number of skilled and unskilled production workers . . . be made available from the adjoining concentration camp for the construction of the Buna plant."[3] The company estimated it would need between eight and twelve thousand construction workers and agreed to pay the SS four marks a day for skilled camp inmates, three marks a day for the unskilled, and one and a half marks a day for any child labor. The workers themselves would receive nothing. The productive capacity of these forced workers was estimated at about 75 percent efficiency. When Himmler agreed to allocate an immediate contingent of ten thousand prisoners, Ambros wrote to a colleague that "our new friendship with the SS is proving very profitable."[4]

It was a marriage of Mammon and the Devil. As Jews stepped down from the cattle trucks into which they had been packed for transportation across Europe, they were met by guards with dogs at an assembly point between two fenced areas of barrack huts at the newly constructed Birkenau, about three kilometers from the original Auschwitz concentration camp. Once inside, the new arrivals were placed in two lines: those fit for work, many of whom would be allocated to the oil and rubber plant, and those pronounced unfit, who would be led straight to the gas chambers.

The SS leaders had created some camps and remodeled others – Chelmno, Treblinka, Belzec, Majdanek, Sobibor, and

Auschwitz-Birkenau were the biggest – on industrial lines where the machinery and operations were dedicated to the obliteration of people. The gas chambers and crematoria they commissioned were conceived as if they were process plants, essential stages in a highly efficient line of human destruction established with all the attention to detail demanded by the principles of scientific management.

Ulrich Wengenroth, a technology historian, described Auschwitz as "the Taylorization of the killing of the Jewish people."[5] Auschwitz-Birkenau and the other extermination camps were the alternate face of mass production, an industry dedicated to genocide that could only contract as it succeeded in its mission. As perhaps 2 million Jews and other prisoners were gassed in the Birkenau complex at Auschwitz, others were allocated as slave labor for IG Farben's oil and rubber business.

Slavery had emerged again almost midway through the twentieth century. But did it ever go away? The Nazis had not been the first of the century's German administrations to employ forced labor. Pressed by industrialists to meet their labor shortages during the First World War, the German High Command ordered the army in November, 1916 to begin the forced transportation of Belgians to work in German factories. Men were loaded into cattle trucks at bayonet point. Some 66,000 Belgians were deported in this way, but the program failed when the Belgians refused to work in spite of threats and promises.[6] The Germans were prepared to bully but would not go to the extremes sanctioned later by the Nazis.

Between the wars Joseph Stalin had established his Gulags, the Soviet Union's version of the concentration camps, where millions were taken and never returned during the terror of the 1930s' purges. The Gulag, an acronym of the Chief Administration of Corrective Labor Camps, part of the Soviet secret police, was, according to the historian Alan Bullock, "an enormous network of penal institutions, inhabited by a population of slaves, who made up some 10 percent of the total Soviet workforce and who could be worked literally to death, at the cost of a third of the average worker's wages."[7] Somewhere between 2 and 4 million people are thought to have been held in the camps at any one time.[8]

The new slave labor was different in one respect from that of classical times – the slaves were not chattels to be traded. They would only be preserved as long as they had some use. In many ways it was much worse, because in the Russian and German labor camps there was little incentive to preserve the worker. People were replaceable. They could be worked and starved to death.

The Nazi attitude to work and imprisonment was ambiguous. To give prisoners work was to offer some hope, because work was part of the Nazi ethos. Work was good. It was uplifting, energizing, the physical embodiment of the spiritual ideal of blood and soil. The Protestant work ethic, long since secularized, had been seized upon and refashioned as a central plank of Nazi idealism. In the new Nazi lexicon, the word *Arbeit*, meaning work, was given an almost mystical status. It was combined with other constructs to create a new series of words. They are explained in *Nazi–Deutsch*, a dictionary of Nazi words and phrases, compiled and published in New York in 1943. There is *Arbeitertum* – workerdom, *Arbeitseinsatz* – the mobilization of labor, *Arbeitsgemeinschaft* – a pool or cartel of factories, *Arbeitslager* – a work camp for students, *Arbeitsmann* – a man in labor service, *Arbeitsmaid* – a woman in labor service, and there is *Arbeitsethos* – the worship of work or ethics of work.[9]

Phrases such as *Arbeiter der Stirn und Faust* (workers of the head and of the fist) were created to demonstrate the notion that workers were accorded a special status in the social order, but they were not seen as a class in the Marxist sense. The idea was that the worker and workmanship had a permanence, a fixed and secure state – neither bourgeois nor proletarian – that did not aspire either to climb the social ladder or overthrow the social order. It was a folksy view of the worker. In the same way, the word *Volk* was quite literally presented as a folksy view of the populace.

The Nazis had taken the concept of *Arbeitsfreude* – joy in work – and added their own gloss. *Arbeitsfreude* was the guiding spirit of the German Werkbund, a 1907 alliance of artisans, craftsmen, and industrialists who aimed at revitalizing German culture by combining industry with artistry. The idea, similar to the craft movement in England inspired by William Morris, was to reject

Victorian excess and revive the craftsmanship that had existed in medieval times. The Werkbund sought to improve the quality of design among German products and, in so doing, restore the satisfaction of the worker in a job well done.[10] But work was far too important to belong to a single creed. Work and the promise of work were the interwar battleground of left and right.

The religious basis of the work ethic mattered not to the Nazis, who drew their inspirations from many sources. In his book, *Why Did the Heavens not Darken*, Arno Mayer points out that Hitler styled certain aspects of the movement on Catholic tradition, arguing, for example, that the campaign against Russia was pursued as a holy war against "Judobolshevism." The Nazis were indiscriminate in their ideological plunder. They pulled their imagery as much from paganism and classical antiquity as from Catholicism. In a country whose industries had made a specialization out of synthesizing materials, Nazism was an "ersatz" ideology from the start, with every constituent designed for its appeal to the most basic – and baser – instincts of humanity. It was acutely conscious of popular desires and popular feeling.

The Nazi Party's full name was the National Socialist German Workers' Party. Work and the search for work were a preoccupation of those who lived through the depression years during the party's embryonic stage. When the slogan, *Arbeit Macht Frei –* Work Makes Free – was fashioned within the wrought iron gateway of Dachau, the first of the concentration camps, in 1933, it was intended not as some cynical taunt, as some have suggested, but as a message holding out the prospect of salvation. It declared that freedom could indeed be obtained through work in a spiritual sense and might occasionally even be attained in the reality of a prisoner's release.[11]

Uppermost in the message was the personal spiritual freedom promised by the Protestant work ethic. The ideal must have seemed remote and unattainable for those restrained within the camp systems. But it was, nevertheless, a constituent of the Nazi Valhalla to which, as far as the party leadership was concerned, its correctional prisoners could aspire, even if their aspirations would be, in most cases, hopeless.

The slogan was certainly not intended for Russian war prisoners. Nor was it intended for the Jews, few of whom were

being thrown into concentration camps in 1933. The first intern-
ees to walk past the sign were Germans, mostly socialists and
other political opponents, rounded up when the Nazis first came
into power. Some have argued that the positioning of the *Arbeit
Macht Frei* slogan over the gates of Auschwitz was part of the
deception maintained to convince the newly arriving deportees
that they were to be put to work. The broad scale of the Nazi
deception is evident in the layout of the extermination camps,
where the use of some buildings was concealed to hide the truth
of the final solution. But *Arbeit Macht Frei* was not part of this
deception. The vast majority of the Jews who died at Auschwitz
were delivered straight to Birkenau and never saw the gate of the
earliest Auschwitz camp.

Even today, there is much confusion over the German concentration camp system, because so many camps had different uses and some were adapted for another role during the war.
Dachau, the converted munitions plant, just ten miles to the north
of Munich, the spiritual home of Nazism, had been the first of
the concentration camps, opened in March, 1933 by Heinrich
Himmler, Munich's then chief of police. Dachau was the proto-
type, described initially as a "concentration camp for political
prisoners." The idea was to concentrate communists, Marxists,
and anyone else considered a threat to the state. The round up of
Jews came later.

Gas chambers were constructed at Dachau late in the war but
were never used. Only four camps – Chelmno, Belzec, Sobibor,
and Treblinka in eastern Poland – were specifically conceived as
extermination camps. None of these operated for more than seventeen months. At least 2 million Jews and 52,000 gypsies were
murdered there. Only 82 prisoners survived these four camps.[12]
Once the camps had served their purpose, the sites were cleared
and planted with trees.

Auschwitz-Birkenau was a series of camps serving different
purposes. The IG Farben plant even had its own camp within the
complex at Monovitz. The camp was administered by company
personnel instead of the SS, but it still had its gallows, and prisoners still died there in their thousands.

Many of the camps in Poland were close to others originally
constructed to hold Russian prisoners of war. The Russians could

have been worked from the start but the Nazi high command preferred to let them starve. Forced labor was not considered initially as a use for Germany's prisoners of war. It is arguable that many more Russian prisoners of war might have survived their internment had the Nazis decided earlier to exploit their labor.

Such exploitation may have done no more than delay their deaths, but delay was the only hope for most of those channeled into the concentration camp system. The decision to use Russian labor in the fall of 1941 was made out of necessity, after the German armies had been checked before Moscow, and losses were being replenished from the ranks of workers engaged in farming and industrial production. But by that time many of Germany's Russian prisoners had already perished.

The Germans took 3,350,000 Russian prisoners in the first six months of the campaign begun in June, 1941.[13] Of these, 2 million would die in prison camps before the end of the war. The Germans had decided before the launch of Barbarossa, the invasion of Russia, that any prisoners would be regarded as "useless mouths," and could not expect adequate provisions. By December, 1941, 1,400,000 of them had died.

As the Russians were being left to starve in their camps, German soldiers were also dying on the Eastern Front, and their replacements were leaving ever broadening gaps in the German workforce. At the start of the year there had been no great labor shortage, but by September the labor shortfall was 2.6 million. The biggest shortages were in metalworking (800,000), agriculture (500,000), and construction (140,000). This was in spite of the use of some 3 million foreign workers across the Reich.

In mid-October, therefore, Hitler abandoned his previous stance against the use of Russian prisoners of war for labor, declaring: "It is necessary to exploit this cheap source of labor, as we would have to feed the prisoners in any case, and it would be absurd for them to remain idle, merely useless mouths to feed in the camps."

Their deployment was slow. By the end of March, 1942 only 166,881 had been put to work. This was not out of sympathy for the prisoners. "The current labor shortage would not have arisen," declared Plenipotentiary for Labor Deployment, Werner Mansfeld, "if a decision to deploy Russian POWs on a large scale had been made in time. There were 3.9 million Russians available; now only 1.1 million are left. Just in the period from November 1941 to January 1942, 500,000 Russians died."[14] But in the camp system the Nazis were never prepared to provide sufficient rations for inmates.

Plans were submitted to Himmler in April, 1942 for other work programs to be established in the network of twenty-three concentration camps. Forced labor was drawn from across Europe. By the end of September, 1944 about 7.5 million foreign laborers had been pressed into service, working for the Third Reich.[15] The Reich's need for labor was so great that in the latter stages of the war it began to use Jews in armaments production. Some people were simply plucked off the streets or were caught in SS cordons as they attempted to go about their daily lives. Others were known dissidents. John Dalmau, a Spanish Socialist, exiled from his own country at the end of the Spanish Civil War, was fighting for the French when he was captured during the German advance in 1940. He and two thousand other Spanish captives were transferred to laboring duties in the Channel Islands. He was among fifty-nine of his countrymen to survive.

In *Slave Worker*, a short account of his experience, he recalls the arrival of Russian prisoners in August, 1942. "Along the road to La Corbière a long column of crawling humanity came into the camp. They were Russians, men, women, and children – two thousand of them, the remains of 150,000 who had walked across Europe, a trophy of the German war machine. Their feet were bare. Only a few of them had rags as footwear. Without exception they were living skeletons, incapable of walking more than half-a-mile an hour."[16]

How Hitler believed such individuals could be capable of constructing his Atlantic Wall defies explanation, but nothing about this slave labor regime makes much sense. The death camps showed the extremes of cruelty that man is capable of inflicting on his fellow man; more than that they showed that people were prepared to utilize industrial efficiency as a means of human extermination and disposal. The fate of the Channel Island slaves, even their usefulness, seemed to be immaterial to their captors. Some starved, some were shot, and some were pushed off cliffs. In the sea wall on Alderney, one of the smaller islands of the group, several hundred Russian slaves are entombed in the concrete. Was this really what the Nazis meant by their slogan *Arbeit Macht Frei*?

Too often we try to apply ordinary common sense to the Nazis, approaching Germany's wartime dilemmas from a point of view that might be expected in a balanced democratic society. It is the same mistake that elevates intellectual brilliance over other aspects of the human spirit. We read admiring accounts of the German war machine and the strategies of its generals, and historians play games of "what if?" as if they almost wished that Hitler's troops had crossed the English Channel or had taken Moscow. They fail to recognize that an ideology so rotten, so corrupt as Nazism was set on a course of self-destruction from the beginning.

The only outstanding question was how much damage this virulent ideology could inflict among all it encountered before it was consumed in the same flames it had itself ignited. When all but Hitler among the Nazi leadership could see that the game was up, some began preparing their escape routes. Others, like Hitler himself, would continue inexorably toward the black hole of their own making, taking with them their enemies in their millions.

Slave labor was used in Germany prior to Hitler's agreement, but it was organized at a corporate level. When Fritz Sauckel was appointed Plenipotentiary General for the Allocation of Labor, putting him in charge of the slave labor program in March, 1942, he was surprised to discover that IG Farben had already been "wildly recruiting foreign labor."[17] As late as 1943 the Reich Minister of Economics was writing to the company's offices seeking suggestions about how to go about recruiting conquered workers. The Farben managers were considered the experts.

In 1941 IG Farben had already assigned to its plants ten thousand forced laborers. In 1942 the slave contingent had risen to twenty-two thousand, by 1943 it was fifty-eight thousand, and by 1945 it numbered well over a hundred thousand.[18] Their method before 1941, when they were scouring the newly conquered territories of Western Europe, was to ask the laborer whom they were pressing into service to sign a contract. Those who refused were forced to go to Germany anyway. Failure to comply would result in the removal of their ration cards. They could work or they could starve. The conscripts were also told that they would be refused further work in their homeland and that members of their families could face reprisals. Those who came to the IG Farben plants had no freedom of movement. If they escaped, the Gestapo were asked to track them down.

As Josiah DuBois, the US prosecutor of IG Farben management at Nuremburg, put it: "Before Fritz Sauckel took over conscription of labor; before Himmler committed the incredibly sadistic deeds that finally led him to suicide; before Hitler announced for the Jews an extermination that was to spread like an instant fever to Poland and then to the whole of Europe; before enforced labor of any kind was a Reich policy, foreigners and prisoners of war had already been enslaved . . . in the IG Farben camps."[19]

Historians have argued about the German motives behind the use of forced labor. Hans Mommsen has rightly pointed out that "the fiction behind which the 'final solution' was concealed was the mobilization of labor." But this fiction could only succeed where there was a genuine need for such mobilization. As war losses increased, there was an escalating need for substitute labor if the Germans were to push ahead with their grand plan.

By the end of the Wannsee conference in January, 1942, there seems to have been consolidated a three-pronged approach to achieving Hitler's objectives: firstly, war as the means of conquest and acquisition of territory; secondly, extermination (with some resettlement of non-Jews) as the means of cleansing the occupied territories of undesirables; thirdly, construction programs, utilizing forced labor, to rebuild the most important cities in the image of the Aryan state.

The Jews were to be annihilated. The skills of some would be exploited, but only as a stopgap. Some have argued that there was a policy, where Jewish labor had been sanctioned, to work the Jews to death – *Vernichtung durch Arbeit*, extermination through labor. Sometimes prisoners were asked to move stones from one pile to another, then to move them back again. This was work as a kind of torture, close to the notion of *Vernichtung durch Arbeit*. Whether or not this was a deliberate policy, there can be no doubt that there was a deep indifference among Nazis to the continuing survival of any Jew. Using work as a form of extermination makes no more sense than using the labor of weakened and starving people.

This seems to have been understood by Mansfeld who, when seeking to organize some effective Russian prisoner labor, pointed out that it was "absurd to transport these workers in open or unheated freight cars, only to unload dead bodies at their final destination." This was not said out of any humanitarian concern; it was the voice of managerial efficiency, the voice of Columella calling down over the centuries from ancient Rome, that informed the remark. Mansfeld urged Reinhard Heydrich, head of the SD, the SS intelligence service, to instigate better treatment and introduce some leisure time for the Russian workers. "Effective treatment, not excessively harsh, was of great and immediate importance," wrote Mansfeld. He might have been whistling in the wind as far as Heydrich was concerned. This was a regime that had long since abandoned any vestiges of predictability or logic in its behavior.

The work at the IG Farben plant offered only the slimmest chance of survival to those selected for labor. Of the thirty-five thousand prisoners taken into the synthetic rubber works, at least twenty-five thousand died. On average some ten thousand Jewish laborers were employed there at any one time. The life expectancy of a worker was three to four months.

The regime was described by one former inmate:

We worked in the huge Buna plant, to which we were herded each morning about 3 a.m. At midday our food consisted of potato and turnip soup, and in the evening we received some bread. During work we were terribly mistreated. As our working place was situated outside the large chain of sentry posts, it was divided into small sectors of 10 x 10 meters, each guarded by an SS man. Whoever stepped outside these squares during working hours was immediately shot without warning for having "attempted to escape." Often it happened that out of pure spite an SS man would order a prisoner to fetch some given object outside his square. If he followed the order, he was shot for having left his assigned space . . . Very few could bear the strain and although escape seemed hopeless, attempts were made every day. The result was several hangings a week.[20]

Germany under Adolf Hitler never seemed to come to terms with its use of manual labor among prisoners. The concentration camp system would not have ended with the killing of every Jew in Europe. There is no evidence that the Nazis considered slave labor or the concentration of prisoners as a temporary remedy. There were plans to double the size of Majdanek, which would have made it capable of holding 200,000 people, almost twice the size of Auschwitz-Birkenau. Who would have been its prisoners? Russians? Poles? Germans?

In *Mein Kampf*, written in 1923, Hitler had characterized the people of eastern Europe as a service population for the "superior races" of Western Europe. He envisaged a slave society – a Slavic society, indeed, if we recall the origins of the word – working for its Aryan masters. Those who would not or could not work would die. The Nazi approach to forced labor was a chilling reminder that the association of work with the restriction of individual freedom is a recurring theme throughout human history. In a poem made famous after his death, Martin Niemoller, the First World War U-boat commander turned Lutheran priest, chided his countrymen for not speaking out.

Business did not speak out. Business went along with the regime. Business, the capitalist employer of labor, did not earn a great reputation for maintaining the lives of slave laborers in the German Reich. This was what made the story of Oscar Schindler and the maintenance of his Jewish workforce so striking. Schindler's factory in Kraków never made anything useful. His enterprise, if it had any aim at all, was that of saving life. This may not have been the reason for its creation – Schindler was an entrepreneur and a Nazi who knew his way around the party apparatus – but the survival of his workforce became the focus of his ambition.

Schindler's imperative was absent in IG Farben, but its directors did not suffer too harshly for their crimes. No one from the company received a prison sentence longer than eight years. Four men, including Ambros and Krauch, were convicted of slavery and mass murder. Josiah E. DuBois, the chief prosecutor, described the sentences as "light enough to please a chicken thief."

It was no more than he had expected. "I was reliably informed that, even before the trial started," he wrote, "one of the judges had expressed the view that he didn't believe it was ever intended that industrialists be brought to account for preparing and waging an aggressive war." It is as if the head of large businesses are exempted from the motives and emotions that drive ordinary mortals.

But industry and industrialists were involved. The techniques for killing people employed in the extermination camps had been devised in the Nazis' euthanasia program. The Zyklon B gas was made by Degesch, an IG Farben-controlled affiliate company. Degesch was reluctant to supply the gas to the SS; not because of its intended use, but because the SS wanted it without any odor, and the odor, or "indicator," to use the terminology of the chemist, was the only constituent to which Degesch held a patent. Degesch directors were not sickened at the end use; they were terrified that another manufacturer might steal the product. This was the morality of IG Farben and the companies under its control. [21]

The Nazis had industrialized murder, and the industrial system was placed at their disposal. Sometimes the system was left wanting. After all the deaths and cruelty at IG Auschwitz, the plant never succeeded in making any synthetic rubber. "Buna Auschwitz was not only the most appalling failure in the history of modern industry – it had no parallel anywhere in history in the uneconomical exploitation of labor," wrote DuBois. He might have saved his breath. In later years, Otto Ambros continued to share his knowledge with executives in Western chemical companies, including some in the US.

The IG Farben executives escaped too lightly. Anyone prepared to work his fellow man to death should be judged with the same severity as that meted out to those who sanctioned the system. "Never Again," it says on the death camp monuments. But history has a habit of repeating itself. How will business leaders react if it does? Is it within the nature of business to cultivate itself as the moral bastion of society, to speak out against despotism, or will it once more sink to the level of willing accomplice? This is a test for the future.

Whatever Happened to Homer Sarasohn?

Had Deming and I stayed at home, the Japanese would have achieved world quality leadership all the same.

(Joseph Juran, b. 1904)

On the afternoon of November 21, 1949, in Osaka, Japan, a young radio engineer from Raytheon stood in front of a classroom full of Japanese telecommunications experts and began to lecture them on the fundamentals of business management. The engineer's name was Homer Sarasohn. He and a few other electronics experts had been co-opted from their companies and assigned to the command headquarters of General Douglas MacArthur in Japan. The victors were teaching the vanquished.

It was not a day too soon. Immediately after the end of the Second World War in 1945 the big family corporations in Japan, the so-called Zaibatsu companies, had been dissolved by the US high command, determined to prevent any re-establishment of the kind of economic and military cooperation that had characterized the Japanese military regime during the war.

This anti-capitalist policy, however, had played straight into the hands of socialist militants and trade unions. Strikes and agitation were commonplace in Japanese companies as they struggled to rebuild their industries. Communism was dominating Eastern Europe and China, and by late 1948 the United States had changed its policy. If Japan was to see off the communist threat, reasoned Washington, it would need a strong capitalist base. The corporate sector needed to succeed, preferably in the American way.

But just what was this American way? What were the Japanese to learn? Scientific management all over again? Japanese companies were in serious trouble. A series of case studies in the telecommunications sector carried out by a group of American engineers made dismal reading. Some 75 percent of Japanese tele-communications infrastructure had been destroyed by bombing. Even where it survived it was not working to capacity. Three years after the end of the war the telephone lines between Tokyo and Osaka were open twenty-four hours a day, but they were only manned for nine hours a day, the duration of a single shift.[1] The companies, the engineers reported, were overstaffed, and their management was inefficient and weak. Delegation of authority was nonexistent. "The weaknesses of management were causing a tide of regression which, allowed to go unchecked, might well culminate in the collapse of the industry," warned the engineers.[2]

The engineers, led by Frank Polkinghorn, a radar and communications design expert at Bell Laboratories, the research arm of AT&T, were attached to the headquarters' Civil Communications Section (CCS). Their study led to a proposal for a series of seminars in Tokyo and Osaka, designed initially for the telecommunications industry. Not everyone among the occupation authorities was supportive of the classes. Officers in the Economics and Social Section (ESS) were worried the seminars could be too successful, giving the Japanese a competitive edge. MacArthur heard the opposing arguments put by Homer Sarasohn, the group's radio adviser, and an ESS official. As the meeting ended the general turned to Sarasohn and said, "Go do it."[3]

With Charles Protzman, the telephone engineering adviser also seconded from Western Electric, Sarasohn put together a textbook for the seminars. Sarasohn covered the section on management philosophy, which he would use for the first lecture. When Sarasohn entered the wooden-framed lecture room to deliver his first class he was just thirty-three years old. In front of him was the cream of Japanese telecommunications talent, people like Masaharu Matsushita, the adopted son of Konosuke Matsushita, the charismatic founder of Matsushita Electrical. It would not be an overestimation of the importance of the occasion to say that when this young American radio engineer mounted the podium, paper in hand, the hopes of Japan were assembled at his feet.

An occasion of such significance demanded something special, but management texts cannot normally be relied upon to deliver anything out of the ordinary. The class was expecting an outline of management processes sprinkled with technical language. Sarasohn was an engineer and young to boot, with little experience of management. But perhaps he felt there was a need to approach the subject from its roots. He was, after all, working with an almost blank sheet. So Sarasohn's lecture began with the most fundamental of questions: "Why does any company exist?" Pursuing the theme, he continued:

What is the reason for being of any enterprise? Many people would probably answer these questions by saying that the purpose of a company is to make profit. In fact, if I were to ask you to write down right now the principal reason why your companies are in business I suppose that most of the answers would be something of this sort.

But such a statement is not a complete idea, nor is it a satisfactory answer, because it does not clearly state the objective of the company, the principal goal that the company management is to strive for. A company's objective should be stated in a way that will not permit of any uncertainty as to its real fundamental purpose. For example, there are two ways of looking at that statement about profit. One is to make the product for a cost less than the price at which it is to be sold. The other is to sell the product for a price higher than it costs to make.

These two views are almost the same. But not quite. The first implies a cost-conscious attitude on the part of the company. The second seems to say whatever the product costs, it will be sold at a higher price.

There is another fault I would find in such a statement. It is entirely selfish and one-sided. It ignores entirely the sociological aspects which should be a part of a company's thinking. A business enterprise should be based on its responsibility to the public, upon service to its customers, and upon the realization that it can and does exert some influence on the life of the community in which it is located. These things are just as important to consider as is the profit motive.

The founder of the Newport News Shipbuilding and Dry Dock Company, when he was starting his company many years ago, wrote down his idea of the objective – the purpose – of the enterprise. He put it this way. "We shall build good ships here; at a profit if we can; at a loss if we must; but always good ships."

This is the guiding principle of this company and its fundamental policy. And it is a good one too because in a very few words it tells the whole reason for existence of the enterprise. And yet inherent in these few words there is a wealth of meaning. The determination to put quality ahead of profit. A promise to stay in business in spite of adversity. A determination to find the best production methods.

Every business enterprise should have as its very basic policy a simple clear statement, something of this nature, which will set forth its reason for being. In fact, it is imperative that it should have such a fundamental pronouncement because there are some very definite and important uses to which it can be put. The most important use of basic policy is to aim the entire resources and efforts of the company toward a well-defined target.[4]

Each member of the class was asked to go away and draft a corporate philosophy for the company, what later became known as a "mission statement." The only member there who had no need of such homework was Masaharu Matsushita. His company was already running to a well-defined philosophy outlined by Konosuke Matsushita some years earlier.

Matsushita's basic management objective is worth noting, because it was drawn up in 1929 when Japan, like much of the West, was in the depths of depression. It was enough, at the time, for most companies to survive, never mind searching their souls for the meaning of their existence. Konosuke Matsushita thought otherwise. "Recognizing our responsibilities as industrialists," he wrote, "we will devote ourselves to the progress and development of society and the well-being of people through our business activities, thereby enhancing the quality of life throughout the world."[5]

There followed the company creed: "Progress and development can be realized only through the combined efforts and co-operation of each employee of our company. United in spirit, we pledge to perform our corporate duties with dedication, diligence, and integrity."[6] Not bad for a company that started with a single simple product – an extension connection to a light-bulb socket. Even today, with a product range numbering in the thousands, the objective, the creed, and an additional seven guiding principles are recited each day like corporate prayers by Matsushita employees as they begin work.

Sarasohn was surprised and impressed to discover Masaharu Matsushita's guiding philosophy. "He alone among all the students who attended the CCS seminar classes knew and understood the essential importance of the basic beliefs of an organization as the starting point for the successful management of any company," Sarasohn later recalled.[7] In the light of subsequent developments it is worth emphasizing Sarasohn's point about quality, when he spoke about the "determination to put quality ahead of profit."

These classes pre-dated the lecture tours of W. Edwards Deming and Joseph Juran that would bring both men fame and recognition in Japan for their contribution to the postwar quality movement. Sarasohn's reputation, like that of his contemporaries schooled in the quality developments pioneered in Western Electric, was eclipsed by the subsequent appearance of Deming. Deming became the first American to be honored with the Order of the Sacred Treasure, an honor later awarded to Juran but never to Sarasohn. So why has Sarasohn's inspirational contribution been so overlooked?

The answer is partly related to Sarasohn's age and status. He was a comparatively junior executive, seconded in mid-career. Deming was an academic thoroughbred, accustomed to making presentations and writing up research. He was certainly no management specialist. As a statistician his first visit to Japan in 1949 was to advise on the census. He received little cooperation at that stage from the Japanese. He returned in 1950 at the invitation of the Union of Japanese Scientists and Engineers (JUSE) to lecture on statistical methods for industry.

Deming blamed the problems of industry on management's failure to eliminate waste. His answer was a process-driven approach that proved both appealing and understandable to Japanese managements familiar with the emphasis on measurement stressed in scientific management. Moreover he had an important sponsor in the Japan Federation of Economic Organizations, an association of Japanese chief executives known as *Keidanren*. He was speaking to the people who could make a difference in their companies.

Deming was strongly influenced by Walter Shewhart, a statistician at Bell Laboratories, and by Joseph Juran, one of the rising stars in Western Electric's community of management excellence. Deming adapted his ideas to recognize the vital contribution of employees who, he argued, should no longer be treated as commodities. He set himself against performance-related pay schemes, which he called "fear schemes," and advocated cooperative problem solving in teams. But Deming remained fundamentally attached to scientific management. He had worked briefly as an intern at Western Electric at the same time as Juran in the 1920s, although their paths did not cross until they met in Washington during the war and, even though they were good friends, they never collaborated professionally.

Unlike Deming, Juran had a corporate background. He began looking at quality when he was asked to help establish a quality inspection team at the Hawthorne works in the 1930s. He defined two areas of quality – quality of design and quality of conformance. The recognition of these distinctions became vital in the innovation and production of goods. Too many companies and too many standards – the European ISO 9000 standard, for example – would concentrate on conformance while ignoring design. Companies, therefore, that produced an average product might be able to boast a high degree of consistency in the quality of their product, thereby achieving a quality standard, without necessarily having produced any great excellence in the quality of design.

Juran explained these differences in his seminal work on quality, the *Quality Control Handbook* of 1951. When Deming drew the attention of Japanese companies to the work, JUSE extended an invitation to Juran, who began to outline his own ideas on quality to business audiences in Japan. Much has been written on the distinctions between the work of Deming and Juran but it has perhaps been exaggerated. The real distinction was in their approach: Deming was the academic, leaning heavily on statistical method; Juran was the corporate manager, schooled on cost controlling and the practical elimination of waste. The stronger recognition of Deming depended on two factors: he was the first to tour Japan, and he had an award named after him – the Deming prize, inaugurated by JUSE in 1951. JUSE, more a professional body than a trade union, wanted the award to increase its influence and market its training programs in Japanese companies.

Juran has dismissed as a popular myth the notion that he and Deming were together responsible for Japan's success in driving quality standards throughout its industries. "In my view there is not a shred of truth in such assertions," he said. "Had Deming and I stayed at home, the Japanese would have achieved world quality leadership all the same. We did provide a jump start, without which the Japanese would have been put to more work and the job might have taken longer, but they would still be ahead of the United States in the quality revolution."[8]

The Matsushita approach would underline this belief. Japan's postwar progress moved in a series of steps. Quality circles, for example, were introduced by neither Juran nor Deming, but by Japanese companies building on the earlier work on quality. By the 1960s the groundwork of these two influential experts had been completed. So had that of the CCS under Polkinghorn.

How did Japanese companies leap ahead under the noses of US industrialists? Why didn't American companies move so rapidly? The answer has everything to do with approach. As already noted, the Japanese were starting from virtually a clean sheet. They had been humbled by defeat. Their industries were shattered. Just as British trade unionists were able to create a model for industrial partnership in postwar German industries – but not in their own – the American engineers gathered in the CCS were schooled in companies that had deliberately promoted management innovation. They were given the time and the opportunity to put their ideas into practice. Rarely are individuals given so much freedom in their working lives.

These were young men working at the cutting edge of management thought. They weren't sitting in the boardroom contemplating the realities of corporate and personal competition. They were able to create a blueprint, unrestrained by the individual foibles, bickering, politics, and entrenched attitudes residing in day-to-day company management. All of them proved capable of synthesizing the best aspects of contemporary American management and presenting them to the Japanese. They had the time to work out their plans and their ideas were refreshing, described by

Bunzaemon Inoue, who became technical director of Sumitomo Electric, as "the light that illuminated everything."[9]

The CCS lectures became famous throughout Japanese manufacturing. Those who attended were sent out like disciples to preach the management message in other sectors. Their names read, according to *Forbes* magazine, like a *Who's Who* of Japan's electronics industry; men like Takeo Kato of Mitsubishi Electric and Hanzou Omi of Fujitsu. Akio Morita and Masaru Ibuka, the founders of Sony Corporation, were schooled separately by Sarasohn.[10] The word fanned out across industry. It meant that Deming and Juran were able to enjoy the advantage of preaching to the converted when they followed on the heels of these CCS pioneers. Sarasohn by that time had returned from what his company would have considered a useful learning experience in Japan. But he did not go back to his old job building radars. He joined Booz Allen as a consultant.[11]

In the United States and Europe, the quality movement was stifled by the concentration among top management on sales. Juran discovered this when he was invited by Rolls-Royce in the UK to deliver a training course for its managers during the 1960s. While touring the aero-engine factories he noticed high levels of waste. He told the then chief executive, Sir Peason Deming, that were he to invest as much energy in reducing waste as he did in the design and build of the engines, he could cut the cost of waste by half within five years. "It was a huge opportunity," said Juran, "but they did nothing. In this company the way for a man to work his way to the top was to increase sales. Reducing costs in the factories was seen as a form of dry drudgery that wouldn't interest most top managers. I was dealing here with a caste system, and the Samurai at the top were the people able to identify sales."[12]

Not everyone in US management had been asleep to the quality movement. Shewhart, Deming, and Juran had shared an obsessive concern for waste that had been recognized, for example, at Western Electric. Henry Ford, too, would have applauded their efforts in another era. Quality, after all, was nothing new – the medieval guilds had introduced hallmarks to certify the quality of their craftsmen's work. But the quality movement, focusing on continuous and systematic improvements throughout the whole organization, had evaded the attention of Western management.

In 1980, against a backdrop of falling sales and performance in contrast with the success of its Japanese competitors, US industry was wondering where it had gone wrong. America's own Samurai cadre was shocked by the answer delivered in an NBC television documentary: "If Japan Can, Why Can't We?" Suddenly America woke up en masse to the Japanese quality revolution. While American companies had been locking horns in a struggle to sell, their Japanese counterparts, concentrating on continuous improvement and value for money, had shed their reputation for cheaply made shoddy goods, winning increasing consumer admiration for dependability and performance. For thousands of US companies the documentary was a revelation of Damascene proportions. And here was the irony – Americans, who had failed to find an enthusiastic response in their own country, had given the Japanese all their ideas. Deming's phone was buzzing continuously the next day.

The quality movement was not stamped on Japan in one easy lesson. It made its way gradually in a series of steps, and these steps, perhaps because of their graduated advances, had been overlooked by Western companies. Companies like Matsushita and Toyota had been quality conscious before the Second World War. Scientific management was also understood and practiced in some Japanese companies before the war. But the spiritual ethic of Bushido guiding the immediate prewar military regime denounced anything scientific and viewed the ideas of scientific management with suspicion.[13] After the war, therefore, Japanese companies were obliged to relearn the scientific management principles that had contributed to their defeat.

Polkinghorn's team laid down the postwar groundwork. Deming and Juran preached it to the most senior people across the Japanese manufacturing sector, outlining their methods of statistical analysis, and big Japanese companies refined and developed the ideas within their own production systems. Toyota, for example, had been looking at the idea of "just-in-time" delivery of parts as a way of reducing inventory and waste, before the outbreak of war, but it did not perfect the idea until Taichii Ohno outlined the principles in the 1960s. Inspired by Henry Ford's concerns to keep his inventory to a minimum, Ohno redesigned the workplace so that workers manufacturing parts could access several operations at once, and parts could be drawn down onto the assembly line as and when they were needed. Ford referred to the supply of parts in transit as the "float."[14] Ohno, attracted to the way supermarket shoppers pulled products from shelves that were quickly replenished, developed the *Kanban* wall at Toyota's Nagoya plants in 1955.

The perfection of these systems means that today the Toyota production line is making cars to order. Instead of a line of uniform models, different models are worked on in succession, depending on the sequence in which they were ordered. There may come a time soon when a car assembly line is an open process allowing access and input by the customer, either directly or via an Internet video link, affording greater customization as the manufacture is in progress. Assembly line work may change, but the line itself remains the most efficient way of producing motorcars.

The processes of scientific management, including quality systems that would have met with the hearty approval of Frederick Taylor, were arguably better fitted to the Japanese production mentality than they were to that of the West, although their importance worldwide must be accepted. As Will Hutton, head of Britain's Work Foundation, recognized in *The State We're In*, a polemic on the pitfalls of contemporary capitalism, Japanese companies can be characterized by their reliance on "trust, continuity, reputation, and co-operation in economic relationships." In spite of these relationships the companies maintain a healthy competition. The Japanese call it *kyoryoku shi nagara kyosa* – cooperating while competing.[15]

Herein lie the clues to the strength of the postwar Japanese revival. But what lies at the heart of such concepts? Should we believe that Japanese workers are somehow more dedicated and industrious than their Western counterparts? Are they imbued with the one-company family spirit that cannot be replicated in the West? Is this the real secret of their success? The answer here is yes and no.

The background to the Japanese work ethic is not so very different to that of the West. There are strong parallels between the rise of the work ethic in Western Nonconformism and the way that different social classes under the Tokugawa Shogunate drew on elements of Confucianism and Buddhism to deal with a strictly imposed social order. The work ethic in Zen Buddhism was used as a kind of coping mechanism after 1603, when the Tokugawa family, based in Edo (modern day Tokyo), seized the power they would hold for more than 250 years. The policies of the earliest Tokugawa rulers were designed to preserve their continuity and prevent the rise of an opposing local ruler among the feudal lords, the daimyo.

The daimyo were forced to alternate their time between their fiefdoms and Edo, where their wives and children were kept. This restriction of family movements was designed to repress rebellious intent. Ieyasu, the first Tokugawa Shogun, threw out Christian missionaries and issued laws preventing Japanese people from leaving their country. Boat construction was limited to vessels no larger than fishing boats. Ieyasu encouraged trade with Europe initially – particularly in firearms – but he began to worry about the destabilizing impact of Christianity and Western politics and decided to curtail European influence. Only one avenue for trade and contact with the West was left open: a Dutch trade mission was maintained in Nagasaki. Social classes were narrowly defined. Even the daimyo were split into three classes, depending on past support for the rulers. Peasants were required to surrender their swords.

Tokugawan rule sought to stifle movement between social classes. It also stifled conflict, neutering the Samurai warrior creed. The more intellectual Samurai explored historical Chinese writings and revived medieval warrior skills such as archery and fencing. Their Bushido code, derived from the teachings of Zen Buddhism, emphasized loyalty, obedience, courtesy, and the importance of learning. The strong moral ethic that emerged melded effortlessly with Confucian principles that stressed a natural order in society. This mixture of Confucian and Buddhist practices was welcomed by the merchant class as a way of accommodating its ambitions in Tokugawan society.[16]

"If it was the decree of heaven that they should remain within the merchant class and do their duty without jealous striving to attain another rank, then their lust for life was, after all, divinely sanctioned and was not merely an imposition of Tokugawa,"[17] wrote the MIT economist, Everett Hagen, who explored the similarity between this ethic and Western Nonconformism in his book, *On the Theory of Social Change.*

Just as Western society cannot escape the Puritan spirit, the Japanese workforce retains powerful links with attitudes framed during the same period that Western Nonconformist sects were overturning the existing social mores of northern Europe in the seventeenth and eighteenth centuries. The big difference between the Japanese work ethic and its Western counterpart is the absence of any accompanying Protestant guilt implied by the burden of religious devotion. On the other hand, traditional Japanese loyalty and acceptance of rank has a much stronger historical underpinning than that expected from the Protestant work ethic.

There has also been the occasional Japanese rebel against the unquestioning acceptance of work. Rarely has the futility and purposelessness of an overblown bureaucratic system been outlined so prosaically as it was in Akira Kurosawa's 1952 feature film, *Ikiru* – Japanese for "to live."

Ikiru tells the story of Kanji Watanabe, a town hall department head who discovers he has terminal bowel cancer. Watanabe has a certificate recording thirty years' loyal service to the authority. But he concedes that in all that time he has been effectively dead, merely rubber-stamping reports and passing them to the next department. The procedure is the same throughout the town hall – problems are passed from one department to another by unenthusiastic officials.

Watanabe wants to experience what life can be like before he dies. He is guided on a drunken tour of immediate postwar Tokyo nightlife that can only offer short-term diversion. He sees one of his department swap her desk job for the sweatshop conditions of a toy factory producing clockwork rabbits. At least here, she argues, she can imagine the joy the product gives to so many children.

What joy do Watanabe or his colleagues give to anyone? In the final part of the film he returns to his desk, but instead of passing the buck he intervenes personally to help a community secure a park on a prime development site where there are plans to build a nightclub. Even in death, however, his achievements go unacknowledged. The kudos is claimed by others, such as the deputy mayor who, but for Watanabe's pleading and persistence, would not have sanctioned the project. Finally Watanabe's colleagues recognize his work and promise to reform their own approaches. The reality is quite different. Back at their desks they quickly return to the safety of the rubber stamp.

Ikiru is a commentary on petty officialdom everywhere. But it also raises questions about the way we live our lives. Is this all there is? Whenever people have questioned the meaning of their existence, the answers have been supplied traditionally through religion. Work adds a physical dimension to the spiritual meaning – the medium of the message. Luther's belief in work as a "calling" had been a strong enough rationale when people devoted themselves to their craft. But industrialization, with its repetitive actions, had, in the words of Studs Terkel, the American social commentator, "perverted the work ethic"[18] in its "planned obsolescence of people."[19] The meaning of work for so many people had been lost in the search for industrial efficiency. One of Terkel's interviewees, Nora Watson, an editor, put the workers' condition like this: "Most of us, like the assembly line worker, have jobs that are too small for our spirit. Jobs are not big enough for people."

The job could be enlarged with a degree of self-management. Peter Drucker made the point at General Motors in the 1940s, but it would be largely ignored for decades. In fact worker participation in production planning was still so rare among Western companies in the 1990s that Masaaki Imai, the Japanese management theorist, used the introduction of participative working at Leyland Trucks in the UK as a case study in progressive production methods.[20] John Oliver, the head of truck production at the company, described the change in attitudes: "We used to expect our workers to hang their brains on the coat hook when they came into work. We didn't want them to think. That's changed. Today they get involved in planning new lines or improvements to the assembly process."[21]

This inclusiveness in approach to the whole workforce dramatically changed employee–management relations. But it did not occur without some often-painful adjustment among managers. It was management, not the production workers, who needed to recognize that the creative potential of a large section of the workforce had been wasted for years.

Why did it take so long for companies to respond to the best ideas of management theorists? The answer lies in the legacy of mistrust and resistance created by assembly line efficiency and the blind faith that would be placed in management throughout the twentieth century. This was the century of management, a hundred years of management dominance in big business. Management's belief in its own superiority had created a seemingly intractable spirit of antagonism among production line workers. Management command and control produced results but it was a wasteful system, wasting most of the human ingenuity residing in the workforce. Tapping this ingenuity would become a lifelong mission for some who became committed to reviving the human spirit at work. In the meantime, only the most thorough examination of the managerial role would create any momentum toward a solution.

CHAPTER 16

Managing the Corporate State

Men have become the tools of their trade.
(Henry David Thoreau, 1817–62)

The tide of the Second World War was turning against the Germans and Japanese in late 1943 when Peter Drucker, an independently minded economics professor at Bennington College in New England, received a telephone call from General Motors. Donaldson Brown, the vice chairman, had been impressed by Drucker's book, *The Future of Industrial Man*, and its conclusion that business enterprise had become the "constitutive institution of industrial society."[1]

Drucker was suggesting that the workings of the large corporation were becoming the organizational model for the whole of society. How a business controlled itself, its governance, and how the individual behaved and operated within that business, had become the standard against which the rest of society could measure itself, said Drucker. It must have seemed that way in a world where conventional institutions had been left wanting, turning to business management as the only system capable of handling the demands of what Drucker called an "industrial war."[2]

The generals had turned increasingly to industry during the First World War, not just for munitions but for supply logistics and for innovation. Germany had come close to defeat in 1915 when its armies were running low on gunpowder.[3] The Royal Navy's blockade had starved German ports of supplies of saltpeter, a vital constituent of gunpowder. The saltpeter came from Chile. This was the reason why the Navy had encountered a flotilla of German warships near the Falkland Islands in December, 1914. The British had no idea why the Germans were there, other than to threaten their possession of the Falklands. Four German warships were sunk in the engagement. In desperation the German government had turned to its growing synthetic chemicals industry, urging that it find a synthetic propellant before its ammunition ran out.

German industry did more than find a substitute; it came up with an alternative weapon – synthetic gas. Gas was an industrial weapon. By the time of the Second World War, Germany had accumulated sufficient stockpiles of the nerve gas, Tabun, to have devastated the cities of its enemies. The only reason Hitler did not use Tabun was that he feared that the Allies had similar supplies. In fact there had been little manufacture of nerve gas outside Germany. "It is terrible to speculate on the holocaust that would have resulted had Hitler known this and ordered a massive nerve gas attack on London, Moscow or Washington. Or worse, Hitler might have found a weapon to win the war," wrote Joseph Borkin in *The Crime and Punishment of IG Farben*. If anyone was ever in doubt about the deterrent value of stockpiles of superweaponry, they need only look at the Nazis' deliberations over the use of Tabun.[4] Even in the darkest days of the world's darkest regime its use was never sanctioned.

Industry made the most terrible weapons, but business leaders could still retreat from the larger moral questions about their application. How long could business preserve this detachment? It had been fighting the war with the generals. Some companies – Ford, for example – even found their manufacturing operations exploited by the military in opposing nations.[5] Business was centrally engaged, driving the industrial juggernaut in a world that had unleashed its most destructive forces as competing ideologies struggled for supremacy across two continents. The customary maneuverings dictated by national interest had been temporarily subsumed in a three-cornered fight between the causes of fascism, communism, and democracy.

The war was not portrayed in this way to the rank-and-file combatants. The soldier in his trench was battling for Britain, fighting for the Fatherland, or defending Mother Russia. But the leaders who gathered at Potsdam and Yalta were playing for higher stakes. They knew that behind their national interests they were fighting for a way of life, a single dominating system of government and control that would best equip the world to go forward. The larger stakes were ideological – capitalism or communism. Which ideology would prevail after the freakish phenomenon of National Socialism had been removed from the stage?

Each of these competing ideologies, argued Drucker, could be viewed as "different concepts in a Big Business industrial society."[6] He perceived that the privately funded business system could stake a claim for the organizational high ground in the postwar climate. He insisted that "the first war really to be fought as an industrial war" should be settled in an "industrial peace – where industry is at the center of peacetime social organizations."[7] The rhetoric (if not the reality) implied by such a statement was music to the corporate ear. No longer could those who ran business be dismissed as pariahs or profiteers. They were ready to take their place at the fulcrum of moral and social behavior. Most of them were not ready, of course, but it was flattering of Peter Drucker to propose that they were. In doing so he had created a context for corporations in society. Companies could no longer distance themselves from the responsibilities borne by other institutions.

Companies not only had to face up to their increasing international presence, they needed to understand their internal structure far better. At General Motors Drucker would define this structure, identifying the constituent parts and the respective roles and responsibilities of corporate management.[8] At the time, the idea that his study would become a management book seemed faintly ludicrous, even to Drucker. "Most managers did not realize that they were practicing management. The general public, while very interested in how the rich made their money, had never heard of management," he wrote in his autobiography, *Adventures of a Bystander*, adding: "A book on such esoteric subjects as organization and structure, the development of managers, and the role of foreman and middle manager, was surely going to go unread."[9]

Drucker's retrospective comment on management is a debatable point. The public knowledge of management may have been limited, but ever since the joint stock company, combined with the acceptance of the principle of limited liability, had allowed a scaling-up of corporate ambitions, directors of the largest companies had become intensely interested in how best to organize and run their businesses. Business was taught in business schools established as adjuncts to universities. The Wharton School at the

University of Pennsylvania had been the first in 1881. Others followed in California, New York, and Boston. Managers were on the ground, working inside companies.

Their understanding of the managerial role was improving, fed by different streams of organizational thinking. In the United States Frederick Taylor's scientific management had created the need for teams of work-study people who organized and then supervised the workplace on more efficient lines. In France Henri Fayol had applied himself ceaselessly in developing effective tiers of administration at the Commentry-Fourchambault and Decazeville mining company, where he began his career in 1866. In Germany Max Weber had outlined a bureaucratic ideal, where organizations were controlled by a mechanistic but efficient chain of authority governed by rules and procedures.

If company bosses were struggling to meld these ideas, particularly in the light of concerns for maintaining human relations, they could call on outside help. Those who had championed the methods of scientific management found they could earn freelance fees taking their know-how into companies as consultants. The engineering company Arthur D. Little found there was growing business in such consultancy. Academics were spotting the main chance too. Elton Mayo had successfully tapped the coffers of business foundations to pursue his studies of human behavior at Western Electric. James McKinsey, a professor at the University of Chicago, had used his knowledge of accounting to help the US Army handle its supply logistics in the First World War, establishing his own consultancy in 1925. There was already a strong body of understanding that companies needed a chain of command and specialist areas of expertise, although the style of management could vary enormously, from Edison's creative collective at Menlo Park to Henry Ford's autocratic generalship at River Rouge.

The transfer of so many managers to war duties brought companies into closer contact with military-style command chains, but the military itself had been evolving during the interwar years, grappling with the science of logistics and supply in order to maintain operations that could stretch across continents. Scale was creating a devolution of management and an understanding that management skills could be learned and applied in different businesses or organizations.

Academic institutions were already venturing into corporations. The work undertaken by university researchers at Western Electric had demonstrated the possibilities and limitations of academic research inside companies. The idea of inviting a lone operator like Peter Drucker instead of a team of researchers who might cause too many waves appealed to Alfred Sloan, General Motors' chairman. He may also have seen Drucker, a man with no previous business experience, as less threatening than a McKinsey consultant. Marshall Field, the Chicago department store founded by its namesake (who had been one of the regulars with George Pullman at the millionaires' dining table), had learned to its cost the consequences of falling too deeply under the consultant's spell. In 1934 the board had invited James McKinsey, the highest paid consultant in the United States at $500 a day, to study the company's problems. A year later he was chairman. Two years after that, succumbing to illness brought on by the pressure of work, the company's declining fortunes, and the threat of forced resignation, he died. According to *American Business* magazine, "he died, as so many businessmen have died, as sacrifice to a job that made impossible demands."[10]

McKinsey, like George Pullman, had found that the work ethic demanded your every waking moment. He spent Saturdays at the office and brought work home on Sundays. His work regime consumed him, leaving little time for his family. "He wasn't much of a Santa," write James O'Shea and Charles Madigan in their book, *Dangerous Company*. "Toys and frivolous purchases were viewed as nonessential."[11] McKinsey was living the ethic of his Puritan forebears. His home was his church, and toys and frippery were unconscious reminders of pre-Reformation ecclesiastical decadence.

The Viennese-born Drucker, son of a senior Austrian economist, had an eclectic enough upbringing to be influenced by a variety of muses and mentors, but he, too, could reflect on the values of a Lutheran background in memories of Bertha Bond, his grandmother on his mother's side. Bertha Bond had been an accomplished concert pianist. In her later years she would disguise her worldliness by prefixing statements with "I am only a stupid old woman, but . . ."

This self-deprecatory remark was often combined with a flattering approach: "You look like an intelligent young man," she would say to disarm her victim. Anyone on the receiving end of such remarks could be assured that they were in for a pummeling, often verbal, sometimes physical. She was not an intellectual, says Drucker, she was more than that. She was wise. Bertha Bond was a legend in her own family. Her ancestors had been silk weavers, then merchants.

> Theirs was a world of skilled craftsmen, of responsible guild members; a small world but one of concern and community, workmanship and self-respect. There were no riches in that world, but modest self-reliance. "I am but a stupid old woman," echoed the self-limitation of the skilled craftsman who did not envy the great ones of this world and never dreamed of joining their ranks; who knew himself to be as good as they, and better at his trade. It was a world that respected work and the worker.[12]

There is a lot of Bertha Bond in Peter Drucker, the first of the management gurus. He has rejected the term "guru," describing himself as a journalist or as a "bystander," the word he uses in his autobiography. But his rejection is disingenuous. He goes to some length in the book to distinguish the Indian term "guru" from that of "teacher." The best teachers at Bennington College, wrote Drucker, were not teachers but pedagogues, programmers of learning like Socrates, whose method was to point the way to learning, to mark out the path for his students to follow. This was Drucker's way – prodding, commentating, criticizing, praising, inspiring, being insightful. He helped to define a new relationship between academics and business, creating an overlap of mutual respect where each could appreciate the concerns of the other.

The overlap was hardly all enveloping. Business would still distrust academia, and academics would still look down their noses at the workings of business. When Drucker wrote up his General Motors study in *Concept of the Corporation*, the only deletions suggested by Sloan were two references to the General Motors technical institute in Flint, Michigan. The General Motors Institute, originally established for apprentices, had been converted by Sloan into an engineering school for hourly paid workers.

But Sloan was afraid to publicize the school because of ingrained prejudice among self-made businessmen at that time against those with a college education.

The exclusion of Nonconformists from academic institutions in seventeenth- and eighteenth-century England had come full circle, creating residual distrust among the descendants of those who prospered without the help of academia. It bred an antipathy toward academia in US entrepreneurs. American entrepreneurism was characterized by equality of opportunity, independent thinking, and the rags-to-riches image of the self-made man. But by the 1940s the world had moved on, and ingrained prejudices were fading, though still real enough. This meant that companies such as General Motors – which had become convinced of the need for well-educated employees, particularly among its managers – nevertheless approached the selection and development of a management cadre with some circumspection.

The prejudice worked both ways. Academia was as cautious and as prejudiced as business about cooperation. When Lord Nuffield, the British carmaker, approached Oxford University with the offer of an endowment to establish a new college, the dons were determined not to soil their hands with the stain of commerce, so they created a social institution devoted to the interests of the working man rather than the employer. Business and learning were as divorced as wine and vinegar in the academic mind.

Concept of the Corporation did not create business management. Nor did it reveal management's existence to a curious world. Unlike Benjamin Franklin's *Poor Richard's Almanac*, it would not be read by the public. But it was read by business people, and it did more than any previous book to popularize management as a learnable discipline. It elevated the role of management in society. In Drucker's own words it "set off the management boom" across postwar industry and beyond. By the 1970s, management was so accepted a part of organizations that Drucker could write that "we even accept the book's assertion that 'management' is not peculiar to business enterprise but is the specific organ of all institutions of modern society."[13] It was another debatable point.

The encroachment of corporate-style management into hospitals, education, and the civil service among Western industrialized nations would be greeted with resistance and resentment by some, particularly in Europe, where social reformers were far from convinced that the business model had become or should become the "representative social institution" to which all other institutions should pay due deference.[14]

Drucker's organizational ideal was drawn from a historic and specifically American perspective, and the ideological battle between capitalism, communism, and fascism had hardly existed in the USA. Even in the troubled times of turn-of-the-nineteenth-century America, when business leaders had hired Pinkerton detectives and shop-floor spies to root out agitators and labor organizers, the cause had been one-sided. American laborers wanted fair wages and reasonable working conditions. They did not want to overthrow capitalism.

Drucker was correct in his perception of the growing importance of management teaching and the Master's degree in Business Administration (MBA) as a management qualification. He was correct also in his reading of business organization, although there remains a fragility in corporations compared to, say, the nation state. This may be no bad thing. Companies settle their differences not on the battlefield or in diplomatic exchanges but in the marketplace, their future – or lack of it – dictated by the often-fickle relationship between buyer and seller. Company managements sometimes forget this. They are fooled into thinking that their relationship with the customer is a given, as if it is some kind of treaty between nations etched in stone or signed in blood. It is not. The seller–buyer relationship is like a living organism that has to be fed and nurtured every single day.

Marks & Spencer, the British High Street retailer, probably knew its customers as well as any business until it began to ignore them, neglecting its bedrock of loyal support, losing touch with their expectations. Once it had stopped treating its customers as special people, a residue of goodwill sustained the relationship for a while. Then, quite suddenly, in 1998, like a partner who gives up on a marriage that has been going nowhere for years, customers began to lose interest, and the Marks & Spencer management was plunged into recriminations, wondering where things had gone wrong.

Drucker was never a man to weep at corporate demise through its own incompetence. "There is no law that says a company has to last forever," he said. After all, Joseph Schumpeter, the Austrian economist and friend of Drucker's father, had promoted a theory of turbulent capitalism, where innovation and growth in one company could destroy a market for others and in the process create a new market and yet more innovation. This process of "creative destruction"[15] would become topical in the accelerated phase of growth, demise, merger, and rejuvenation that occurred in 2000. It was as if the economy had become engaged in some sprightly Dance of Siva absorbing and pacifying every new horror that came its way. Meanwhile technology stocks were falling like mayflies, confirming Drucker's self-evident observation.

Peter Drucker was hailed as a corporate visionary. Henry Ford II, after reading Drucker's book, would seek to emulate the federated arrangements of Alfred Sloan (building, it should be said, on groundwork pursued by Sloan's predecessor, Pierre du Pont) where GM divisions were allowed to run their own operations, guided by a centralized policy-making committee. Ford was not alone. According to Tom Peters, the management writer and consultant, Drucker could be credited with "moving 75 to 80 percent of the Fortune 500 to radical decentralization."[16] If this is true, it shows the extent to which companies are driven by the herd instinct.

General Motors was not decentralized because Alfred Sloan thought it a great management model, but because he could see no better way to organize and control a corporate empire built from acquisitions. Once they were within the General Motors fold the independently minded founders running these acquired companies would continue to take exception to some higher authority telling them how to go about their business unless that authority could be clothed in the structure of federalism. This structure involved an interlinked network of divisions, committees, and subcommittees in which everyone appeared to have some say but which ultimately always deferred to the wisdom of Alfred Sloan. Sloan's style of leadership was Socratic, posing the difficult question which, in the asking, suggested a solution. Beneath the theory it was the cussedness of the American entrepreneur that created the decentralized structure of General Motors. Alfred Sloan looked at what he had and developed a system that made it work.

Drucker understood this. He himself was not prescribing the decentralization pill, not for healthy companies, anyway. But he recognized its strength, comparing it to the structure of the Catholic hierarchy and of the Prussian general staff between 1800 and 1870. Corporate imitation might not have been so enthusiastic had he highlighted these examples in anything broader than a footnote. Only Drucker could have conceived such an unlikely triumvirate as Field Marshal Helmuth von Moltke, Alfred Sloan, and the Pope. In fact Drucker's own ideas on corporate organization went further than those of Sloan. Drucker was seeking to influence new styles of factory working that would only be adopted by the most progressive of manufacturing managements some forty or fifty years later. In particular he was proposing "self-managed plant communities."

It was the concept of empowerment or, in his words, "the assumption of managerial responsibility by the individual employee, the work team, and the employee group alike for the structure of the individual job, for the performance of major tasks, and for the management of such community affairs as shift schedules, vacation schedules, overtime assignments, and, above all, employee benefits."[17] The idea would evolve partially and independently in quality circles developed by manufacturers in postwar Japan. But the principle was the same. Drucker envisaged a workplace where the worker was the master of his or her own job.

It seemed that neither managers nor workers were ready for such employee autonomy, not at General Motors anyway. Management viewed the idea as encroachment on to their turf. Likewise, labor unions were unenthusiastic. They wanted a "visible boss" who could be identified as the enemy. But Drucker knew he was on to something. He had noticed how work teams covering wartime projects, when there were too few supervisors to go around, had assumed responsibility for their jobs, often with superior results. Why couldn't this be replicated in peacetime? "Of all my work on management and 'the anatomy of industrial order,'" he wrote later, "I consider my ideas for the self-governing plant community and for the responsible worker to be both the most important and the most original."[18]

The idea may not have been quite as original as Drucker suggested. In his book, *Workers' Control in America*, David Montgomery reminds us that unionized teams of iron-rolling workers at the Columbus Iron Works in Ohio were negotiating overall rates for the company for each of its contracts between 1873 and 1876. The company management would propose a contract, and the rolling teams would state the price at which they were prepared to undertake the work. They would then decide among themselves how much each worker would receive for his or her contribution. They also decided the workload on any particular day and worked out the way workers could progress in their jobs. "To put it another way," wrote Montgomery, "all the boss did was to buy the equipment and raw materials and sell the finished product."[19]

These nineteenth-century iron-working practices do not seem far removed from self-managed teams. The ability of unions to organize such work may well have been a significant deterrent to companies such as General Motors accepting Drucker's proposal. Managers were fearful of instigating anything that appeared to be handing over power to the workers. Not until the latter part of the twentieth century, when re-engineering became the big fashion, did companies begin to fall over themselves to hive off whole areas of nonessential or "noncore" business on a contractual basis. Shorn of its union association, self-management was suddenly acceptable.

The idea of the self-managed worker had appealed to Charles Wilson, General Motors' company president and chief operating officer, who would succeed Sloan as chief executive officer. But Wilson did not think it would be welcomed in a workplace characterized by adversarial relations between management and employees. After the end of the war he decided to canvass the workers to tap into their concerns. His staff came up with a competition, which they thought would be better received than a survey. Employees were asked to submit essays outlining "My Job and Why I Like It" with prizes for the best entries. Almost 200,000 employees, two-thirds of the workforce, responded. The response was so great that the judges – Drucker was one of them – read no more than a few thousand. The rest were labeled and cataloged.

Those entries that were read by the judges revealed that the obvious rewards for work, such as pay and promotion, were part of employee expectations. If these factors were not handled well they could demotivate workers. But they were not, in themselves, important incentives. Frederick Herzberg, another student of motivation, would later call such issues "hygiene factors." The most powerful motivators, said Drucker, were achievement, contribution, and responsibility. People, he found, wanted to find satisfaction in their work. "They resent nothing so much as not to be allowed to do the work they know they are being paid for, whatever it may be," he wrote.[20]

The employees wanted to respect their company but believed there was no conflict between this desire and their membership of a trade union and did not see an allegiance to both as mutually exclusive. Drucker described the data as "the richest research material on employee attitudes and worker values ever brought together."[21] Whatever their value, the essays were boxed away and forgotten, not at the management's instigation but at the insistence of the stewards at the United Automobile Workers. The union was so suspicious of the exercise, its officials insisted that any further work on the data be shelved as a condition of its pay claim in 1948. Another opportunity to tease out the constituents of employee motivation had been lost. Wilson had found that the only way to achieve union acceptance for a management idea, even for something that would benefit employees, was for the union to perceive that it had won something for its members. Wilson, however, may have been too pessimistic about union opposition and Drucker too ready to absorb this pessimism.

The incentive plan devised in 1938 by Joseph Scanlon, a union official at the La Pointe Steel Company, had some of the hallmarks of the self-governing plant concept. In this case both company and employees were desperate to secure a formula that would save the company and its jobs by increasing production. The Scanlon plan was centered on a suggestion scheme and production committees in which workers and management discussed ideas together. No single individual benefited from a good suggestion, but cost savings were rewarded by bonuses paid across the workforce. The Scanlon plan, which saved the business, showed that something close to the self-managed plant was achievable where there was a mutual desire to bring about management and worker cooperation, even during the 1930s.

Drucker's ideas on self-managed work groups would have to wait to find a more willing audience. But in every other respect, the timing of *Concept of the Corporation* was perfect. Only later would Drucker discover that some of his ideas had been pioneered quite separately by Mary Parker Follett, a management prophet. During her lifetime her views had been sought out by business leaders hungry for guidance on human relations, and today she is revered by management academics, but her observations were forgotten and ignored for decades after her death in 1933. Warren Bennis describes her as a "swashbuckling advance scout of management thinking," and for Drucker she is "the brightest star in the management firmament."[22] Yet when Drucker began to grow interested in management in 1941 her work was overlooked by those he canvassed for references. Harry Hopf, an expert on managing insurance companies, passed on a reading list that included the work-study pioneers Taylor, Fayol, Gantt and the Gilbreths, the humanists Owen and Mayo, and the psychologists Cyril Burt and Hugo Munsterberg. But Follett's name was omitted, even though her books were in Hopf's extensive library.

Drucker rejects the idea that she was overlooked for so long because of her sex. Many women had risen to prominent positions in the United States by the 1930s, he points out. The reason that Follett had become, to use his phrase, a "nonperson," he believes, is that the 1930s and 1940s ushered in an era of conflict; not the Follett concept of constructive conflict – an approach to negotiation designed for the resolution of differences – but the notion that any fight at that time was a fight to the finish. The right of might had overtaken any idea of negotiated settlements.

That Follett was ahead of her time, far ahead of her time, is significant, but Drucker is too ready to overlook not only male prejudice but business prejudice, too. Follett, like Drucker, had no business background. How could she know how to react when the competition decided to cut up rough? Surely only an experienced, hard-nosed businessman knew how to mix it with a rival when the gloves were off. Andrew Carnegie knew this. Why else, he told himself, should he have respected and admired George Pullman so much? Neither was it reasonable to believe that women's views on management were as respected as those of men. Lillian Gilbreth's publishers understood the marketplace for ideas and recommended that she use her initials, so that readers would be none the wiser about the sex of the writer.

Follett was a social scientist. Her interest was the behavior of people in groups, an interest shared by business leaders who were attracted to the idea of a workforce moving with a common purpose in the same direction as management. "Labor and capital can never be reconciled as long as labor persists in thinking that there is a capitalist point of view and capitalists that there is a labor point of view," she wrote in *Creative Experience*. "There is not. These are imaginary wholes which must be broken up before capital and labor can co-operate."[23]

Follett was influenced by Max Wertheimer's *Gestalt* school of psychology, which conceived of an event viewed from different angles creating different interpretations or "imaginary wholes." The whole event was greater than these different interpretations, greater than the sum of its parts. *Gestalt* theory was the forerunner of group theory or the idea of a thinking mass. It helps to explain certain human behavior such as mass hysteria or what Charles Mackay called *Extraordinary Popular Delusions and the Madness of Crowds* in his book of the same name.

Mackay tracked illogical speculative events such as Tulipomania in the seventeenth century and the South Sea Bubble in the early eighteenth century. Follett believed that group experience need not have such calamitous consequences but could be channeled creatively for the common good of an organization. But it could only succeed, she argued, if managers were prepared to amend their approach to authority. Her idea was that those in authority should develop the idea of *power with* those they sought to influence rather than *power over*.

As Drucker rightly pointed out, with rare exceptions such as the Scanlon plan, where managements were forced to look at any avenue that might save a failing company, business leaders were unwilling to accept anything that could be construed as power sharing in the 1930s. They did not reject Follett's ideas outright, because they could appreciate there was something of substance worth pursuing, if only it could be made more tangible. The idea of constructive conflict had some appeal. Anyone could recognize that Follett had a point when she argued that compromise was an unsatisfactory solution to a conflict of interest, only postponing the issues that still needed to be resolved. Her idea was to pursue the differing interests by analyzing the premises on which they were built and seeking some common ground on which to establish a mutually beneficial outcome. It might not work every time, she conceded, but, she argued, "integration involves invention, and the clever thing is to recognize this, and not to let one's thinking stay within the boundaries of two alternatives which are mutually exclusive."[24]

Follett overlooked the one ingredient that might have made her ideas more digestible, although probably not at that time – the idea of trust. Without trust there could be no exploration of a common purpose. But any initiative involving trust would be viewed as a weakness within the adversarial relationships of business or, indeed, of society during the 1930s, as Drucker understood. Admiration came from respect – Carnegie's respect for Pullman, Stalin's respect for Hitler, the Duke of Wellington's respect for Napoleon Bonaparte – the recognition by a potential adversary that here was a smart operator, a sharp cookie (the language of the macho arena is studded with suitable descriptions), here was someone who would put one over on you if you let your guard down. The same mistrust was apparent in the Cold War. Equally it fed antagonism between the Ulster Unionists and the Irish Republican Army (IRA), Israel and the Palestinians, and the Turks and the Greeks in Cyprus. As each side struggled to produce an inventive solution to these standoffs, trust was viewed as a weakness, not a strength.

A great thinker, then, was largely forgotten after her death. Even today Follett's ideas are attracting too little attention. But she and Drucker had carried the torch that would insist that humanity remained at the center of human endeavor. Finding the key to human motivation had become a legitimate area of study, a Holy Grail of management, defining the growing field of occupational psychology. The stage had been set for Abraham Maslow and his lifelong determination to identify what it was that made people tick.

CHAPTER 17

The Wanting Animal

We do what we are and we are what we do.
(Abraham Maslow, 1908–70)

The Second World War had created an upheaval in the way people worked. Millions of servicemen had moved out of full-time jobs into the armed forces. Millions of men and women in the occupied countries had been subjected to forced labor. Millions of people had tasted something different in their lives that would change their attitudes irreversibly. Men had labored in prison camps and in the jungle, women had done men's work and had done it well.

After the war everything was supposed to revert back to the prewar pattern, and many people, including thousands of women, did go back to their old way of life. But attitudes did not revert so readily. People were more confident and in many cases more militant. They wanted change so badly in Britain that they were prepared to vote out their cherished war leader, Winston Churchill, for a socialist government headed by Clement Attlee. People wanted to get back to work, to get on with their lives, but none would forget their wartime experience.

There was so much work to do and plenty of willing hands. The Germans set about rebuilding their shattered and partitioned nation in the west with a vigor that would amaze those nations that had inflicted their defeat. The same happened in Japan. It was as if in defeat they were determined to bury their past, wiping the slate clean through sheer hard graft. Some things had not changed. The boss–worker relationship was as fragile as ever in Britain, and its industries were soon beset by strikes. West German industry, on the other hand, was experimenting with shop-floor democracy, creating works councils in which trade unions were represented in company committees alongside management. The system was established with the help of

British trade unions and had a lasting influence on German labor relations.

Trade unions in the United States continued to set themselves against management, but managers were getting the upper hand in the new, top-heavy, divisional style of command. Scientific management, which the larger companies had been introducing between the wars, was quickly consolidated in postwar management practices throughout the industrialized nations. The system operated on an arrogant and intellectually wasteful assumption that demanded knowledge and initiative from only one small section of the workforce – the managerial class. Worker efficiency – the worker as a vital but temperamental part of the machine – was the bedrock on which management practices were founded. The increasingly complex combinations of people and machines in factory-based manufacturing led to a broadening and elevation of management across industry.

Economies were strengthening once more, and many countries were reaching full employment, or as near as damn it, in what some would later regard as a golden age of productivity. The consumer society was swelling as families began to enjoy more leisure time. People were buying cars, televisions, and holidays. British Prime Minister Harold Macmillan told the public that they had "never had it so good," while Dwight Eisenhower reminded the American people where the money was coming from: "This world in arms is not spending money alone," he said. "It is spending the sweat of its laborers, the genius of its scientists, the hopes of its children."[1] The United States and the Soviet Union were beginning to believe they could reach for the stars.

Others were wondering where they might catch the stardust that made some people shine in business. The goal of managerial and corporate excellence was creating new avenues of research, supported by the profits of capitalism. Elton Mayo and Peter Drucker, for example, had struck academic gold when they began to research the human equation that made corporations successful. But companies were looking for something tangible from such research. They wanted material they could use and exploit for competitive advantage: anything that could tease out some extra production on the shop floor or deliver some winning strategy among the leadership was worth investigating. Academics did not necessarily share these goals. Some, like Drucker, may have been in search of the perfect economic and social community. Others, like the behaviorists, began searching for the elixir of success, studying the relationship between achievement, endeavor, and motivation.

If psychologists had not yet identified the substance of achievement, there were others, driven more by the instincts of the gut than by the pursuit and extrapolation of statistics, who believed that they knew excellence in a person when they saw it. Military leaders had often been dismissed as donkeys in the Great War, but the Second World War, a much more fluid conflict, had shown that leaders could make a difference, whether it was Erwin Rommel in North Africa, Bill Slim in Burma, Grigori Zhukov at Stalingrad, or George Patton in the Ardennes.

In peacetime companies needed their own leaders. They wanted tough men, yes, but not necessarily charismatic entrepreneurs. The analytical approach bred by a college education was beginning to be appreciated as an asset rather than a handicap. They wanted builders, organizers, corporate stewards who could manage the business efficiently, delivering growth and dividends to the stockholders. And the boards of these companies wanted help in finding these people.

The same people who were willing to offer management solutions were willing to find the managers themselves. Booz, Allen & Hamilton, the management consultancy, had its own executive recruitment division. Sydney Boyden, one of its earliest managers, would break away to specialize in recruitment alone. Jack Handy, a McKinsey man, did the same. Both of them were following in the path of Thorndike Deland.

Deland, a former part-time magician, had run an "executive placement bureau," finding managers and executives for buying and merchandising members of the Retail Research Association. In 1926 he set up his own recruitment business, outlining a fee basis that would become the model for the modern executive search industry.[2] Deland charged a retainer for the search, which was deducted from a commission he charged on the recruited executive's first year's salary. His business took off when he was asked by the US War Department to recruit executives for the Army Services Forces. Headhunting had been born.

Top executives were finding that they had a price, and the best of them seemed worth every penny. When Harold Geneen was brought in by Sydney Boyden to head the struggling International Telephone & Telegraph in 1959 he turned the business around. Geneen was a numbers man, an intimidating boss who pinned down his executives with the most searching questions about their divisional figures at the monthly financial meetings.

It is not surprising that company bosses should have been valued for their generalship during the 1950s and early 1960s. Capitalism was, after all, engaged in an economic war to the death with those nations that believed socialism, combined with economic planning, was a fairer system, redistributing wealth across society rather than concentrating profits among a wealthy elite. Peter Drucker was acutely aware of the struggle. He had lived through its gestation and birth and would witness its denouement. Abraham Maslow, whose ideas on motivation would inject a stronger human dimension into Drucker's thinking, was also a child of his time.

The experience of the Vienna-born Drucker, who left his homeland and did not go back after the banning of one of his books singled him out as a marked man, was directly absorbed in the events surrounding the rise of Nazism. Maslow had no such direct experience, but as a Brooklyn-born Jew, witnessing from afar the depredations of the Holocaust, he felt a deep emotional connection with concentration camp survivors. This helped to clarify his thinking on the psychological thresholds that must be surpassed if people were to achieve self-fulfillment. The idea of self-fulfillment on the part of an employee, be it the maintenance engineer or the boss, might not have been uppermost in the minds of managers within most manufacturers. But the notion that different levels of psychological development could influence creative decision-making had its attractions.

Maslow belonged to that group of motivational thinkers, along with Douglas McGregor, Frederick Herzberg, and David McClelland, who, while contributing to corporate philosophy, were capable of detaching themselves from the profit-driven goals of competition and production. For the minority of psychologists in postwar America it was not so much socialism but concerns for the social welfare of shop-floor workers and unhappiness with the mechanistic processes of Taylorism that motivated a small number of them to search for better ways of working, associated with improving the self-esteem and job satisfaction of the production-line worker.

Maslow drew a link between production and the product in the mind of the worker. If employees could preserve the idea that their work was important, it could enhance their self-respect and self-esteem. "The more I think about it," he wrote, "the more difficult I find it to *conceive* of feeling proud of myself, self-loving and self respecting, if I were working, for example, in some chewing gum factory, or a phony advertising agency or in some factory that turned out shoddy furniture."[3] He argued that "if you take yourself something important into the world, then you yourself become important thereby."[4] Maslow had noticed that concentration camp survivors had often been driven by some inner purpose, "some duty to live for, or some other people to live for." Those who gave up and sank into apathy, he said, had died without resistance.

The wartime experience of Stanislaw Szmajzner, a Polish Jew, bears out Maslow's point. Szmajzner, one of thirty-two inmates who survived an uprising in the Sobibor extermination camp, owed his initial survival during the gas chamber selections to his skills as a goldsmith. Although a boy at the time, he carried tools in his backpack and was able to fashion some metal to prove his abilities in front of the German selecting officer. The possession of a skill and the tools to do the job were no coincidence. The learning of a skill as something to fall back on, even if it were not needed as a primary source of income, was an important part of the knowledge passed on to a Jewish boy by his father. "I knew that work was the only security we had," said Szmajzner in an interview with Gitta Sereny. "We worked day and night. The trick was to make oneself indispensable."[5]

Prisoners worked to survive. Their captors claimed that they, too, worked to distract themselves from the business of killing. Franz Stangl, the commandant of Sobibor, told Sereny that to avoid thinking about the daily gassing of Jews it was necessary "to concentrate on work, work, and work again."[6] In both cases, for the murderers and the murdered, work was invoked as a means of self-preservation.

This idea of harnessing the psychological benefits of work as a strategy for survival or as a means of screening yourself mentally from the horrors of your surroundings was explored in Pierre Boulle's controversial novel, *Bridge on the River Kwai*, later made into a feature film. The central character, Colonel Nicholson, played in the film by Alec Guinness, believes it is in the best interests of morale among his men to work hard to earn the respect of their Japanese captors. Nicholson becomes obsessed with the bridge as a feat of engineering in its own right, to the extent that he is prepared to expose an attempt by Allied saboteurs to blow it up.

The book was controversial, because the fictional colonel was based on a genuine character, Lt.-Col. Philip Toosey, the commander of those British prisoners who worked on the construction of the Kwai Bridge. The bridge – in reality there were two bridges: a wooden construction and a later bridge made from concrete and steel – was part of the notorious Burma–Thailand Railway, built by Allied prisoners of war and contracted Malaysian and Burmese laborers. These slave laborers died in their thousands from starvation, disease, debilitating ulcers, and heat-exhaustion. The film was a distortion of the real events. There had been no attempt at sabotage, and the idea that a man like Toosey would override his duty in the way that was portrayed in the fictional Nicholson was a gross misrepresentation of character. But the concept of work as a means of preserving dignity, as a means of survival, was shared by the fictional Nicholson and the real-life Toosey.

"Toosey understood from the very beginning that the only real issue was how to ensure that as many of his men as possible should survive their captivity," wrote his biographer, Peter Davies. "He appreciated to the full that the bridges would be built with or without his co-operation and set himself the task of mitigating the terrible conditions under which the work was to be completed."[7]

Maslow understood there was a relationship between work and an individual's psychological health. His book, *Eupsychian Management* (republished as *Maslow on Management*), explores some of the thinking behind his most lasting concept – the hierarchy of needs. Maslow's theory was inspired partly by the work of

Henry Murray, a psychologist who outlined a list of twenty needs that all people, he believed, strove to satisfy. Maslow refined and distilled the idea, identifying five categories of human needs: the *physiological*, such as hunger, thirst, and sex; *safety*; *love*; *esteem*; and lastly (at the top of the order) *self-actualization*.

The satisfaction of the lowest of these needs allowed the pursuit of the next step in the hierarchy, and so on. When the most basic physiological needs had been met, he argued, human concerns turned to those of safety, such as warmth, shelter, personal defense, and the establishment of financial supports. The "love" needs included the need for affection and acceptance by others, whereas esteem involved the recognition and praise of others and the freedom to work without external interference. The highest need identified by Maslow, the need he called self-actualization, pursued the idea that an individual can identify and then seek to fulfill some inner need. "What a man can be, he must be," he wrote, by working "to become everything that one is capable of becoming."[8]

The outplacement industry that emerged during the 1980s drew on these ideas to encourage people to explore future career paths. Outplacement came out of corporate restructuring, when companies sought to cushion the impact of layoffs among thousands of their white-collar workers. The outplacement company was engaged by the employer, for a fee, to help redundant managers and executives cope with their job loss and find new work. (No such service was available initially for the rank and file worker.) For the first time in their lives some people would discover that the career they had followed from school or college had never satisfied anything more than their financial needs, or what Maslow would call their safety needs, with perhaps some "esteem" peaks of recognition.

The demands of the work ethic did not always permit self-actualization. This higher need might seem a psychological luxury beyond the unremitting grind of honest hard work. Yet, as Maslow saw it, one could not be achieved without the other. The work ethic was very much an ingredient of the self-actualized individual. In fact it may have been the prime ingredient. There is a problem here that Maslow does not appear to have considered. If you don't work, you will never achieve self-actualization, but you may find yourself working so hard that you are denied the freedom to fulfill your dreams. It is Joseph Heller's *Catch 22*, transferred to the workplace. "The test for any person," wrote Maslow, is "does he bear apples? Does he bear fruit?" But supposing the apples are crab apples, the stunted achievements of the work-obsessed environment? You could call it achievement of a sort, but hardly self-fulfillment.

Maslow, nevertheless, saw no other route beyond the path that had been outlined in Kurusawa's film, *Ikiru*.[9] *Ikiru*, he argued, outlined a path to "salvation via hard work and total commitment to doing well the job that fate or personal destiny calls you to do." Kanji Watanabe, the town hall official, does indeed find self-actualization, but only after his terminal cancer awakes in him the desire to use his skills, connections, and previously unrecognized determination to achieve some public good – the creation of a children's playground. His full-time job had become a drudge, unappreciated and unrewarded beyond his pay check; he displayed no greater ambition than getting through the day. *Ikiru* was highlighting the unlikelihood of achieving self-actualization in a steady nine-to-five job.

Watanabe needed to be released from the mental imprisonment of moribund management. The work ethic alone was not enough. He might have rubber-stamped twice the amount of paperwork as his neighbor, but he would still have been shifting paper. The real apples, the apples worth eating, were not part of his job description and demanded an initiative that went way beyond the requirements of his management job. Watanabe had become trapped in a stale system that would do all in its power to stifle any personal commitment to self-actualization.

The hierarchy of needs made so much sense, but what could it mean to the average production worker or junior manager? Maslow criticized those of his young students who, he said, thought self-actualization could be achieved without effort. But at least they had hope. Their desires and dreams had not yet been ground down in the corporate machine. He could count himself fortunate that he had students who still knew how to dream, who had not been dulled in a teaching system that rewarded effort over inspiration.

Maslow understood there were obstacles to self-fulfillment. He wrote of "healthy selfishness," of listening to one's impulses, of "embracing one's own nature" as a means of achieving one's highest plan. The unemployed laborers queuing for work at the dock gates would have loved to embrace their own nature, but the reality for many people in and out of work in the perpetual cycles of the capitalist system was a continual balancing act on the first rung of Maslow's ladder. As he recognized himself, "to do some idiotic job very well is certainly not real achievement." But what do you do when the unfulfilling job in Maslow's chewing gum factory example is the only job there is? Is all paid work justifiable simply because it is work? Is all paid work justifiable simply because it is rewarded? Or should there be some broader justification, a test to sort the apples from the crab apples?

None of these questions troubled Douglas McGregor. In his studies, work was a given, because man would be constantly engaged in attempting to satisfy his needs. As Maslow had put it, man was "a perpetually wanting animal."[10] McGregor's emphasis was on the control and organization of work. Should it be authoritarian, the traditional form of top-down management by decree, or could better results be achieved by consultative management? What did a contemporary model of management look like? What could an alternative model look like?

The first model he described, a model familiar to managements in 1960 when he framed his proposition in *The Human Side of Enterprise*, he called "Theory X"; the second, he named "Theory Y." The theories were based on different assumptions about human behavior. The traditional Theory X assumed that the average person was naturally disinclined to work and had to be cajoled into working. Theory X assumptions were that people, in general, preferred to be directed, craved security, and displayed little ambition or desire for responsibility. Authoritarian management was the customary response to such assumptions. Theory Y, the theory that McGregor wanted to see applied in the workplace, assumed that people had no in-built aversion to work, that mental effort in work was as natural as play or rest, and that people were capable of self-control and self-direction when they were working at something to which they were committed. In the right conditions the average person was quite capable of accepting and even seeking responsibility. Furthermore, said McGregor, the capacity for creative problem solving in organizations was widely distributed among the population, not narrowly confined within a decision-making elite.

McGregor felt that people behaved in response to the way they were treated. They were perfectly capable of applying self-discipline, seeking responsibility, acting creatively, and problem solving if they were trusted to do so. It was a bold theory. Drucker said it should not be regarded as a form of "soft" management, since it required individual discipline, strong performance goals, and high standards, if people were to meet its demands. McGregor and Drucker were beginning to sing in tune.

There were parallels between these ideas and those of Mary Parker Follett. McGregor was advocating Follett's proposal for "power with." Follett had also been attracted to the idea of managers giving workers scope to develop some responsibility. "Managers . . . should give the workers a chance to grow capacity or power for themselves," she wrote. [11]

Frederick Herzberg, professor of management at the University of Utah, believed that "job enrichment" – enlarging an individual's job by creating greater responsibility and providing broader scope for on-the-job learning – was one way that companies could achieve Follett's ideal. In one study he looked at secretaries working for the Bell Telephone Company. Their job – responding to letters from shareholders – involved working under close supervision to standardized formulas. Herzberg found that their morale was low and their work was prone to errors. The job was redesigned, assigning the secretaries specific areas where each could become the resident expert. At the same time they were asked to organize their own workloads, and supervision was reduced. Productivity fell at first but soon rose well above previous levels. The quality of the work improved too.

In another study for his 1959 book, *The Motivation to Work*, Herzberg surveyed some two hundred engineers and accountants in Pittsburgh, asking them to list the times they felt good about their work and the times they disliked their work and to explain the reasons behind their feelings. The good feelings were produced by achieving something, receiving some recognition, the knowledge of a job well done, having some responsibility, making some progress, and achieving some personal growth. Dissatisfaction with the job was invariably related to issues such as pay, working conditions, management and management policy, job security and prestige, or to personal problems outside work.

Herzberg called all of these issues "hygiene factors," aspects of the job or of life that had to be right if people were going to stay motivated in their work. The factors of satisfaction – what he called "actualization factors" – were essential for long-term employee well-being. The hygiene factors were important but not intrinsically so. Their influence was temporary and not always as expected. A pay raise, for instance, might trigger a negative feeling if it was lower than a worker thought he or she deserved.

These various theories of motivation were useful to managers but they tended to simplify the complexity of human needs and aspirations. As Peter Drucker admitted much later, Maslow was showing that "different people require different ways of managing."[12] Maslow discussed this when he outlined an approach to "Enlightened Economics and Management" in *Eupsychian Management*.[13] The thirty-six points he listed under this heading, drawn from his own work and the work of others in the same field of study, are probably the most illuminating and succinct collection of assumptions covering human behavior and good management ever published. They deserve to be chiseled in stone. The first and most important of all of them is: "Assume that everyone is to be trusted." Two other points may be emphasized here: "Assume the preference for working rather than being idle," and "All human beings prefer meaningful work to meaningless work."

The human relations school was enlarging throughout the postwar period, but many Western companies were apprehensive about putting its ideas into practice. Japanese companies had been more receptive. Their leaders had had their fill of an authoritarian, militaristic regime that had embarked on an ill-conceived campaign of conquest and domination that had ended so ignominiously in 1945. The ground had been prepared for more consultative working practices in the future.

Companies in the United States had experienced no comparable brush with humility. American managers were reluctant to consider the idea that they should sacrifice some of their authority for a more consultative workplace. Authority was power. But more than thirty years after Follett had urged managers to give workers the chance to involve themselves in shop floor decision-making, a California company accepted the challenge.

Non-Linear Systems of Del Mar, an aerospace company, began to apply the ideas of Drucker, Herzberg, McGregor, and Maslow in the early 1960s. Andrew Kay, its president, got rid of the assembly line and organized the workforce into self-managed teams that learned every aspect of the production. The teams decided their work hours, work schedules, and break times. Quality inspectors were dispensed with and work cards were replaced by salaries across the workforce. Kay also paid employees 25 percent higher than the going rate and introduced an options scheme for company stock.

Many of these systems have been introduced in companies today but at the time they represented an untried, pragmatic attempt to apply management theories from the human relations fold. When the business experienced a downturn in the early 1970s, Kay reintroduced traditional management practices, made changes to the production line, and cut his workforce. Did this mean that the idea of self-managed teams was a failure? That might be one interpretation. Another interpretation is that the company's business took a nose dive and management had taken its eye off the ball. Whatever the case, it was not the first time and would not be the last that a company shed jobs in response to worsening trading conditions, or that crisis-inspired pragmatism overruled idealism.

Nor would it deter managements from exploring the implications of Theory Y. There was no chance of that with hundreds of new consultancies putting some varnish on these theories which they would soon be peddling as progressive management techniques promising the earth. Volvo, the Swedish carmaker, experimented during the 1970s with team-built cars at its workshops in Udevalla and Kalmar. The idea was that a single work team would build a model from scratch, seeing the production through from start to finish.

The system created the same type of job variety among production workers that Kay was seeking to create at Non-Linear Systems. The experiment was abandoned in 1992. The teams made good cars but the system could not approach the manufacturing speeds attained by assembly line production. Whether we like Ford's assembly line or not, it remains the most economical way of making mass-produced cars.

Volvo might have failed in its attempt to get rid of the moving assembly line but during the 1990s assembly-line manufacturers were increasingly accepting the challenge of self-managed teams and job variety. The Toyota production system gives workers theoretical control over production with a pull-cord running above their heads, the whole length of the line. Pulling the cord summons a supervisor to investigate the problem, and if the line needs to stop then it stops.[14]

The long-term US resistance to allowing greater worker involvement in car production began to diminish after General Motors instigated its own experiment in employee participation, when it established a new program to develop a small family car. The Saturn Project was launched in 1984, from an engineering study ordered two years earlier. The engineers were asked to work from a clean sheet and to explore ways of integrating people and technology in car manufacture. Saturn's philosophy would be based on a belief "that all people want to be involved in decisions that effect them, care about their jobs, take pride in their accomplishments, and want to share the success of their efforts."[15] The Saturn management dropped time clocks, emphasized teamwork, ensured that team members had a voice in decisions, and entered into a unique partnership with the United Autoworkers Union based on an agreement to consult the union in every aspect of the business. Saturn must have done something right. In the summer of 1998 Saturn was the only General Motors plant in the United States producing cars as an industrial dispute shut down every other plant.

Worker involvement in manufacturing decisions became more common in the 1990s. Since the late 1990s assembly-line workers at Leyland Trucks in Preston, Lancashire, have been sitting down with production engineers to discuss potential improvements. "I remember when everything that was ever planned was planned and implemented by technical engineering people," said Allister Butler, the plant's manufacturing engineering manager. "I guess that in our minds we didn't trust people on the shop floor. The one thing that we have learned is that the real experts are those who build the trucks."[16] Leyland Trucks says its changes were brought about in a spirit of enlightenment and a desire to implement innovative management practices because the old practices, based on Taylor's contention that the worker should be under the direct control of the manager, had failed to maintain competitiveness.

Worker participation can be a two-way process. Just as assembly-line employees can become involved in production planning, those in executive management can immerse themselves in assembly work. James Dyson, who almost single-handedly demonstrated to disillusioned British manufacturers in the 1990s that a well-designed domestic product could still be manufactured in a high wage earning economy, insists that everyone who works at the Dyson Company makes one of his vacuum cleaners on their first day at the company. "This is true from the lowliest member of staff to a non-executive director," he says.[17]

In many companies, however, empowerment of the workforce in the closing years of the twentieth century was driven less by these enlightened approaches and more by the desire to cut costs and distribute the workload among fewer people. Improvements in technology throughout the 1980s had highlighted the cost of people, as technology became cheaper and companies sought to offload many of their nonessential functions. Employees were invariably exposed as the most expensive asset on a company's books, however vital their contribution. In fact, as far as accounting convention was concerned, people were a cost, not an asset. But not until the ideas of corporate reengineering had come along did companies begin to look at the costs of management.

Reengineering was a simple concept. It was all about flattening the hierarchical pyramid, taking out layers of management and contracting out most operations that were not at the core of the business. If, at the same time, you handed over increased responsibility to your front-line workers, it followed that you would need fewer people to supervise them. Since supervisors were often among the most expensive employees, with their long service records delivering regular pay increments, there was an added financial attraction to thinning their ranks.

Layoffs had been a harsh fact of life for many in manual employment, alleviated briefly among those born into that generation of steady economic growth after the Second World War. But layoffs among white-collar management were almost unheard of until the axe began to fall in the late 1980s and early 1990s. It fell in the service sector, perhaps more heavily than it did in manufacturing. It cut a swath through the middle of large corporations, taking with it middle-class, middle-aged, middle management. Arthur Miller's vision of white-collar obsolescence had come home to roost, as thousands of managers contemplated Willy Loman's nightmare of rejection in *Death of a Salesman*.

Frederick Reichheld, a director of Bain & Company, the management consultancy, bemoaned the destruction of loyalty implicit in layoffs. Loyalty, he argued, was essential to the long-term prospects of extracting value from a business.[18] But writers like Reichheld and Jeffery Pfeffer of Stanford Business School (another advocate of strong corporate commitment to employees) were voices in the wilderness during the 1990s. Far more common was the manager's comment quoted by Charles Heckscher in his book, *White-Collar Blues*: "If you want loyalty go get a dog."[19] This kind of contempt for the middle manager had been implicit as far back as 1955, when Sloan Wilson wrote *The Man in the Gray Flannel Suit*, an unsettling novel about the way that men were prepared to bury their emotions and values in the name of corporate conformity.

Reengineering was the great corporate leveler, portrayed nowhere more starkly and bitingly than in the 1997 film, *The Full Monty*. One scene shows out-of-work laborers and their former manager sharing the same queue for unemployment benefit. The manager has been unable to discuss his redundancy with his wife and maintains a charade, leaving for the office every day, carrying his briefcase. His wife, meanwhile, is spending money as if her husband's income will never run dry. Only when the bailiffs arrive for their furniture does she become aware of the crisis in their lives. The manager has further to fall than his former underlings. Finally he confronts the ultimate humiliation of the jobless executive, shedding his clothes to music before an audience of rapturous women as he joins a group of other laid-off workers who decide that stripping on stage can earn them some money.

Everything is laid bare – class distinctions, gender differences, male dominance – and none of it really matters. There is a triumph in the performance – the triumph of shared humiliation, of common adversity. Each man in his own way finds something special in the experience. Film distributors in the United States were worried that American audiences would struggle to understand the strongly accented language, but they understood the story all right. It was an all too common experience on both sides of the Atlantic.

Like all good fiction, *The Full Monty* told so many truths. The truths were repeated across the Western world. Reengineering had changed the face of unemployment. In 1994 I was handed a sheaf of letters that had been sent to an Oxford-based recruitment magazine in response to a campaign it was running against ageism in the workplace. The letters all told the same story.[20] They were from people in the forty to fifty-five age bracket with many years of experience in their chosen careers. Typically they had been working in middle management, drawing good salaries at the time – between £30,000 and £40,000 ($47,500 to $63,250) with commitments and a lifestyle to match. The *Full Monty* manager was writ large in their expressions of shock as they found themselves too old and too expensive for the needs of their employers.

One writer who had committed "the cardinal sin of getting old" said that he and his fellow job seekers had become so accustomed to rejection letters that they held a "lottery as to what excuse will be in the standard three paragraphs." In another letter a forty-seven-year-old man who had lost his job five years earlier said he had never signed on for unemployment benefit and after a series of part-time and temporary jobs had become "resigned to never having a proper job again."

Some of the letters were from highly qualified people. An engineer said he had "worked very hard through engineering apprenticeship, engineering studentship, and university to achieve Master of Science and Chartered Engineer status, and for the last two years I have been jobless like many other people in my situation. I could have pretended I am a self-employed consultant like many professionals do to hide the shame of being unemployed."

The letters were the cries of England's suburbia, a groundswell of resentment otherwise hidden within the poplar-lined avenues and neatly manicured lawns of open-planned executive housing developments. The same story, the same pain was being experienced in similar developments across the manufacturing regions of the USA. White-collar angst was the self-inflicted corporate disease of the 1990s as shareholders turned on the stewards of their investments and demanded quick returns. It all came down to the bottom line.

Reengineering was the brainchild of Michael Hammer, a former computer science professor at MIT. He used the term originally in the late 1980s to describe the way that information technology could transform business processes. By the time he and James Champy, chairman of the CSC Index consultancy, wrote *Reengineering the Corporation* in 1993, he was defining the term as "the fundamental rethinking and radical redesign of business processes to achieve dramatic improvements in contemporary measures of business performance."[21] This was quite a mouthful for something that equated to the removal of thousands of jobs, of people's livelihoods, from thousands of corporate registers.

Reengineering went further in paring away the flesh of companies down to the pure white bones of profit, much further than Peter Drucker had ever ventured. It pursued the implications of an empowered workforce in corporations where computer software systems could handle much of the information and deliver know-how directly to the front line. It questioned the necessity of the top-heavy structure of corporations modeled on the system created by Alfred Sloan at General Motors and suggested that a lengthy chain of command was unnecessary.

Links in the chain could easily be removed by stripping out layers of management. Board directors were happy to go ahead with this because it saved money and it rarely affected their particular layer, not the top job anyway. The apparent effectiveness of the top job was usually enhanced, since the cost savings that could be achieved were translated immediately to the bottom line. This had the attractive knock-on effect of increasing the company share price, which reflected handsomely on the potential earnings of top executives through share options.

The share option was a method of payment invented by pay consultants as a financial incentive for executives in publicly owned companies. Executives were granted a number of options to buy shares in their company from a certain date. The price of the option was fixed at the sum paid when the company purchased the shares for the incentive scheme. But the option would be exercised at the share price pertaining when it was cashed in. If the company and the markets had performed well in the interim period it could deliver a significant gain to the executive.

Why executives should have a greater incentive in receiving options than other workers is one of the mysteries of corporate reward systems. There seems to be a prevailing attitude that workers who are not executives would prefer to be paid in cash, the theory being that they live such a hand-to-mouth existence they need every penny they can spend. The same theory claims that workers would not like to see any of their pay exposed to the risks associated with the stock market. This is a peculiar assumption when it is recognized that the biggest risk associated with any worker is the loss of their job, something they live with continually.

Reengineering the Corporation was arguably the most influential management book since Drucker's *Concept of the Corporation*. While Drucker had described a model of administration that had created jobs, that had built a social system within the large corporation, Hammer and Champy were prescribing a low-calorie recipe for corporate anorexia. The system brought with it a whole new lexicon of management jargon that quickly became assimilated within the American language and eventually found its way into the English language. The contracting out of work became "outsourcing," the removal of layers of management became "delayering." Removing jobs was called "downsizing," putting them back after removing too many was "rightsizing." The mid-1990s were crazy alarming years for the one-company career manager.

Managers who cut jobs were lionized by their peers, who gave them nicknames reminiscent of the fearsome warriors who rampaged across Europe at the end of the Roman Empire. There was "Neutron" Jack Welch who shed some 100,000 jobs within five years of his appointment as chief executive of General Electric in 1981.[22] The "Neutron" was dropped later, when Welch revealed his skills as a corporate builder. But Al "Chainsaw" Dunlap would never get rid of his own *nom de guerre*. This was a man who cut his way through a cluster of companies until the formula lost its potency. At Scott Paper he walked into a struggling company and laid off a third of the workforce within a year. More than two-thirds of the headquarters staff, half of the management, and a fifth of the hourly paid employees lost their jobs. He then sold the company to its rival, Kimberly-Clark, for $6.8 billion, returning a 225 percent profit on their investment to the shareholders of Scott Paper. Dunlap had earned himself almost $100 million in salary and stock profits in a single year.

When he walked into his next job as chairman of the Sunbeam Corporation, its stock rose by 49 percent on the day his appointment was announced.[23] But when Sunbeam continued to struggle, even after job cutbacks, the buzzsaw was turned on Dunlap himself. The old hacker was unrepentant. It had all been necessary, he claimed. Few people shed any tears at Dunlap's demise. Even his own son said he had it coming.

But Dunlap had a point. His argument was that the overstaffed companies that had called him in were in severe trouble. Had he not cut staff the whole enterprise and thousands more jobs would have disappeared. His job was to keep the balloon aloft by throwing passengers out of the basket. Reengineering was a corporate reckoning. Never again could people assume that board directors were acting in the interests of the company's employees. The boards answered to external shareholders, and the shareholders wanted value for their investment – continuous value. Shareholder value became the new corporate language repeated at every opportunity like grace before breakfast, lunch, and supper. Shares, the lifeblood of the publicly quoted company, were a tradable commodity, and the market was fickle. The market was human. It did not see the corporation as Drucker's social enterprise, merely as a vehicle for increasing personal wealth. In fact the market system questioned whether a company could ever be more than that. Was there an alternative? Some company bosses – a tiny minority – thought there was. They had asked themselves a simple question. Supposing the people who owned the company were the people who worked there? Wouldn't that make a difference?

CHAPTER 18

Sharp-suited Philanthropists

> To secure for the workers by hand or by brain the full fruits
> of their industry and the most equitable distribution thereof
> that may be possible upon the basis of the common owner-
> ship of the means of production.
>
> (Clause Four of the British Labour Party's
> constitution, 1918; removed 1995)

John Spedan Lewis was a man alone in a nation of shopkeepers. Some may have thought him subversive, even dangerous. Others may have wondered if he had taken leave of his senses, all because he wanted his company's workforce to share the advantages of corporate ownership. Lewis was a successful British capitalist, the head of a growing retailing empire, an autocrat obsessed with his business. But his obsession had some unusual characteristics. While he was determined, like other entrepreneurs, to create an ever-expanding business empire, he questioned why the profits from the business should be concentrated among a minority of wealthy shareholders. Shouldn't the people whose labor contributed to the company's success have a fairer share of the profits? Shouldn't they experience, collectively, the rewards and responsibility of ownership? He thought they should, so he placed his company in the hands of its workforce.

The same questions had troubled Karl Marx in his analysis of the capitalist system, but Marx was reared on the philosophy of Hegel, not the hard-nosed realities of profit and loss. Marx could inspire a revolutionary movement that would grip half the world, dedicated to seizing control of the capitalist system. Lewis's vision was far more benign. It did not rely on force of arms but placed its faith in a spirit of benevolence and an understanding that wealth creation was a mass movement, a social movement, not the sport of an entrepreneurial elite played out for the benefit of a privileged minority. In capitalism Lewis backed the winning horse, and yet his experiment failed to create any groundswell of enthusiasm. The plutocrats were not lining up to scatter their winnings among the working classes.

John Lewis knew what it was to be privileged. He headed a growing chain of high street stores that had started life as a drapery shop on London's Oxford Street. The business had been established by his father, the original John Lewis, a former draper's apprentice. John Lewis had been raised by his aunt, Ann Speed, hence the unusual name chosen for his first son. Trading under the slogan "Never Knowingly Undersold," the company earned a reputation for fairness and value for money. John Lewis grew his business from a determination to make available to the customer a wide range of goods at reasonable prices. He was, in effect, establishing a relationship of trust with his customer. It would be repeated in other ways by Marks & Spencer in the UK and Nordstrom in the USA.

Both Marks & Spencer and Nordstrom made a virtue out of their refund policies. If goods were not acceptable for any reason, a customer could return them for a full refund. This brought untold business for Marks & Spencer in the practice of present-buying on birthdays or at Christmas. It meant that people could safely buy something at Marks, advising the recipient that they "could always take it back and change it." It meant high rates of returned goods, but each return brought people into the stores and often created more business. In the same way John Lewis customers were attracted to its principled stance on fair trade.

But fairness has many facets. Spedan Lewis was given a £50,000 quarter share in the business on his twenty-first birthday in 1906. His brother Oswald received another quarter. Between them the two young men and their elderly father were sharing profits of £16,000 a year. At the same time the annual wage bill for the three hundred employees came to the same figure – £16,000. It didn't take a Marx to work out the inherent inequities in the way that earnings were being shared. Spedan Lewis thought this was wrong.

As a second-generation entrepreneur he couldn't even claim that his share of the profits was a just reward for some initial risk or the product of his sweat and sacrifice. He was simply enjoying the good fortune of his birth. A two-year period away from the business, convalescing after a serious fall from his horse, gave him time to think about his future, to think about the business and how it might be shared more equitably among the workforce. The brothers had already begun to concern themselves with the interests of the employees, encouraging sports and creating a staff magazine. The magazine would become a cornerstone of staff communications and remains a remarkable forum for employee debate and criticism almost a century on.

The process of creating a workable worker democracy was achieved by Spedan Lewis over a number of years, after his father had died and his brother had relinquished his own shares. Gradually the majority of the company's shares were vested in a trust protected by a carefully worded constitution designed to maintain the business as a partnership of employees. To parody the United States Constitution, the principle was to create a *business by the employees, for the employees.* The John Lewis constitution, drawn up in 1928, can be compared in its idealism with the corporate creed of Konosuke Matsushita, written one year later. Matsushita's creed promoted the "well-being of people" and quality of life. Matsushita was "united in spirit" with its employees. John Lewis's constitution uniquely focused its concerns on its employees. "The partnership's supreme purpose," it said, "is to secure the fairest possible sharing by all its members of the advantages of ownership – gain, knowledge, and power; that is to say their happiness in the broadest sense of the word so far as happiness depends on gainful occupation."

The concept was nothing short of revolutionary. Here was a company declaring that its prime purpose was the happiness of its employees. The Protestant work ethic is firmly planted within the company's definition of happiness – in the words "gainful employment" – but the ethic seems to have undergone some modification. It can hardly be interpreted as work for work's sake. It can be seen instead as work in order to gain happiness. This is a higher order of ambition than mere job satisfaction. It recognizes that there is something other than joy in work, that there is joy outside work, joy beyond work.

John Lewis, the company, has stuck to those principles. Sir Stuart Hampson, its former chairman, believes that the partnership structure has created a strong sense of belonging among employees.

"We are in this role for the long term, and I'm absolutely convinced that the only way to sustain success is to have a company with a happy workforce. Do they come in just for their pay or do they come in because they identify with the business?" he asks.[1]

Spedan Lewis elevated the corporate perk to a different plane, introducing his workforce to the pastimes of the aristocracy. The company bought two ocean-going racing yachts and secured the use of the Island Sailing Club on the Isle of Wight, one of the snootiest clubs in what was still, in the 1950s, one of the snootiest sports. Workers were able to enroll in the company sailing club for a nominal fee and go sailing every weekend for the price of pitching a family tent on a public campsite. Today the company has five yachts, and membership of the yacht club costs £1 a year. A day's sailing costs about £13. It has three staff golf courses and offers subsidized accommodation at four of England's most sought-after holiday retreats. There are twenty company-based special-interest clubs covering pastimes such as skiing, riding, pottery, drama, photography, and gliding. The company even secured a stretch of the River Test, one of England's finest chalk trout streams. It also makes a commitment to employees, promising job security to any who have more than five years' service.

John Lewis seems to offer the ultimate in employee security, everything that people had craved during the job clearouts of the early 1990s. So has it succeeded in its aims? Are employees happy? Well, not all the time. In 1999 there was a heated debate in its magazine, when employees began to suggest selling out so that they could cash in on the windfall from its vastly increased market capitalization. Although the suggestion was dismissed by the chairman as "carpetbagging" inspired by the greed of a minority, the company magazine's subsequent mailbag revealed that there were other arguments behind the proposals.

Some employees thought that the company's management was rooted in a hierarchical system that was not prepared to invest sales employees with any great responsibility. Why should the existing management, wondered some writers, assume that the company could not be run better as a publicly owned business answerable to outside shareholders? How could the chairman uphold the principle of employee democracy and yet refuse a referendum on the sale proposal among the company's forty thousand employees? If John Lewis really was an employee partnership, why didn't its management behave more democratically and put the company's future to the vote? The vote could not have changed the company's partnership structure, tied up in a trust, but it would have given a definitive indication of employee opinion.

The chairman did not regard the debate or any referendum as helpful in running the business. The position was clear, said Hampson. John Lewis wasn't his or any other partner's to sell. It belonged to the trust set up on behalf of the partners, not the partners themselves. Trust ownership means that employees bring nothing into the company but their labor and ideas and leave with nothing other than their pay and pensions. Ownership in this case is a transient concept related entirely to their labor. Their work conveys ownership. The real relation of the employee to the company might be called "workership."

We all live in a state of workership to some extent, influencing the world we live in by the work that we accomplish. The John Lewis Partnership has given this state some definition. The trust will not run in perpetuity. It is a finite entity. The original trust deed of 1929 fixed an expiry date for the trust twenty-one years after the death of the last descendant of King Edward VII alive at the time that the trust was established. The two surviving descendants of the King alive at that time are Queen Elizabeth II and her cousin, Lord Harewood. If the Queen has inherited the longevity and constitution of her mother, the carpetbags are likely to be moth-eaten before they can bulge with the gains from a sale of John Lewis. In the meantime, however, the company must begin to confront its mortality, possibly with some modernizing of its rigid hierarchical structure. But there is no reason why it should not carry on under sound management, providing services and employment well into the future.

In his book, *The Hungry Spirit*, the management writer, Charles Handy, discussed the role of companies in society. Inheriting the ideas of Peter Drucker's company-as-a-social-institution, Handy has pursued the implications, suggesting that if companies are to take their place in the social system they must adopt the role and responsibilities of other social structures; they must become good corporate citizens. Handy has become disenchanted

by the way that a company's market capitalization can fluctu-
ate on the whim of shareholders whose only concern is seeing a
quick return on their investment.

His latest thinking has explored the idea of a company as a
community of interest. "It's ridiculous to think of a company as
a piece of property which is owned by outsiders who, in many
cases, don't even know they own it because they own it through
a pension fund," he says. "I'm really arguing that we have to
change our concept of the company very radically and to return
to a sense of community with interest groups, and that means
diminishing the power of the shareholders."[2] Handy has toyed
with the idea of nonvoting shares for investors, but when large
blocks of shares are held by single investors or investment funds
the mere threat of disinvestment may be enough to force a management's hand.

A broader question needs to be answered by the investors. Is
it in the interest of a pension fund to force a company into knee-
jerk reactions to problems that may require longer-term plans?
Investors need to have almost as strong an understanding of
the company and its marketplace as the board itself, hence the
increasing inclusion of investor representatives on the advisory
boards of US corporations. How close should investors be to their
company? Is it best for business that a company reflects the interest of outside investors, or is there greater merit in the business
that works in the interest of internal investors, where employees
and shareholders are one and the same? Wouldn't this create
that magical alignment of interests between a company and its
employees so desired by chief executives when they ask their pay
consultants to work out incentives for their management teams?

Jeff Gates has championed the potential of businesses owned
by their employees in his book, *The Ownership Solution*. He
envisages a capitalist society in which those who participate are
given more responsibilities and a fairer share of the profits. To
some extent Peter Drucker anticipated a movement toward such
a society when he pointed out that shareholdings of large public corporations were increasingly held by mutual funds and pension funds.[3] But these investment blocks were held indirectly on
behalf of the workers; they were not held by the workers or in
any way controlled by workers except in rare examples where

they were co-opted as pension fund trustees. This was nowhere near direct ownership of the means of production by the workers. However, once private pension schemes began to dominate investment capital, particularly in the United States, it gave the employees of big business a tiny wedge. When this wedge became organized into influential voting blocks such as the California Public Employees Retirement System (Calpers) and Teachers' Insurance and Annuity Association – College Retirement Equities Fund (TIAA/CRF) – a benefit plan for teachers and researchers in the United States – the wedge was transformed into an important lever of corporate governance. A capitalist society that had always depended on workers' muscles had become increasingly dependent on the workers' wealth.

This did not mean so much for the worker, as disenfranchised from the seat of power as he ever was. Companies have been reluctant to countenance the idea of worker democracy, but the European Union's employment reforms have begun to make a difference, introducing the German works council model into those large multinationals with a presence in the member states. Many companies complained beforehand, but the councils were introduced in 1998 without so much as a whimper of unrest.

Gates places his faith in the Employment Stock Ownership Plan – the ESOP – as the conduit for conveying company ownership to employees. The concept was introduced in the 1950s by Louis Kelso, a San Francisco lawyer who began to study economics in an effort to understand why so many American workers had been laid off in the Great Depression. Here were people who wanted to work because they needed the things made in factories, but they could not buy goods without the earnings they made in their manufacturing jobs.

The virtuous cycle of production, earnings, and consumption triggered unwittingly by Henry Ford and explained by John Maynard Keynes in his 1936 treatise, *The General Theory of Employment, Interest, and Money*, had reversed itself during the Depression. Keynes had proposed large-scale public works to restore employment, earnings, buying power, and therefore demand. President Franklin D. Roosevelt put the idea into practice in a public works program he called the New Deal, and it worked, to a degree.

But the New Deal did not reduce the broadening inequalities between rich and poor. The rich did not appear to have suffered at all during the Depression. Roosevelt's administration lurched to the left in 1935 after a presidential rethink that led to new wealth taxation, increases in inheritance tax, the establishment of a graduated corporate income tax, and the Social Security Act.[4] Louisiana governor Huey Long, whose grandiose public works programs had influenced government policy, was assassinated that same year, but his son, Russell Long, began to forge his own career in politics and became chairman of the powerful Senate Finance Committee in 1964.

Attracted to any idea that might promote a fairer society, Long was persuaded by Louis Kelso to promote tax benefits for ESOPs in employment benefit legislation in 1973. This and subsequent legislation has created in the ESOP a tax-efficient method for business owners to transfer their corporate shareholdings to employees. By 2000 the National Center for Employee Ownership estimated there were 11,500 ESOP plans worth $400 billion and covering about 8.5 million employees across the United States. By 2009, the number of employees had risen to nearly 14 million with assets worth $925 billion.

While the ESOP increases employee share ownership, in most cases the employee shareholding remains a minority one, typically between 5 and 20 percent of a company's stock. In terms of employee numbers the biggest employee-owned companies in the USA are Publix Supermarkets (145,000 in 2009) and Hy-Vee supermarkets (55,000 in 2009).

The ESOP was designed as a tax-efficient form of corporate finance that could benefit both employees and owners. The way it works is that the company sets up a trust fund for employees. The company then either puts shares into the plan or contributes cash to buy company shares. Alternatively the plan may borrow money to buy shares and the company then makes payments into the plan to repay the loan. These contributions can be deducted from corporation tax. Employees pay no tax on the shares until they retire, when they can either sell their shares on the market or sell them back to the company. If the ESOP owns 30 percent of the stock, the company owners who are selling their own stock to the employee trust can defer taxation on their capital gain by reinvesting the proceeds in other corporate securities. The tax benefit of the ESOP is both its strength and its weakness. It means the ESOP has become a relatively popular tool for raising finance, either to undertake a management buyout from a parent company or to extract some value from shares for an owner in a partial sale to employees.

It does not mean, however, that the ESOP has delivered some kind of utopian worker democracy. A minority of managements whose adoption of ESOPs has been accompanied by some power-sharing idealism have experienced difficulty making their ideas work. Jerry Gorde converted Vatex, a company based in Richmond, Virginia, into an employee-owned cooperative, using an ESOP, but he abandoned the arrangement ten years later, buying out the shareholdings of the fifty-four employees for $750,000, after concluding that the workers had not understood the demands of capitalism.

Under the cooperative system the company created an employee-elected board. It was the responsibility of the board to select a president and a chief executive. Worker committees set pay rates and employment policy. The idea was that the checks and balances built into the company – its governance – were organized democratically while hierarchical management relying on a chain of command would be maintained.

The system did not work, said Gorde, because workers were constantly rebelling against authority. "They don't realize they are the authority," he said. The comment was injudicious. Gorde was the authority. He had no belief in the employees' ability to read balance sheets or understand the business, and the employees ultimately had no belief in themselves. This is the dilemma of worker democracy. The culture of adversarial relations – the mindsets of managers who believe they know best and workers who shy away from responsibility, thereby confirming their mutual prejudices – is not easily broken.

Gates writes of a unionized company, Clark of New Jersey, bought out using an ESOP. This former General Motors roller bearing plant could not shake off labor disputes even after employees became shareholders. On one occasion they instigated a go-slow in pursuit of a profit share-out when the company had wanted to use the profit for investment. The industrial action wiped out the profit and with it a badly needed plant upgrade. Ultimately all the jobs were destroyed when the business failed.[5]

The Clark case highlights another problem of the ESOP – it has sometimes been used as a last-gasp source of finance for a struggling company or as an escape mechanism for owners who can see no future for the business. This was true of the employee buyouts instigated by the steel industry unions. Steel has a special place in the history of the American economy. Steel and railroads working in harmony were the driving forces of the late-nineteenth-century US economy, pushing expansion westward. Oil and automobiles became the pistons of the early twentieth century but steel, which reached its employment peak of 650,000 in 1953, remained a vital industry until the 1980s, when cheaper high-quality Japanese imports began to eat into the US steel market. Suddenly US steel companies found themselves dated and uncompetitive. New processes helped stave off the technological decline but could not prevent industry contraction. Neither could they prevent layoffs, since the new technology was inevitably labor-saving.

The steel trade unions took the gamble of negotiating ESOP plans in the steel businesses for their members. In 1997 some 60,000 of the remaining 163,000 American steelworkers were shareholders in ESOP plans. Worker ownership began to change the union–management relationship. As shareholders the union members were more willing to accept flexible working practices that made the plants more efficient. Their new ownership perspective also made them more demanding of their union leadership, expecting it to display a greater understanding of business. Labor disputes became a thing of the past. But whether the arrangement is strong enough to stave off the forces involved in industry decline remains to be seen.

The same question was faced by Tower Colliery. As one of the last remaining coal mines in South Wales, the colliery was bought out and run by its workers when every other of its neighboring mines had been closed down by the state-owned National Coal Board as uneconomic. Tower Colliery, which finally closed in 2008, was a bold experiment in worker ownership, extending a way of life that was precious to the people of South Wales. The jobs that replaced those in mining were typically low-paid, low-skilled warehousing or assembly manufacturing. The miners at Tower restored their pride and asserted their independence. But theirs was a fragile capitalism, not an expansionist enterprise. The mine's lifetime was finite, depending on coal resources and available markets.

The most successful ESOP arrangements have involved the simultaneous introduction of more participatory management styles. Companies that began to trust their employees, explaining their business plans and sharing monthly sales and profit data – so-called open-book management – began to reap dividends in big improvements to their business performance.

Management at Springfield ReManufacturing in Springfield, Missouri, disproved Gorde's arguments when they introduced training for employees so that they could read financial and production figures. Work groups are encouraged to analyze financial statements and look for possible improvements. When Springfield launched its employee ownership plan in 1983 its share price stood at 10¢. By 1993 the price had risen to $21. Like many companies who have introduced ESOPs, Springfield has worked at developing closer cooperation and consultation between management and workers.

The employee-share-owned companies appear to have become the proving ground for Drucker's theories on self-managed groups. The most successful of them are harnessing the creativeness of their employees, using quality circles, project teams, and suggestion schemes. A study in 1987 found that ESOP companies that increased worker involvement in decision-making grew more rapidly than they would have done otherwise.[6]

The danger of employee-owned companies is that they may be seen as a way of amassing a fortune rather than as a going concern that can, with prudent and skillful management, provide livelihoods for generations. This was the idea of Spedan Lewis. It was also the idea of David Erdal, the former owner of Tullis Russell, a Scottish paper manufacturing business. Erdal sold his shareholdings to a trust that now owns the business on behalf of employees. The sale was financed by a loan that is being paid off over a number of years out of profits. Severed from his family business connection, Erdal has used his new independence to undertake a study comparing the quality of life in a cooperative community run on egalitarian lines with that of a community dominated by private business.

He chose for his comparison Sassuolo and Imola, two small towns not far from Bologna in northern Italy. Imola, a town of about 60,000 people, is supported by a large number of cooperative ventures, many of them more than a hundred years old. Some 18 percent of its population works in cooperatives, and about a third of the town's families have at least one member working in a co-op. Just forty miles away in Sassuolo, a town of 40,000 people, no one works in a cooperative. One of the first differences Erdal noticed among his population samples, drawn for comparison, was that Imola had no great divide between rich and poor, whereas the divide in Sassuolo was much sharper.

Erdal wanted to test his theory that cooperative ventures promote stronger, more peace-loving, and healthier communities. The evidence pointed to greater involvement in voluntary work and more employee training in Imola. But one of the most striking discoveries was that people in Imola were living considerably longer than those in Sassuolo, with a 14 percent lower mortality rate over the six years prior to the research which started in 1998. "Employee share ownership makes you live longer. That's the main thing I want to bring out," said Erdal, shortly after analyzing his preliminary results in 1999.[7] As he pointed out, "Sassuolo is a good place to live by international comparisons – but Imola is better."

There is some supporting evidence for this finding in a long-running study of hierarchies in the British civil service. A study of the health prospects among Whitehall mandarins, carried out by Michael Marmot, director of the International Centre for Health and Society at University College, London, has discovered that people lower down a hierarchy are more likely to suffer heart attacks than those in the upper echelons.[8]

The cooperative employees of Mondragon in the Spanish Basque region would need no convincing by academic research that their way of life is preferable to that of employees in conventional businesses. Mondragon is one of the success stories of the cooperative movement. The movement itself began in 1844 in Rochdale, Lancashire, when a group of tradesmen pooled their resources to form the Rochdale Society of Equitable Pioneers. The Rochdale pioneers, inspired by the ideas of Robert Owen, the Welsh-born textile entrepreneur turned utopian dreamer, were at the vanguard of a movement that would spread worldwide, influencing the working practices of millions.

But can this kind of enterprise prevail in a capitalist system where only the strong succeed and the weak either go to the wall or find themselves absorbed by a merger? The story of Mondragon suggests that it can. Cooperative working was established quietly in this Basque town in 1941, when Spain's European neighbors were at war. Father Jose Maria Arizmendiarrieta, a Catholic priest and a veteran of the Republican cause in the Spanish Civil War, arrived in Mondragon intent upon carrying out a mission on behalf of his bishop to help the town's young people.

His proposal to enlarge a school for apprentices run by the town's largest industrial employer, the Union Cerrajera steel company, was rejected by its management, so the priest made plans instead for a separate school. He placed urns, like ballot boxes, on street corners and asked people to drop letters pledging cash or any other support they might give to the proposal. The six hundred replies represented support from a quarter of the families in the town's 8,000 population.[9] As Robert Oakeshott points out in his book, *Jobs & Fairness*, a strong community involvement and spirit of self-help were engendered among the students and their families from the start.

Five of his original graduates who continued their studies, gaining engineering degrees at Zaragoza University, returned to Mondragon, where they worked in management at Union Cerrajera. They wanted the company's senior managers to restructure the business on the cooperative social model that had been outlined to them as students by Fr Arizmendiarrieta. When the company rejected their ideas, they left to set up their own cooperative factory in 1956, making oil stoves and heaters. By the end of the century the Mondragon Co-operative Corporation was one of the largest corporations in Spain, being the country's largest supplier of domestic appliances and machine tools, and an important supplier of car parts, employing twenty-six thousand people in a hundred industrial, financial, and retail companies. Eighty of these businesses are cooperatives.

Woven into this network of businesses are worker education and training centers, universities, research centers, and service cooperatives. The cooperatives are worker owned and democratically managed. Each worker has the right to vote colleagues onto a general assembly that elects the board. No one in the company earns more than six times the salary of the lowest paid worker. Typically, when a company grows to more than five hundred employees, the parent finances another start-up company to ensure that each unit remains relatively small and manageable.

Mondragon is a giant among cooperatives, but at the other end of the scale some businesses have learned to live with even more democratic and idealistic principles. SUMA Wholefoods, a sixty-strong cooperative based in Halifax, England, was created in the 1970s by a group of lentil-eating hippies who became attracted to vegetarian lifestyles and wanted to ensure a continuing supply of wholefood. The business has proved determinedly idealistic in its principles, interchanging management roles with those of production work and paying the same pay packages to everyone, whether they sweep the floors or look after the accounts. No one is rich at SUMA, but the business sustains itself and the pay is reasonable in a low wage area with higher than average unemployment.

Cooperatives take many forms, but many of them tend to have a dated image with histories steeped in the ideology of socialism and worker equality in the factory system. More recent manifestations tend to be founded on a desire for more equitable working arrangements. Loch Fyne Oysters is owned and run by its employees through the Loch Fyne Oysters Trust that lists as its aims: "relief of poverty, the advancement of education and the protection of the environment particularly within Scotland and the area around the head of Loch Fyne."

Employee shareholding ideals also led to the establishment of the London advertising agency, St. Luke's, an employee-owned business that feeds off its collective imagination and channels its creativity into advertising campaigns. St. Luke's started life as the London office of Chiat Day, the US advertising agency known for its colorful open-plan offices exploiting the fashion for "hot desking," where employees who only spend part of their working week in the office are encouraged to share desks. Andy Law, the London-based executive responsible for finding new business, David Abraham, the account director, and a group of other colleagues were asked by their head office to look at ways of renewing the company. They wanted to explore the concept of running the business on strong ethical principles. The idea was rejected by the US parent, but Law and Abraham went ahead with their idea anyway, working with clients in a more open way, who warmed to the approach. But when Chiat Day sold out to Omnicom, one of the largest advertising businesses in the United States, neither Law, Abraham, nor their London colleagues wanted to be part of the new set-up. In a company where people are the only real assets their views carried considerable clout. Omnicon agreed to sell them the London business for £1 in return for a £1.2 million share of its profits over the next seven years.[10]

Law and Abraham were the ostensible owners of this new business, but how could they pursue a policy of openness, trust, and cooperation with their talented colleagues if these people were merely employees earning profits for a two-man partnership who simply got lucky? It didn't seem fair or particularly sensible if they wanted to retain the best people, so they set up the business as an employee-owned cooperative. They, too, opted for the trust method of ownership, distributing shares to employees but retaining a majority ownership in trust.

In its early days the atmosphere of St. Luke's was trendy beyond belief, with special rooms for clients called "brand meeting rooms" and a round room called the "womb," used as a retreat. Strip away the fancy furniture and there may not have been much difference between this business and many other professional partnerships – Law himself left in the mid-2000s to set up a networked franchise-based company called The Law Firm – but it showed that employee ownership and partnership, backed by a sense of idealism, could thrive in an economy dominated by multimillion dollar share-option deals for chief executives and telephone-number bonuses for investment bankers. This disconnected world of fat-cat salaries caused deep concern and government approbation in the 1990s, yet deep down many of us continued to harbor desires for wealth and riches. When Gordon Gekko puffed out his chest in Oliver Stone's 1987 film, *Wall Street*, and announced "Greed is good," it was supposed to invite contempt. But too many of us believed him.

CHAPTER 19

The End of Management

So much of what we call management consists of making it
difficult for people to work.

(Peter Drucker, b. 1909)

London's Houses of Parliament, the Gothic revivalist creation of
Charles Barry and Augustus Pugin, were built for a period when
the spoken word carried far more influence than it does today.
Pugin's magnificent interiors, with their bold William Morris
prints, are a constant reminder of the history embedded in the
building's walls. It has a humbling, majestic, and sometimes
intimidating atmosphere, and it was here, in committee room
15 in January, 1995, that fifty-nine-year-old Cedric Brown, the
head of one of the UK's largest companies, faced charges placed
before him in the gravest tones by his parliamentary inquisitors.
Brown, the then chief executive of British Gas, was accused of
making too much money, of agreeing to a pay raise that was
wholly unacceptable.

Brown had risen through the ranks at British Gas, starting
in what had been the publicly owned Gas Board as a fitter after
leaving school at age 16. His was a story of a hardworking young
man who made good after years of solid effort, the type of
story that is admired and celebrated in the United States. But
Americans do not suffer from envy to anything like the same
degree as their British cousins. Envy is part of the British disease. When stirred together with equal measures of self-righteous
indignation and the British sense of fair play it creates a potent
cocktail worthy of a newspaper's front page.

Brown's pay details had been reproduced in the company's
annual report, a legal requirement covering British-registered
publicly quoted companies. A journalist had queried the size of
the raise, and a British Gas press officer had explained that it
amounted to a salary increase of 75 percent, from £275,000 to

£475,000. Any further explanation was superfluous in terms of tabloid column-inches.

The 75 percent raise in basic pay was quite correct, but it did not tell the whole story. The figure had been skewed by some financial manipulations. Brown was approaching retirement, and his pension would be calculated as a proportion of his basic pay. His overall pay, including bonuses, was much higher than his basic pay, and the board wanted to consolidate some of this unpensionable bonus pay into basic pay in order to boost his pension. This kind of manipulation was perfectly legitimate and not uncommon. It was regularly used to guarantee an agreeable send-off and a comfortable lifestyle to the chief who had made it through to retirement. It might not have been perceived as fair by some, but such arrangements were par for the course in the relationship between top people in big companies and their pay advisors. The raise in overall pay – the real raise in effect – was 28 percent over two years, enough for most of us perhaps. The problem was that the basic figure stood out in the report like the proverbial sore thumb, and an irritating journalist had the presence of mind to question it.

The result was a scandal, the sort of newspaper feeding-frenzy in which the British press delights. Cedric Brown was branded a fat cat. Brown became the representative whipping boy for all top UK executives perceived to be overpaid, particularly those former public servants who now headed privatized utility companies. Once their utilities had entered the private sector they saw their pay awards spiral to levels that more closely matched those in competitor companies. Pay is emotional, and Cedric Brown's pay raise was starkly translated in newspaper headlines.

There were plenty of obvious metaphors. Some newspapers described him as a pig with his snout in the trough. The unions were only too happy to lend a hand. Lest the public were in any doubt about this analogy, the GMB general workers union acquired a pig it named Cedric. The pig was paraded before the press in organized photo opportunities. Brown, the former public servant turned capitalist, was pilloried. And this was only the start.

The Employment Committee – a parliamentary investigatory committee comprising eleven sitting Members of Parliament of different political hues – decided it was time to look at executive pay arrangements. When Brown sat before the committee that January day he knew what lay in store. It didn't help that for the previous few months British Gas had been seeking to reduce the basic pay of many of its employees, while increasing their variable pay, placing more emphasis on the element that could be earned in commission – a reversal of the changes made to Brown's pay.

Politicians can work with this kind of material. First they softened him up with questions on the staff pay negotiations, then they went for his enhanced pension. Brown confirmed that his improved pension entitlements would cost the British Gas pension fund an extra £750,000, according to calculations made by actuaries. There was more. How much did he earn in a day, asked one committee member who had calculated the figure at around £1,000, and how much did his lowest-paid workers earn? Brown reckoned he earned more than a thousand a day. A sales assistant, he said, would earn between £10,000 and £13,000 a year. It was clear what was coming next. Would he be happy to work for £10,000 a year? Brown said it was a matter of differentials, so the committee discussed differentials. The average ratios of top-to-bottom pay in Japan, they noted, were about 7:1. "Do you not think that is a more fair and equitable system for running a business? It certainly seems to be a successful one, since the Japanese are the competitors who we are all chasing, for productivity, efficiency, and all the rest of it, in the world market," said Angela Eagle, who had taken over the questioning.

Brown hit back with US ammunition. He could think of the boss of a much smaller American competitor who earned ten times his own salary. The question of differentials, he said, was a matter for politicians. But, as he also suggested, the chief executive's pay was an important figure to get right in a privatized company. Implicit in his argument was the possibility that in a few years' time the company might be seeking to fill the post from outside, and it would need to offer a rate of pay that would attract candidates from its competitors.

None of this mattered much to the committee. The harrying continued, increasing in intensity when the baton was handed to the chairman, Greville Janner. Other committee members had already highlighted a voluntary redundancy program. Janner mentioned one or two other little embarrassing coincidences occurring around the time the pay raise came into the public domain. On top of the start of a restructuring program that would shed the jobs of 25,000 people (a third of the workforce), the company had announced an increase in the price of gas and the closure of many of its showrooms. There had also been a leak of plans to cut spending on safety surveys of gas mains, and complaints to the Gas Consumers Council had risen considerably. Did he not agree, asked Janner, that it had been insensitive and tactless to handle the pay raise in the way that it was handled? "I think it could have been handled better," said Brown.

But that was not enough for Janner, who administered the *coup de grâce* with a verbal flourish: "Mr Brown, it was insensitive, tactless, and a grave mistake, and you were chief executive at the time?" Brown's reply was a simple "Yes."[1] If there is such a thing as Judgment Day, surely it could not offer anything as severe as this.

American pay consultants were incredulous at the hullabaloo over Brown's pay. There had been some ructions in the United States, but over much vaster salaries. In late 1992, for example, Michael Eisner, the chairman of Walt Disney, exercised $202 million of share options. The presence of these options packages has made the basic pay rates of senior US executives almost insignificant in comparison. Since then, Eisner's earnings through share options have soared even further into the stratosphere. Shortly after he had realized another $551.6 million before tax from cashing in share options in 1998, *Fortune* magazine estimated the total value of Eisner's options, both exercised and unexercised, at $1.43 billion and suggested that his pay deal might have made Eisner the "highest-paid hired hand in history."[2]

Making money had always been a perfectly respectable and thoroughly laudable exercise in the USA, whereas British society had been weaned on seventeenth-century amateurism, academic indifference, and professional snobbery that preferred to emphasize the notion of vocation over grubby commercialism. The poorer working masses went along with this system, arguing that wealth and privilege were "not for the likes of us."[3] It did not help any when American commentators like Gary Hamel, the management writer and academic, pointed to the lack of entrepreneurialism among public company chief executives, many of whom had never known what it was to build a company from scratch, unlike those who ran the technological power-houses of Silicon Valley in California.

Cedric Brown retired soon afterwards. His work steering British Gas into the private marketplace had been eclipsed by the infamy of his pay raise. A committee was formed to look at exec-utive pay policy throughout the UK. It met under the tough and uncompromising control of Richard Greenbury, the chief execu-tive of Marks & Spencer, Britain's best-loved retailer. Greenbury was one of the most respected business chiefs in the country. Within two years his committee had made its recommendations for even greater clarity in corporate reporting of salaries, greater independence of remuneration committees in the deliberation of pay awards, and increased clarity in the fixing of pension arrangements (a point that was later fudged after submissions from actuaries).

Suddenly corporate governance was a hot topic on both sides of the Atlantic. Within a further two years Greenbury had retired form Marks & Spencer amid growing consternation and board-room battles among his fellow executives about the future direction of the company, as its sales and profits plummeted. If Marks & Spencer was in trouble, it seemed that no one was safe. Other giants began to falter, relying on mergers to maintain market dominance.

Nevertheless, chief executive salaries continued to climb ever upwards, attracting forthright comments from people like John Edmonds, general secretary of the GMB union, who, when presi-dent of Britain's Trades Union Congress, quite simply called their recipients "greedy bastards."[4] If it wasn't inflated pay increases it was overblown payoffs for a job done badly. When the board of British Airways agreed a £1.98 million payoff and a handsome pen-sion for its former chief executive, Bob Ayling, who lost his job after the company ran up losses of £244 million in the financial year 1999–2000, shareholders rebelled and forced the board to review its arrangements.[5] It looked like Ayling, a former civil servant, was being rewarded for failure. Where was the justice in that?

It seemed particularly improper that large rewards were avail-able for people who had never known what it was to build a company from scratch or who had never displayed an ounce of entrepreneurial or innovative sparkle. Gary Hamel has described disparagingly the heads of large public companies as a generation of "stewards" whose main role is to concentrate on efficiencies and return value to shareholders.[6] Stewardship, he argues, does not involve risk or entrepreneurialism. On the contrary, it is risk averse.

In the late 1990s the position of these boardroom stewards seemed unassailable. In 2000 they found themselves under attack, as many of them saw their company's stock market capitalization begin to stagnate. Financial journalists, stirred by the performance of Internet stocks in the first few months of the new century, began to partition the business sector into the old and new economies. In writing of solid manufacturing or service sector businesses as "old economy" enterprises, there was an implicit suggestion that these were solid, slow-moving, boring old businesses not worth the candle when compared to the nimble, agile, youthful and sexy dot.com start-ups of the "new economy."

Hamel helped to compound the slur, describing these solid multinationals and their obsession with mergers as "dinosaurs mating."[7] Even then the analogy was ironic since dinosaurs were hugely successful animals who lived on the planet for 160 million years. Subsequent events would prove the accuracy of this observation. At the time, however, Hamel was using the word "dinosaur" as a metaphor for an outdated, lumbering giant. He went further in his dismissal of these merging multinationals, commenting: "I'm not sure that two drunks make a stable person."[8] Investors seemed to concur with him in 1999 and early 2000, switching their loyalty to emerging technology stocks, but the euphoria couldn't last, and by the end of 2000 many of the stalwarts were beginning to reassert themselves as technology stocks nose-dived.

Worse still, Enron, the energy company that Hamel had championed as a business revolutionary, a paragon of innovation and an "open market for talent,"[9] collapsed amid one of the biggest business frauds in history. Other prominent business frauds, including those of WorldCom and Tyco, led to the 2002 Sarbanes-Oxley Act that tightened regulatory controls on companies in the US.

The companies that could adapt to harsher trading conditions after the 1990s era of excess, argued Richard Pascale, the management writer, were behaving like the kind of "complex adaptive systems" found in nature. "'Living Systems' isn't a metaphor for how human institutions operate. It's the way it is," he wrote in *Surfing the Edge of Chaos*.[10]

As companies attempted to come to grips with this new Darwinism, it was no surprise to find that tried and trusted management methods, perfected and refined for a century, were running aground. Were we beginning to witness the end of management as we knew it?

The signs had been there for several years in the vogue for flatter hierarchies, single-status workplaces, and bosses who called themselves colleagues, associates, or partners. While these more egalitarian-looking company chiefs may have been on first-name terms with their staff, the fundamental power base in most companies did not change. There are still hierarchies supported by ambitious managers and formal reporting structures. Some of these managers, like Andy Grove at Intel, would sit among their staff in tiny offices, sharing the work experience – but he was still an autocrat. And top management remained a male-dominated world.

Women have found it tough to penetrate what they describe as the "glass ceiling," a layer of management beyond which few emerge to rub shoulders with the executive elite. One who has is Marjorie Scardino, the American chief executive of Pearson, the London-headquartered media and information conglomerate, who won her spurs increasing the circulation of the *Economist* business magazine in the United States.

It was a big jump to take over the helm of an FTSE 100 company, and Scardino's arrival was regarded with initial suspicion, particularly when she seemed slow to act. But when she did move, she demonstrated a boldness that earned the admiration of her peers. She set ambitious targets and talked the language of the Internet teeny-boppers. Pearson moved with apparent ease from the old economy into the playground of the new. But her success did not trigger a feminine revolution. In September, 2000 less than 2 percent of executive directors in the FTSE 100 – the UK's largest quoted companies – were women.[11]

At the top of the largest US companies the presence of women was not much stronger. *Fortune* 500 companies had only two women chief executives in the year 2000. It took Carleton S. Fiorina at Hewlett-Packard more than twenty years at companies like AT&T and Lucent to get to the top. Andrea Jung had been passed over once for an outside candidate, before she eventually became chief executive at Avon.

Women had greater success in dot.com start-up companies. The initial investor appeal of these businesses offered a bypass of the traditional boardroom. Suddenly women could get to the top through the entrepreneur route, not the route that was controlled by the headhunter who had mastered the game of boardroom musical chairs.

Each of these developments tended to disguise other forces pounding away at traditional workplace relationships. One of these was technological. The modem, the Internet, and speedier electronic connections were enabling increasing numbers of people during the 1990s to work from home. The extent of this practice was difficult to gauge, because the work was often done quietly. This was a silent movement, not normally arranged in a systemized or organized way – people were reasoning that as long as the work was done, why should their managers complain? Sometimes it had the approval of managers, sometimes it did not. Sometimes it was pursued by the managers themselves, retreating to dens at home for some solitude away from the unceasing demands of their offices. Occasionally, combined with a reduction in desks to save on office overheads – the hot-desking system introduced at St. Luke's – it was part of a planned regime of working. This system began in computer companies but had become so commonplace (and so unpopular) in 2001 that *Fortune* magazine thought it worth highlighting the "benefits" of offices with a door, desk, and computer for each staff member at Plante & Moran, a Michigan accounting firm, listed tenth in its "100 Best Companies to Work for" feature, without a trace of irony.[12]

Teleworking – the name given to this mixture of home and office work – demanded different attitudes to work. Firstly it demanded a degree of trust that workers were not shirking. Beyond that it needed a reassessment of what was perceived as shirking. If workers were saving two hours a day on their daily commutes, and if they chose to spend some of that time watching the TV, wandering in their gardens or running the odd errand, what did this matter to their bosses, as long as they delivered results? After all, most office workers would take natural breaks throughout the day to gossip around the coffee machine or go for a smoke. Even at their desks they might be exchanging personal emails or trawling the Internet. In many offices the amount of real productive work taking place seemed to be dwindling, yet hours spent at work appeared to be lengthening.

No such changes were apparent among assembly workers tied to their workbenches. The processes of scientific management remained apparent, also, in the proliferating use of call centers for servicing customers, often based in large, anonymous sheds – the battery cages of the information industry. Nor was life much different for those whose days were governed by strict timetables and deadlines, such as teachers, postal workers, and train drivers. But, to the authoritarian mind, new technology appeared to have delivered unprecedented opportunities for shirking as well as for work.

There were two approaches to this dilemma: to police the technology and the worker's day – a costly use of managerial time and which is technically difficult – or to outline clearly the expectations that went with the job and monitor the results. The second option placed the responsibility on workers to manage their job as they saw fit. It was not quite so straightforward, because it would be incumbent on the employer to ensure that employees were well trained and appraised of the company's policies and culture. But extending greater freedom and scope to the employee might bring added dividends of innovation and creativity. The idling or incompetent worker could be quickly weeded out, or, better still, could be taken in hand and helped or redirected into work that was better suited to his or her potential.

The increase in online working was soon forcing the issue. In late 2000 the intimate contents of an email sent by a sometime girlfriend to a junior lawyer at Norton Rose, a large London firm of solicitors, was passed between the lawyer and some of his colleagues. Within two days the message had been seen by millions around the world.[13] The Norton Rose website received so much traffic in response that it crashed. Suddenly, workplace email policies and protocols became an urgent issue, as companies woke up to the power of this Pandora's Box they had introduced as a tool.

Incidents such as this emphasize the urgency of the need for businesses to establish relationships of trust with their employees. Big Brother-style controls, recalling the days of the factory overseer, may be the knee-jerk answer but are hardly likely to increase job satisfaction or improve workplace morale. In the online workplace it will be incumbent on an enterprise to ensure that work is meaningful. When the tool is also a toy, when it works like a television set allowing workers to download their favorite film or music, the real work had better be absorbing if it is to distract the on-screen worker from tarrying within the Internet.

In spite of the growing literature and theory of the empowered workplace, *The Dilbert Principle*, a book of cynical cartoons, is one of the world's most popular business books, because it recognizes the reality of the workplace and the disingenuousness of so much modern management theory. We are told about job enrichment and self-management on the one hand, but on the other hand we still run up against the boss–minion relationship.

"Subordinate" is such an archaic word; it should be banished from the workplace lexicon. But the "subordinate" still exists. Archie Norman might have introduced the term "colleagues" to engender a sense of equality when he was chief executive of Asda supermarkets, but he was still the boss. If the boss said that meetings would take place standing up, as Norman did, then that was the rule. Managers, like the craftsmen of Midvale, instinctively work to the rule. In this case it is a hierarchical rule with lines of authority. The more senior of them have been invested with power and budgets, and many are poorly equipped, behaviorally, to exercise the relationship with their staff in a spirit of openness and trust.

The inadequacy of management in trying to implement Drucker's self-managed work teams is at the heart of much workplace tension today. Many managers feel uncomfortable with the language of "bosses" and "subordinates," but this language and the concepts that go with it are tremendously resilient. It is not only managers but employees, too, who need to adjust. Self-management means just that. If you go to a boss and ask for work, you are perpetuating a relationship that must change in the creative workplace. Stephen Barley, a professor at Stanford University, says this conditioning is perpetuated in "western images of work rooted in several polarities: mental/manual, clean/ dirty, educated/uneducated, white collar/blue collar, manager/ worker."[14] The first and last terms of each of these polarities, wrote Barley, anchored "the upper and lower end of a system of status and prestige."

But the fastest growing technical jobs in the United States – those of programmers, systems analysts, operations researchers, computer operators, and computer repair technicians – were, he argued, fundamentally altering the organization of work, since the roles did not fuse easily with traditional offices manned by managers and secretaries. The newer jobs, staffed by technical experts, would require management to take on a coordinating role between teams of professionals.

Barley also noticed that a study of secretaries at Cornell University had revealed that the spread of computers was developing the secretarial job into that of an administrative or research assistant. It appeared that the jobs of the secretary and the manager were beginning to merge, yet there remained a gulf between the reward and qualifications for – and status of – the two jobs. Barley predicted, however, that technology would produce more horizontal divisions of labor, with significant consequences for management. "Management's traditional source of legitimacy will begin to wane," he asserted, concluding that "the likelihood is that managers, unable to make knowledgeable decisions autocratically, will find themselves relegated to the important but less heady role of coordination."

Barley may well be on the right track in his thinking, but his conclusion demands some greater analysis of the managerial job. Henry Mintzberg described the job accurately as something of a juggling act in his 1973 book, *The Nature of Managerial Work*. A manager's time, he wrote, was perpetually interrupted. Far from the portrait of managerial work outlined by Henri Fayol, [15] emphasizing planning, organization, coordination, and control, the manager was constantly handling interruptions, each of which, typically, would be delegated and disposed of within ten minutes.

While the coordinating role remains important in management, other functions such as planning and organization are increasingly being handed over to employees. This can only happen if there is a relaxation of control. But there is another significant role for managers working closely with professional employees who by the nature of their work will exercise high degrees of self-management. Advertising, education, the media, marketing, finance, and research and development are all sectors where this relationship is evolving. This is the concept of the customer-manager, whose relationship with the professional is transactional rather than commanding.

A relationship on these lines has existed for years in English barristers' chambers, where the clerk offers work to the barristers, who choose whether they want to take it. The clerk is an important coordinating and administrative figure, but he does not have the same status or earnings power as the senior barristers. In other organizations, where departmental demarcation lines have been reduced by reengineering, the customer-manager will undoubtedly need to have technical knowledge and some experience to make a fair assessment of the product. He will also begin to notice that he is in competition with other managers in the same organization.

I have been involved in these transactional relationships inside newspapers and seen them working among colleagues. A newspaper comprises several sections, each run by a separate editor. At the *Financial Times* there are numerous page editors responsible for the day-to-day content and appearance of these pages. A story may by "sold" by a writer to any one of these editors he or she thinks most appropriate. If he thinks the story strong enough for the outside pages, he could sell it further or let it establish its own strength as it is evaluated throughout the day. Often a feature idea is discussed before it is researched, to assess the willingness of an editor to use it or the willingness and suitability of a writer to undertake the work.

Relationships between writers and editors are important, because each will use past experience to make a judgment about the willingness of the other to keep his or her side of the bargain. The bargain is not always recognized as such explicitly, but it is implicit. Often the contract is precise, expecting a certain number of words by a certain deadline. There has to be flexibility in these arrangements. Pressure of space may force a story aside. But, like the boy who cried wolf, the writer soon recognizes the editor who overcommissions or who hacks back a good story. When this happens the writer will try to "sell" his material elsewhere and he will go to someone who he knows will handle his story sensitively and use it sensibly.

The contract works both ways, and an editor will mark the card of an unreliable writer, commissioning him less frequently. But editors may not always realize the two-sidedness of the relationship, that they have become customers. They may still see themselves as originators using writers as suppliers, but they cannot always count on a writer who may be working for someone else. It can be seen, therefore, that the editor–writer relationship is quite fluid, relying heavily on mutual understanding, trust, and professionalism. The same relationships are emerging elsewhere. The manager who expects his charges to drop everything at the sound of his command is fossilizing before our eyes.

That said, it's all very well relating the experience of a newspaper, but can a more open transactional relationship exist between managers and employees in manufacturing? Ricardo Semler, the chief executive of Semco, the Brazilian white-goods manufacturer, has proved that in a country noted for its traditional boss–worker autocracies, it is possible to originate innovative management styles. When Semler inherited the business from his father, his first action was to purge the top management of all those who were not prepared to align their views with his. His second step was to recruit a solid finance head and an aggressive head of sales. Those who departed may have judged Semler as no less ruthless than any previous corporate demagogue. He was growing the business by acquisition through leverage – supporting his bids on the promise of future profits. Managers were putting in long hours to achieve their goals, rarely seeing their families. "Work hard or get fired. That was the ethic of the new Semco," he conceded later.[16] But Semler had other ideas once the company had secured its survival with a sound financial base, a healthy order book, and a collection of businesses that had promising prospects of growth. People had been pushed forward, he wrote. Supposing he tried to create a "self-propelled" workforce.

Change to a more democratic workplace at Semco started with a crisis. At the age of twenty-five Semler felt seriously ill. His vital signs were fine, but his doctor told him that his was the most advanced case of stress he had encountered in someone of Semler's age. Semler decided to rebel against the most ingrained ethic of his business regime – the gospel of hard work that concentrated on quantity over quality. "Executives feel pressure from their bosses to outwork colleagues and build their image and career," he wrote. "By this reasoning, having a heart attack because of work leads to true glory, and keeling over at the office is even better – a sign, a Calvinist might say, of being among The Elect."[17]

His tactic was to move first on the little things, the details: ending factory searches of employees and getting rid of time cards to check up on workers' arrival and leaving times. Formal dress codes were abandoned and signs of status, such as embossed business cards, personal parking bays, and private executive dining rooms, were removed. Secretaries were shared, and offices were no longer fitted out in size and decor according to seniority. Participative management was encouraged rather than consultative management.

Semler was careful to stress this difference, which is key to the changing managerial role. Participative management, says Semler, does not merely involve listening to people's opinions but involves handing over decision-making responsibilities. At last someone had grasped Drucker's fifty-year-old plea for self-managed plants. "It's only when the bosses give up decision-making and let their employees govern themselves that the possibility exists for a business jointly managed by workers and executives," wrote Semler.

Management as managers knew it for most of the twentieth century has all but disappeared at Semco. The trail blazed by this Brazilian manufacturer is the model for the future. Semler has opted for common-sense management, throwing out the procedures and rulebooks. His common-sense approach, based on what is right and proper, has transformed the way Semco goes about its business. At the core of this transformation is a reliance on trust, a belief that most people in the workforce will not rip off their employer if they are treated decently and fairly. Anyone who wants to know about the business can look at the books, and if they don't understand the figures there are training courses to explain what they mean.

Where Semco has ventured, others may follow. Within the next twenty or thirty years we may well see the disappearance of conventional management and reporting structures, replaced by interdependent networks engaged in transactional relationships. Complex adaptive systems demand responsive front-line employees, as Richard Pascale has pointed out.

If old-style management becomes extinct, management itself will flourish, because it remains an organizational foundation of human society. Management wasn't invented. It has existed from the earliest times. Only its definition changes periodically. Work will remain in tomorrow's enterprise and will still need to be managed. But people will increasingly manage themselves.

Wages will become more erratic, reflecting good years and bad. Many people will work from a base line, with possibilities to increase their wealth through bonuses and incentives and by working on specific projects. But there will be no accusatory finger pointed at those workers who want a more balanced life. In fact balanced workers will be desired, because it will be perceived and accepted that they are pacing themselves. As the demographic curve begins to swell the numbers of people in Western society at or near retirement age, it will become more natural and desirable from both employers' and employees' standpoints for people to ease their way into retirement, working less hard but perhaps working later into their seventies.

The demographic shadow created by falling birth rates in the West and Japan has created a new caucus of doom-mongers, worried about pension fund deficiencies and falling sperm counts. But they rarely seem to factor into their arguments the large injections of inherited wealth that the late twentieth-century middle classes began to enjoy with the death of their parents, often around the time their offspring would be approaching retirement. This is not to say that Western governments and businesses can ignore demographic trends. These trends will cause problems.

Ken Dychtwald, a psychologist and specialist on aging, has warned that, unless some cure is found, some fourteen million Americans will have Alzheimer's disease by the middle of the century.[18] But Dychtwald is more positive than negative, describing the "age wave" swelling the world's elderly population as a new economic and political powerhouse. Many of the elderly will work by choice, because their views will carry some clout. But they will not work long hours. They will not need to do so and will have no desire to do so. Employers will have to create flexible part-time positions to meet these requirements. They will not do so out of charity but out of necessity because the older employee will be the memory, the wisdom, the conscience and the cultural standard-bearer of the company. Employers must change their attitudes to the older worker. It is an imperative.

Adjusting to this changing profile of society will not be helped if Western employers persist with the kind of overwork that has become endemic in Japan. Death from overwork is not uncommon among Japanese employers. They even have a word for it – *Kaoroshi*.[19] Do we really want this *Kaoroshi* to spread like a disease throughout the West?

CHAPTER 20

Melting the Frozen Assets

> Nature has not provided ready-made all the things necessary
> for the life and happiness of mankind. In order to obtain
> these things we have to Work. The only rational labor is
> that which is directed to the creation of those things. Any
> kind of work which does not help us to attain this object is a
> ridiculous, idiotic, criminal, imbecile, waste of time.
>
> (Robert Tressell, pseudonym of Robert Noonan, 1870–1911)

The end of management was the last thing on the mind of Peter
Drucker when his book, *The Practice of Management*, was published for the first time in 1955. This, after all, was the book that
was supposed to be inventing management.[1] And yet, at the same
time, the book was presaging the end of managers. In a way he
was saying: "Management is dead, long live management!"
Drucker was attempting to define a new beginning with management, organization, and planning incorporated into all jobs.
Nowhere is this struggle for meaning more apparent than in his
dissection of personnel management.

Drucker was scathing in his criticism of the personnel role.
In the 1950s personnel management was something of a schizo-
phrenic profession, torn between human relations and employee
administration. *Plus ça change.* There had been no great changes
in personnel administration, he wrote, since its foundations were
laid down shortly after the end of the First World War. In human
relations there had been little progress since the original insight
on human motivation at Western Electric's Hawthorne works. In
a telling remark that seems to have as much resonance today as it
did half a century earlier, he wrote: "The constant worry of all personnel administrators is their inability to prove that they are making a contribution to the enterprise. Their preoccupation is with
the search for a 'gimmick' that will impress their management
associates. Their persistent complaint is that they lack status."[2]

He didn't stop there. He added a joke, that personnel management had been described as an amalgamation of "all those things that do not deal with the work of people and that are not management." Then he added his own attempt at a job description: "It is partly a file clerk's job, partly a social worker's job and partly 'fire-fighting' to head off union trouble or to settle it." Other parts of the job – looking after health and safety, pension plans, and union grievances – were "necessary chores." But the two most important areas of employment – the organization of the work and the organization of people to do the work – he said were generally avoided.

Drucker's assassination of personnel's character was almost complete, but not quite. His gravest charge was that the personnel role assumed that people did not want to work. Here he was agreeing with a point made by Douglas McGregor, that work was viewed as "a kind of punishment." This was contrary to the spirit of human relations, which started out with the assumption that people wanted to work. This was the correct assumption, said Drucker. It recognized that the "human resource is a specific resource."[3]

The attack achieved some results, but not those desired by Drucker. Within a few years American personnel managers had begun to describe themselves as human resource managers. The job had not changed significantly. It was still attracted to what some might call gimmicks. Family-friendly policies, 360-degree or all-round assessment, employee assistance programs, mentoring, and benchmarking are just a few of the processes in vogue today. It is a process-oriented job, and the title Human Resource Manager seemed to stress the process side of the job. What's more, it tended to convey more status, backed by the prospect that its processes could produce measurable results.

If anything, the new job title dehumanized human relations. This had not been Drucker's intention but at least it exposed the underlying dishonesty of human relations – the suggestion that its exponents might be in some way concerned about the welfare of employees. Human resources was about sweating the most valuable assets of the company. It still is.

Drucker, however, was concerned about employee welfare or, rather, the job in hand, recognizing that the well-being of employees was linked to productivity. He had never let go of the concept of the self-managed plant. This, he decided, would require job integration using some of the processes already developed, such as scientific management. Assessing the impact of scientific management, he made the analogy of the alphabet. Taylorism could break a worker's job into its constituent parts, just as the alphabet had broken down language. But the alphabet was impractical unless the letters were reassembled into pronounceable words that had their own sounds.

The key to management, he reasoned, was to assemble the constituent parts of a job in a way that fitted the talents and desires of the worker. Job placement was the thing – putting the right individual into the right job. Taylorism had separated planning from doing. Drucker was saying that they needed to be handled as a whole. He decided that planning – a vital part of management – did not need to be carried out by some designated manager. It could be achieved by workers themselves if they were given the necessary information.

As an example he pointed to the way that workers at the Chesapeake and Ohio Railway had involved themselves in remodeling the workshops.[4] The railroad managers did not need a personnel assistant to explain to them the theory of empowerment. They simply sat down with employees and listened to their ideas. "We have overwhelming evidence that there is actually better planning if the man who does the work, first responsibly participates in the planning," wrote Drucker.[5]

His book was hailed by reviewers as "a tour de force," the seminal work on management, and yet this particular message was largely ignored in the West until Japanese companies – with their quality circles and close worker participation in continuous improvement – began to set the standard. Drucker could not have spelled his message out any more plainly. He even urged his readers to look at the work of Joseph Juran.[6] Drucker's writing was illuminating but subversive. Personnel management, he said, was "insolvent," preferring to ignore the "the frozen assets" of scientific management and human relations in favor of "techniques and gadgets."[7] Perhaps he bruised too many egos, not only of those in personnel management but also those in general management. After all, he had written that "many workers of tomorrow may have to be able to do more planning than a good many people who call themselves managers today are capable of."[8] Like Frederick Taylor before him, he was undermining the rule, only this time it was the management rule. Here he was writing about the practice of management but carrying the message of management to the shop floor. It wouldn't do.

There may have been too much in one book to take on board at once. And Drucker wasn't right about everything. In describing employees as stakeholders in the business, he was years ahead of his time.[9] Yet he was dismissive of employee-share ownership, suggesting that it would not overcome "the employees' resistance to profit." On the one hand he was saying that employees were quite capable of organizing their work, but on the other hand he seemed to think they had a natural disinclination to think of profits. The observation lacked consistency. Drucker was, however, capable of a remarkable prescience, noting, for example, the way that employees, indirectly, were assuming ownership of publicly quoted companies through pension trusts, investment trusts, and life-insurance funds. But he did not, at that time, envisage the personal share ownership that is beginning to define popular capitalism today.

The Practice of Management was a milestone in the understanding of work. It demolished the idea of a worker as an automaton and reinstated the thinking worker. Later Drucker would build on this theme, outlining the concept of the knowledge worker. The book also highlighted the importance of selection. Some employers were already aware of this. Psychometric testing and links with universities and assessment centers had been growing increasingly popular among more progressive employers before and after the Second World War. But the vast majority of employers – the small businesses run by people who had neither the time nor the inclination to immerse themselves in management theory – continued to rely on gut feeling when they interviewed candidates for a job. Western government offices would be drawn increasingly to sophisticated selection processes, but most careers continued to be founded on relationships. It was still possible to go in at the shop floor and work your way up if you displayed some initiative and a willingness to work.

Psychology had moved on. Selection had become institutionalized in the education systems of the West. By 2000, in the USA alone, some 2,000 million tests of intelligence or achievement were being administered every year,[10] as children undergo continual assessment in a range of subjects. Intelligence tests such as Stanford-Binet, however, do not test the work ethic. In response to what some have regarded as an omission, the work ethic has begun to play a much greater role in school examination systems. It is not enough simply to be "clever" or "bright." Indeed, many employers are suspicious of the brightest graduates, often preferring a second-class degree to a first. The suspicion is that the academic star might not have any great grasp of reality. Few manufacturing companies would be able to make much use, for example, of John Stuart Mill.

There are exceptions. Investment banks want the best mathematicians to work out ever more complex derivatives – the financial instruments first conceived as a way of hedging an investment but which were later valued simply for their money-making potential. Oil companies want scenario planners. Software companies want focused but lateral-thinking geeks. Increasing corporate complexity is demanding increasing complexity in the area of placement. Team building has become an amalgamation of science and art. People are mixed like complementary ingredients in a human recipe, and there seems to be a test for everything under the sun.

First there were ability tests that looked for different thinking skills. Later there were personality questionnaires, aimed at discovering individual behaviors. Today the marketplace is awash with personality tests produced by large commercial publishers such as Saville & Holdsworth, ASE, and Oxford Psychologists Press. The 16 Personality Factor (16PF) questionnaire devised by Raymond Cattell and originally published in 1949 was the first to be developed for commercial use. It has various forms but typically it asks upwards of 180 questions and takes about forty minutes to complete. The questions seek agreement or otherwise to various propositions such as: "I prefer going to parties rather than reading a book at home." Depending on your opinion you mark a box indicating whether you believe the statement to be true, false, or questionable.

The test, and others like it, is looking for the strength of various personality traits or factors. To arrive at these factors Cattell sifted out all the words he could find in the English language to describe human behavior. Then he sifted out the synonyms, until he was left with words which each carried a different meaning. The next step was to ask assistants to rate a sample of students over six months, using the traits he had listed. This allowed him to analyze their observations and arrive at the most significant traits. The traits included such qualities as warmhearted, abstract thinker, aggressive, enthusiastic, gregarious, suspicious, and insecure. A questionnaire was assembled to test for these and other factors and further analysis of these results picked out a total of sixteen traits – twelve from the original list and four new ones.

Factor analysis, the statistical method used in devising such tests, involves comparing and correlating the scores among a large number of people who have undertaken the test with those of people who have taken other similar tests. The more these results have in common – the more they correlate with each other – the more likely it is they are testing for the same trait. Psychologists refer to this as validity – proof that the questionnaire is finding what it set out to find. Validity has become the cloak behind which the success or otherwise of personality testing has hidden itself ever since.

There is nothing wrong with factor analysis per se. The technique was developed, like many others, from the separate and not always interrelated work of several people, namely Karl Pearson, who had been working on Francis Galton's ideas for correlation, Charles Spearman, a former army officer who arrived at a theory of general intelligence published in 1904, and Cyril Burt, the man who introduced psychometric testing into the British education system.

Burt's examination meant that millions of schoolchildren would be sorted at the age of eleven according to their intellectual promise. This "11-plus" selection test, to determine whether a child went to a state "grammar" school or a "secondary modern" school, was introduced at the end of the Second World War and abandoned in the 1970s. The system was widely criticized for labeling so many children as failures at an early age. On the other hand, for the first time, it gave thousands of working-class children the opportunity to obtain a grammar school education.

Many of these same children would find themselves as adults undertaking occupational psychometric tests to measure their suitability for a particular line of work. But are these tests fool-proof? Some critics have pointed to the danger of the "Barnum Effect," named after the showman Phineas T. Barnum, who believed that you could "fool most of the people most of the time."[11] The Barnum effect is a popular device of mediums and fortune-tellers, who derive credibility by voicing some obvious comment that people are convinced is a reasonable description of themselves. Other worries have been voiced over the potential for ethnic bias in some tests.

Beyond these worries the test publishers must confront a further, more fundamental question: can a personality question-naire predict future job performance? Unfortunately, the validity scores of these tests are too often not so much measures of their predictive worth as of their ability to assess the personality traits of the candidate. There is a parallel with the ISO 9000 qual-ity standard. It can ensure that products are made to a defined standard, but it cannot say whether the products are worth buying. So an employer can discover, from testing, the type of candidate he is getting – whether the job applicant is a loner or gregarious, for example – but tests will not necessarily reveal whether the candidate is up to the job.

This point was raised by Stephen Blinkhorn and Charles Johnson, two British occupational psychologists whose criticisms caused uproar among test publishers during the 1990s. Writing in *Nature* magazine, they said: "We see precious little evidence that even the best personality tests predict job performance and a good deal of evidence of poorly understood statistical methods being pressed into service to buttress shaky claims."[12] Saville and Holdsworth psychologists hit back at these claims with two related validation studies of the Occupational Personality Questionnaire, the company's most popular test. The studies, on groups of British bank managers, provided proof, they said, that such tests could indeed predict future job success.[13]

The controversy over the effectiveness of personality testing looks likely to run and run. In the meantime Blinkhorn, work-ing with a team of researchers at his company, Psychometric

Research & Development, has devised a series of tests that are defining a third way in occupational testing. These are the Able Tests, published by Oxford Psychologists Press. The Able Tests are job specific and incorporate an element of training. The idea is that they are testing a candidate's ability to learn. This is particularly important for a specialized job that may require some specific skills training. It is also useful for assessing the potential of young people who, for whatever reason, may have had a poor education. If their latent learning skills are evident, their early disadvantages can, in theory, be swept aside by intensive on-the-job training by employers who want to recruit people for their potential.

Another problem with testing, and with selection and recruitment generally, is the determination of the behaviors or skills that the job requires. Employers often think they know both what they are looking for and how to find it, but they can be mistaken. Some years ago recruiters at Chemical Bank advertised in *Flight International* magazine for "numerate, risk-oriented, confident, and highly ambitious professionals" to train as dealers.[14] The bank was seeking to attract air traffic controllers who, it reasoned, were accustomed to reacting under pressure to movements on screens. Perhaps these people would make good money market dealers. What the bank did not appreciate was that air traffic controllers must be risk averse. A large part of their job involves minimizing risk. Money market traders, on the other hand, are constantly taking risks. They, too, should be minimizing their risk, in theory. In reality, however, they live with risk, and as the events of 2008 would demonstrate, when risk-taking behavior is allowed to dominate an industry it can bring an entire financial system to the brink of collapse. Fail-safe risk management remains, it seems, an ideal to which organizations can only aspire. But can it ever be achieved in an industry that relies on a complex betting system for its beating heart?

When job requirements are drawn up by managements, therefore, they can be prone to flawed assumptions. David McClelland, the American behavioral scientist who advanced the study of ambition – he referred to it as the "need to achieve" – in motivation, understood this when he began to observe the factors that went into the job performance of individuals. In an effort to determine the factors of superior performance he interviewed people who were considered by their peers or managers to be the best in their particular field. He then interviewed those considered to be average. He canceled out the common features in both groups, leaving him with certain traits, abilities, or work habits that determined the success of the best workers.

In one exercise looking at the crews of US naval ships, for example, he wondered why one ship's crew appeared to be more successful than other crews in making their vessel ready to go to sea. The determining factors were dishonesty, sneakiness, and negotiating skills. The most effective crews would beg, borrow, or steal to get the equipment they needed from the stores. This was not the information that the naval authorities wanted to hear, but it was the truth.

McClelland called these traits, abilities, and work habits that differentiated work performance "competencies." The way he himself defined competencies was: "A little bit higher than a skill, more of a motive and a trait, a human characteristic that differentiates outstanding from typical performance."[15] McClelland questioned the reliance placed by employers on academic qualifications. Knowledge and skills, he believed, could be developed, but it was much more difficult to develop basic human motives.

Specifically the motive that fascinated him most was the need to achieve, and he knew, from the work of Hagen and Tolles on the Nonconformist origins of so many eighteenth- and nineteenth-century business leaders and innovators,[16] that this quality was closely associated with the Protestant work ethic. McClelland devised what he called the Behavioral Event Interview, a rigorous process designed to sift out the crucial competencies defining excellent work in a particular field.

It was as if the work ethic had somehow found its way into the human genome, creating a competitive advantage for those who possessed it. Could this possibly have happened? Could those people who work the hardest have inherited their motivation? This is a critical issue. It introduces the eternal debate of nature versus nurture – whether intelligence is something we inherit from our ancestors or whether it is derived from our immediate environment. A curious feature of this debate is the polarization of opinion. Very few of the protagonists on both sides of the issue seem prepared to concede that the argument may be looking at questions of degree – the degree to which people's intellectual performance is influenced by upbringing and environment and the degree to which their intellectual capabilities are inherited.

John Locke's "blank sheet" in infanthood still has its adherents. Equally there remains a strong vein of support for Galton's ideas on inherited intelligence. Richard J. Herrnstein and Charles Murray's elitist and controversial 1994 book, *The Bell Curve: Intelligence and Class Structure in American Life*, claimed that hereditary factors governed various social ills such as poverty and crime. Not for the first time this type of study was used to point to the disproportion of black Americans in the lower half of the curve. Opponents of the authors' ideas, however, pointed out that the gap between the educational attainment of white and black Americans was narrowing, as educational opportunities and social conditions among black Americans improved.

The problem with Galton's theories, then as now, is that they are distasteful to most liberal-minded people. They formed the basis of the discredited science of eugenics and influenced Nazi ideas of Aryan supremacy. At a time when society was fearing Malthusian predictions of catastrophic overpopulation there may have seemed some merit in selective breeding to preserve the best of the human species. In his futuristic work, *Anticipations*, H. G. Wells explored the ways in which a world state in the year 2000 might seek to phase out Europe's "vicious, helpless and pauper masses."[17] But all these discussions were subsumed by the evils of Nazism.

Today the debate is once again hotly contested, with evolutionary psychologists on one side and "environmentalists" on the other. Nigel Nicholson, professor of organizational behavior at the London Business School, pursuing the argument of evolutionary psychology, has argued that people are predisposed to certain types of behavior that may have been adopted as far back as the Stone Age. These behaviors, he believes, are so ingrained in our genes that to deny their influence is futile. "There is little point in trying to change deep-rooted inclinations," he wrote in an article that poured scorn on the idea of leadership training. "The most important attribute for leadership," he said, "is the desire to lead."[18]

In his favor he has the colloquial recognition by parents of familiar traits displayed by their children, the sort of recognition that prompts remarks like: "He has his father's sense of humor," or "He has a good memory for names, just like his mother." This kind of recognition seems far more persuasive of hereditary behaviors than the various long-running studies of identical twins. The studies of twins tend to be vulnerable to arguments that similarities in their behaviors, responses, and intelligence test results have been influenced by environmental factors such as contact with their parents or with each other. Very few twins in these studies have been denied contact from birth.[19]

Diametrically opposed to the idea of hereditary intelligence are environmentalists such as Michael Howe, professor of psychology at Exeter University, who believes that excellence is not inborn but determined by factors such as opportunity, encouragement, and endless hours of practice.[20] Howe found that waitresses could remember far more drinks orders than a control group of students in a comparative study. The ability of the waitresses, he concluded, depended on practice. The same applied to violinists. Violinists who achieve the level of skill necessary to perform at the highest level have practiced in their careers thousands of hours longer than those who go into teaching. The same can be said of many sports stars. As Gary Player, the golfer, once said when he was asked about his good luck in holing a put: "It's funny, but I find that the more I practice the luckier I get."

More recently, in his book, *Talent is Overrated*, Geoff Colvin has written about the need for highly skilled people to engage in what he calls "deliberate practice" – working on the minutiae of a specific skill, perfecting and then moving on to the next aspect of a skill that needs to be improved.

Whichever way you look at it, however, practice takes time, involving countless hours of repetition. It's hard work. The Protestant work ethic, therefore, remains central to the issue of nature verses nurture. Another more fundamental issue is the nature of intelligence. What is intelligence, and how important is this ability? What do we mean when we say someone is smart or bright? In recent years some academics have begun to investigate different aspects of intelligence. Robert Sternberg, professor of psychology and education at Yale University, likes to illustrate different approaches to thinking with this story:

> Two students are walking in Yellowstone Park when they come across a grizzly bear. The first, an Ivy League graduate from the top drawer of academic achievement, calculates that the bear can reach them in seventeen seconds. "We can't outpace him," he tells his companion, who is pulling on his running shoes. The other boy, who never went to college, says to his friend: "I don't need to outpace the grizzly. I just need to out-pace you."[21]

"Both boys were smart," says Sternberg. But while the Yale student was intelligent in the analytical way used to define excellence in universities, the second was intelligent "to the extent that you define intelligence as the ability to adapt to the environment." Sternberg's environmentalist argument has taken the issue to its roots by seeking to define intelligence in a variety of ways. He outlines three definitions of intelligence – analytical, practical, and creative. The first is understood and emphasized by academic institutions, but the other two, he says, tend to be neglected or ignored. "You need more than IQ skills to get through life," he says. "In U.S. society, if you're good at IQ-like skills – the type of things that get you As in school – you are extremely highly rewarded by the system. These systems promoted you from an early age, so there is no incentive to acquire creative and practical skills."

Sternberg calls those systems that concentrate on a single feature of attainment "closed systems." These become self-selecting societies that shut out other useful features. Instead of focusing on one type of intelligence, says Sternberg, society should be seeking to recognize what he calls "successful intelligence," something that combines the analytical, the practical, and the creative.

Here again, however, there is room for argument. When I used Sternberg's example of the bear and the students to begin a column in the *Financial Times*, a reader wrote in afterwards, suggesting that the "smart" response to the dilemma was mor-ally flawed. The reader was an Arab. In his culture, he pointed out, it would have been dishonorable and morally unacceptable to leave your friend to the bear. It was a sound point. Sternberg's example of practical intelligence stressed the idea that in a crisis it is every man for himself. But it has been a long-accepted hallmark of humanity that in a sinking ship, the priority is women and children first.

It is tempting, when discussing intelligence, always to pursue the so-called intellectual argument. This may be the reason for the polarity of opinions in this field. Is it possible that some people can be too intelligent for their own good? Edward de Bono, the man who introduced the concept of lateral thinking, says that "a lot of people with high IQs get stuck in the intelligence trap." He adds: "They have a point of view and the more intelligent they are the better they are likely to be at defending their argument. Many excellent minds are trapped in poor ideas. That is not excellent thinking."[22] What is the point of intelligence, after all, if it supports a conviction that turns out to be wrong? Wasn't it Keynes who admitted: "When the facts change I change my mind. What do you do, sir?"

In *The Ascent of Man* Jacob Bronowski lamented the way some academics were "in love with the aristocracy of intellect." He wrote:

> That is a belief which can only destroy the civilization that we know. If we are anything, we must be a democracy of the intellect. We must not perish by the distance between people and government, between people and power, by which Babylon, Egypt, and Rome failed. And that distance can only be conflated, can only be closed, if knowledge sits in the homes and heads of people with no ambition to control others, and not up in the isolated seats of power.[23]

Of course there is no reason, other than simplicity, that Sternberg should have settled on just three forms of intelligence. Howard Gardner, the Harvard psychologist, for example, lists seven types of intelligence.[24] This thing called intelligence is a slippery substance. It seems to be something broader than the ability to get all the questions right in the school exam. What should we call this broader, practical form of intelligence, this intelligence that combines qualities such as common sense and nous with inventiveness and worldliness, what we might once have called "wisdom"?

In 1996 Daniel Goleman described a type of thinking called *Emotional Intelligence* in his book of the same name. The idea of emotional intelligence, as Goleman acknowledged, belongs to John Mayer, a psychologist at the University of New Hampshire, and Peter Salovey of Yale University. Mayer defines emotional intelligence as "the ability to perceive, to integrate, to understand and reflectively manage one's own and other people's feelings."[25] So there we have it. Emotional intelligence demands oodles of empathy and self-awareness. A number of management consultancies have decided that this kind of ability is just what is needed to run large companies, hence a whole new field of psychometric testing and leadership profiling.

There has never been so much choice in selection testing, or so much awareness of what makes people tick. The problem today is not so much the motivation to work but understanding the nature of work – sorting the necessary, worthwhile, and satisfying work from the frivolous. Each of us must ask ourselves: What are we achieving with the work that we do? Is it worth the candle? Is it making a better world? Is it making a difference? Some years ago Studs Terkel carried out a series of lengthy interviews with people in a wide variety of jobs for his book, *Working*. Many of the interviewees found little to celebrate in their work but one of them, Tom Patrick, a fireman, thought differently about his job. "I can look back and say: 'I helped put out a fire. I helped save somebody. It shows something I did on this Earth.'"[26] How many of us can be so certain about the value in the work that we do? How can we rationalize our working lives? Do we need a new work ethic, an ethic that questions the content of work, that does not value prolonged hard work above everything? Isn't it time we began to concentrate on results? Surely a job should be a job well done. If work is neither well done nor worthwhile, why work at all?

CHAPTER 21

The Road to Panama

To make employment regular is to invite industrial decay.
(Henry Ford, 1863–1947)

Religion is the medium through which a large proportion of the world's people seek meaning in their lives. Its power is so strong that when many of us speak of faith we need no other explanation. Belief, in and of itself, is the anchor that tethers our lives within the universe. Lying behind our beliefs – the generator of belief – is an innate desire to understand at the very core of our being. To harness this desire to corporate thinking seems inappropriate when we know there is much more to life than business. But when we see business as one of the most important fulcrums of change, or as a social institution, as Peter Drucker regarded the large corporation, there seems some merit in grappling with the mysteries of corporate evolution.

If Carlyle was right in describing all true work as religion, it helps to explain the fervor with which so many of us go about our work. This doggedness and determination to persevere, this pilgrim's progress of hard work which informs our outlook on almost every aspect of our lives, has served the Western industrialized nations well in a world that measures itself by the standards of economic growth outlined by Adam Smith. But will it continue to serve us well in a society of rapid change? Perhaps we should sit back and analyze whether we are indeed living in a time of great change, as so many people insist.

Change, like evolution, is a constant. It makes life livable. But we can't always see it and sometimes when we can see it we choose to ignore it. Today we can almost smell it, just as those who lived through the Industrial Revolution were conscious of that whiff of change they called progress. If we are living through a period of change on a par with the Industrial Revolution, when

did it start? Are there similar characteristics? And what will be
its consequences for the way we run our lives?

The late twentieth century was thickly populated with change
merchants peddling an often-fuzzy futurology. But most of them
were tailgating the ideas of others. Daniel Bell was the first of
these seers to write of the "information age" in his 1973 book,
*The Coming of Post-Industrial Society: A Venture in Social
Forecasting*. Then, in 1980, Alvin and Heidi Toffler launched
their interpretation of the information revolution in *The Third
Wave*. Their observations leaned heavily on the changing face of
the labor market and advances in technology. Well before person-
alized computers were occupying every desk, and years before
the Internet would begin to influence commercial practices, the
Tofflers were insisting that society had embarked on a wave of
change as significant as two earlier waves. The first wave was
that of agriculture, which transformed people from nomadic
hunter-gatherers to settled farmers. The second wave was the
later Industrial Revolution, which concentrated employment in
factories.

The Tofflers dated the beginning of this third wave to 1956,
when, for the first time, the number of white-collar employees
in the US labor market outnumbered those in blue-collar jobs.
While they pointed to computing as a big influence, they also
highlighted the significance of other social factors, such as the
availability of the contraceptive pill and the advent of the commercial jet airliner. The pressures and conflicts arising from
these waves of change, said the Tofflers, had led to warfare in
the past. The American Civil War, they maintained, was a war
between a second-wave society – the industrial North – and a
first-wave society – the agricultural South. The nature of these
societies meant that they were supported by different employment
systems – slavery and wage-earning workers.

The simplicity of the picture is useful, but the reality is more
complex than the Tofflers' interpretations. Agriculture in the Deep
South of America had industrialized by the time of the Civil War.
Although the cotton gin was a labor-saving device, its impact was
to increase the demand for slaves, as cotton producers prospered
and expanded their plantations. So the second wave had impacted
on the South in a way that was socially unsustainable. The South

had industrialized its cotton production without industrializing its society.

The failure to recognize the impact of change is common throughout most societies. Rapid change creates a phenomenon that we might call "social drag." This social drag is one of the most significant features of change as society struggles to adapt. I use the term "social drag" rather than "social lag" because "lag" implies that part of society is playing catch-up, while "drag" recognizes that much of society is resistant to change.

We can see this resistance to change in our nostalgia for recent history. It helps explain why paintings by John Constable or the Impressionists are more popular on chocolate boxes than those of Mondrian or Matisse. It explains why Manet's paintings of contemporary nudes in the nineteenth century were relegated to the *Salon des Refusés* in Paris. Ian Dunlop, the art historian, called it the *Shock of the New.*[1] And yet creativity demands newness. Art must experiment or the very substance, the lifeblood, of the artist is diminished. So the creative world continues to push out the frontiers of experience in the arts and technology, while the receptive world – that's most of us – comfortable in the familiarity of our surroundings, our habits, and routines, tends to look at change with some suspicion, even hostility. In the film, *Shirley Valentine*, Shirley's husband is angered when she cooks him "chips and egg" instead of the steak he *always* has on Thursdays.

The extent of change, therefore, is difficult to interpret in a society that perpetually lives in denial. Change is also relative. An insurance broker who left the old headquarters of Lloyds, the London-based insurers, for the replacement "outside-in" building designed by Richard Rogers, was always going to feel alienated from the comfort of his former environment. In fact the Lloyds board was so attached to its Adam-style boardroom that it had it transferred – the plaster work, the paneling, the paintings, the table, the lot – to a location high up in the new stainless-steel structure.

Walking into the boardroom is like stepping back in time to a former era of life in the City of London, when a gentleman's word was his bond. That may be part of the allure, a nostalgia for a way of life that many regarded as better than the one they see around them today.

This nostalgia is a feature of social drag. We remember selectively. Although I was born in 1957, I grew up hearing so many stories of the Second World War that it might as well have been continuing around me. Whenever my relatives were gathered together for some occasion, such as Christmas, a birthday, or a funeral, they would begin to reminisce about the war. The stories were not about tragedy or death but of the many good times they enjoyed in the bonding that only seems possible when people are experiencing adversity collectively. The stories became familiar – my father losing his helmet, in which he had stored his French francs for safe keeping during the D-day landings, my mother falling into the air raid shelter during the blackout, my uncle fraternizing with the Fräuleins in Berlin. Everyone had heard them before and everyone wanted to hear them again. The war was the biggest thing that happened in the lives of my parents and probably in the lives of most of their generation. They would never have sought war, but having survived they held onto the good times and shut out the bad.

The psychological condition that creates a need in most of us for comfort and nostalgia may be evolutionary in nature. Pioneering is dangerous. The Oregon Trail, the route of the largest mass migration in history, has been described as the longest graveyard in the world. One report estimated that almost eleven people died for every kilometer.[2] But the potential rewards eclipsed the fear of failure for those facing an uncertain future in an economic depression.

Pioneering is a human and corporate necessity – something that its exponents sometimes accept with reluctance, fearful of the consequences of staying where they are. And pioneers do not always survive. In the event of catastrophe those who have stayed behind are the survivors, a holding pool from which future discoverers will set out. A love of nostalgia and the comfort of the familiar should not, therefore, be seen as regressive traits. They are necessary and they are probably manifest in all species to a certain degree, if only in the concept of safety in numbers.

We can understand what drove those pioneering American settlers. The life they were leaving was far from satisfactory. Some groups, like the Mormons, were seeking freedom from religious persecution with the same conviction that had persuaded their

Pilgrim forefathers to cross the Atlantic two centuries earlier. But the underlying motivation of those who change jobs or move house today out of a constantly nagging sense of dissatisfaction is more difficult to understand. Sometimes the driving force is an irrational belief that life is better somewhere else. Most people seem to possess a romantic concept of paradise.

In *The Trip to Panama* by Janosch, the pseudonym of Horst Eckhert, a bear and a tiger live in blissful harmony in their small rural cottage by the side of a river, until one day they find a box that has been floating down the river.[3] The box smells of bananas, and on its side is the word *Panama*. The smell of bananas is overpowering. Panama, they conclude, must be a wondrous place, the land of their dreams. But where can they find it? They use the boxwood to make a sign that points the way, and they set off with a few sandwiches. On their travels they meet more animals and make new friends. One friend has a particularly comfortable sofa. Every now and again they see a message in a bottle floating down the river, but it always goes by, unopened and unread. Finally they find a house, slightly overgrown and tatty. Beside the house is a fallen-down sign on which they can see the word, *Panama*. Here it is, the land of their dreams. Of course it's their old house, but they don't recognize it. They buy a sofa just like the one they had admired, and they are blissfully happy.

But then they were happy in the first place. The land of their dreams was the life they had. Well, not quite. A few important things had changed. They had made new friends and they now possessed a comfy sofa. In this simple story Janosch created a metaphor for many of our lives, including the opportunities that pass us by like messages in bottles. We are all of us seeking Panama in our different ways. This is good and admirable. It is what keeps the world turning. But we should not be blinded by our ambitions or yearnings to the good things of life that we may already possess.

There are moments – we all experience them – when life is as good at it gets. The trick is to recognize them when they come along and to savor the moment for all it's worth. For Charles Foster Kane in Orson Welles's cinematic masterpiece, *Citizen Kane*, it was the good times that he had enjoyed as a child with his sled, called *Rosebud*, symbolizing a mother's love that was denied him when he was sent away to be reared outside his natural family home.

Citizen Kane was more than a commentary on the empire-building acquisitiveness of Randolph Hearst, the newspaper baron. It was, in part, an exposé of the damage people can inflict upon themselves when they fail to recognize their individual Panamas. Instead they march on in pursuit of ever-changing unfulfilling goals. The large estate and towering castle modeled on Hearst's San Simeon are dismissed by Kane's bride, Susan, as "forty-nine thousand acres of nothing but scenery and statues." She is lonely. She doesn't want a palace full of grand possessions. She wants friendship.

Kane spent his life searching for the love that had been taken away in childhood. But love was the one emotion he could not understand. Every friendship he ever had, he lost. The Panama of his early career had been his newspaper and the hard work and dynamics of the newspaper industry. His life on the newspaper was as good as it would get. But he couldn't see it. Janosch and Herman J. Mankiewicz, the film's scriptwriter, are almost soul-mates in their common insight.

We all recognize something in Charlie Kane's unquenchable ambition. And yet so often we seek to repeat Kane's journey. We see a vision of the perfect life that never measures up in reality. This gulf between image and reality was explored in Alex Garland's book, *The Beach*. The book was made into a film, and hundreds of young people were drawn to the movie location, only confirming Oscar Wilde's observation that "each man kills the thing he loves."

Our ceaseless pursuit of economic growth is not only killing the things we love, but killing the things we need. We should not ignore the forces that sent people onto the street in Seattle and London, protesting at the way the capitalist system appears oblivious of the biosystem that maintains the health of the planet. But it is not just pollution and trade imbalances that are undermining society. There are imbalances too in our approach to work.

The Protestant mind is tortured by the need to achieve. Success must be earned. We work hard because we must, because we hear but cannot identify that unseen Puritan whispering in our heads. We used to take deep pride in our work for this same reason.

When we practiced a craft, this pride was fulfilling in itself. But the deskilled flexible workplace that, like Frederick Taylor, views "the rule" – that special knowledge of the skilled and experienced exponent of a trade – as an unnecessary cost, has removed the intrinsic joy in work. So we continue to work long hours in pursuit of something that is no longer attainable and slowly, inexplicably, we are suffocating.

The Mexican artist Diego Rivera portrayed the role of production workers in the relentless progress of industry very effectively in a set of murals commissioned by the Ford Motor Company for the Detroit Institute of Arts. The journey portrayed in the four frescoes is not of people but of a machine given life by the hundreds of people who partake in its creation. Most of the workmen are rooted to the floor of the giant River Rouge factory. Significantly, perhaps, the finished product, a 1932 Ford V-8, is obscured by the workmen, as if they are engaged in some elaborate ritual. This indeed is the way Rivera saw the process, comparing the car plant with the Aztec temples of his native Mexico. The factory had become a twentieth-century temple of human sacrifice. As far as Rivera was concerned, for thousands of immigrants, the Panama dream, the search for some better way of life, had ended in factory exploitation.

Others have expressed Janosch's Panama-need in different ways. Russell H. Conwell, the Baptist minister who founded Temple University in Philadelphia in 1888, found his personal Nirvana in an inspirational speech, which he repeated many times before enthusiastic paying audiences. He spoke of a man who sold his land to search for diamonds, only to discover later that there had been diamonds in his own backyard all along.[4] The message was simple, says Joanne Ciulla, a fellow of Harvard University, in her book, *The Working Life*. "Work," she writes, "was part of a quest in life, but in America you didn't have to travel far."

Today this quest has become a burden for all involved. But the burden is viewed differently from different perspectives. Business is concerned about the cost of employment, whereas government concerns itself with the cost of unemployment. European Union leaders, therefore, were jubilant in the spring of 2000 when they could declare a "strategic goal" of creating 20 million jobs within a decade.[5] Why should it be the goal of any institution to create work? Governments seem to take the view that a society of full employment is a healthy society, both socially and financially, with fewer people drawing welfare from the state. Business is happy with this picture as long as it is able to profit from the labor. But what of the individual? How happy are we with the make-work society? Shouldn't we be looking forward to more leisure than work?

The extent to which working time has eaten into the average American's leisure time was explored by Juliet Schor in *The Overworked American*. Trade unions on both sides of the Atlantic had fought from the beginning of the Industrial Revolution for fewer working hours, gradually shortening the working day over a hundred-year trend. But in the rapidly improving economic conditions after the Second World War, working time in the USA began to buck the trend. By the early 1990s manufacturing employees in America were working about eight weeks a year more than workers in Germany or France.[6]

At one stage, during the 1930s Depression, it seemed that a working week of thirty hours was within the unions' grasp. "Mass unemployment became the route to leisure," writes Schor. The idea was that a shorter working week would allow employers to reengage many more of the workers they had laid off.[7] Legislation for a thirty-hour week was passed by the US Senate but, under pressure from employers, President Roosevelt scrapped the idea. Business leaders were worried that a big reduction in the pool of unemployed labor would increase competition for employees, thereby pushing up wage costs. Some argued that the same forces would undermine discipline in the workforce, since employees would be less fearful of losing their jobs.[8]

Businesses used the same arguments against the shorter working week as they did against the minimum wage – that it would increase their costs. The argument is as vigorous today as it was then. Opposition to the minimum wage in the UK reached fever pitch during the General Election campaign of 1997. But there was little if any evidence of an adverse effect on business after its introduction.

Its opposers were grudging in their acceptance, arguing that its lack of impact was due to the "sensible" limit at which it was set. The British government steered a middle course, insisting on the minimum wage but ignoring trade union demands for a rate higher than the one that was fixed. The British also delayed their acceptance of the European Union's Working Time Directive that would limit the working week to forty-eight hours. Its introduction included voluntary opt-out arrangements. This seemed a sensible policy, since the right to work is just as important as the right to take time off.

We must ask ourselves, however, whether any of these policies are radical enough to meet the changing demands that information technology is placing on the workplace. What do the change merchants say? Charles Handy, whose work on modern organizations has put him among the most predictive of all contemporary management writers, delivered a convincing analysis of the evolving company in *The Age of Unreason*, where he described the "shamrock organization."

Handy was describing a core structure of expertise consisting of essential managers, technicians, and professionals forming the nerve center of the organization. Embodied within this first leaf are the organization's culture, its knowledge, and its direction. The second leaf of the shamrock comprises the nonessential work that may be farmed out to contractors. The third leaf is the flexible workforce – temporary and part-time workers who can be called on to meet fluctuating demands for labor.

A world of shamrock corporations, reasoned Handy, requires a different relationship between employers and employees. His solution was the "portfolio career." Instead of working all your life for one employer, you would "collect" relationships and contracts with different employers. The idea is that you decide where you want to work and how much you want to work.[9] The interim management industry has created an important contracting niche from this concept.

The interim or temporary manager belongs to an agency that hires the manager out at a daily rate for the duration of a project. Typically the interim will be caretaking a full-time management job after a sudden departure, to give the board breathing space before it makes a permanent appointment. Alternatively a company might need someone from outside to lead a special project of a limited duration. The supplier of these interims is providing options in flexible management. Companies must pay a premium for this service, since the supplier takes a commission and the temporary manager must be compensated for the sacrifices made in order to be flexible. It may not be possible, for example, to take a vacation between assignments.

Interim management began in the Netherlands in the late 1970s at the Boer and Croon Group, a management consultancy that needed experienced executives to run some of its programs in client companies. Dutch employment laws insisted on lengthy periods of notice so companies saw potential in using temporary executives as a way of increasing management flexibility. Today it has spread across Europe and into the United States. Job tenures fell so markedly among executives in US companies during the early 1990s that many jobs began to look like temporary assignments.

By the late 1990s the real innovation was happening in the small start-up companies that had begun to attract increasing interest from venture capitalists and get-rich-quick investors. This dot.com phenomenon that had been gathering pace during the late 1990s enveloped the markets in early 2000, putting the share performance of hitherto reliable businesses into the shade. While Alan Greenspan at the Federal Reserve and Sir Howard Davies at the UK's Financial Services Authority began to worry that Internet stocks were taking the form of a speculative bubble, many commentators were hedging their bets, writing of Shumpeter's creative destruction, regarded by some as a necessary constituent of dynamic change.

Yes, agreed the optimists, some companies launching their services on the Internet would most probably perish in the struggle for ascendancy, but, like salmon climbing a waterfall to reach their spawning grounds, the strongest would succeed. Not only that, they would transform the way people bought things and the way companies did business. The pessimists were thin on the ground but continued to regurgitate their cautionary tales of Tulipomania and the South Sea Bubble. Tulipomania – the Dutch speculation in tulip bulbs during the seventeenth century – was a particularly striking comparison because, although many speculators lost fortunes in the financial euphoria that valued some bulbs beyond the price of a house, the trade in tulips transformed the Netherlands, both geographically and agriculturally. The bulb industry continues to be a mainstay of the country's agriculture.

Whatever the future of technology stocks – they suffered a steep decline in value during 2000 – continuing commercial activity on the Internet seemed to favor the Schumpeter model. The success of some Internet businesses like eBay, a website that conducts Internet auctions, would ensure the continued vigorous spawning of thousands if not millions of hopeful knowledge workers with salmon-like aspirations to grow their web businesses into corporate adulthood.

Peter Drucker had begun to explore the concept of knowledge workers in his 1959 book, *Landmarks of Tomorrow,* although he did not use the term until 1969, when he drew the reference from Princeton professor Fritz Machlup's description of knowledge industries.[10] The knowledge workers – Drucker describes them as "people who get paid for putting to work what one learns in school rather than for their physical strength or their manual skill"[11] – would inherit the computer age. As Alain Cotta, professor of economics at the University of Paris-Dauphine, observed in 1994: "More than half the people are now employed in sectors where they create, release, transfer, receive, and utilize information. The crossing of the frontier between muscle and neuron may have as many consequences as the rise of industry."[12]

Given their Taylorist heritage it should not be surprising that some of the earliest efforts by large companies to exploit systematically the human knowledge in their companies involved the creation of a concept called "knowledge management." Knowledge management from the start was almost wholly exploitative. Companies wanted their employees to transfer their knowledge to the corporate database so that employees with less experience or with different experience could tap into this knowledge bank and use it for the general good of the business. It was touted as something new, but Ralph Waldo Emerson had sensed a desire for such exploitation in the nineteenth century, when he wrote: "I hate this shallow Americanism which hopes to get rich by credit, to get knowledge by raps on midnight tables, to learn the economy of the mind by phrenology, or skill without study, or mastery without apprenticeship."

Knowledge management was exactly that – an attempt to obtain skill without study, and mastery without apprenticeship. Again this supposedly modern concept came up against "the rule." After a period of heavy staff cutting across industry during the late 1980s and early 1990s, those that remained were hardly enthusiastic about handing over their meal tickets. It was tantamount to asking a journalist to disgorge the contents of his or her contacts book. Too often knowledge management was a crude attempt to mechanize relationships. Too often it did not reward employees for their personal "intellectual capital." Neither did it recognize that knowledge alone is no more attractive than an uncut diamond. Knowledge is a commodity. The real value is in the way it is applied.

The underlying challenge of the Internet is its useful applications as a medium. This is why there is so much work ahead of us. When I look at the Internet I see an unquantified mass of work, an unraveling of human minds, translated into a hotchpotch of type and images, some of it stimulating but much of it, like the labels on sauce bottles, of little more than passing interest. Advertising litters websites in the same unplanned way that signposts and billboards clog the arteries of American cities. The commercial image, the logo, the brand, flashing from every street corner and video screen, are as polluting to the mind as exhaust emissions are to the atmosphere. The Internet started out as a useful means of conveying information between academics. Later, in adolescence, it became an unregulated playground for disaffected, rebellious youth, for extremists, wackos, and pornographers, for those on the fringe of society. By the early 2000s it was displaying all the hallmarks of immaturity – self-belief, hopes, and idealism mixed with naivety, rawness, and incompetence. There must be something in these qualities that stirs our juices, because the businesses that began to exploit this medium created a new gold rush, fueled by the belief that much of future society was going to spend its time in dialogue with a video screen – and today it's beginning to pay off.

Is the rise of the Internet as significant as the Industrial Revolution? Or should we think of it as an information and communications milestone akin to the one that appeared before recorded history, when people first achieved the spoken word?

These milestones are more frequent than the Toffler waves. The second big step in communications was the development of writing. Some of the earliest written records involving a mixture of numerals, pictographs, and ideograms are records of business arrangements made by Mesopotamian priests about 3,500 BC.

Message and medium seem to be common factors in these step changes. Stone was replaced by paper. Paper, one of the greatest technologies ever discovered, has still not been replaced adequately. Its cheapness and utility are unmatched. Printing created an explosion of the printed word. Computers, and today the potential of cloud computing, has created massive storage potential, response speeds, and new options for collaboration. Their influence cannot be denied. Gradually, slowly, sometimes imperceptibly, computing and the Internet is changing the way we live. When fast broadband communications are available evenly in rural villages some of us may be tempted back in to the communities our ancestors deserted in the Industrial Revolution.

This may be the biggest change effected by the Internet. Will it take away our wanderlust? As travel costs diminish and the world becomes available to all, will we tire of our search for *The Beach*? Will we nestle in our comfy sofas and find contentment in a simpler life or in a complex internal domestic life servicing our household gizmos? Will we play God on the computer, spending more time in a virtual Second Life that simulates domestic scenarios? Will we turn our homes into mini museums, schools, zoos, and laboratories, drawing on our ability to tap in to a vast sea of online knowledge? Will we rediscover the pub and the corner shop and return to those who clung onto these institutions, those who had no desire to go out West?

Isaac Newton defined the basic law of motion. For every reaction there is an equal and opposite reaction. Sometimes the law applies in society. For every Ferrari capable of clocking 200 mph there is a traffic jam, a driving ban, or a speed bump; for every alcohol inspired binge there is a hangover; for every cream cake a layer of fat. Every development in society has its consequences, both good and bad. There has been too much Internet euphoria. We should prepare for the fallout. Marshall McLuhan, who introduced us to the "global village," also declared that "the medium is the message."[13] Today the medium is destroying the message, as the cuckoo Internet absorbs corporate aspirations and the rest of us bow in daily homage before the computer screen. Martin Luther King warned us of the dangers of technology in 1963 when he wrote that "the means by which we live have outdistanced the ends by which we live. Our scientific power has outrun our spiritual power. We have guided missiles and misguided men."[14]

The same Newtonian principles governing reactionary forces apply to work. In the early 1990s Juliet Schor concentrated on the overworked American, but Europe soon followed, with the UK heading the charge into the long-hours culture. Did it deliver fantastic benefits for business? Work increasingly took on the appearance of a treadmill where, however quickly we ran, we didn't get anywhere any faster. People stayed in the office because they felt they should. Suddenly there was voicemail to catch every incoming telephone call to the desk and to the mobile phone; then there were emails to cover the unanswered telephones, faxes, and postal deliveries.

When everyone was given the ability to send emails the messages multiplied in their millions. The desk was under siege. The first thing to suffer under this deluge of communication was work itself. Information was spinning into our laps like junk mail, like discarded litter. This wasn't information but information pollution. Unsifted, unregulated, uncontrolled information was gumming up our brains. No sooner had we begun to experience this social phenomenon of information overload than surveys began sprouting like dandelions confirming everything we could see. Then there were the malicious, destructive, software-eating viruses – Melissa and the Love Bug – disguised as innocent email messages. Like the cavalry charge on the back of the artillery barrage came advice sheets and books on the email menace and how to deal with it. It was time management all over again. And this was all before social networking demanded even more of our attention, before Twitter and the automatic newsfeed and the bleeping BlackBerry. The message is there: sliced, diced, and delivered a hundred times a day so that we are swamped with information. The message, any message, has become a tiny insignificant voice in a cacophony of communications, an email maelstrom. Work? The chance would be a fine thing.

CHAPTER 22

One Life. Live it.

> We are moving from the workplace to work done any place.
> (Alvin Toffler, b. 1928)

Every weekday morning in downtown Mumbai (Bombay), long after the rush hour, when most office workers are looking forward to lunch, it is possible to witness the first signs of an extraordinary operation at each of the city's mainline train stations. As the trains begin to arrive around 11.30 a.m., you can see men in their hundreds carrying long wooden trays on their heads, struggling to extricate themselves from the passenger cars. Each tray contains about thirty round cans, like tall paint cans. Each can, or *dabba*, contains the home-cooked lunch of spicy meats, vegetables, rice, and chapatis for an office worker.

The cans are handled by *dabbawallahs*, men whose job it is, every day, to collect the lunch-boxes from the office workers' wives or mothers at their suburban homes, bring in the lunches, then collect the empty cans and repeat the distribution process in reverse. Every *dabba*, or tiffin box, is marked with small painted symbols identifying where the owner can be found. The *dabbawallahs* are expert at sorting and distributing the cans, working like links in a chain, passing the cans between them at various stages. Some estimates reckon that as many as 100,000 lunches are delivered in this way in Mumbai every working day.[1] Why does it happen?

The *dabbawallahs* are unique to Mumbai. Their business originated from the desire of a single British office worker more than a hundred years ago, during the British Raj, to have his lunch cooked by his wife and brought to his desk. The fashion caught on and today, even though fast food is beginning to appear in Mumbai, this "slow food" tradition continues. Those who use it say it provides an important social link with their home and with their colleagues, since the arrival of the *dabba* is one of the few opportunities employees have each day to break off and sit around a table and talk to each other.

Labor in Mumbai is cheap, which means that the delivery system and cost to the customer are also cheap. It could be equated with the price of mailing a letter. The *dabba* is cheaper than a meal taken outside in a restaurant, but it is hardly cheaper than sandwiches or a prepared meal and fruit in a Tupperware box. In some ways the service doesn't make much sense. Why, for instance, can't people take their empty *dabba* back home with them? Looking at the system logically there seems to be much unnecessary work, particularly to Western eyes schooled on maximizing the efficiency of every job. Some may view the system as a form of entrapment for women, keeping them at home, rather than encouraging their entry into the labor market. But the system is not some form of government job creation scheme. It is private enterprise. The *dabbawallahs* themselves rarely see their families except for two weeks a year when they go home to their villages outside Mumbai, and the city is left to pine. The *dabba* system is a remarkable exercise in logistics among men who have never learned to read or write. It functions perfectly. It relies neither on digital technology nor on the written language.

A counter-argument in support of the system says that the 2,300 *dabbawallahs*, all members of the Union of Tiffin Box Suppliers, would be begging on the streets without their work. It gives them a role in society and brings in an income for their families; it makes the office workers happy – although wives might not like the way that it confines them to the kitchen – and it works. It is a perfect example of work driven by fashion and social need, where economic considerations play a secondary role.

Nowhere, perhaps, is labor such an important national economic factor as in India. With a population of 1 billion people, keeping a plentiful supply of work has become essential to maintaining order and keeping incomes at sustainable levels. Much of the work, however, seems unnecessary, less significant, in fact, than *dabba* work. The state sector is bulging with bodies filing bits of paper on dusty shelves, passing forms from one desk to another, often getting in the way of projects that could inject genuine economic life into the country.

The free market is viewed with suspicion in India, partly as a result of the legacy of administration under the East India Company and partly due to a fear of cultural dilution by Western ideals, something that is already happening. Additionally there is a belief that any solutions to poverty emerging from the capitalist system have been by-products of the system rather than stemming from values embodied in any capitalist ethos.

It used to be the case that the West looked guardedly at countries like India, seeing them as potential threats to its manufacturing base because of the ready supply of cheap labor. It has been argued that part of the Indian labor movement had its roots in a desire by nineteenth-century British textile manufacturers to suppress competition.[2] The idea was that India would be less competitive if its manufacturers were forced by unions to pay workers higher wages. If this was true, all it succeeded in doing was to delay the inevitable. Mohandas Gandhi played the economic counterpunch, urging his followers to burn their imported British clothing. Today the West might look again at India as a market for its goods, but not as a dumping ground. The only way that India can become a market for expensively produced Western goods and services is to provide the Indian employee with purchasing power, in the same way that Ford workers received more pay in 1913, enabling them to buy their own Model Ts.

Not only are the West's future export markets emerging in developing countries, these countries are also beginning to provide high technology labor. The Indians have become aware of their human potential in the field of information technology. Bangalore is the Silicon Valley of the East. Although some of the most computer-literate Indians have moved to California to take advantage of high wages in American technology companies, others are preferring to stay in India. Cheaper labor in countries such as India, China, the Philippines and Indonesia has led employers to become increasingly attracted to offshoring products and services seeking out what some have called the "China price" – the lowest level of labor cost (although China's economic rise means it has probably already lost this benchmark status). In this developing wellspring of employment, labor-sourcing is beginning to go to the places where it is most needed. It is no longer realistic for Western governments to fear the search by the largest companies for the cheapest labor. The advantage of sourcing labor in developing countries is to create spending power and wealthier internal markets which will become export markets for Western countries that never existed before. Business has begun to seek out labor globally, and the means of doing so has become simpler through the Internet. This should not be seen as a threat by governments inclined toward protectionism but as an opportunity for Western manufacturers in creating new export markets for their goods and services. There has to be a trade-off between businesses and international governments. In exchange for a government's willingness to liberalize trade, large international companies must be willing to set new market rates by paying higher wages than the existing market level. The economic effect would be that of Ford's five-dollar day but multiplied onto a global scale.

The developing world has been dismissed for too long as a drain on Western capital in economic aid, much of it pocketed by corrupt rulers. But if earnings, not aid, were placed separately in the pockets of thousands, indeed millions, of individuals the West would be creating a market for the future. Jobs created abroad will create jobs at home in the cross-fertilization of business. This is an international argument. "Home" can be anywhere. The World Wide Web is the Main Street of the global village, creating massive opportunities for countries with few natural or manufacturing resources to begin marketing the know-how of their people.

But we move too soon to make Western-style economic judgments. There are parts of the world that just do not want much to do with Western-style capitalism. Perhaps the Western democracies should respect their wishes. Who is to say that economic progress and everything it brings with it – want and waste – is the one best way for all humanity? Western capitalism was forced on some nations. Perhaps the model of social capitalism, fostering increasing worker-ownership of businesses, would mean much more to many developing economies. These countries cannot expect to receive much encouragement from Europe.

The Lisbon summit in 2000, with its promise to create 20 million new jobs in the European Union, remained anchored to the policies of social protectionism implicit in the old agenda rhetoric of job creation. The philosophy of job creation is as flawed as Henry Ford's idea of creating a bird reserve on his homestead. Building birdhouses and putting down birdseed was a waste of time and money. Birds want to fly free and make their own way. So do people. Birds seek to congregate in environments rich in the basics they need to thrive – food, shelter, social groups, and reasonable safety from predators and the elements. People have slightly more complex needs but not dramatically so if you remove the manufactured "wants" of consumerism from the equation.

In fact, if the futurists are right in their reading of a fundamental sea change in society, enabled by the almost instantaneous transfer of information, some of our consumerist hunger may well recede. The very fact that almost anything is attainable may restrain our desires. With fewer financial, political, or legislative caps on personal ambition, people can begin to confront an ambition as a realizable dream. Will this mean that the dream loses its luster, because it is no longer special, testing, or unique?[3]

The futurists write of a paradigm shift. A paradigm shift is a shift in attitudes or beliefs so significant that it changes the way we see the world. The realization that the world was round, not flat, involved a paradigm shift, particularly for sailors. Michael Dunkerley points to several others in his book, *The Jobless Economy*. Charles Darwin's *The Origin of Species* forced people to rethink their concept of the Creation, and Louis Pasteur's discovery that bacteria transmitted disease revolutionized the understanding of diseases. "Changing just one belief can force on to people a completely new world view, and that is a very disturbing experience. People will hold on to old, even outmoded beliefs, just to avoid this experience," writes Dunkerley.[4] He is writing about the phenomenon of social drag. This is the phenomenon that can blind us to what is happening around us.

Dunkerley's book, published in 1996, was written before the explosion of the Internet, when companies such as America Online, Yahoo!, Amazon.com, and eBay were barely on the radar screen. Yahoo! – some suggest its initials stand for "yet another hierarchical officious oracle" – was founded in 1994 by two Stanford University electrical engineering students as an Internet directory for websites. It became a stock market quoted company in 1996. Netscape, a provider of Internet browser software, was founded the same year. It also came to the market in 1996.

Amazon.com sold its first book over the Internet in 1995. Google, the company that has come to dominate the Internet in today's new age of the search engine, was not founded until 1998. Facebook, the social networking internet phenomenon, was created by Mark Zuckerberg in 2003, Twitter, the microblogging site, in 2006. Wikipedia, the online information service that relies on updates from millions of volunteer contributors worldwide – challenging our thinking on knowledge-based transactions – was launched in 2001. The history of so much that we take for granted today is barely out of kindergarten.

The speed and impact of Internet-based information technology has been so staggering that Don Tapscott, a writer and consultant on Internet businesses, is convinced that the paradigm shift is for real. "We're moving into a new period of human history. It's not about dotcom. We're beginning to see some fundamental changes in how we create value and how we govern ourselves," he says.[5] Some of these changes, says Tapscott, involve the way that people will work in the new economy. Far more people, he believes, will have freelance or partnership arrangements with new technology companies. He quotes Steven Behm, the former vice president of global alliances at Cisco Systems. "We have 32,000 employees but only 17,000 of them work at Cisco," said Behm.[6]

It is difficult for many people who started and retain their careers in traditional employment – programmed as it is with career ladders and certain expectations – to appreciate the way the corporate and employment landscape is changing. Thomas Malone and Robert Laubacher, writing in the *Harvard Business Review* in 1998, illustrated the way that the ratio of employees in the biggest companies relative to other companies has been falling. Fortune 500 companies employed one in five US workers in the 1970s. By the late 1990s this had fallen to one in ten. As Malone and Laubacher pointed out, "the largest private employer in the United States is not General Motors, IBM or UPS. It's the temporary employment agency, Manpower Incorporated."[7]

Are we witnessing another wholesale redefinition of the job? Will we look back in twenty to fifty years' time at the structured employment of twentieth century big business, founded on practices developed in the previous century, as the era of the job?

Should we think of the job as nothing more than what William P. Bridges, the author of *JobShift*, called a "historical artifact"? Up to about 1800, he says, "people *did* jobs but didn't *have* jobs."[8] In a 1993 *Time* magazine article called the "Temping of America," Lance Morrow decided that the "great corporate clearances" and "ruthless restructuring efficiencies" of the nineties were creating a "just-in-time" workforce of "fluid, flexible and disposable" part-time and temporary workers.[9]

Tom Peters, the management writer, was dismissive of Morrow's article, preferring to be upbeat about the nature of change. A few years later he was less dismissive. In a lurid prediction published in *Time* magazine in May, 2000, Peters was forecasting that 90 percent of white-collar jobs in the United States would be either "destroyed or altered beyond recognition in the next 10 to 15 years. That's a catastrophic prediction, given that 90 percent of us are engaged in white-collar work of one sort or another," he wrote.[10] It was also way off the mark.

The predictions were accompanied in the magazine by a list of jobs expected to disappear. It was alarming stuff. Destined for the dump, according to *Time*, were teachers, printers, truckers, housekeepers, orthodontists, stenographers, stockbrokers, car dealers, insurance agents, real-estate agents, and prison guards. For good measure it included the role of the chief executive. It was a deliberately provocative piece of journalism. Surely there will always be someone who calls the shots, someone who has the casting vote. But need it be the same person all the time? Perhaps the role of the chief executive will change to one of coordinator or choreographer. In an organization run on the principle of Follett's *power with* there could be combinations of experts who will take center stage at different times. "All the world's a stage and all the men and women merely players," wrote Shakespeare in *As You Like It*. "One man in his time plays many parts."

When power is democratized, there is no reason why leadership cannot interchange. It already happens within partnerships. It happens within government. The president of the United States would not presume to overrule the head of the Federal Reserve or the Attorney General. Yet so many companies are still run like personal fiefdoms responsible to anonymous shareholders.

Behind the scenes power is wielded by the controlling managers of large pension funds. Some of these have become king-makers. This could not happen in a company run on behalf of its employee and pensioner shareholders. Some may argue that such an institution would be slow moving and unwieldy. Constant voting prevents crisp decision-making. But it is the way we run Western democracy, and consultation by government is increasing. Besides, a company does not own its people, and it may not even formally employ its best people. You don't order these people to do something, you ask them nicely and they see if they can fit the project into their schedule. An artisan independence is returning to the workplace. Relationships are growing in importance. Whatever Dilbert may say, the command-and-control philosophy is not going to work in the information age.

Peters's argument for change appeared to be founded partly on an observation – he had been talking to an old dockhand in London – that an awful lot of blue-collar jobs had vanished. I remember the blue-collar jobs disappearing in the 1970s and 1980s. I watched the textile mills close down in the town where I grew up. I saw the steel industry melt away in Sheffield. I interviewed out-of-work shipyard workers on Teeside and miners in the Welsh valleys who complained that the only work left for them was "women's work."

More recently I visited manufacturing sites where the blue-collar and white-collar distinctions were blurring. In some it was difficult to tell workers from management. Managers had abandoned their ties and jackets, and workers had abandoned their overalls, and both groups were spending more time in each other's company. In the early 1990s Rover, the former car manufacturer, deliberately mixed the roles for a while in an attempt to preserve jobs. As some white-collar jobs disappeared, the people who did these jobs were offered work on the assembly line. The idea was not popular. The biggest problem for white-collar workers was psychological, associated with the stigma of losing the trappings of the office job. No longer did they leave for work in the morning clutching their briefcase. Jobs take on trappings, and these trappings become part of an individual's identity, affecting not only how they see themselves but how they are seen by others.

The trappings of the white-collar job in many cases are the office, the telephone, the secretary, and the company car. These tend to convey status, and in the past these status symbols have been expanded or elaborated to extraordinary degrees. In British Civil Service jobs a higher grade would at one time attract a larger desk and several more square feet of office space. A property executive at Mobil Oil, when trying to make cost savings in office space at the company headquarters, found that many of the company's senior executives liked to have extra space for a couch. "In my own office I worked out that 35 percent of the office was status space – the place where the couch went," said Joe Licameli, the company's vice president for real estate in 1995.[11]

These examples are historic, but many other status trappings still exist, and the desire to possess them has not disappeared. I was told of one executive who turned down a job move in the 1990s because he was refused a request to have wire wheels on his company BMW. In his book, *Liar's Poker*, Michael Lewis, a former bond trader at Salomon Brothers, the investment bank, ridiculed the way a spirit of pettiness can develop in the pampered executive and the way that service organizations fall over themselves to pander to this spirit. After achieving some early success in his dealings, Lewis finds himself yelling at a bellhop about the inadequacies of his hotel room. There were no bath robes, no fruit bowl with apples and bananas, and, worst of all, the staff had forgotten to form a little triangle on the first sheet of the roll of bathroom tissue. It's just a dream, he explains. In fact it was a nightmare – the fear of a world without perks, without those little frills that symbolize special treatment. "Sometimes I dream I have been downgraded by British Airways from Club Class to Economy. Other times it's even worse," he wrote.[12]

Many such perks still exist – airline, hotel, and restaurant businesses thrive on them – although one of the healthier consequences of reengineering and the flattening of hierarchies was a move, often for the sake of economy rather than ideology, toward single-status working. A new generation of younger executives got rid of named parking spaces and individual offices. Some even got rid of desks. One UK office of Digital, the computer company, increased its worker–desk ratio to 12:1.[13] In these hot-desking environments the office furniture and office space were changed to reflect the desired mobility of the job, where the office became no more than a drop-in station. Christopher Jones, a consultant at Unisys whom I interviewed in 1995, said the only drawback of the change was the hefty barrister's briefcase he had bought to lug around his papers. His few other office possessions and files were kept in a box-on-wheels that could be trundled out when he needed a desk.

The biggest resistance to these transformations came from managers who found it difficult to make the psychological adjustment to the way their job was changing. Stephen Jupp, a specialist in change management at Digital, contrasted the difference in managerial attitudes at the time: "Good managers manage by results. Sloppy ones assess your contribution by your presence and how long you are there."[14] The concept of bums-on-seats, of being seen to be working in white-collar offices, remains one of the most persistent obstacles to the introduction of flexible working patterns. Too often flexibility is one-sided. The employee is expected to be flexible with no quid pro quo from the employer.

Big-time gurus must make big-time predictions. Peters might have been right about some aspects of change, but it will not be catastrophic. The fundamentals of the job will remain. Teachers will still be needed to teach, but they may no longer stand, autocratically, in front of classrooms dispensing knowledge in syllabus-driven packages. The role will be modeled around the needs of the children. Education, like the job, is due for an overhaul. The changing expectations of the job, indeed, will feed through to education providers. But education, like other areas of society, remains in the grip of social drag. Here's a test. How many jobs today require keyboard skills? How many schoolchildren receive typing lessons? Typing has become as fundamental to communications as joined-up writing, perhaps more so, and yet the education system continues to neglect this basic area of training.

Most of Peters's predictions, like most of those concerning the changes in work, were principally about packaging. Arguments about the packaging of the job remain relevant. Repackaged work needs to be supported by a new and more flexible financial infrastructure that appreciates the value of freelance workers moving from project to project. The packaging and support for these new jobs has been slow to improve. A freelancer, for example, needs variable arrangements to look after mortgages and other lines of credit. These issues are beginning to be addressed by the financial services industry, but the industry still prefers to focus its products on the so-called permanent workforce.

More important questions for society revolve around our attitudes to work. If we ask ourselves, "Is there work to do?" we must conclude that in the new century there is more work than ever. Technology designed to save labor invariably creates work. The internal combustion engine and the car led to vast new industries, from petrochemicals to road construction. It led to new laws, new living patterns, new leisure patterns. The advent of the mass-produced car, in fact, was as significant a social revolution as that which accompanied the steam engine, but no eminent historian ever chose to favor it with a label.

Perhaps it is because historians have become tired with the concept of revolutionary change in social history. Social history, after all, is not about events but about continuity. As one country invades another, the social history is bound up in the streams of refugees, their thoughts, their fears, and their aspirations. The tide of war shifts them this way and that. Sometimes the war creates a vortex into which are sucked whole strata or groupings of people – the kulaks in Russia, the Jews in Europe, the Armenians in Turkey, the Muslims in Bosnia. Those who survive are capable of a ferocious resistance to integration, such is the evolutionary power of diversity. Their traditions live on, often in another geographic location.

Social continuity transcends revolution, transcends geography. It is not about kings and queens or despots or conquests. It is about people making the best of their lives, looking out for themselves and for those who come after them, and work is so central to the human continuum. Where there is humanity there is work. Where there is life there is work.

We must look carefully, then, at the work before us, the work we have created for ourselves, and deliberate over how much of it is necessary and useful. As we deliberate on the best way to organize and accomplish the necessary work, however, we must also begin to confront the enduring presence of the work ethic. If we are indeed in the middle of some change in the way we look at work, some paradigm shift, to use the phrase so beloved of the modern guru, should we be thinking of ditching the work ethic as something that has served us well in the past but which has outgrown its usefulness? Has it become redundant? The idea sounds absurd.

The work ethic seems to be buried as deeply within Western society as the chemical reaction that pumps us with adrenaline in the event of sudden danger. Adrenaline gives us the physical preparedness for the fight or flight. Which is it to be? We must make the decision ourselves and in an instant. We have a little longer to deliberate over our work. So should we work ever harder or should we try to ease up on the accelerator? Were the question so simple. Some of us are psychologically incapable of easing up. The work ethic is so ingrained.

When I say "we" in this context I am referring to you and me, not to some government agency or some anonymous employer. We cannot expect capitalism to dispense with the work ethic. The capitalist system, as Adam Smith, Max Weber, and R. H. Tawney understood so well, was founded on the Protestant work ethic. To remove the work ethic is to remove the foundation of capitalism. So the work ethic will stay within the body corporate. Many companies will continue to view people as employees, as work units, as cost items to be factored into the price of a product or service. But some of the newer Internet companies are finding that they can obtain the products of work without paying for them. Amazon.com, for example, runs thousands of book reviews contributed willingly by customers.

Great work is not about ergonomically styled offices in different shades of blue and green. It is certainly not about all the processes of human resource management. It is not about leadership – not leadership from above, anyway. It is not about technology. It is about kindling the inner human spirit that makes us the people we are. We may well be inspired by the work or the example of others but only we, as individuals, can generate the glow that illuminates the achievements of our ancestors and sparks the achievements of our heirs.

If we want to refer to this glow as work, then well and good, but I think it is more than work. Some work has dimmed this glow to nothing more than a flicker in the human soul. If work cannot create the fire that fortifies every human spirit then that work has lost its meaning and should be discarded. We need to recover the spiritual in our lives and harness it to the way we work. Work has become the one-eyed monster that invades our dreams, but we can learn to love it.

We have come a long way in the two and a half million years since our ancestors found some merit in fashioning tools to improve their lives. The very act of creation, whether Biblical or evolutionary, involved work. But God was allowed to rest. Man has become increasingly restless. Whatever the severity of his original sin, he must have served his punishment by now. Yet man continues to punish himself in the way to which he has become accustomed – by heaping upon himself ever more complex levels of work.

Our society will always reward the industrious and long may it continue to do so, but hard work alone is not going to deliver either employee or employer satisfaction. It must be purposeful work, rewarding in and of itself. A job not worth doing should be ignored. The irony is that much technology has gone to war on work, replacing jobs (and therefore costs) with machines. Yet technology creates work because it feeds our desires, stimulating economic demand. People must learn to inhibit their desires. They must learn the lesson of Panama – that the land of their dreams is the land that they live in. At the same time they must continue to dream and to search in the knowledge that that search itself is the adventure.

The lesson is psychological. Today we have become deaf to what Martin Luther described as the "calling." If we hear something like it today, we hear a siren song. The sirens are so seductive; they are riches and possessions, gizmos and fashions, products and brands. In the commercial exploitation of the human genome, life itself becomes a brand. Shall we opt for a quality brand or shall we settle for a vacuous label that only delivers unhappiness, an empty exercise in gratification?

Taylor's production methods and Weber's bureaucracy did much to damage the human spirit. They compartmentalized work and, in so doing, they compartmentalized leisure. C. Wright Mills wrote in *White Collar: The American Middle Class* that office work had created a new leisure ethic. He argued that people in dull white-collar jobs during the 1950s were no longer driven by the work ethic but by a leisure ethic wrapped up in the promise of the weekend. "Work has been split from the rest of life, so the idols of work have been replaced by the idols of leisure," he said.[15] This new attitude of "Thank God It's Friday" was noticed by F. Scott Fitzgerald. "The rhythm of the week end, with its birth, its planned gaieties, and its announced end, followed the rhythm of life and was a substitute for it," he wrote.[16]

Work and leisure have been artificially divided for too long. Lewis Mumford believed that "in origin, work and play have the same common trunk and cannot be detached; every mastery of the economic conditions of life lightens the burden of servile work and opens up new possibilities for art and play."[17] So why don't more of us begin to explore these possibilities? Work and leisure can be fused together once more in the new working patterns of the future if employers and individuals are prepared to let go of the ingrained attitudes anchoring them to worn-out systems. It is the forces of social drag that hold them back. Nothing else.

A new generation of businesses – and this may well include those in dot.com and technology enterprises – must show the way. If they don't, then it is up to individuals. The World Wide Web means that we no longer need the safety of the old job. We just need an idea, and that idea might be something as simple as selling homemade jam through the Internet.

We may need to look to the Internet generation for a new work ethic. Unlike their Baby Boomer parents reared on a diet of television, a new generation is emerging that immerses itself in interactivity of the Web. Don Tapscott says that these children display different attitudes to their parents, rejecting the idea of conventional employment. "Every kid with a computer is creating his own radio station," he says. "They want to share the wealth they create. Tell them you'll give them a job and a corner office? I don't think so. Offer them lifelong, full time exclusive employment? I don't think so. This huge demographic change is like a tidal wave. These kids are going to shake the windows and rattle the values of every company. If you really want to have security, be an entrepreneur. That's the way these kids think. The real security is working for yourself."[18]

Frederick Taylor's scientific management was the Protestant work ethic harnessed to one man's bidding, taking control of our working lives. It helped to secure the factory system of production. Automation and the Internet have the potential to release us from this system if only we can summon the courage to take the leap from our institutionalized workplace to a fluid working pattern merged with the lifestyles we choose and the homes and communities we inhabit. But we must be careful about the work we select. Much new work has become repetitious. Information found in newspapers or in books is repeated on the Internet. Instead of one news channel there are hundreds of them, each employing newscasters relating the same news to fragmented audiences.

This fragmentation cannot last. Quality has suffered in the ubiquity of the information industry. It will only return when excellence begins to attract a discerning audience. Then we may be able to celebrate the value of creative work once more. As Mumford put it: "The function of work is to provide man with a living; not for the purpose of enlarging his capacities to consume but of liberating his capacities to create. The social meaning of work derives from the acts of creation it makes possible."[19]

Not since the Industrial Revolution has it been so important for individuals to explore the nature of their work. A poor decision today can lead to a lifetime of unfulfilled ambitions. How much can we rely on institutions, on government, and on traditional employers to provide us with fulfilling work? Can there be welfare in workfare? Historically, the prospects for relying on public- and private-sector employers to deliver worthwhile employment do not look encouraging. Historically, most manual work has been undertaken for the enrichment and life enhancement of a privileged few. If it wasn't the lord of the manor, it was the plantation owner, the factory boss, or the tribal chieftain. Was there ever a world when communal work was undertaken for the benefit of the whole of society?

The theories of the archeologist Marija Gimbutas are compelling. The idea that people once worked for each other, that decisions were taken democratically, mediated possibly by women, is easily dismissed by those of us who cannot conceive of a society that is not dominated by people who lead, in the words of Nigel Nicholson, because they desire to lead. But Gimbutas was not alone in her observations. Mary Parker Follett saw sense in a society run on the basis of *power with* rather than *power over*. When *power over* is abandoned as a desirable ambition, the alternative becomes attractive.

Of course there will be those who dismiss such notions as "too much like communism," refusing to acknowledge the historical precedents of economically successful communist models such as New Harmony, created by George Rapp. His was a flawed society, denying the natural state of the nuclear family, but it channeled work efficiently while celebrating the working spirit. There are lessons to be learned from Rappist organization. There are lessons, too, from Robert Owen's learning society, if only that learning alone cannot sustain a successful standard of living. But cooperation in society delivers healthier lifestyles, according to David Erdal's study of Italian cooperatives. In these societies, as in the Rappist towns, the members were stakeholders. Does this make a difference? We shall soon see. We are all capitalists now.

Within two generations most people will own financial shares in the ventures or institutions for which they work. The values of the workers will become the values of the corporation. Only then will companies have become the representative institutions of society, as employers and employees evolve their relationship through the conditions of "workership" – ownership vested through work. Even then, companies will lay claim only to commercial society – as far reaching as that may be. The corporation will continue to be subordinate to the family as a social unit, because the family must survive if society is to prosper. Society without the family ceases to be society.

The evolution of workership should be easier to achieve in a world where ideological differences have ceased to dominate elections, where the difference between political parties is determined by their electoral appeal. It is time to rid ourselves of ideological blinkers. The old ideologies are dead. Capitalism won and communism lost. People prefer capitalism. They prefer the opportunity to better themselves as individuals in the way they see fit. But this does not mean that selfishness will abound or that it cannot be directed at communal effort.

Work should be a means to an end. But work has got out of hand for so many of us. Our attitudes have become institutionalized by the secularized mindset of the Protestant work ethic, transferred down the years in cultural expectations and teachings of families and societies. Its importance needs to be diluted in our perspectives. It is part of life, not life itself. Voltaire described labor as "the father of leisure,"[20] yet today we strangle the child at birth. Work must be fused with our leisure, playing a more balanced role in our lives. Leisure should not be treated as idleness. The granting of public holidays should be celebrated, not damned. Greater leisure time can be an economic boon, allowing people to spend more of their earnings on leisure pursuits. It will also allow greater opportunity for those who wish to pursue other work, and sometimes this work will be voluntary. But we should have no more desire to create a leisure society than we should desire to create a world that is dominated by work.

The ancient Greeks pursued the concept of a leisure, or learning, society (the ideas are intertwined) and it worked – for the privileged citizens of Athens. The Greeks thought six hours were sufficient for a day's labor.[21] I would agree with the Greeks. But theirs was a two-tier society supported by slavery. The most free-thinking civilization the world has known was a state wrapped in chains. The only acceptable Greek revival today would be one in which machines were the slaves, and that seems beyond our wildest aspirations.

But we do need a revival of the Greek vision. The Greek scholar Edith Hamilton reminded us that "the exercise of vital powers along lines of excellence in a life affording them scope" was a Greek definition of happiness.[22] She called it a concept "permeated with the energy of life." The definition holds well for a fulfilling life today. It could almost be a definition for the future of work. No employee or employer could ask more of a job. Neither, in choosing a career, could they go wrong in adopting the two pieces of advice said by Plato to have been inscribed on the temple of Apollo at Delphi: "Know Thyself" and "Nothing in Excess."[23]

Work and leisure are vital ingredients in the soup of life. They can run together as a single fulfilling experience. This is what should inform our ambitions – a varying flow of experience, barely separable as work or play, not the telephone-number salary. Pay will continue to feature strongly in people's expectations, but it must not dominate expectations. Increasing numbers of people in the Western industrialized nations can look forward to greater fluctuations in income. These variable incomes, containing higher proportions of performance-related pay and bonuses, will be boosted occasionally by share dividends, interest from savings, pension annuities, and inherited wealth.

Our identity will no longer be framed by a single source of income or a single employer. They may be defined partially by a skill or set of skills or changing skills as we adapt throughout life; they may be defined by our values, and they may be defined by our circumstances. But in future our world will no longer be dominated by virtuous work. We have become conditioned to the idea of living for work. But the changing workplace, gradually undergoing transformation through the forces of flexibility, teleworking, home working, and work/life balance, aided by constantly improving remote communications, is influencing a change in attitudes, and the job opportunities today seem greater than they have ever been before.

Technology is the great leveler. Technology is handing us the capability of packaging our work in a way that suits us. We begin to look at choosing a career in the same way that we choose a holiday. We can find one "packaged" through an agency, or we can do some research and go our own way, tracking down and shaping work to fit our needs like modern-day hunter-gatherers. The essential lesson is that the choice is ours.

"Choose life," says Renton, the young Scottish reprobate, in the film *Trainspotting*. But working life offered such few prospects that he confesses, "I chose not to choose life. I chose something else." His choice was a dissolute existence addicted to heroin. How many others have chosen this path in preference to a fast-food counter or machine-watching in a factory? Work and the prospect of work must offer hope of something better if it offers nothing else. In future, work will need to earn its place in our lives. We cannot live for work. Instead we must take control of our lives. But the choice is ours. We cannot expect anyone to make it for us. If we choose wisely, if we follow our hearts, we may just begin to experience something called living. In the end it's up to us; our work, our play, our learning. We only get one life. Let's live it.

CHAPTER 23

Age of the Search Engine

The Earth is nobler than the world we have put upon it.
(J.B. Priestley, 1894–1984)

The first decade of the twenty-first century has passed since I first wrote this history of work. Our children have been reared in the new age of the Internet, an age of instant communications and democratized knowledge, but also an age of extremes where grinding poverty at one polar end of society contrasts with fabulous wealth at the other. It is a world where governments persist with economic solutions to recession and unemployment that may have worked in the twentieth century but which are ill-suited to the growing challenges of environmental degradation in the shadow of climate change.

Recession-tainted banks, meanwhile, seek to justify the telephone number bonuses of their highest paid employees, demonstrating breathtaking indifference not experienced since Nero chose to play his fiddle as Rome burnt around him. Some governments have promised clampdowns, but will it lead to a lasting change in behaviors?[1] I doubt it.

The world I described in the later chapters of this history was one where capitalism had triumphed. The celebrations of that triumph had barely subsided, however, before the devastating attacks on New York's World Trade Center in 2001 sent a shiver through the new world order. But it took a near financial meltdown of the Western banking system in 2008 to shake the capitalist system to its very foundations. While governments reacted swiftly to shore up the system, they failed to paper over the fissures that exposed an ugly side to corporatism.

How much did those who sought to enrich themselves in the financial system really care about the world beyond their crystal and steel high-rise towers? As banks shed staff – including some who had only joined from university two or three years earlier – students and graduates among tomorrow's generation could be forgiven for thinking that the system in which they had invested their hard-earned education had failed them.

This failure of corporatism, not only through its self-serving introspection, but also through its reluctance to explore or to innovate new working relationships, has been one of the most egregious examples of lassitude among employers during the formative years of the new century. At a time when the Internet was liberated by search-engine technology in ways that transformed the dissemination of knowledge, many companies fell back on old fashioned protectionism, attempting but often failing to ring-fence their intellectual property and copyrights in stubborn defiance of a new spirit of openness and information-sharing.

The established corporate sector did not invent the Internet, nor did the old order have the vision or the inventiveness to exploit the new medium in any novel way. The real breakthroughs of the information age have been the province of the entrepreneur and the start-up venture, taking corporate form in most cases because capitalism is the only game in town for those who need finance to achieve their ambitions. If corporatism can be condemned for inertia, so can governments, blinkered against changes in society that demand fresh thinking in labor market policy. To shed some light on emerging themes that are influencing attitudes to work, I embarked on a second book, *The Future of Work*, designed as a companion to this one. It sought not only to explain the way that work is changing, but also to outline a case for reform within antiquated labor markets.

It has become clear in the past decade that demographic change and the aging of Western populations is demanding new approaches in health care, retirement, and pensions. With as yet insufficient guidance, large sections of society are searching for ways to engage with work beyond the parameters of conventional employment. Nowhere is this more apparent than among the aging population. But policy has been slow to respond.

Take, for example, the decision by the UK's High Court in late 2009 to uphold a European Court of Justice ruling, allowing British employers to maintain default retirement ages. High

Court judges, who can work in post until they are seventy (with discretionary year-on-year extensions to age seventy-five), might be forgiven for seeing some merits in imposing limitations on the working age. But their own working age limits are set much higher than those for most other people in work.

Why did they insist on delaying the inevitable? As Dianah Worman, diversity adviser to the Chartered Institute of Personnel and Development, pointed out: "The High Court has missed a trick to resolve this issue once and for all. The government itself has admitted that the days of the default retirement age are numbered. It seems counter-intuitive to drag this decision out even further while thousands of older people will be forced out of work in an already difficult jobs market."[2]

Just as important as these economic arguments for reforming labor markets around an aging society is spiritual reform. Today our lifestyles are defined by "two-of-everything" materialism ensuring that Sunday car boot sales are more popular than church services in the UK.[3] A 2008 report by Christian Research, the statistical arm of the Bible Society, claimed that by 2050 Sunday congregations within the Church of England would fall below 88,000, compared with just under a million now.[4] The Church may have lost its battle to keep Sunday special but society will be the poorer if it allows the creeping demands of corporatism to destroy opportunities for shared communal leisure time and rest at weekends.

The point was made in a discursive exploration of historical and religious influences on the evolution of work undertaken by the Rt Rev. & Rt Hon. Richard Chartres, Bishop of London, in a lecture he gave in 2007.[5] His lecture explored many of the themes I have covered in this book, portraying two very different understandings and experiences of work, the first aligned to the doctrines of the ancient Greeks as understood by Plato and Aristotle, the second relying on an Old Testament interpretation where, he noted: "The idyllic picture of harmonious work conjured up in Genesis II lasted in Luther's striking phrase 'about as long as the first afternoon.'" Work became toil because it was abstracted from the connections and relationships which give it meaning, according to Chartres, who argues that work needs balance in the same way that the Sabbath maintains relativity and balance between labor and leisure. The Bishop continued:

> Work goes far beyond any utilitarian calculation and is meant to express and to bring into being our potential. Toil is what is experienced when work loses its connections and its meaning. Miners very understandably used to rail against the toilsome character of their work but, hard as it was, it also gave them dignity and established the values of strength and solidarity on which their communal life was based.
>
> In modern conditions it is easy to lose the connection between our work and the meaningful life and so we have to be distracted by a hectic pace and bribed by the accumulation of things to conceal the draining away of meaning.

Families too had been impoverished by the demands of work, he said. "The absent father has been joined by the absent mother on the treadmill of the work-and-spend cycle. No one on their death-bed ever expresses regret that they did not spend more time in the office. More often, in my experience, people regret that they did not pay more attention to family relations and friendships. The two things which bring joy in life are love and work but the balance between them has to be right."

The Bishop is one of a number of high profile individuals in the UK who have lent their support to a Work Foundation campaign called the Good Work Commission, seeking to define the meaning of and broaden the potential for good work. Good work has always been recognized in the sense of achievement we experience over a job well done. But there are so many deadening aspects of modern offices and manufacturing plants that both this sense of good work and any sense of our individuality can be drowned in the processes of management and corporatism.

Sometimes these processes can come to dominate a job, eclipsing the end product. In a recent routine from the popular BBC TV sketch series, *The Armstrong and Miller Show*, one of the actors is portraying a harassed executive spending his time during a flight struggling to coordinate his meetings within a hectic travel schedule. His fellow passenger asks him what he does for a living and the executive replies: "I have no idea." The best humor is always grounded in truth.

The way that employees of large companies can become lost in the system was observed by the philosopher Alain de Botton in his book, *The Pleasures and Sorrows of Work.* "It is surely significant that the adults who feature in children's books are rarely, if ever, Regional Sales Managers or Building Services Engineers. They are shopkeepers, builders, cooks or farmers – people whose labour can easily be linked to the visible betterment of human life," he wrote.[6]

One of the most curious aspects of de Botton's project – that involved spending time observing people at work among various employers – was the reticence of large companies to open their doors. Some 90 percent of his requests to go inside companies and look at how they went about their day-to-day business were rejected. Could it be that companies sensed they had a heretic in their midst bent on ridiculing their strategy trees, mission statements, management jargon, and sterile employment systems? It would not take long for corporate executives in conversation with de Botton to realize that here was a man who they might reasonably describe as "not one of us."

Such suspicion smacks of a tawdry homogeneity within the tiers of white collar management – a "them and us" division between the body corporate and those in the arts and academia. The way this is manifest in corporate jargon is apparent when de Botton quotes the chairman of a large firm of accountants replying to a question asking how the firm differs from its competitors: "Our people are our brand in our clients' eyes and a differentiated client experience can only be created through our people living our values," said the chairman.

The sadness is that fellow managers nod in passive acquiescence at such statements because their senses have been anesthetized by prolonged exposure to the same tribal language. What George Orwell in *1984* once defined as Newspeak has materialized in the workplace as "Corpspeak." The lack of meaning in Corpspeak, it seems, is less material than streaming the words together in sentences that give the impression of cohesion but which will not stand up to any serious analysis. No one dies when people communicate this way, but something in the human spirit dies, enough to influence an imperceptible drooping of the shoulders that begins to weigh heavily over the years.

It was with this sense of weariness that, in his final column as Management Editor of *The Observer*, that Simon Caulkin concluded that the management model in place for the past thirty years was "bust, dead, finished."[7].

Not everyone in the capitalist system, however, is weighed down under the burdens of bureaucracy, blandness, and banality endemic in modern management systems. Take Warren Buffet, probably the world's richest man if he could ever be bothered to count his wealth. The so-called sage of Omaha still skips to work as an 80-year-old.

Buffet enjoys his work because he understands that business is about getting things done. He invests, therefore, in those who do things well. He also understands himself – that his joy in life is making money and spending sensibly where the end is related directly to the means. His greatest gift to his children has been to pass on this understanding. The vast bulk of his wealth will go elsewhere – mostly to helping third world development through the Bill and Melinda Gates Foundation.

Buffett's brain seems to be hardwired to the business of investing in order to make a gain. In as much as he has developed an ethical philosophy it seems, today at least, to be based on a singularly humane preference – that he would prefer to make money in a way that is mutually beneficial to others to the alternative of profiting to the detriment of others. His approach to human relations is also simple – he believes that it's good to have them. This means that his head office is small so that he knows all of his colleagues; his house is relatively small (by multibillion-aire standards), and he lives in a small city in the Midwest where home-spun ideals mean that people know what they like and like what they know.

In the *Future of Work* I discussed an idea that has informed the way I have lived for some years now. For want of a better phrase I called it the "Economics of Enough." It is not a fully rounded principle underpinned by complex economic theory. In fact I find it difficult to illustrate because I am not talking about being satisfied with our lot in a way that extinguishes ambition – far from it. What I'm really talking about is understanding the wasteful profligacy underpinning a desire to accumulate that is bordering on addiction among those who live to shop.

If anyone embodies this concept of enough – and no one can fail to capture the irony here – it must be Warren Buffet who regularly eats in the same simple restaurant, usually ordering the same meal, drives a relatively modest car, and embodies values that measure people by their intrinsic human worth and character, not by the size of their bank accounts. For Buffet money is a utility. For many of us today, however, it has become a source of reverence.

This means that wealthy individuals can come to be lauded not for who they are but for their wealth and possessions. The comedy writer and actress Caroline Aherne raised this suspicion mischievously when in character as "Mrs Merton" in her spoof 1990s chat show she asked magician's wife Debbi Magee: "What was it that first attracted you to millionaire Paul Daniels?"

Unfortunately the rich too readily interpret calls for restraint as cries of envy without recognizing that unbridled acquisitiveness does not guarantee happiness. There will always be someone with a bigger boat.

David Cameron, leader of the Conservative Party in the UK, underlined the direction of the party's future employment policy in a wide-ranging speech that emphasized the need to improve the well-being of people at work. In what amounted to a backlash against long-hours working and the kind of working practices that have encouraged hastily consumed snack lunches in front of computer screens, the Conservatives promised to concentrate on a series of policies that emphasize effective, purposeful work. It was significant, perhaps, that Cameron used the language of economics, stressing something he called General Well Being beyond wealth-producing metrics such as Gross Domestic Product.[8]

Measures of happiness would seem to make much more sense if we are to gauge fulfillment in life in terms of how we feel about ourselves rather than by how much money we have made or how many cars or houses we posses. In his book *Happiness: Lessons from a New Science*, Richard Layard described what he called the Hedonic Treadmill. This refers to the insatiable appetite for material possessions in order to "keep up with the Joneses": "When I get a new home or a new car, I am excited at first. But then I get used to it, and my mood tends to revert back to what it was before," he writes. "Now I feel I need the bigger house and the better car. If I went back to the old house and car I would be much less happy than I was before I had experienced something better."[9] Layard has identified what he calls the "big seven" factors that influence well-being: family relationships, financial situation, work, community and friends, health, personal freedom, and personal values.

The influence of these factors has been measured in the World Values Survey carried out by the University of British Columbia, covering ninety thousand people in forty-six countries. The survey, run four times since 1981, asks people to rate their happiness on a scale of one to ten against various factors. The two biggest single ratings (each rated at six) are apportioned to work and health. It cannot be coincidence that both of these issues are related. Overwork, particularly without maintaining compensating fitness levels and a sensible diet, creates stress and, in some cases, a poor physical condition.

Employers could and should do more in actively helping employees to stay fit and healthy. It is as important today as it was in the factories of early industrial society. For some this will mean overcoming the attitude among managers that equates the constant occupation of workstations with productivity. If people are happy to spend lunchtimes sitting in front of a screen, eating packets of crisps and sandwiches, that may be fine, but if they are doing so in order to meet their deadlines, or for fear of breaking ranks, and if this practice becomes consolidated in daily routines, they and their employers could be storing up health problems for the future.

People have been willing to make compromises because their careers are important to them. As Layard stresses, work provides both income and meaning in life. "That is why unemployment is such a disaster: it reduces income but it also reduces happiness directly by destroying the self-respect and social relationships created by work. When people become unemployed their happiness falls much less because of the loss of income but because of the loss of work itself," he writes.

But the answer to job security is not more employee protection. Europe has enough of this as it is. The answer has to be in promoting more fluid ways of working. Why should work always be rewarded by money? Why not use more time off as a reward if time off is valued by an employee? The suggestion is made by Ken Hopper, joint author with his brother William of *The Puritan Gift*. Longer periods of time off tend to become attractive to employers only during recessions as ways to reduce production while retaining necessary skills. As soon as a recession ends and demand increases then the pressure for people to work longer hours increases. The frequently criticized European Working Time directive was introduced in an attempt to avoid this concentration of work, spreading it out among more people. While it may have been viewed as something of a blunt instrument, curtailing people's choices to work longer hours, it did at least establish the idea that not everyone wants to work all hours or, indeed, should be compelled to do so.

The option to work fewer hours should be enshrined within employee rights. This would help to break down the idea that everyone should have a single employer that is owed their undivided attention all of the time. People should not be viewed like sticks of Blackpool Rock with the name of their employer imprinted from end to end almost as an assumption of ownership.

Up to now, however, European employment legislation has done too little to relax labor market restrictions that are less apparent in North American employment. Lower levels of job protection in the US have allowed more fluidity in the workplace, creating more temporary or project work that can be appealing to those with the right kind of skills. Too many European workplaces have become tied to rigidities embedded in twentieth-century attitudes to jobs and employment, whereas in the emerging second generation Internet industries people are collaborating and learning new skills beyond the boundaries imposed by their existing employer, if indeed they have one.

In future, therefore, it's important that employers become more conscious of the need for a diversity – not simply the diversity of minorities but a diversity of options – that recognizes the different demands of different people at different stages of their career. The needs of a dual-income, childless couple, with no mortgage, for example, are different from those of a single mother in rented housing. Diversity thinking in employment has to be extended into accommodating the varying personal circumstances of employees. Attitudes to work change within a working lifetime during different life stages. But life should not be stereotyped in to a modern-day interpretation of Shakespeare's seven ages of man. Today's sixty-year-old, free from family commitments, mortgage paid perhaps, may feel invigorated and ready for anything; and that includes a readiness to engage with workplaces in different ways.

Organizational or brand identity still matters but it need not be expressed any longer solely through the job. Jobs will continue to define working relationships for the vast majority of people for some time. This is because, as David Cameron acknowledged, they underpin an important sense of commitment on both sides of the contract.

But jobs do not suit every working arrangement. Employment policy therefore should not be focused on the right way to package work but on creating the skills and opportunities to undertake meaningful work. If an economy of well-being is to be something more than a Conservative Party sound-bite on a day short of news, it will depend on good work producing good products and services, and on earnings invested in personal relationships, health, and those values that emphasize the things that matter in life.

Building such a virtuous circle is the biggest job of all. Unfortunately the new work of the Internet has failed as yet to influence general workplace reform. Bishop Chartres says he has yet to see improvements. "If anything the quality of life for office workers over the past ten years has deteriorated," he says. "The asceticism of so many modern office workers is remarkable. Like ancient votaries we take our places before our screens and tune in like mediaeval monks going about the Opus Dei."

It might have been hoped that new techniques in performance management would have offered some respite for those engaged on screen for much of their working days, but the Bishop interprets developments differently:

> The reduction of staff and new techniques for extracting more work from human resources also diminish the time for creative thought and there is a hardening of corporate arteries. The work that needs to be done today is performed more

efficiently but the erosion of space to contemplate tomorrow makes our organisations very vulnerable.

This is very much exacerbated by the new puritanism. Trust and profound communication are learned in the lunch hour but macho-management creates an atmosphere in which people are induced to graze on salad wraps with non-fat Mayo without leaving their screens.

In response to these developments, Bishop Chartres has called for

small incremental ways of changing the atmosphere at work. We must insist, particularly to ourselves, on having a proper lunch break preferably in congenial company.

In order to divert the pressure of the passing moment we might try beginning the day with a half hour's meditation and treating this time as seriously as we would any other business engagement in the diary. Once established as a daily habit it is possible to take five minute breaks throughout the day at convenient times to re-establish a healthy equilibrium. How the message would reverberate around the business world if the receptionist asked us to ring back in a couple of minutes because the CEO was meditating.

We are engaged in a life and death struggle. It is no good putting off the day when we give ourselves time to do justice to love as well as work. If there is no struggle today then when tomorrow comes the inner life will be too impoverished to bear much fruit.

I have quoted liberally from Bishop Chartres's lecture because it is such a refreshing antidote to the make-work society. His fear of "cultural impoverishment in the midst of abundance" dovetails precisely with my own fears and those I suspect of millions of others worldwide; and his demand for a better understanding of the way we work is a clarion call echoed throughout this history and my later book.

We shouldn't be surprised, perhaps, to find such clarity of understanding within the Church that historically has concerned itself intimately with the direction of human endeavor. In the past this concern has been focused on human and spiritual relations. Today, however, it must be coupled with our new understandings of the forces creating environmental impoverishment. Employers in what we should now recognize as post-industrial society must learn to refocus their institutions to the shape of tomorrow's society, and that means evolving attitudes just as much as technical innovation.

We move forward with a dangerous sense of complacency if we invest our faith in purely technical solutions to environmental depravation, world poverty, overpopulation, and dwindling oil reserves. These developments lie at the very heart of the new work and they are coloring and informing attitudes to materialism that need to be digested in government.

Governments need to be taking a lead in conservation beyond token systems of recycling and financial and legislative support for alternative and renewable energy sources. They need to reform and refocus their economic systems that continue to depend on the generation of consumption. If consumption is the lifeblood of economic growth, then the answer has to be to redirect consumption into regenerative and renewable resources.

A second area of potentially healthy growth is the generation of intangibles such as the stuff of leisure – music, literature, the arts, and the transfer and dissemination of information and knowledge. Much of this work need not be so resource-hungry as the creation of bigger airplanes, faster cars, grander buildings, and the concrete, asphalt, and steel citadels that house much of the world's population.

A concentration on this concept of having enough, emphasizing needs rather than wants, may well be viewed as economic heresy since most of our economic systems depend on creating more than enough. Tailoring work toward need is a venture into the unknown, at least for modern society, and could be interpreted as a regressive step. It is, after all, the philosophy of the hunter-gatherer.

But it's a modern philosophy too. Dame Ellen MacArthur has switched her attention from round-the-world racing in recent years to issues of sustainability informed by her own approaches to thrift and need, shaped partly by her childhood and partly by the ultra-conservationist approach needed to ensure that a long-distance racing yacht has no more equipment and supplies than it needs. "Why tear a piece of kitchen towel at the perforations just because the manufacturer puts them there. We might need no more than a fraction of that tear-off piece to do the job," she says.[10]

One consideration when contemplating a more minimalist society is that a reversion to something akin to subsistence living might limit our ability to innovate. As Jared Diamond points out in *Guns, Germs and Steel*, the production of food surpluses was essential for the evolution of writing: "Writing was never developed or even adopted by hunter-gathering societies, because they lacked both the institutional uses of early writing and the social and agricultural mechanisms for generating the food surpluses to feed scribes."[11]

In other words, surpluses are essential for developing societies. So the idea of a new economics that no longer venerates consumption must accommodate the principles of wealth creation. Perhaps, as Richard Layard has suggested, we need to redefine what we regard as wealth, moving away from material riches to alternative riches such as fellowship, community, mutuality, health, knowledge, and art.

Another danger of simply meeting needs, rather than generating a surplus, is that of miscalculation that will leave us genuinely impoverished. But if corporatism has achieved anything it is an understanding of efficiency. Is it beyond our competence to create a "just-in-time" society on the lines of a Japanese *kanban* wall? To develop the concept of enough, however, we need to define the meaning of the word just as we may need to reappraise what constitutes wealth. The biggest hurdle of all, perhaps, is in changing attitudes. But people have been here before. My grandmother, mentioned at the beginning of this book, had her own aphorism: "Enough's a feast," she used to say. But she was born into a nineteenth-century society that pre-dated mass production.

In the twentieth century the tenets of mass consumerism, feeding what became known as the disposable society, destroyed understandings of need, endorsing instead the desire that replaces needs with wants. As greed became good, people abandoned any historical sense of restraint and sufficiency, supplanting contentment with acquisitiveness and ambition that could be adequately described as enlightened self-interest.

Unfortunately this celebration of self-interest, condoned by the likes of Ayn Rand in works that outlined her objectivist philosophy, placing the pursuit of happiness at the very center of our moral compass, was to blind-side society to the kind of environmental crisis envisaged in Garrett Hardin's article, "The Tragedy of the Commons," first published in the journal *Science* in 1968.[12]

Hardin argued that an objective pursuit of self-interest on a grand scale would ultimately destroy limited resources, thus damaging the long-term interest of all. The power outages that disrupted companies in Silicon Valley during 2001 are just one consequence of unbridled growth. Deforestation, over-fishing, shortages of drinking water, and soil erosion are among the more critical examples of Hardin's tragedy in the making.

Society, therefore, is faced with two choices: regulatory restrictions on the selfish exploitation of resources or voluntary restraint, induced by a widespread understanding that wealth is both finite and relative. Some may argue that voluntary restraint is unrealistic. But there are numerous historical examples of managed societies and good husbandry, such as the mediaeval three-field system that allowed land to regenerate, just as there are examples of the mismanagement of resources leading to societal collapse. The Polynesians who discovered and settled on Easter Island, survived for 1,000 years before deforestation reduced their ability to sustain themselves. Their society had collapsed before the first Europeans arrived in 1722.

Could Western society be heading for a similar collapse but on a much more catastrophic and terrifying scale? The warning signs were there to see in the late 1990s when George Carlin, the late US comedian, puzzled over the contradictions of his overly materialistic nation: a nation of "bigger houses but smaller families; more conveniences but less time; wider freeways but narrower viewpoints; taller buildings but shorter tempers; more knowledge and less judgement." Carlin was quoted by Peter Whybrow in his 2005 book, *American Mania: When More is not Enough*, a book that highlighted the damage that today's "fast new world" is doing to the average American citizen.

Are we really prepared to tolerate a future of growing obesity and rampant diabetes fueled by overindulgence and untrammeled consumerism? Obesity is not simply about body fat. Today we are suffering from obesity of the mind, our thought patterns clogged each day by the information donuts we graze from the Internet. When Homer Simpson complained that "every time I learn something new, it pushes some old stuff out of my brain," we may have chuckled at the absurdity of his analysis. But it was symptomatic nevertheless of the sense of mental overload we sometimes feel when dealing with multiple information streams channeled over the Internet in emails, tweets, and newsfeeds.

The way we live, the way we spend, the way we eat, the way we work, and the way we look at ourselves and our world, must all change if we are to leave any worthwhile inheritance for the unborn generations to come. Advances in genetics, health care, technology, and environmental approaches ensure that change is inevitable. Wealth creation is fundamental to this change, but it is our appreciation of wealth itself that needs some revision. We must begin to think beyond the salary and the bonus and to the way that financial wealth is engaged in the broader well-being, not just of people, but of the entire planet.

In the past decade many of the nascent communications technologies at the turn of the century have been consolidated. The power of the search engine meanwhile has transformed the way that people transmit, retrieve, and disseminate information. Human creativity has proliferated over the Web where information consumers are still learning to sift the genuinely useful and the innovative from a sea of mediocrity. In the information gold rush millions of people are striving to establish their individual entities on social networking sites such as Facebook and Twitter. Nowhere, however, has the democratization of knowledge been more apparent than in the growth of Wikipedia – the online encyclopedia.

Meanwhile, evidence of climate change through global warming is hardening, thereby shaping the attitudes of a new generation. These changing attitudes are filtering into the workplace as potential recruits question employers' environmental credentials, seeking indications that prospective employers have a genuine commitment to sustainable development.

At the same time performance measurement is growing more sophisticated and attitudes generally seem to be toughening as younger employees become inured to a more competitive work-place. Demographic shifts, heralding an aging society in most Western industrialized nations, is forcing governments to rethink their pensions and retirement systems. Amid all this change, the structure of jobs and careers has proved remarkably resilient, remaining the dominant system of delivering and accomplishing work. The Protestant work ethic has proven equally persistent as a virtue among those who seek to prosper in their chosen careers. Hard work and commitment continue, rightly, to be prized among employers, but too many are interpreting performance management as a blunt-edged instrument, continually demanding higher workloads in order to maintain competitiveness. Employers need to realign their management thinking around a few old-fashioned principles such as mutual trust and purposeful work that is rewarded by a sense of achievement in a job well done as much as it is by the year-end bonus.

Yet new understandings have inspired some deeper thinking about our relationship with work. Work should not be disengaged from meaning and purpose. Drudge work continues and so does unemployment. So too does industrial action and all the different forms of illegal discrimination. Work itself, however, should no longer be seen purely as a means to earn a living but as a source of personal development. Today, increasingly, it is chosen for its intrinsic value. If work is a living, then people are living their work. The kind of work we can accept as central to our lifestyle is lending us a sense of vocation.

Employers need to see themselves as enablers for those who seek this vocational path. Companies that score highly on various "best places to work" rankings seem to do just that. There should be a duty, therefore, among those who profit from work to ensure that the work is both rewarding and well managed. Too much existing work is deficient on both counts. Will it remain so or can we look forward to the day that all work is a source of stimulation as well as earnings?

Societies can never return to the Garden of Eden. But work can be good again. We owe this much to ourselves.

Postscript: New Century, New Ethic

> I go on working for the same reason that a hen goes on laying eggs.
>
> (H. L. Mencken, 1880–1956)

The gestation period for this book was about six years. That's six years spent grappling with the idea of change within permanency, the idea that we are undergoing a revolution in society without needing to venture out of our sitting rooms to see it. It's a quiet revolution. Or at least it has been quiet up to now.

Looking back has helped me to be clearer about one thing. Change creeps up on you. The concept of revolution is one of hindsight. It should remain where it began, as a description of sudden, violent, political change. It is wholly inadequate in describing the changes in the way we live and this thing we call work. We cannot divorce work and life. They go together. Work can be fun, but the fun had gone out of it for so many people. When I looked around me, so many people seemed to be dissatisfied with their work. There seemed to be a common suspicion, a realization among some, that if they were working to live, they were working in a way that was ruining the way that they lived. Many did not even allow themselves this reflection. They took their work for granted; they had become consumed by work. They were living to work. They were the ones, to varying degrees, who could not remove themselves from the psychological, historical grip of the Protestant work ethic.

I must number myself here. Work avoided, work done badly, could only fan the smoldering coals of Protestant guilt. If only I could confess my sin and receive absolution. If only I could be carefree about laziness, like Jerome K. Jerome, pottering through life in a state of fascination. In *Three Men in a Boat* he writes: "I like work: it fascinates me. I can sit and look at it for hours. I love to keep it by me: the idea of getting rid of it nearly breaks my heart."

But a work-obsessed society would have no truck with that idea. Any remaining Jeromes in the corporate sector were winkled out in those fastidious exercises of personnel grooming called reengineering.

It may have been reengineering, however, that indirectly inspired my approach to this book. The first time I encountered the word "outplacement," in 1994, I had no idea what it was. As someone who had never been unemployed, had never lost his job, had never been downsized, I did not know there was an industry dedicated to helping people out of their old jobs and into new ones. Outplacement was aimed initially at management, because industry was traditionally conducted in a spirit of "us" and "them" – management and workers. It was considered all right to lay off workers. Their jobs had never been secure. But management was different. Managers had an unwritten psychological contract: in return for their loyalty, they could expect a steady career moving up the ladder until retirement. Reengineering beggared that dream. It was hard for top management to break the news among the people who shared their offices. Outplacement was a way to say it with flowers, to cushion the pain of saying goodbye on both sides. Outplacement recognized that when you took away a manager's job, you were taking away a piece of his or her identity.

For a small investment a company could buy its departing executive an outplacement program designed to fill the void between one corporate life and the next. To make this period of limbo familiar, the outplacement companies could provide an office and secretarial support. Some companies provided psychological support. Out of interest for my newspaper column I attended some of these sessions.

There were different techniques all with the same aim – discovering what you really wanted to do with your life. One psychologist who relied on so-called guided imagery demanded that the subject close his or her eyes and think of something, an object or an experience, that would then be woven into a story. The story would be viewed as a metaphor for whatever it was that lay at the seat of the subject's desires.

For some the sessions were plainly a waste of time. These were people who had a good idea of what they wanted. For many, however, they were a revelation. An accountant realized he had always wanted to be a magician, a merchandiser knew he could enjoy the challenge of running his own corner shop. Sometimes the session would point to a vague interest – bird watching, perhaps. The next stage was to explore the possibilities of a career working with birds or harnessing the skills and behaviors adopted in bird watching.

Easier said than done, perhaps. How do you step away from one successful career and pursue what some might call a pipe dream?

In mentioning birds, I must have been recalling Josep del Hoyo. Del Hoyo didn't lose his job. He was very happily employed as a family doctor in a village in Spain. Often people would visit his clinic only to find a sign on the door saying "In the Woods. Back Soon." Del Hoyo's real passion was wildlife. Gradually bird watching began to predominate. It might have remained a hobby, but there was something niggling him: nowhere could he find a book that listed and described every species of bird known to man. So he decided to create one.

The *Handbook of the Birds of the World* really is an act of creation. Del Hoyo isn't writing it all – that would be far too great a task – but he is making it happen. He is the editor. It is his project. By the time it is finished in 2011, it will consist of sixteen volumes. If some people had been skeptical initially, the first volume changed their minds. Suddenly anyone who was anyone in ornithology wanted to contribute. Del Hoyo commissions plates from some of the world's finest painters of birds. He buys the work, so by the time the project is complete he will have a unique collection of artwork depicting every one of the nine to ten thousand types of bird we know to exist. Not even Nathan Rothschild, the nineteenth-century banker, had that. Rothschild built up the world's largest collection of bird specimens but had to sell half of it to pay off a former mistress in what today would be described as a palimony suit.

"I feel very grateful to birds because they have given me the chance to travel the world doing the things that I enjoy," says del Hoyo, whose personal philosophy is inspired by a quote from Pablo Neruda, the Chilean poet and Nobel prize winner: "Bird by bird I knew the world." What a wonderful way to launch a new career. Del Hoyo isn't Superman. He simply discovered what he wanted in life and decided to make it happen.

Yet so many people never achieve these levels of fulfillment. They cannot let their dreams soar with the birds. That way invites ridicule. The real world demands work, not dreams. That said, the psychotherapy offered by some outplacement companies is daring people to dream once more, then pointing to ways they may clothe these dreams in reality.

I could not divorce my own dreams from these outplacement sessions. Writing my weekly column – meeting some of the best brains in the field of management writing, people like Peter Drucker, Warren Bennis, Rosabeth Moss Kanter, C. K. Prahalad, and Gary Hamel, and at the same time dealing with the issues faced daily by the recruitment and personnel industries – began to shape my own thinking while feeding my frustrations. Something was happening to the job, but what was it? It wasn't simply an abandonment of the "job for life" concept. The job for life was a modern myth circulated by those who had cruised through the civil service or the middle reaches of some large corporate monolith. It never existed in journalism.

Books like Charles Handy's *The Empty Raincoat*, William Bridges's *JobShift*, or Jeremy Rifkin's absurdly titled *End of Work* were trying to make sense of the changes, but every new discussion seemed to have its academic detractors who churned out figures suggesting that the job market was changing far less markedly than some were suggesting.

Without taking sides, one thing seemed obvious: a lot of people were doing some serious navel-gazing about the concept of work. I wanted to do more than add my own two cents worth in a weekly column, so I decided to invest my savings, to buy for myself a year of my life, to organize and use it as I saw fit, to investigate the merits and drawbacks of working at home, to enter a world of social isolation, to cut myself off from the corporate expense account and the monthly pay check, to read some books, to sit and think, and to write.

I chose a time when the business world began to turn upside down. Old reliable blue-chip stocks floundered as hoppity-hopeful Internet stocks soared upward in a shiny, growing bubble, gleaming with anticipation and dripping with greedy speculation. Every fifteen-year-old schoolboy wanted a website that would earn him instant millions. Sitting in the tiny home-based cube I call my office, it was like watching an episode of the 1970s television spy fantasy, *The Prisoner*, in which people lived an unreal existence of harmony and contentment, separated from the real world by a giant bubble. Every time they grew curious, the bubble would steer them back toward the candy-striped existence of their model town. But in this real-life episode everyone was sitting inside the bubble.

The Internet bubble had all the characteristics of previous waves of financial euphoria. Internet stocks were being valued in the way the Dutch once valued tulip bulbs. People could see the speculation, but they fervently believed it would pay off or that the strongest would prevail at the expense of the weak. This is the price of transformation. The bubble didn't burst. It deflated to more acceptable proportions. Dot.com has not disappeared, but it appears to have learned some humility.

Guided by an affinity with Jerome's remark that "work fascinates me," I have tried to shed some light on the question, Why do we work? Looking back, it's tempting to conclude: "It's the Puritans wot did it"; or, as some will continue to insist, "It's the pay, stupid." But that doesn't explain Stonehenge or the Pyramids or the extraordinary constructions of the Incas. It doesn't explain the paintings at Lascaux and Chauvet.

Perhaps none of these achievements were viewed as work. I think we work because we want to leave something better for those we leave behind, some signpost of our existence, of our potential. Our work is an instinctive recognition of human greatness. Modifying the way we work, as Taylor did, was as misguided as the genetic modification of plants. There were benefits, but our personal skills and capabilities are characteristics of our individuality. To alter or to regiment human ability is to distort life's infinite variety, and that is an offence against humanity for which we must all pay a price. Do we want human variety or do we want Aldous Huxley's industrial clones?

If we opt for variety, then we must begin to change our society from the roots, starting with education. The dominant system of education is designed for the industrialized world of Frederick Taylor and the rational systems of Max Weber. A teacher, a figure of authority, stands in front of a class and pours forth information. The children sit in rows of desks and struggle to digest like oversoaked sponges. Teaching is barely one step removed from Gradgrind's barrage of meaningless facts. Stir in a bit of Socratic method and there you have it. Maria Montessori, the Italian educator, believed that children were trapped in the classroom "like butterflies mounted on pins."[1]

Traditional teaching in schools is command-and-control learning: I speak and you listen; you ask a question and I tell you the answer, or I force you to think with another question and we arrive at the answer together. Just as we're getting somewhere in French class, the bell goes, and it's over to history, more facts, a bit of discussion, a smidgen of interpretation, set the homework, books closed, and off you go. Command-and-control learning produces boredom and unrest. It closes minds. As I once heard a conference speaker say, children go into school as question marks and leave as full stops.

Real life isn't like this. Left to ourselves we are open to hundreds of influences. A day develops. We may grasp just one of a myriad of colorful threads and we begin to weave, picking up information and understanding as we go along. The more we learn, the more we want to learn. We may need guidance, and one of our guides may well be a teacher, but another may be a parent or a book or a TV program or a movie or a game or a conversation with friends. We may even learn something from the Internet, but we should not hold our breath.

I don't teach my children in any formal way, but, like many parents, I help them to learn when they seek my help and I work with them on their homework. So does my wife. But we don't push the teaching, because the children are being driven hard enough at school; too hard, perhaps. Educational expectations are rising. Schools and teachers must realize their students have a life outside the classroom. Companies, too, must realize their employees need a life outside the workplace. Often this outside life provides a platform for creativity denied in the institution, be it employment or education.

Creativity is our future. It may not be the future of big companies, because most big companies have stifled the creativity of their employees by insisting on processes, on time sheets, by constantly measuring or by boxing in the creative process in brainstorming sessions. I have been to brainstorming sessions and I have thought alone in the bath. The bath is better. Isaac Newton enjoyed the stimulation of his Trinity College colleagues at Cambridge University, but his best thinking, his most focused thinking, occurred when the university was closed down in 1665 for fear of the Great Plague. Newton went home and mused in his orchard, and that's how we know about gravity.

The work ethic, this historical relic of Nonconformism, has been transformed by capitalism into a corporate ideology controlling our lives. But it has not always dominated our concerns. The ethic should not be viewed as a permanent feature of life. It waxes and wanes. It strengthened in the wake of corporate engineering, and its influence has spread with that of the Americanization of commerce. The working breakfast, the alcohol-free lunch, the staying late in the office, are all part of this pervasive American business influence.

Even political correctness is Puritanism in disguise. Tina Brown's *Talk* magazine referred to the most significant symptom of the new Puritanism as "anhedonia" – the inability to find pleasure in leisure.[2] "We're too busy achieving and fretting about what we've yet to achieve," said *Talk*. The work ethic, it admitted, had invaded almost every facet of life. Leisure time is devoted to productive pursuits such as fitness programs and workouts, children's play time is increasingly organized to reflect its educational possibilities, even sex has become invested with the pressure to achieve peak performance, like competitive figure skating before card-holding judges. What are we doing to ourselves? There is madness in this work.

Once we could celebrate the social side of the workplace. Today we are damned if we don't work, drained if we do. To balance our lives in this new century we need nothing less than a new ethic. We need to take the old ethic, dismantle it, analyze it, then reconstruct something which makes more sense. We need an ethic that leans far less on its religious antecedents but which concentrates on the needs of society; not the needs of the job which might have been outlined in some dry job description, but on the work that needs doing to ensure we can maintain a healthy society. If our work is not making a difference, to quote the fireman in Studs Terkel's book, we shouldn't be doing it.

Slavery, whether enforced by inhuman societies or disguised as a wage-earning job, should not be encouraged by the philosophy of job creation. Job creation is a corruption of wealth creation. If we believe we have become slaves to our jobs we should examine our own value systems and make some adjustments. We cannot rely on employers. Most employers have only ever seen workers as costs. Any self-made employer will remember the cost–benefit equation he or she makes when considering the need to employ someone else. The employer may develop social cares. He or she may begin to identify with his employees, but, when the chips are down, in times of financial crisis, it is every man and woman for themselves.

There are occasional exceptions. Aaron Mordecai Feuerstein became a national hero in the United States when he decided to rebuild his ninety-year-old Massachusetts textile factory after it burned to the ground in 1995. Few would have blamed him had he simply retired. He was sixty-nine at the time. Instead he rebuilt the plant while paying the salaries and benefits of the 2,400 employees during the time the plant was shut down. His decision was viewed by many as a rare philanthropic gesture. Feuerstein's philosophy that "if you pay people a fair amount of money and give them good benefits to take care of their families, they will produce for you," made so much sense it was regarded as rather quaint.[3] It seems extraordinary that a commitment to a business should have caused so much surprise. But in a world where values have become aligned with an uncompromising service-driven economy, such examples tend to evoke a nostalgia for a way of life and work that is fast disappearing.

The new work ethic will not be apparent among most conventional employers. It will not be found on management courses. But it is there, in all strata of the corporation, in all strata of society. It is something that resides within us, that only we as individuals can develop. Inevitably it will borrow heavily from its Nonconformist heritage. It would be unrealistic to think otherwise. It may even appear as a new Puritanism in some. It will certainly rely on individuality and require an element of self-will. But it must be inclusive, not exclusive, harnessing the selfish gene of self-help and extending itself to helping others.

It involves letting go of some reassuring habits. It may involve letting go of a lifetime career. It will involve careful evaluation: a personal soul searching, an understanding of what makes us tick, what it is in life that we really value, what we love doing, and what needs doing in the wider environment. There are many ways of taking this step. Some utilize a form of personal psychoanalysis – the sort sometimes used by outplacement practitioners – some draw on the insights to be gained from personality testing, and some involve careful questioning of our nearest and dearest.

This does not mean we should go rushing out for the nearest self-help book. That would be pandering to the damaging obsession with perfection that characterizes our work-focused lives. We must not sacrifice ourselves to the anhedonia syndrome. We must learn to relax, to "chill out," to do less, to recognize the essentials and skim away the froth, to live with imperfection; more than that, to celebrate imperfection. There is more to life than six-pack stomachs and cellulite-free thighs. Fashion has brought total quality, six-sigma lifestyles into the domestic arena. It's time to say "enough." So one of your dinner plates has a chip on the rim. Let's hear it for the chip.

Act we must, and quickly. At the very least we can try to engineer a break for a period of reflection. The world is changing so quickly, we don't have time for that, you say. Speed and change, speed and change. It's the latest fashion. Change is like a river. The flow is fastest in the middle, but if you swim to the side you can paddle in the slack water by the bank. That's where you find the messages in their bottles. Stay in the current and you'll be swept out to sea.

Of course change is a constant, but rapid change is an illusion. The most important things in life – our beliefs and values – are tremendously resilient to changing fashions, and much of today's so-called change is wrapped up in fashion. It is essential for our sanity that we filter the good and the wholesome and the important from the transitory hype and hysteria.

The career break I took to research and write this book was the best move I ever made. Not only did I enjoy that year more than any other, I have probably worked harder than at any time of my career; but the work was focused and organized and fun. I read books, I traveled, and I learned. Work became a joy. So much so it no longer seemed like work.

"You won't want to go back to work," said some people. But I never left it. On the other hand the work never became so burdensome that it dominated my every waking moment. There was always time for a change of scenery. There was always time to stand and stare. The difference was – and this will be recognized by some who are self-employed – I was setting my own pace and it worked.

I set out to write a book about something that has run through human society like an unbroken thread from the dawn of our history. It's a book about work. It's a book about the organization and the management of work. But most of all it's a book about people, the men and women who created the world we live in and the inner soul-deep sense that pushes so many of them ever onward. Jerome K. Jerome was right about one thing. Work is fascinating when you look at it. But we shouldn't become obsessed with it. We shouldn't become slaves to work.

NOTES

Introduction

1. Max Weber, *The Protestant Work Ethic and The Spirit of Capitalism*, Routledge, 1992 (first published 1930), p. 181.
2. Juliet Schor, *The Overworked American*, Basic Books, 1992, p. 29. Schor's estimates are based on labor force statistics during 1969–87.
3. Valerie Bayliss, *Redefining Work*, Royal Society for the Encouragement of Arts, Manufactures and Commerce, 1998.
4. *Daily Telegraph*, September 26, 1998. A random poll of 1,178 adults carried out by ICM for BBC Radio 4 found that 55 percent described themselves as working class and 41 percent said they were middle class. Just 1 percent said they were upper class.

1 Hands to the Grindstone

1. For the definitive study of the Langdale axe workings read B. Bunch and C.I. Fell, *A Stone Axe Factory at Pike of Stickle*, Great Langdale: Westmorland, 1949; see also *Prehistoric Society Proceedings*, vol. 15, pp. 1–20.
2. Some conjecture on this point is raised by T.H. McK. Clough and W.A. Cummins in *Stone Axe Studies*, CBA Research Report No. 23, 1979, p. 10.
3. Michael D. Lemonick and Andrea Dorfman, "Up From The Apes," *Time*, August 23, 1999.
4. Graham Richards, "Freed Hands or Enslaved Feet?" *Journal of Human Evolution*, pp. 143–50, quoted by Clive Gamble in *Timewalkers: The Prehistory of Global Civilization*, Penguin, 1995, p. 101.
5. According to Timothy Bottoms, the Cairns historian, the first aboriginal contact with Europeans in the Cape York area was in 1623 when Dutch ships sailed down the west coast of Cairns. Cattle drovers pushing into the peninsula in 1864 killed at least 30

Yir Yoront tribesmen in the Battle of the Mitchell River. Like most such "battles" the encounter was one-sided.

6. Edward H. Spicer, ed., *Human Problems in Technological Change*, Russell Sage Foundation, 1952, p. 75.

7. Richard B. Lee and Irven De Vore, *Kalahari Hunter Gatherers: Studies of the !Kung San and Their Neighbors*, Harvard University Press, 1976, p. 102. Also quoted in Michael Pitts and Mark Roberts, *Fairweather Eden*, Arrow, 1998, pp. 152–3.

8. Barry Alpher, *Yir-Yoront Lexicon: Sketch and Dictionary of an Australian Language*, Berlin: Mouton de Gruyter, 1991. Alpher considered whether "woq" might have been a derivation from the English "work" but, other than noting the possibility, he cannot be definitive on the point.

9. Author's interview with Jerry Mission, member of Yir Yoront tribe.

10. Gamble, p. 66. The leading proponent of the scavenger interpretation of early hominid food gathering is Lewis Binford.

11. *Daily Telegraph*, February 2, 1997. A photograph of the spears with a fossilized horse skull is featured in *National Geographic*, July, 1997, p. 113.

12. Interview with the author.

13. Pitts and Roberts, *Fairweather Eden*, p. 298.

14. Interview with the author.

15. Interview with the author. Flint knapping techniques are described by John Lord in *The Nature and Subsequent Uses of Flint*, John Lord, 1993.

16. Pitts and Roberts, *Fairweather Eden*, pp. 202–3.

17. E. Paul G. Bahn, *The Story of Archeology*, Weidenfeld & Nicolson, 1996, pp. 54–5.

18. Brigitte and Gilles Delluc, *Discovering Lascaux*, Sud Ouest, 1990, p. 38.

19. Rick Gore, "People Like Us," *National Geographic*, July, 2000, vol. 198, no. 1.

20. Ibid. Evidence of textiles has been discovered at Dolni Vestonice and Pavlov in the Czech Republic. The sites belonged to the Garvettian people who lived about 7,000 years after the Chauvet paintings were executed.

21. Gore, "People Like Us," p. 95.

22. Ibid., p. 152, quoted from Lee and De Vore, *Man the Hunter*, New York: Aldine Publishing, 1968.

23. Richard Rudgley, *Lost Civilizations of the Stone Age*, Century, 1998, p. 20.

24. Ibid., p. 352.

25. Gore, "People Like Us," pp. 110–11.

26. Pitts and Roberts, *Fairweather Eden*, p. 168.

27. Genesis 4:19.

28. Rudgley, *Lost Civilizations*, p. 159.

29. Ibid., p. 14.

2 Fettered Lives

1. Paul Johnson, *A History of the American People*, Phoenix, 1998, p. 37 (first published 1997).

2. Fustel de Coulonges calls slavery a "primordial fact, contemporary with the origin of society." Quoted by M.I. Finley in *Ancient Slavery and Modern Ideology*, Pelican, 1983, p. 67.

3. Ibid., pp. 131–2.

4. Keith Bradley, *Slaves and Masters in the Roman Empire*, Oxford University Press, 1987, p. 21.

5. Ibid., p. 22, quoted from the Loeb translation of *De re rustica*, 1919.

6. Ibid., p. 22.

7. Ibid., p. 33.

8. Frederick Douglass, *My Bondage and My Freedom*, New York, 1855, quoted in M.I. Finley in *Slavery in Classical Antiquity*, Man, 1961, p. 67.

9. *Germanica*, ch. 15.

10. Adam Smith, *Wealth of Nations*, Book I, ch. viii and Book III, ch. ii, quoted by John Kells Ingram in *A History of Slavery and Serfdom*, Adam and Charles Black, 1895, p. 281.

11. William Lim Westerman, *Slavery in Classical Antiquity: Views and Controversies*, ed. M.I. Finley, W. Heffer, 1960, pp. 26–7.

12. Finley, *Slavery in Classical Antiquity*, p. 68.

13. Ibid., p. 30.

14. *The Art of Rhetoric*, 1367a 32.

15. Franklin Roosevelt's message to Congress, January 6, 1941, in *Public Papers*, vol. 9.

16. 2 Thessalonians 3:10, Authorised Version of the Bible, 1611.

17. Bradley lists three major slave revolts between 140 and 70 BC. The most serious of these was the one led by Spartacus in Italy from 73 to 71 BC.

18. Quoted by Finley in *Slavery in Classical Antiquity*, p. 160.

19. The lever theory was advanced by Peter Hodges in *How the Pyramids Were Built*, ed. Julian Keable, Warminster: Aris and Phillips, 1993. I.E.S. Edwards discusses pyramid construction methods in *The Pyramids of Egypt*, Penguin Books, 1972, pp. 254–95. Edwards noted the use of ramps in some pyramid construction and ventured that a single ramp may have been used for the Great Pyramid. But he also notes that Herodotus wrote that machines were used for lifting the single blocks of stone (p. 270). The precision employed by the Egyptian builders is illustrated by Edwards in a discussion of their expertise in leveling the site of the Great Pyramid to an overall deviation of just over half an inch.

20. Gimbutas, *The Civilization of The Goddess*, HarperCollins, 1994, p. 341.

21. Adriano Tilgher, *Work: What It Has Meant Through the Ages*, George G. Harrap, 1931, p. 3.

22. Edith Hamilton, *The Greek Way to Western Civilization*, Mentor, 1954, pp. 25–6.

23. Finley, *Slavery in Classical Antiquity*, p. 72.

3 Job Creation

1. Two of the three portraits are reproduced in *Ancient Faces: Mummy Portraits from Roman Egypt* by Susan Walker and Morris Bierbrier, British Museum Press, 1997. The first on p. 44 is dated AD 55–77. The second on p. 88 is dated AD 100–140. The third, of a bearded man, not pictured in the book, is dated AD 250.

2. Quoted in ibid., p. 21.

3. The Sutton Hoo treasure is exhibited at the British Museum. One of the most impressive pieces of Anglo-Saxon jewelry is the King Alfred jewel in the Ashmolean Museum.

4. Adriano Tilgher, *Work: What It Has Meant to Men through the Ages*, tr. Dorothy Canfield Fisher, George G. Harrap, 1931, p. 39.

5. Sarah Leigh and Simon Taylor, eds, *The Livery Companies of the City of London*, The Corporation of London, 1997, p. 6.

6. Ibid., p. 5.

7. R.H. Hilton, *The Decline of Serfdom in Medieval England*, Macmillan, 1969, p. 53.

8. The Julius Work Calendar is preserved in the British Library, London. The Calendar was used as a basis for Robert Lacey and Danny Danziger's description of life at the end of the first millennium in *The Year 1000*, Little, Brown, 1999.

9. According to John Wade's *History of the Middle and Working Classes*, London: Effingham Wilson, 1834, p. 9, the selling of slaves openly in the market was made illegal in England in 1102. A Papal Bull had been issued for the emancipation of slaves in the 11th century.

10. Ibid., p. 24.

11. Hilton, *The Decline of Serfdom*, p. 15.

12. Ibid., pp. 55–8.

13. Frances Davenport outlines how rents for leased land gradually became more important than the land's produce for the landlord in "Decay of Villeinage in East Anglia," a study published in E. Carus-Wilson, ed., *Essays in Economic History*, vol. II, Edward Arnold, 1962.

14. David Knowles, *Christian Monasticism*, Weidenfeld & Nicolson, 1969, p. 213.

15. Ibid., p. 41.

16. Ibid., p. 221.

17. There are several accounts of this incident. One of the most detailed I found was Philip Lindsay and Reg Groves, *The Peasants' Revolt 1381*, Hutchinson, 1941(?). I make no apology for favoring a portrayal of Tyler as the good guy and Sir William Walworth, the Lord Mayor, as the oppressor, but I was reminded on a recent visit to Fishmongers' Hall, London, that some view this differently. A statue of the fishmonger Walworth, sword in hand, stands on the stairs, with a plaque commemorating the intervention of "Brave Walworth."

18. Statute of Labourers, 1351.

19. This and earlier poll taxes are analyzed by Rodney Hilton in *Bond Men Made Free: Medieval Peasant Movements and the English Rising of 1381*, Methuen, 1973, p. 162.

20. This proverb was the catchphrase of the revolt and cannot be attributed to Ball alone. It was widely used by priests supporting the peasants.

21. Ball was captured, then hanged, drawn, and quartered at St. Albans, July 15, 1381.

22. E.M. Carus-Wilson, *Essays in Economic History*, vol. I, Aberdeen: University Press, 1854, pp. 41–60.

23. Lindsay and Groves, *The Peasants' Revolt 1381*, p. 18.

24. Tilgher, *Work*, p. 50.

25. R.H. Tawney, *Religion and the Rise of Capitalism*, Penguin, 1990, p. 114 (first edn John Murray, 1936).

26. Ibid., p. 119.

27. Tilgher, *Work*, p. 51.

28. Back in the good old days when More was a trusted adviser of Henry VIII, he was asked to refute Luther's criticism of Henry's defense of the sacraments that had been attacked by Luther at Wittenburg. More went about his task with gusto in a tirade of name-calling, using the earthiest of scatalogical language, all written in Latin. Luther, he said, was an "ape, an arse, a drunkard, a lousy little friar, a piece of scurf," and these were some of the milder expressions. The response is detailed in Peter Ackroyd's *Life of Thomas More*, Vintage, 1999, p. 226. The 18th-century Church man, Francis Atterbury, called it "the greatest heap of nasty language that perhaps was ever put together."

29. Tilgher, *Work*, pp. 36–7.

30. Tawney, *Religion and the Rise of Capitalism*, p. 198. He uses the phrase "most fundamental movement of the seventeenth century."

31. Ibid.

4   The New Religion of Work

1. Christopher Hill, *The English Bible and the Seventeenth Century Revolution*, Penguin, 1994, p. 15 (first published Allen Lane, 1993).

2. Ibid., p. 10.

3. Ibid., p. 11.

4. *Dallas Morning News*, April 24, 1998.

5. Paul Johnson, *A History of The American People*, Phoenix, 1998, p. 31.

6. Juliet Schor, *The Overworked American*, Basic Books, 1992, p. 70.

7. I would love to claim this observation as my own but it belongs to David L. Edwards in *A Concise History of English Christianity: From Roman Britain to the Present Day*, Fount, 1998, pp. 29–30.

8. Robert Greenleaf, *The Power of Servant Leadership*, San Francisco: Berrett-Koehler, 1998.

9. Maurice W. Thomas, *Young People in Industry 1750–1945*, Thomas Nelson, 1945, pp. 60–1.

10. Ibid., p. 61.

11. Everett E. Hagen, *On the Theory of Social Change: How Economic Growth Begins*, London: Tavistock Publications, 1964, pp. 295–309.

12. David C. McClelland, *The Achieving Society*, The Free Press, 1967, p. 367.

13. Frederick B. Tolles, *Quakers and the Atlantic Culture*, Macmillan, 1948, p. 58.

14. George Unwin, *Industrial Organization in the Sixteenth and Seventeenth Centuries*, Oxford: Clarendon Press, 1904, pp. 196–227.

15. J.U. Nef, *Essays in Economic History*, Methuen, 1954, p. 90.

16. David L. Edwards, *Christian England*, vol. II, Collins, 1983, p. 348.

17. Neither should we forget the Jews, least of all Haym Salomon who, after helping to finance the American Revolution, was left destitute for his efforts. His loans were never repaid.

18. Speech in Philadelphia, August 1, 1776.

19. Quoted in *Harper's Monthly Magazine*, September, 1932.

5 The Most Important Pile of Bricks in the World

1. W.H.G. Armytage, *A Social History of Engineering*, Faber & Faber, 1966, p. 62.

2. Maxine Berg summarizes the arguments in *The Age of Manufactures: Industry Innovation and Work in Britain*, Routledge, 1994, pp. 13–21 and concludes that applications of economic calculations are insufficient to explain the changes in society during this period.

3. G.M. Trevelyan, *Illustrated English Social History*, vol. III, Pelican, 1964, p. 182 (first published by Longmans, Green, 1942).

4. Ibid.

5. Arthur Raistrick, *Dynasty of Ironfounders*, Sessions Book Trust in association with Ironbridge Gorge Museum Trust, 1989, p. 20 (rev. edn; first edition 1952).

6. Ibid., p. 22.
7. By 1620 a series of patents had been granted for coking coal so that it might be used by brewers and maltsters, see W.H.G. Armytage, *A Social History of Engineering*, Faber & Faber, 1961, p. 62.
8. Abiah Darby, quoted in Raistrick, *Dynasty of Ironfounders*, p. 38.
9. This refers to the so-called "potwalloper boroughs" still represented in Parliament during the eighteenth century. To claim the right to vote in these boroughs the inhabitant had to establish that he had a family and had boiled a pot there. The potwalloper franchise was a relic of earlier times when freemen would take their meals in public to demonstrate their independence from the lord of the manor. See J.L. Hammond and Barbara Hammond, *The Village Labourer 1760–1832*, Longmans, Green, 1911, p. 9 (paperback edn 1987).
10. Interview with the author.
11. Raistrick, *Dynasty of Ironfounders*, pp. 38–9.
12. From Abraham Darby's cash book and accounts, held in the Elton Collection, Ironbridge Gorge Museum, Shropshire.
13. Barrie Trinder, *The Industrial Revolution in Shropshire*, Phillimore, 1981, pp. 207–9.
14. Some mill and mine owners were prepared to exploit the system themselves, opening their own truck shops.
15. An example of a two-faced clock is held in the collection of the Museum of Science and Industry in Manchester. The museum quotes an entry in the records of Quarry Bank Mill, Styal, for September, 1818, stating: "Ten days lost time to be worked up in half year, 256 spindles or two drums upon an average of want of water."
16. E.P. Thompson, "Time, Work-Discipline and Industrial Capitalism," *Past and Present*, vol. 38, 1967, p. 86.
17. Lewis Mumford, *The Lewis Mumford Reader*, ed. Donald L. Miller, The University of Georgia Press, 1995, pp. 325–6.
18. R.S. Fitton and A.P. Wadsworth, *The Strutts and the Arkwrights, 1758–1830*, Manchester University Press, 1958, p. 67.
19. Maurice W. Thomas, *Young People in Industry, 1750–1945*, Thomas Nelson & Sons, 1945, p. 3.
20. The story is related in a history of the silk mill on the Derby City website: www.derbycity.com.
21. Fitton and Wadsworth, *The Strutts and the Arkwrights*, p. 62.

6 Secrets of the Dumb Steeple

1. Frank Peel, *The Risings of the Luddites, Chartists and Plug-Drawers*, 4th edn, Frank Cass and Co., 1968; also quoted in J.L. Hammond and Barbara Hammond, *The Skilled Labourer, 1760–1832*, Alan Sutton, 1995, p. 307.
2. Charlotte Bronte, *Shirley*, Collins, n.d., p. 296.
3. *The Penny Magazine*, December, 1843, p. 508.
4. Ibid.
5. R.S. Fitton and A.P. Wadsworth, *The Strutts and the Arkwrights: 1758–1830*, Manchester University Press, 1958, p. 101.
6. Philippe Aries, *Centuries of Childhood*, Penguin, 1973, pp. 125–30 (first published 1960).
7. Fitton and Wadsworth, *The Strutts and the Arkwrights*, pp. 234–6.
8. K. Marx, *Capital*, vol. 1, Harmondsworth: Penguin, 1976 (first published in German in 1867).
9. Laws were introduced in Elizabethan England to curb domestic wood burning so that timber could be preserved for ship building.
10. An idea of the complexity of chimney systems in large houses can be gleaned from the sectional view of the drying room chimney at Buckingham Palace, reproduced in Maurice W. Thomas, *Young People in Industry, 1750–1945*, Thomas Nelson & Sons, 1945, p. 46.
11. J.L. Hammond and Barbara Hammond, *The Town Labourer 1760–1832*, Alan Sutton, 1995, p. 182 (first published 1917).
12. Ibid., p. 179.
13. Ibid.
14. Ibid., p. 185.
15. Ibid., p. 188.
16. Thomas, *Young People in Industry*, p. 43.
17. Hammond and Hammond, *The Town Labourer*, p. 173.
18. Ibid., pp. 190–1.
19. E.P. Thompson, *History of the English Working Class*, Penguin, 1991, p. 237.
20. J.L. Hammond and Barbara Hammond, *The Village Labourer 1706–1832*, Longmans Green, 1911, p. 38.
21. The story is told concisely in *The Story of the Tolpuddle Martyrs*, London: Trades Union Congress, 1991.
22. *The Unknown Mayhew, Selections from the Morning Chronicle 1849–1850*, ed. E.P. Thompson and Eileen Yao, Penguin, 1971.

7 The Silent Monitor

1. The town plan was based on the Phalanstery, or communal palace, concept of Charles Fourier.
2. There are varying accounts of the price paid by Owen. This figure is based on Posey County records quoted with other figures by William E. Wilson in *The Angel and The Serpent*, Indiana University Press, 1964, p. 110.
3. Donald E. Pitzer and Josephine M. Elliott, "New Harmony's First Utopians," *Indiana Magazine of History*, vol. 75, no. 3, 1979.
4. Karl J.R. Arndt, *America's Communal Utopias*, ed. Donald E. Pitzer, Chapel Hill, 1997, p. 74.
5. The information on the Kirkburton fire was supplied partly by Denis Kilcommons, a journalist at the *Huddersfield Examiner*, and partly from newspaper accounts in the *Examiner* archives.
6. The sale may have been agreed in July, 1799 when two of Owen's partners had visited New Lanark.
7. Gregory Claeys, ed., *Selected Works of Robert Owen*, vol. 4, London: William Pickering, 1993, p. 155.
8. Address delivered to the people of New Lanark, January 1, 1816, quoted in Robert Owen, *A New View of Society and Other Writings*, Penguin, 1991, p. 120.
9. L. Urwick, *The Golden Book of Management*, London: Newman Neame, 1956, p. 7.
10. Ibid.
11. Karl J.R. Arndt, *America's Communal Utopias*, ed. Donald E. Pitzer, University of Carolina Press, 1997, p. 81. According to Arndt, John Duss, a musician whose mother had worked for the Rappists, secured a position as a junior trustee and spent his way through millions of dollars accumulated by the society.
12. Ian Donnachie and George Hewitt, *Historic New Lanark*, Edinburgh University Press, 1993, p. 94.
13. Described in the *Penny Magazine*, December, 1843, p. 501.
14. *Financial Times*, Survey of Leeds, December 1, 1989.

8 The Last Puritan in a Nation of Amateurs

1. Quoted by Crispin Tickell in *Mary Anning of Lyme Regis*, Lyme Regis: Philpot Museum, 1996, p. 3.

2. Ibid., p. 26. The tongue twister is taken from a 1908 song by Terry Sullivan.

3. Ibid., p. 3.

4. Ibid., p. 27.

5. T.H.S. Escott, *England: Her People, Polity and Pursuits*, London: Richardson, 2009 (1885), quoted by Martin J. Wiener in *English Culture and the Decline of the Industrial Spirit*, Penguin, 1987 (first published by Cambridge University Press, 1981).

6. Wiener, *English Culture and the Decline of the Industrial Spirit*, p. 22.

7. Kenneth Clark, *Civilization*, BBC and John Murray, 1979, p. 247 (first published 1969).

8. Paul Johnson, *A History of the American People*, Pheonix Giant, 1998, p. 137.

9. The two raised fingers – a popular gesture of abuse in Britain, used in the same way as the middle finger in the United States – has its origins in Anglo-French medieval warfare. The index finger and the middle finger were used by English archers as drawstring fingers. Sometimes these fingers were severed if a bowman fell into the hands of the French, so the two-fingered gesture became an act of defiance and remains so today. Winston Churchill used it, apparently without irony – but maybe not – as a sign of victory. The V for Victory sign, however, was usually reversed in the same way as the hippie Peace sign.

10. Weiner, *English Culture and the Decline of the Industrial Spirit*, pp. 14–15.

11. Anthony Trollope, *Doctor Thorn*, Chapman & Hall, 1858, pp. 11–12, quoted by Wiener, *English Culture and the Decline of the Industrial Spirit*, p. 31.

12. Quoted by Weiner, p. 32, from *Fraser's Magazine*.

13. Thomas Carlyle, *Latter Day Pamphlets*, Chapman & Hall, 1858, p. 21.

14. "Mark Twain's Christmas Book," *New York World*, December 10, 1899.

15. Paul Johnson, p. 413.

16. *Past and Present*, Routledge, date unknown, p. 26.

17. Ibid., p. 29.

18. Ibid.

19. Ibid., p. 197. See also Simon Heffer, *Moral Desperado: A Life of Thomas Carlyle*, Weidenfeld & Nicolson, 1995, p. 230.
20. Ibid., p. 264.
21. Ibid., p. 263.
22. Ibid., p. 265.
23. Simon Heffer, *Moral Desperado*, p. 153.
24. Wiener, *English Culture and the Decline of the Industrial Spirit*, p. 33.
25. Ibid.
26. Anthony Bimba, *The History of the American Working Class*, London: Martin Lawrence, 1927, p. 23.
27. Ibid., pp. 14–15.
28. Charles Johnson, Patricia Smith, and the WGBH Series Research Team, *Africans in America: America's Journey through Slavery*, Harcourt Brace, 1998, p. 39.
29. Ibid., p. 40.
30. Ibid.
31. Bimba, *The History of the American Working Class*, p. 18.
32. Stanley M. Elkins, *Slavery: A Problem in American Institutional and Intellectual Life*, University of Chicago Press, 1968, p. 7 (first edition, 1959).
33. Ibid., p. 21.
34. Ibid., p. 24.
35. "Occasional Discourse on the Nigger Question," London: Thomas Bosworth, 1853, p. 7.
36. Ibid., p. 12.
37. *A Social History of England*, Penguin, 1991, p. 272.

9 The Yellow Dog Unleashed

1. O.D. Boyle, *History of Railroad Strikes*, Washington: Brotherhood Publishing, 1935, pp. 8–10.
2. Ibid., p. 11.
3. Ibid., p. 7.
4. Ibid., p. 23, supported by accounts of the Baltimore and Pittsburgh disturbances in the *Baltimore Sun*, from July 20, 1877 to July 26, 1877.
5. Ibid., p. 26.

6. Ibid., pp. 27–8.

7. Ibid., p. 33.

8. From a photograph in the permanent exhibition of the Chicago History Society.

9. Liston E. Leyendecker, *Palace Car Prince: A Biography of George Mortimer Pullman*, University Press of Colorado, 1992, pp. 29–30.

10. The palace car idea was originated by Plyman B. Green but, like many inventors, Green profited little from the concept; see Boyle, *History of Railroad Strikes*, pp. 53–4.

11. Ray Ginger, *Eugene V. Debs: A Biography*, Collier, 1962, p. 125.

12. Christopher Hill, *The English Bible and the Seventeenth-Century Revolution*, Penguin, 1994, p. 73.

13. Leyendecker, *Palace Car Prince*.

14. Stanley Buder, *Pullman: An Experiment in Industrial Order and Community Planning, 1880–1930*, Oxford University Press, 1967, pp. 68–9. Buder writes that the Pullman company reported an 8 percent return from its farm investment in 1885.

15. W.F. Burns, *The Pullman Boycott: A Complete History of The Great Rail Road Strike*, The McGill Printing Company, 1894, p. 22.

16. Ibid.

17. Ibid., p. 21.

18. Quoted by Buder, p. 36.

19. Buder, *Pullman*, p. 132.

20. Ibid., p. 42.

21. Ibid., p. 133.

22. John Tebbel, *From Rags to Riches: Horatio Alger Jr. and the American Dream*, New York: Macmillan, 1963, p. 12.

23. Title of an article by Carnegie published in the *Pall Mall Gazette*. He advocated dispensing wealth during the life time of the giver to either found or support various institutions in the following order: universities, free libraries, hospitals and hospital extensions, parks, concert and meeting halls, swimming baths, churches. Wall writes that "ministers were outraged to find churches seventh on the list" (Joseph Frazier Wall, *Andrew Carnegie*, New York: Oxford University Press, 1979, p. 808).

24. Wall, p. 808. When Carnegie's will was disclosed it showed that he had given away $350,695,653, leaving a residue of $30m, two-thirds of which was left to the Carnegie Corporation. The remaining $10m

comprised gifts and annuities for various friends and relations in Dunfermline where he was born (Wall, p. 1042).

25. David Ray Papke, *The Pullman Case: The Clash of Labor and Capital in Industrial America*, University Press of Kansas, 1999, p. 5. Andrew Carnegie did the same. It was a popular way for the wealthy men to avoid the draft.
26. Burns, *The Pullman Boycott*, pp. 17–18.
27. Ibid., pp. 17, 23.
28. Ibid., p. 42.
29. Ibid., pp. 40–1.
30. Paul Averich, *The Haymarket Tragedy*, Princeton University Press, 1984, pp. 205–8.
31. Burns, *The Pullman Boycott*, pp. 300–4.
32. Ibid., p. 306.
33. Buder, *Pullman*, p. 3, quoted from Carnegie's *Triumph of Democracy*, C. Scribner's Sons, 1888.
34. *Chicago Dispatch*, May 14, 1894, quoted in Buder, *Pullman*, p. 170.
35. Pinkerton guards were privately recruited uniformed guards run by the agency established by Allan Pinkerton.
36. Louis Adamic, *Dynamite: The Struggle of Class Violence in America*, Peter Smith, 1960, p. 12 (first published 1934).
37. Joanne B. Ciulla, *The Working Life*, Times Books, 2000, p. 103.
38. Daniel A. Wren, *The Evolution of Management Thought*, John Wiley & Sons, 1994, p. 169.
39. Ibid., p. 170, quoted from Whiting Williams, *Mainsprings of Men*, Charles Scribner's Sons, 1925, p. 147.
40. Adamic, *Dynamite*, p. 23.

10   The Philadelphia Catechism

1. Henry Dana, Jr., *Two Years before the Mast*, Wordsworth, 1996, p. 14 (first edition 1840).
2. Ibid., p. 56.
3. Robert Kanigel, *The One Best Way*, Viking, 1997, p. 100.
4. Ray Wild, *Mass-Production Management*, Wiley & Sons, 1972, p. 27.
5. Some have claimed that Pittsburgh-born William Kelly was the first to perfect the Bessemer process, but Kelly was short of the

mark. He discovered, like Bessemer, that blowing air through molten cast iron could control the temperature of the melt by burning out carbon. But, crucially, he did not realize how important it was to stop the blow. Nor, unlike Bessemer, did he devise any method to deoxidize the steel before it was poured. So Kelly went bankrupt and Bessemer didn't. But Kelly's lawyers did have some success in challenging Bessemer's 1856 US patents, and a royalty-sharing deal was struck after protracted legal action. To insist that Kelly invented the Bessemer process, however, is to get involved in the type of semantics that could be used to promote the case for Elisha Gray against Alexander Graham Bell over the invention of the telephone or Joseph Swan against Thomas Edison on the incandescent lamp. In all these cases the losers were beaten to the Patent Office, lacked some vital ingredient, or lacked the essential big picture or the wherewithal to apply their discovery commercially.

6. Robert Kanigel, *The One Best Way: Frederick Winslow Taylor and the Enigma of Efficiency*, Viking, 1997, p. 74.
7. E.P. Thompson gives several examples of such practices in "Time, Work-Discipline and Industrial Capitalism," *Past and Present*, vol. 38, 1967.
8. Ibid., pp. 202–3.
9. Quoted by Morris S. Viteles in *Industrial Psychology*, Jonathan Cape, 1933, p. 9, from Dupin, *Cours de Geometre et de Mécanique Appliquée*.
10. Ibid.
11. David S. Landes, *Revolution in Time: Clocks and the Making of the Modern World*, Belknap Press of Harvard University Press, 1983, p. 130.
12. M. Cutmore, *The Pocketwatch Handbook*, David & Charles, 1985, p. 92.
13. Charles D. Wrege and Ronald Greenwood, *Frederick W. Taylor: The Father of Scientific Management, Myth and Reality*, Business One Irwin, 1991, pp. 83–8.
14. Fred Taylor, *Shop Management*, Harper & Brothers, 1911, pp. 150–6. *Shop Management* was first read as a paper to the American Society of Engineers in June, 1903.
15. Kanigel, *The One Best Way*, pp. 226–7.
16. Ibid., p. 319.
17. Ibid., p. 320.

18. Ibid., p. 317. Kanigel says the house was demolished in the 1960s. Taylor refers to Noll's house building in his book, saying that he was working on the house at the same time as he was carrying out the pig iron loading, but Wrege and Greenwood, *Frederick W. Taylor*, p. 104, say that Noll's house had not been built until after the experiments had been completed. A sign has been erected at the now disused Bethlehem Steel Works in recognition of Noll's achievement. Today an industrial museum is being installed on part of the site.

19. Wild, *Mass-Production Management*, p. 20.

20. George Dodd, *Days at the Factories: The Manufacturing Industry of Great Britain Described*, E. P. Publishing, 1975, p. 137 (first published 1843 by Charles Knight, London).

21. Maxine Berg, *The Age of Manufactures 1700–1820: Industry, Innovation and Work in Britain*, Routledge, 1994, p. 267.

11   Modern Times

1. Quoted in David A. Hounshell, *From the American System to Mass Production, 1800–1932: The Development of Manufacturing Technology in the United States*, The Johns Hopkins University Press, 1984, p. 241.

2. Daniel A. Wren and Ronald G. Greenwood (*Management Innovators: The people and Ideas that Have Shaped Modern Business*, Oxford University Press, 1998, p. 44) point out that Ford's system of mass production evolved by trial and error among a team of engineers, including Peter E. Martin, Charles E. Sorensen, Harold Wills, Clarence W. Avery, and Charles Lewis.

3. Wren and Greenwood, pp. 44–5, outline the difference as they see it: At Ford "the workers were required to 'adjust to the line' rather than designing the line to fit the worker. That was the difference between the assembly line and scientific management – the former was conveyor-paced, the latter, worker-paced."

4. Hounshell, *From the American System to Mass Production*, p. 252.

5. Robert Lacey, *Ford: The Men and the Machine*, Heinemann, 1986, p. 17.

6. Horace Arnold quoted in Hounshell, *From the American System to Mass Production*, p. 241.

7. Lacey, p. 107.

8. Hounshell, p. 249.
9. Robert Kanigel, *The One Best Way: Frederick Winslow Taylor and the Enigma of Efficiency*, Viking, 1997, p. 496.
10. Lacey, *Ford*, p. 9.
11. Kanigel, *The One Best Way*, p. 212.
12. The press reactions and that of Ford are outlined by Lacey, pp. 118–22.
13. Frank B. Gilbreth and Ernestine Gilbreth Carey, *Cheaper by the Dozen*, Consul Books, 1961, p. 10.
14. Wren and Greenwood, *Management Innovators*, p. 143.
15. Kanigel, *The One Best Way*, p. 525.
16. Ibid., p. 18.
17. Carey Scott, *Sunday Times Magazine*, November 17, 1996.
18. Oliver Pritchett, *Daily Telegraph*, October 18, 1988, and Rupert Cornwell, *The Independent*, October 17, 1988.
19. Alexei Stakhanov, *The Stakhanov Movement Explained*, Moscow: Foreign Languages Publishing House, 1939, pp. 7–8.
20. Ibid., p. 11.
21. Ibid.
22. Ibid., pp. 29–30.
23. Rosabeth Moss Kanter, "Power Failures in Management Circuits," *Harvard Business Review*, July/August, 1979.
24. Alan Bullock, *Hitler and Stalin: Parallel Lives*, BCA, 1991, p. 1003.
25. Ford R. Bryan, *The Fords of Dearborn*, Harlo, 1997, p. 174.
26. Kanigel, *The One Best Way*, p. 433.
27. L. Urwick, *The Golden Book of Management: A Historical Record of the Life and Work of Seventy Pioneers*, Newman Neame, 1956, p. 75, quoting from Frank Barclay Copley's *Frederick W. Taylor*, Harper & Brothers, 1923.
28. Lacey, *Ford*, pp. 342–4.
29. Peter Drucker, *The Practice of Management*, Butterworth Heinemann, 1999, p. 274 (first published 1955).
30. Quoted by Stuart Crainer in *The Ultimate Book of Business Quotations*, Capstone, 1997.

12 Western Electric Discovers Motivation

1. Charles D Wrege, *Facts and Fallacies of Hawthorne: A Historical Study of the Origins, Procedures, and Results of the Hawthorne*

Illumination Tests and Their Influence upon the Hawthorne Studies, Garland Publishing, 1986, p. 62.

2. Andre Millard, *Edison and the Business of Innovation*, Johns Hopkins, 1993, p. 32.
3. Ibid., p. 24.
4. Warren G. Bennis and Patricia Ward Biederman, *Organizing Genius*, Nicholas Brealey, 1997, p. 15.
5. David E. Nye, *Henry Ford: "Ignorant Idealist"*, Kemikat Press, 1979, p. 100.
6. Ibid.
7. Wrege, *Facts and Fallacies of Hawthorne*, p. 7.
8. Ibid., p. 36.
9. Ibid., p. 67.
10. Ibid., pp. 670–1.
11. Ibid., p. 106.
12. Ibid., pp. 107–8.
13. Ibid., pp. 237–54.
14. Ibid., p. 299.
15. Louis Adamic, *Dynamite: The Story of Class Violence in America*, Peter Smith, 1960, pp. 341–3.
16. Author's interview with Joseph Juran, May, 2000. The story is also told by Stephen B. Adams and Orville R. Butler in *Manufacturing The Future: A History of Western Electric*, Cambridge University Press, 1999, p. 161.
17. Wrege, *Facts and Fallacies of Hawthorne*, p. 666.
18. Wrege's *Facts and Fallacies of Hawthorne* is by far the most comprehensive study available of the original lighting experiments, drawing on documents in General Electric's archive.
19. Ibid., p. 695.
20. From newspaper files, Chicago Historical Society.
21. Charles D. Wrege, *Facts and Fallacies of Hawthorne*, New York: Garland, pp. 209–10.
22. Stephen B. Adams and Orville R. Butler, *Manufacturing the Future: A History of Western Electric*, Cambridge University Press, 1999, p. 119.
23. Ibid., pp. 240–1.
24. Ibid., p. 120.
25. Ibid., p. 124.
26. Adams and Butler, *Manufacturing the Future*, p. 126.

27. Ibid., p. 127.
28. Quoted by Stuart Crainer in *The Ultimate Book of Business Quotations*, Capstone, 1997, p. 322.
29. Quoted by Pauline Graham in *The Handbook of Management Thinking*, International Thomson Business Press, 1998, p. 248.
30. Daniel A. Wren and Ronald G. Greenwood, *Management Innovators: The people and Ideas that Have Shaped Modern Business*, Oxford University Press, 1998, p. 176.
31. Ibid.
32. Pauline Graham, in *The Handbook of Management Thinking*, p. 442, says that "between 1923 and 1943, Mayo and his colleagues received grants totalling $1,520,000 from the Rockefeller Foundation."
33. Bernard M. Bass and Gerald V. Barrett, *People, Work, and Organizations: An Introduction to Industrial and Organizational Psychology*, 2nd edn, Allyn & Bacon, 1981, p. 56.
34. Ibid., p. 443.

13   Unnatural Selection

1. Morris S. Viteles, *Industrial Psychology*, Norton, 1932, p. 41.
2. Ibid.
3. Edwin G. Boring, *A History of Experimental Psychology*, Prentice Hall, 1950, pp. 134–5.
4. "Death by Cannibalism and Coconut," *Financial Times*, October 4/5, 1997.
5. Adam Smith, *An Inquiry into the Nature and Causes of the Wealth of Nations*, W. Strahan and T. Cadell, 1776, Book I, ch. II.
6. Descarte's *Le Discours de la Methode* was published in 1637, but the quote "*Cogito, ergo sum*" is taken from the 1641 Latin edition.
7. Raymond E. Fancher, *The Intelligence Men, Makers of the IQ Controversy*, W.W. Norton & Co., 1987, pp. 61–2.
8. Ibid., p. 65.
9. Ibid.
10. Boring, *A History of Experimental Psychology*, p. 574.
11. Fancher, *The Intelligence Men, Makers of the IQ Controversy*, pp. 142–3.
12. Ibid., p. 119.

13. Stephen B. Adams and Orville R. Butler, *Manufacturing the Future: A History of Western Electric*, Cambridge University Press, 1999, p. 120.
14. Quoted in Walter Dill Scott, *Increasing Human Efficiency in Business*, New York: Macmillan, 1911, p. 5.
15. Ibid., p. 6.
16. Ibid., p. 15.
17. Viteles, *Industrial Psychology*, p. 43.

14 *Arbeit Macht Frei*

1. IG Farbenindustrie was a chemical and dyestuffs conglomerate created in 1925 from the merger of the following companies: Bayer, Hoeschst, Badische Anilin und Soda Fabrik (BASF), A G fur Anilinfabrikation (AGFA), Cassella, Kalle, Griesheim-Elektron, and Weiler-ter-Meer.
2. Josiah E. DuBois, *Generals in Grey Suits*, Bodley Head, 1953, p. 155.
3. Joseph Borkin, *The Crime and Punishment of IG Farben*, Andre Deutsche, 1979, p. 117.
4. Dubois, *Generals in Grey Suits*, p. 172.
5. Robert Kanigel, *The One Best Way*, Viking, 1997, p. 528.
6. Borkin, *The Crime and Punishment of IG Farben*, p. 23.
7 *Hitler and Stalin: Parallel Lives*, BCA, 1991, p. 320.
8. Ibid., p. 320.
9. Heinze Paechter, Karl O. Paetel, and Berta Hellman, *Nazi–Deutsch: German–English Dictionary*, New York: Office of European Economic Research, 1943.
10. Joan Campbell, *Joy in Work, German Work: The National Debate, 1800–1945*, Princeton University Press, 1989, p. vii.
11. This explanation for the slogan is offered by Campbell, ibid., p. 347. She writes that Rudolf Höss, the commandant, first of Dachau, then later of Auschwitz, regarded labor as "essential to counteract the degrading effects of prison conditions and could help to develop the qualities of character that would prepare inmates for eventual freedom." She adds: "For Höss, at least, *Arbeit Macht Frei*, was more a statement of faith in a widely proclaimed national principle, than an expression of cynical disdain for those held in subjection."

12. The figure is given by Gitta Sereny in *Into that Darkness* (Pimlico, 1974, p. 100), her portrait of Franz Stangl, the former commandant of Treblinka. According to Martin Gilbert in *The Holocaust* (HarperCollins, 1986, p. 287) there were just two survivors from Belzec, three from Chelmno, sixty-four from Sobibor, and "less than forty" from Treblinka.

13. The figure is taken from Herbert Ulrich's *Hitler's Foreign Workers*, Cambridge University Press, 1997, p. 157 (first published in German in 1985). In the same book, however, he quotes Werner Mansfeld claiming he had 3.9 million Russians available (p. 161; see also Bullock, *Hitler and Stalin*). The latter figure may have been Mansfeld's mistake.

14. See Bullock, *Hitler and Stalin*.

15. William L. Shirer, *The Rise and Fall of the Third Reich*, Secker & Warburg, 1959, p. 946.

16. John Dalmau, *Slave Worker in the Channel Islands*, Guernsey Press, 1956.

17. DuBois, *Generals in Grey Suits*, p. 50.

18. Ibid.

19. Ibid.

20. Borkin, *The Crime and Punishment of IG Farben*, p. 113.

21. Ibid., p. 123.

15 Whatever Happened to Homer Sarasohn?

1. Author's interview with Masaharu Matsushita, June, 1999.

2. Memorandum on the need for management training courses in the communications and manufacturing industry, August 6, 1949, Research and Development Division, General Headquarters, Supreme Commander for the Allied Powers Civil Communications Section, declassified document.

3. Will Hopper interview with Sarasohn, May 22, 1993. A version of this meeting is recalled in Robert Chapman Wood's feature, "A Lesson Learned and a Lesson Forgotten," in *Forbes*, February 6, 1989. The feature, rightly, credits Kenneth Hopper, a British-born management consultant who lives and works in the US, with much of the original research into the CCS. A detailed article by Hopper, covering the work of Sarashon, Polkinghorn, and Protzman, was published in *Human Resources Management*, summer, 1982. Ken's brother, Will, has been assisting him in his researches.

4. Text of the lecture supplied by Masaharu Matsushita.

5. Quoted from the Personnel Policy of Matsushita Electrical.

6. Ibid.

7. Typed recollections of Homer Sarasohn supplied to Masaharu Matsushita.

8. *Financial Times*, December 30, 1993, quoted in *The Handbook of Management Thinking*, ed. Malcolm Warner, International Thomson Business Press, 1998, p. 337.

9. Chapman Wood, "A Lesson Learned and a Lesson Forgotten," *Forbes Magazine*, February 6, 1989.

10. Interviews and correspondence with Ken and Will Hopper.

11. Ibid.

12. Interview with the author, May 6, 2000.

13. This view about the impact of Japanese militarism is sourced to the author's interview with Toshio Goto, professor at Shizouka Industrial University in Tokyo in May, 1999. According to Goto the adoption of several US management ideas, including scientific management and standard cost accounting, came to their peak in Japan in 1935 when the military set itself against these ideas. "The military people were against anything named 'scientific,'" he said. But some companies quietly resisted this military opposition. Sumitomo, for example, persisted with standard cost accounting for its cost control, concealing its methods from the attention of the military.

14. Ford factories did not achieve just-in-time delivery. In practice the workshops built up overlarge inventories.

15. Will Hutton, *The State We're In*, Vintage, 1996, p. 269.

16. E.E. Hagan, *On the Theory of Social Change*, Tavistock, 1962, p. 341.

17. Ibid.

18. *Working*, Pantheon Books, 1972, p. xxiii.

19. Ibid., p. xviii.

20. Gemba Kaizen, *A Commonsense, Low-Cost Approach to Management*, McGraw-Hill, 1997, pp. 237–47.

21. Interview with the author, June, 1997.

16   Managing the Corporate State

1. Peter Drucker, *Adventures of a Bystander*, Heinemann, 1979, p. 256. Drucker's autobiographical observation is not quite accurate. In *The Future of Industrial Man* he was arguing the case for business

as a social institution (pp. 50, 205) while not accepting that it had already made this transition.

2. Ibid., p. 1.
3. Josiah DuBois, *Generals in Grey Suits*, Bodley Head, 1953.
4. Joseph Borkin, *The Crime and Punishment of IG Farben*, Andre Deutsch, 1979, pp. 131–3.
5. Robert Lacey, *Ford, the Men and the Machine*, Heinemann, 1986, p. 388.
6. Peter Drucker, *Concept of the Corporation*, Transaction Edition, 1995, p. 9.
7. Peter Drucker, *The Future of Industrial Man*, William Heinemann, 1943, p. 1.
8. In his own words Drucker became a "nonperson" (*Concept of the Corporation*, p. xii) at GM for pointing out the company's problems. Neither he nor his work was mentioned in Alfred Sloan's book, *My Years at General Motors*. In this book Sloan went to some length to explain that the decentralized structure was his idea and his idea alone, based on a study he carried out in 1919.
9. Peter Drucker, *Adventures of a Bystander*, Heinemann, 1979, p. 262.
10. James O'Shea and Charles Madigan, *Dangerous Company*, Nicholas Brealey, 1997, p. 24.
11. Ibid., p. 22.
12. Drucker, *Adventures of a Bystander*, p. 21.
13. Ibid., p. 263.
14. Drucker, *Concept of the Corporation*, p. 5.
15. Francis Fukuyama, *Trust*, Penguin, 1996, p. 159.
16. Carol Kennedy, *Guide to the Management Gurus*, Century Business, 1993, p. 41.
17. Drucker, *Adventures of a Bystander*, p. 273.
18. Ibid., p. 273. Andrea Gabor takes issue with this point in her book, *The Capitalist Philosophers* (Times Business, 2000, p. 312), pointing to a later remark by Drucker that the idea was an "intellectual Edsel." Drucker, however, was commenting on the impracticality of the idea *at that time*. Gabor, like John Tarrant, author of *Drucker: The Man Who Invented the Corporate Society*, believes Drucker was "wedded to the notion of hierarchy." This is simply not correct. Drucker was a pragmatist, working with and for hierarchical organizations. His books interpreted management in a hierarchical fashion because this was the way management worked. His self-governed

plant represents his idealism whereas his acceptance of hierarchy reflects his realism.

19. David Montgomery, *Workers' Control in America*, Cambridge University Press, 1979, p. 12.
20. Ibid., p. 276.
21. Ibid.
22. Mary Parker Follett, *Prophet of Management*, ed. Pauline Graham, Harvard Business School Press, 1996.
23. Mary Parker Follett, *Creative Experience*, 1924, pp. 167–8.
24. Henry C. Metcalf and Lyndall Urwick, eds, *Dynamic Administration: The Collected Papers of Mary Parker Follett*, New York: Harper & Row, 1940, pp. 32–3. A concise summation of Follett's contribution to management theory can be found in Daniel Wren, *The Evolution of Management Thought*, John Wiley & Sons, 1994, ch. 14.

17 The Wanting Animal

1. Speech in Washington, April 16, 1953.
2. The origins of the headhunting industry are outlined in John Byrne, *The Headhunters*, Kogan Page, 1987.
3. Abraham Maslow, *Maslow on Management*, John Wiley, 1998, p. 16.
4. Ibid., p. 10.
5. Gitta Sereny, *Into that Darkness: from Mercy Killing to Mass Murder*, Pimlico, 1995, p. 127.
6. Ibid., p. 200.
7. Peter N. Davies, *The Man Behind the Bridge: Colonel Toosey and the River Kwai*, Athlone, 1991, p. xiii.
8. Quoted by Daniel Wren and Ronald Greenwood in *Management Innovators: The People and Ideas that Have Shaped Modern Business*, Oxford University Press, 1998, p. 179.
9. See Chapter 15, p. 213.
10. Wren and Greenwood, *Management Innovators*, p. 178.
11. Henry C. Metcalf and Lyndall Urwick, eds., *Dynamic Administration: The Collected Papers of Mary Parker Follett*, 1940, New York: Harper & Row, 1940, p. 80.
12. Peter Drucker, "Management's New Paradigms," *Forbes, Global Business and Finance*, October 5, 1998, p. 56.

13. Maslow, *Maslow on Management*, pp. 20–42.
14. There is a common misconception that the pull cord allows the worker to stop the line. It does not. If the supervisor, once summoned, believes the problem is serious enough to warrant a line stoppage, only then will the conveyor system be brought to a halt.
15. Vicki Lenz, *The Saturn Difference: Creating Customer Loyalty in your Company*, John Wiley & Sons, 1999, p. 12.
16. Interview with the author, *Financial Times*, July 9, 1997.
17. James Dyson, *Against the Odds: An Autobiography*, Orion Business Books, 1997, p. 256.
18. Frederick F. Reichheld, *The Loyalty Effect: The Hidden Force behind the Growth, Profits and Lasting Value*, Harvard Business School Press, 1996, p. 5.
19. Quoted in "Loyalty Bonus Should not be Devalued," *Financial Times*, November 1, 1995.
20. "Redundancy Reigns in Metroland," *Financial Times*, July 27, 1994.
21. Quoted in *Management Thinking*, ed. Malcolm Warner, International Thomson Business Press, 1998, p. 268.
22. *Business Week*, August 8, 1998.
23. Jeffrey Pfeffer, *The Human Equation*, Harvard Business School Press, 1998, p. 150.

18 Sharp-suited Philanthropists

1. Sir Stuart Hampson, speech at the Centre for Leadership Studies Conference, London, November 1998, reported in *Financial Times*, November 18, 1998.
2. *Financial Times*, September 4, 1997.
3. Peter Drucker, *Managing in a Time of Great Change*, Butterworth Heinemann, 1995, p. 215.
4. Jeff Gates, *The Ownership Solution*, Penguin Books, 1998, pp. 52–3.
5. Ibid., p. 63.
6. NCEO study, *Harvard Business Review*, September/October, 1987.
7. "La Dolce Cooperativa," *Financial Times*, January 20, 1999.
8. Ibid.
9. Robert Oakeshott, *Jobs & Fairness: The Logic and Experience of Employee Ownership*, Michael Russell, 2000, p. 457.

10. The story is told briefly by Charles Leadbeater in *Living on Thin Air*, Viking, 1999, pp. 65–9, and in greater detail by Andy Law in *Open Minds*, Orion Business Books, 1998.

19 The End of Management

1. House of Commons Employment Committee, minutes of evidence, Tuesday January 24, 1995, HMSO, pp. 8–21.
2. *Fortune*, August 6, 1998.
3. This expression is the common retort of workmen in Robert Tressell's *Ragged Trousered Philanthropists* (Grant Richards, 1914) when Frank Owen, the intellectual among them, attempts to describe the iniquities of the capitalist system.
4. *The Guardian*, September 15, 1998.
5. *Financial Times*, July 12, 2000.
6. Address by Hamel to Hay Management Consultants conference in Amsterdam, March 30, 2000.
7. I am paraphrasing an introduction Gary Hamel used to a *Financial Times* article, suggesting that the pages of the newspaper "may be the only place outside Jurassic Park where you can watch dinosaurs mate." The phrase was removed in the editing, possibly for reasons of taste. He has used it frequently since in addresses at management conferences.
8. Both of these comments were made at the Amsterdam conference.
9. Gary Hamel, *Leading the Revolution*, Harvard Business School Press, 2000, pp. 258–9.
10. Richard T. Pascale, *Surfing the Edge of Chaos*, Texere, 2000, p. 7.
11. Kerry Townsend, "Knock, Knock, Knocking on Boardroom Doors," FTCareerPoint.Com, December 22, 2000.
12. *Fortune*, January 8, 2001. The absurdity of this apparent development was highlighted by Lucy Kellaway in her *Financial Times'* column, January 15, 2001.
13 *New York Times*, December 24, 2000.
14. Stephen Barley, *The New World of Work*, British–North American Research Association (UK), 1996, quoted by the author in the *Financial Times*, March 6, 1996.
15. Carol Kennedy, *Guide to the Management Gurus*, Century, 1993, p. 105.
16. Ricardo Semler, *Maverick*, Arrow Books, 1994, p. 51.

17. Ibid., p. 60.
18. Ken Dychtwald, *Age Power: How the 21st Century Will Be Ruled by the New Old*, Tarcher Putnam, 1999, p. 79.
19. John Micklethwait and Adrian Wooldridge, *The Witch Doctors: What the Management Gurus are Saying, Why it Matters and How to Make Sense of It*, Heinemann, 1996, p. 232.

20 Melting the Frozen Assets

1. Jack Beatty, *The World According to Drucker: The Life and Work of the World's Greatest Management Thinker*, Orion Business, 1998, p. 104.
2. Peter Drucker, *The Practice of Management*, Butterworth-Heinemann, 1999, p. 269.
3. Ibid., p. 272.
4. Ibid., p. 302.
5. Ibid., p. 303.
6. Ibid., p. 281.
7. Ibid.
8. Ibid., p. 280.
9. Ibid., p. 310.
10. Richard Goss, *Psychology: The Science of Mind and Behaviour*, 3rd edn, Hodder & Stoughton, 1996, p. 708.
11. Charles Jackson, *Understanding Psychological Testing*, BPS Books, 1996, p. 37.
12. S. Blinkhorn and C. Johnson, "The Insignificance of Personality Testing," *Nature*, vol. 348, 1990, pp. 671–2.
13. 'Work and Personality', Special Issue, guest ed. Nigel Nicholson, *Applied Psychology*, vol. 45, no. 3, 1996, pp. 243–62.
14. *Financial Times*, July 6, 1994.
15. *Financial Times*, October 12, 1994.
16. See Chapter 4, pp. 51–2.
17. Quoted by John Carey in *The Faber Book of Utopias*, Faber & Faber, 1999, p. 368.
18. "How Hard Wired is Human Behaviour," *Harvard Business Review*, July/August, 1998.
19. Nicky Hayes, *Foundations of Psychology*, Thomas Nelson, 1998, p. 141 (first published 1994).
20. *Financial Times*, September 16, 1998.
21. *Financial Times*, September 23, 1998.

22. *Financial Times*, "Nurture v. Nature," September 16, 1998.
23. *The Ascent of Man*, British Broadcasting Corporation, 1973, p. 435.
24. Richard Gross, *Psychology: The Science of Mind and Behaviour*, 3rd edn, Hodder and Stoughton, 1996, p. 717.
25. *People Management*, October 28, 1999, pp. 49–50.
26. Studs Terkel, *Working*, Pantheon Books, 1972, p. 589.

21 The Road to Panama

1. Ian Dunlop, *The Shock of The New: Seven Historic Exhibitions of Modern Art*, American Heritage Press, 1972.
2. CBS report, September 7, 1993.
3. Janosch, *The Trip to Panama*, Andersen Press, 1978.
4. Joanne B. Ciulla, *The Working Life*, Times Books, 2000, pp. 61–2.
5. *Financial Times*, March 25, 2000.
6. Juliet Schor, *The Overworked American*, Basic Books, 1992, p. 7.
7. The Alabama senator, Hugo L. Black, who introduced the Thirty Hour Week bill estimated it would create immediately about 6.5 million jobs.
8. Schor, *The Overworked American*, pp. 74–5.
9. The idea sounds enticing but in reality it is difficult to achieve. Henry Ford experimented with something similar in the 1930s when he created a string of "village industries": automotive supply businesses spread among village communities in Michigan. The idea was that farmers could work part of their time in these industries then return to their farms for crop planting and harvesting. In reality farmers abandoned their farms to work in the supply companies full-time rather than mix the two forms of work. The village industries were never profitable and were phased out after Ford's death.
10. Peter Drucker, *The Age of Discontinuity*, Heinemann, 1969, p. 247.
11. Peter Drucker, *Concept of the Corporation*, Transaction, 1995, p. xvii. Note that in the Preface added later to this book, Drucker states that he coined the term in his 1959 book, *Landmarks of Tomorrow*. In fact he did not use the term in this book but he did stress the importance of knowledge in productive work, emphasizing the significance of employees who he would subsequently call knowledge workers.
12. Speech at Hay Management Consultant's Conference, Prague, November 10, 1994.

13. Marshall McLuhan, *Understanding Media: The Extensions of Man*, McGraw-Hill, 1964, title of Chapter I.
14. Martin Luther King, *Strength to Love*, Harper & Row, 1963, Chapter 7.

22   One Life. Live It.

1. *Financial Times*, "Lunch Survives a Hard Journey," June 19, 1995.
2. *Financial Times*, "Union Power is Eroded," June 19, 1995.
3. I pursued this argument at greater length in *Twenty-First Century Leadership: A Fairy Tale Future*, a report published by Hay McBer in May, 2000.
4. Michael Dunkerley, *The Jobless Economy: Computer Technology in the World of Work*, Polity Press, 1996, p. 131.
5. Presentation at Canada House, London, June 1, 2000.
6. Don Tapscott, David Ticoll, and Alex Lowy, *Digital Capital: Harnessing the Power of Business Webs*, Nicholas Brealey, 2000, p. 170.
7. Thomas Malone and Robert Laubacher, "The Dawn of the E-Lance Economy," *Harvard Business Review*, vol. 76, no. 5, 1998, quoted by Tapscott, Ticoll, and Lowy, *Digital Capital*, p. 172.
8. *Financial Times*, "No More Jobs Please," December 23, 1994.
9. Quoted by John Micklethwait and Adrian Wooldridge in *The Witch Doctors: What the Management Gurus are Saying, Why it Matters and How to Make Sense of It*, Heinemann, 1996, p. 212. Morrow's article was published in *Time* on March 29, 1993.
10. *Time*, May 29, 2000.
11. *Financial Times*, "Tales of the Office Nomad," May 29, 1995.
12. Michael Lewis, *Liar's Poker*, Penguin, 1989, p. 185.
13. *Financial Times*, "Tales of the Office Nomad," May 29, 1995.
14. Ibid.
15. C. Wright Mills, *White Collar: The American Middle Class*, New York: Oxford University Press, 1956, p. 236.
16. Ibid., p. 237.
17. Lewis Mumford, *The Conditions of Man*, New York: Harcourt, Brace and Co, 1944, p. 4.
18. Interview with the author.
19. Lewis Mumford, *The Conditions of Man*, p. 5.

20. Voltaire, *Discourse*, no. 4.

21. "Six hours are most suitable and the four that follow, when set forth in letters, say to men 'live.'" Unknown author, from the *Home Book of Quotations*, p. 1,062.

22. Edith Hamilton, *The Greek Way to Western Civilization*, W.W. Norton, Mentor, 1954, p. 21 (first published 1930).

23. Ibid., p. 25.

23 Age of the Search Engine

1. Consider the words of Gordon Brown: "Our bank bonus regulation will be the toughest in the world." *The Guardian*, September 27, 2009.

2. CIPD statement in response to the Heday case decision ruling in favor of default retirement ages, September 25, 2009.

3. "Return of the Car Boot Sales" reported that more than 19 million Britons were expected to attend three or more car boot sales in the summer of 2008. Femalefirst.co.uk, July 11, 2008.

4. "Church Attendance to Fall by 90 Percent," *The Observer*, September 21, 2008.

5. Alan Rogers memorial lecture, June 17, 2007, St Mary's Church, Twickenham.

6. Alain de Botton, *The Pleasures and Sorrows of Work*, Hamish Hamilton, 2009, p. 80.

7. Simon Caulkin," Farewell, with a last word on the blunder years," *The Observer*, June 14, 2009.

8. Speech to Google Zeitgeist Europe, May 21, 2006.

9. Richard Layard, *Happiness: Lessons from a New Science*, Penguin, 2006, p. 48.

10. In conversation with the author, June 20, 2009.

11. Jared Diamond, *Guns, Germs and Steel*, Vintage, 1998, p. 236.

12. "The Tragedy of the Commons," *Science*, December 11, 1968.

Postscript: New Century, New Ethic

1. George Ochoa and Melinda Corey, *The Fitzroy Dearborn Chronology of Ideas*, London: Fitzroy Dearborn Publishers, 1999, p. 190.

2. *Talk*, August, 2000.

3. *Financial Times*, June 8, 1998.